Brief

Encounters

Brief Encounters

Meetings with remarkable people

Gyles Brandreth

First published in Great Britain 2001

Politico's Publishing
8 Artillery Row
Westminster
London
SW1P 1RZ

Tel 020 7931 0090
Fax 020 7828 8111
Email publishing@politicos.co.uk
Website www.politicospublishing.co.uk

A catalogue record of this book is available from the British Library.

ISBN 1 902301 95 1

Printed and bound in Great Britain by Creative Print and Design.

Contents

Introduction:
Name dropping

In the summer of 1957, in a sloping, loopy hand, I wrote in my diary, 'Met Charles de Gaulle today. He is very tall and President of France.' For as long as I can remember – which is from about the age of six – I have been fixated with the famous. For more than forty years now, relentlessly, I have been pursuing brief encounters with the great and the good, and the notorious. I like to think I have some impressive scalps in my collection: Nelson Mandela, Michael Jackson, Pope John Paul I (the Pope who reigned for thirty days: quite a catch that one), Bob Hope, Francis Bacon, Roald Dahl, Barry Manilow, Sir Stanley Matthews, Bill Clinton, Richard Nixon, Victoria Beckham, Diana Dors. When I was seven, and a server at St Stephen's Church in London's Gloucester Road, T. S. Eliot stroked my head; when I was twenty-seven, and standing in the foyer of the Midland Hotel, Manchester, I sensed Johnny Rotten of the Sex Pistols was going to butt my head. I said, 'Lovely to meet you, Mr Rotten.' He said, 'F*** off, f*** face.'

I have self-made rules about what constitutes a genuine celebrity encounter. On the whole, fleeting meetings in public places don't count. In the US Senate I once travelled in a lift with Robert Kennedy; in a London hotel, I was once caught in a lift with Harry Corbett and his glove-puppet, Sooty. Kennedy smiled at me and Sooty waved, but words were not exchanged on either occasion and, for a meeting to register, there needs to be some kind of conversation, however limited. Not long before his death in 1990, I met Sir Rex Harrison. I was in Mayfair, walking down Arlington Street, on my way to Le Caprice restaurant for lunch. As I passed the steps of the Ritz Hotel, Harrison was coming down them. He raised his Professor Higgins hat to me and I told him how much I admired his work. Together we walked down the street and into Le Caprice. It was only when I had helped him off with his coat and hat, that he turned towards me and said, 'Who are you and why have you brought me here?'

Harrison was a performer of extraordinary skill and charm, but not, by most accounts, a terribly nice or easy man. (I have met two of his wives and interviewed one of them.) During the first year of the London run of *My Fair Lady*, at the stage door of the Theatre Royal, Drury Lane, he was approached by an admiring autograph hunter, a well-meaning English-woman of riper years. Harrison brushed her aside without so much as a nod or a glance, but she wasn't to be ignored and, as he made for his limousine, she tapped him sharply on the arm with her autograph book. Stanley Holloway, following Harrison out of the stage door, witnessed the scene and pondered out loud, 'Is this the first recorded instance of the fan hitting the shit?'

I treasure celebrated signatures (my prized correspondents include Field Marshal Montgomery of Alamein and Samuel Beckett), but I do not collect autographs. And, wary of rejection, I do not approach people out of the blue. An admirer once accosted James Joyce at Zürich railway station and asked, 'May I shake the hand that wrote *Ulysses*?' 'No,' said Joyce, 'it did a great many other things as well.' Occasionally, I contrive a chance encounter. When on holiday with my children, some years ago, I happened to see John Diefenbaker (prime minister of Canada, 1957–63) sitting alone in a deck chair on a beach in Barbados, I sent my two-year-old daughter to trip over his outstretched feet so that I had an excuse to go over and apologise. Courteously, Mr Diefenbaker engaged me in conversation. I told him of my ambition to become a member of parliament. He told me that, when I made it to Westminster (he was confident I would), 'For the first six months after you arrive, you will wonder how you ever got there. After that, you will wonder how the rest of the members ever got there.' (I had not heard the line before.)

I have shaken hands with a variety of prime ministers, presidents, princes and potentates, as well as with assorted known killers (including the actor Leslie Grantham), with Christine Keeler (and John Profumo), with Keith Moon (and with a man who has been to the moon), with James Stewart and Jackie Stewart and Ed 'Stewpot' Stewart, but there are some hands I should have shaken and didn't.

My encounter with General de Gaulle came about because, in the late 1950s, I was a pupil at the Lycée Français de Londres when de Gaulle came to London on a state visit. His itinerary included lunch at 10 Downing Street, dinner at Buckingham Palace and, in between, tea at the French Lycée in South Kensington where a selected band of pupils was to be presented to him. For weeks we were drilled in anticipation of the great day. We memorised all seven verses of the French National Anthem (yes, seven) and carefully rehearsed the firm handshake that was to be accompanied by a smart bob of the head. At long last *le jour de gloire est arrivé* and, at the given hour, I and half a dozen other representatives of Anglo-French youth were lined up outside the Lycée awaiting the arrival of the presidential limousine. On schedule, the great man stepped from his car, was greeted reverentially by our headmaster and led towards the line where we boys and girls were waiting. I was fourth to be presented. President de Gaulle shook the hand of the first pupil. Then he shook the hand of the second pupil. Next he shook the hand of the third pupil and even exchanged a few words with her. Then he shook the hand of the fifth pupil. And then the sixth. And then the seventh. And then he was away, into the building and out of my life. I knew I was small, but I hadn't felt that small before. At first I consoled myself with the thought that the slight had not been deliberate, that the President was so tall he simply had not noticed the shrimp standing fourth in the line-up, but later I came to have my doubts.

Ten years after this non-event, when I was an undergraduate at Oxford, I was invited to have tea with Harold Macmillan, then Chancellor of the University. Realising that 'Supermac' and de Gaulle had known each other over half a century, I hoped the anecdote of my unconsummated encounter with the champion of the Free French might amuse the former prime minister. When I arrived at the tea party I discovered Mr Macmillan was already there, ensconced in an armchair by the fire, dozing gently. My hosts said it would be a shame to disturb him. I waited more than two hours for the great man to rouse himself. I enjoyed three toasted tea cakes and several sandwiches, but no small talk with Harold Macmillan. He slept throughout the afternoon and I slipped away without even shaking him by the hand. That night I decided that he and de Gaulle had been in it together.

Physical contact is important. I have been in the presence of Barbara Streisand, but I have not touched her. I can boast, however, that I once held Marlene Dietrich's left thigh. In the 1960s, after a performance at the Golders Green Hippodrome, Miss Dietrich, wearing a black mini-skirt with a slit up the side, was teetering on top of her limousine throwing signed photographs of herself to the fans surrounding the car. When all the pictures had been distributed and the final kisses blown, a police officer and I eased the legend off the roof of her vehicle onto the ground. For fully fifteen seconds, I had half of Dietrich in my arms.

I have a weakness for beautiful women. I have been nose to nose with Raquel Welch (great bone structure, peachy skin) and Diana, Princess of Wales (beaky nose, skin with slight pebble-dash effect). I have been privileged to know – and even kiss – all the great television beauties of my lifetime, from Katie Boyle to Ulrika Jonsson. On Valentine's Day in 1984, when I was a presenter with TV-am, Britain's first breakfast station, I attempted to break the world record for the longest-held screen kiss. My accomplice was Anne Diamond and we were on the edge of earning our place in the *Guinness Book of Records*, when our osculatory marathon was interrupted by the sudden need to take the viewers to Moscow for live coverage of Leonid Brezhnev's funeral. (These were the early days of the station when we still felt we had 'a mission to explain'.) I secured the on-screen kissing record a year later, with the help of Cheryl Baker of the pop group Bucks Fizz. The erotic charge of the encounter was blunted by the cold sore on Cheryl's top lip and the little drip on the tip of her nose, but for three minutes forty-five seconds we can claim to have made television history, of a sort.

I realised recently that one of the reasons my love life has lacked adventure is that I am a coward. I flirt indiscriminately but haven't the courage to follow through. In 2000, for radio, I interviewed the ITN newcaster Kirsty Young. We were alone for the recording (in the office of our mutual friend, Sir Trevor McDonald, as it happens) and, in the course of the interview, Kirsty told me about her husband and what a marvellous kisser he is. At once (and all too fruitily) I said how much I envied him. A few minutes later, the recording concluded, I was packing away my microphone, when suddenly I sensed Kirsty's face close to mine. 'Shall I show you what I mean?' she murmured. She was calling my bluff, of course. She was sending me up, I know. But even if she had meant it, would I have had what it takes to seize the moment? I think not. Indeed, I know not. Only a few weeks later, for the same programme (but in a different room) I was interviewing the lovely Melinda Messenger, formerly the *Sun*'s 'Page 3 Girl for the Thrillennium' and now a successful television presenter. Throughout our conversation I kept saying how fanciable she was. When I turned off the recording equipment, she put her head to one side and laughed, 'Shall I get my kit off now? I think we know what you're after.'

While I may have a soft spot for beautiful young women, it seems that only elderly comics have a penchant for me. As a child in England in the

1950s, once I had graduated from *Muffin the Mule* and *Mr Turnip*, my favourite television programmes were, from the United States, *Circus Boy* and *The Lone Ranger*, and, of home-grown fare, *Billy Bunter* and *Whack-O!*.

Whack-O! was a situation comedy set in a minor public school in which 'Professor' Jimmy Edwards starred as the irascible, blustering headmaster who took to the cane and the bottle with equal ease. Years later, when I was in my mid-thirties, I worked with Jimmy Edwards on his war memoirs (*Six of the Best* by Flight Lieutenant J.K.O. Edwards, DFC) and he invited me down to his house in East Sussex. He met me at the railway station mid-morning and drove me to his home at great speed down narrow country lanes and via two pubs. At the first pub, he downed a pint, at the second, two Bloody Marys. Once home, and before lunch, he opened a bottle of champagne, mixed it with a carton of orange juice, and quaffed the lot from a silver tankard. He grilled us a pair of substantial steaks and we eased ourselves through two good bottles of claret before moving on to generous balloons of brandy. After lunch, he told me how unhappy he was and suggested we would both find it a cheering experience to take off all our clothes and clamber together into his new hot tub.

Until that moment I hadn't realised that this great bull of a man, with his booming voice and bristling moustaches, was what Barbara Windsor later described to me as 'Tommy Two-ways'. Awash with alcohol, moist-eyed, sprawled like a beached whale on the banquette in his unkempt kitchen, he was a touching sight, but not an enticing one. I declined the hot tub. He snorted, and offered me another drink.

Frankie Howerd was not so easily put off. We had enjoyed a not noticeably liquid lunch at Al Gallo d'Oro in Kensington High Street, and after it, rather than go around the corner to his house in Edwardes Square, he suggested we would work more efficiently at his agent's office in Mayfair. As we passed the receptionist, he growled at her, 'This young man and I have a lot of work to do. We do not wish to be disturbed. Is that understood, madam?' The girl gave a little giggle ('Titter ye not') and we proceeded up the stairs and into a spacious panelled room that appeared to be more drawing room than office. Frank ('I like my friends to call me "Frank"') gestured towards a leather sofa and, to my surprise, locked the door and pocketed the key. 'We don't want intruders,' he muttered.

I opened my briefcase and hurriedly pulled out the manuscript we were to work on. 'Yes,' I said quickly, 'there's lots to get through. I told my wife I would have a busy afternoon, but I'd be back in time to bath the children. I've got three children you know.'

'Never mind that,' said Frank. Then, as he made to sit down beside me on the sofa, his face suddenly contorted, he clutched his thigh and yelped with pain. 'No, no,' he whimpered, his eyes screwed up as though Hattie Jacques were about to plunge in the syringe.

'What is it?'

'It's my groin! No, ooh, ah, ow . . .' he grimaced.

Continuing to clutch the affected part, Frank slowly pulled himself across the room towards the large partners' desk by the window. He opened a drawer and produced a jar of ointment. 'This is what we need,' he muttered. He then slowly staggered back towards me, thrust the jar of ointment into my hands, undid his belt, pulled down his trousers, lowered his underpants and collapsed in a heap at my side.

He closed his eyes and sighed, 'You know what to do.'

'I don't,' I said hoarsely.

'You do,' he murmured.

'I don't,' I yelped.

'Apply the ointment,' he barked 'Rub it in.'

'Where?'

He sat up, opened his eyes, exposed himself and said, 'There!'

'Where?' I gulped.

'There!' he repeated. 'Haven't you seen one before? It's perfectly harmless. Treat it like a muscle!'

Unhappily I couldn't make my excuses and leave because Frank had locked the door and the key was in his right trouser pocket and his trousers were round his ankles on the floor. Instead, I averted my gaze, got to my feet and stood looking out of the window while I waited for him to get dressed and release me from his lair.

Telling this story to Barry Cryer the other day, he said, 'You know, excactly the same thing happened to me – in 1955. It happened to Griff Rhys Jones too, you know.' And to Bob Monkhouse. And, I imagine, to any male of any age, shape, or persuasion who happened to cross Frank's path.

There is a message here for younger readers: beware of older men bearing ointments. Indeed, beware of older folk altogether. People get to an age when anything that is young is appealing. Sir John Gielgud told me the tale of Sir Herbert Beerbohm-Tree, the turn-of-the-century actor-manager, famous for his Hamlet (described by Max Beerbohm as 'funny without being vulgar') and infamous for his extra-marital dalliances. One night Lady Tree came home to find her husband dining *à deux* with a breathtakingly handsome young actor. She said goodnight, and, as she closed the dining-room door behind her, murmured, 'The port's on the sideboard, Herbert, and, remember, it's adultery just the same.'

About ten years ago, at a reception in the Durbar Room at the Foreign Office, I found myself standing with a pair of recently retired diplomats. 'In a long career,' mused the first, 'you are bound to meet any number of remarkable people; some you recall quite vividly, others have slipped your memory completely, but, as a rule, I have found that no one ever forgets their first head of state. Mine was George V. Who was yours?' he said, turning to his colleague. 'The Emperor Haile Selassie, oddly enough.' Both of them turned their beady eyes on me. 'And how about you?' 'The President of Switzerland,' I said. 'Ah,' they smiled in unison. 'Yes, well . . . why not?' I felt to have offered Charles de Gaulle would have been wrong since, in effect, the great Frenchman had cut me, but, for a few hours, back in 1965, the President of Switzerland and I were really quite close.

I was seventeen and managed to secure myself a well-paid summer holiday job by default. Actually, it was a case of deflowering rather than default. At my school (Bedales, a co-educational boarding school in Hampshire) a young master had developed a tendresse for a girl in my class. It was a tendresse that turned into a rather hasty wedding during the summer holidays, which meant that the errant teacher was unexpectedly unable to take up his August assignment as tutor to two children in Switzerland. As I was available and willing (he liked his pupils to be available and willing), he passed on the job, and his railway tickets, to me.

I set off from Victoria Station and, eighteen hours later, emerged, bewildered and dishevelled, on the empty platform of Sion Station in the Valais region of Switzerland. I was expecting to be met, but I was not expecting to be met by two smartly uniformed soldiers and a military limousine sporting a fluttering Swiss flag on the bonnet. I sensed that I was underdressed and unprepared for the role I was to undertake. The soldiers sensed it too, but they had their orders and they obeyed them. They saluted me, relieved me of my rucksack, ensconced me in the car and drove me off to my new employer.

It turned out that I was to be tutor and companion to the offspring of the head of the Swiss Army, a splendidly grizzled old soldier with a delightfully vivacious second wife. The Brigadier (I believe he was actually a Marshal, but we called him Brigadier) had seen service (if not necessarily very active service) over four decades and was evidently as tough as they come. Our day began at five when he led the entire family out into the woods to gather mushrooms for breakfast. He explained that you had to eat what you picked. He had found this rule very effective in ensuring that his troops learnt quickly and correctly which fungi were poisonous and which were not.

During that August and September we spent time in Berne, time on the road (visiting military establishments, in what seemed like complete villages built within mountains), and time at the Brigadier's holiday retreat in the hills outside Sion. It was to the holiday home that the President of Switzerland came to dinner. He was an old crony of the Brigadier's and it was made clear to 'Madame' (he called his young bride 'Madame') that all that was wanted was something very informal – '*un repas bien simple et puis un jeu de cartes*'.

Madame set about preparing the most elaborate simple supper you can imagine. The Brigadier set about teaching me the President's (and his) favourite game of cards.

Even in Switzerland, even when he's an old mucker of your husband's, having the head of state to dinner is none the less an ordeal. There were to be six of us: the President and Madame la Presidente, the Brigadier and Madame, another old soldier (who knew the family and the card game equally well) and me. I am afraid the evening when it came was not a total success, although it taught me several valuable lessons. The culinary calamities included a soufflé that wouldn't rise and savoury jellies that wouldn't set. (Lesson No. 1: When entertaining old soldiers 'safe and simple' is always the better bet. Besides, a simple failure is less noticeable than an elaborate one.) Happily, the wine flowed. (Lesson No. 2: Old soldiers never die, but they are happy to float away.) Unhappily, when one of the bottles was emptied I invited the President's wife to kiss the bottom of it, telling her I had heard that if you did there was an old Swiss tradition that said you would be married within the year. I was meaning to help, but far from lightening the mood this vulgar touch on my part only served to increase the *froideur*. (Lesson No. 3: It is not the duty of the most junior guest to be the life and soul of the party.) When dinner was over and we men settled down to cards I happened to win the first game – and the second – and, *mon Dieu*, the third. (Lesson No. 4: Never play to lose, but don't always play to win. There is a difference.) We had just embarked on a fourth game, and this was the one it looked as if the President might win, when Madame took us by surprise, tinkled a little bell, and suddenly announced the *Son et Lumierè*. '*Quoi?*' barked the Brigadier, '*Le Son et Lumierè? Oû? Quand?*'. '*Ici! Maintenant!*' simpered Madame.' '*Mais non!*' expostulated the Brigadier. '*Mais oui!*' cooed Madame.

It transpired that our thoughtful hostess had arranged a command performance of the Sion Son et Lumierè at 10 p.m. as a special presidential treat. (Lesson No. 5: Old soldiers don't like surprises. Not many people do. And the more elaborate and carefully prepared the surprise the less welcome it will be.) The Brigadier was not accustomed to his wife taking executive decisions (he told me that when women were first allowed a referendum on whether or not they wanted the vote he had locked Madame in the bathroom for the day), but the President showed the courtesy that becomes a head of state, laid down his cards and got to his feet. (Lesson No. 6: 'Uneasy lies the head that wears the crown.' There is always a price to be paid for life at the top.)

We clambered to the foot of the hill and the President glad-handed the few villagers who had turned out to cheer. The six of us sat together on the same bench to watch the show. It only lasted three-quarters of an hour and it hardly mattered that there was no roof to the auditorium as the drizzle was light and there were umbrellas for all.

At the end of the performance, the President and his lady applauded gamely, but, despite being pressed, declined the offer of a nightcap and one last game of cards. Somewhat stiffly we all embraced one another and the presidential pair stepped into their motor and were sped away. By ten the following morning the President's chauffeur was back. Madame answered the front door to find him standing there holding the biggest, most elaborate, grandest, grossest box of chocolates you have ever seen. The moment she set eyes on them, poor Madame burst into tears. (Lesson No. 7: If you overdo the thank-you present you give the game away.)

For a celebrity-groupie like me, Bedales was an ideal school: so many of the parents (from Oscar Wilde to Laurence Olivier) were household names. In my day, distinguished Bedalian parents included Robert Graves, Cecil Day-Lewis, Lawrence Durrell and the photographer Eve Arnold. (She was a particular favourite of mine: she had photographed Marilyn Monroe.) It was while I was at school that I first got the idea that a good way of meeting interesting people – and of getting into their homes – was to interview them. I began modestly, with the local vicar ('Why do you believe in God?'

'Because he is ultimately unavoidable'), moved on to the Chairman of Hampshire County Council, then to the school's founder (John Badley, a contemporary and friend of Oscar Wilde – see page 227), then went international with what I billed in the *Bedales Chronicle* as a 'world exclusive': a no-holds-barred interview with the President of Switzerland.

At Oxford, I began to run riot. If there was a someone I wanted to meet somehow I got hold of their address (usually from *Who's Who*) and wrote to them. My interviewees (for *Isis*, the undergraduate magazine, then edited by my friend Anthony Holden and handsomely subsidised by the local Labour MP, Robert Maxwell) included Bruce Forsyth ('Nice to see ya, Gyles, to see ya nice!': my first dressing-room interview), Sir Gerald Nabarro MP (noted for his handlebar moustache and deft way with words: 'Would you like your daughter to marry a big buck nigger?'), and my political hero, Iain Macleod (my first interview with a serious politician; my first visit to a House of Commons office: I could not believe how tiny his room was). At Oxford I really did secure a world exclusive: the first-ever interview with the Aga Khan. I read in a newspaper that he did not give interviews. I found his address in *Who's Who* and wrote to him, asking him to make an exception in my case. He did. At the time, I thought it was because I wrote him such a persuasive letter. Now I realise it was simply that I had youth and nerve on my side.

At Oxford, through *Isis* and *Cherwell*, through the Dramatic Society, through the Union, I met a wonderful range of famous people. A number of them – James Robertson Justice, Michael Redgrave, Beverley Nichols, Lord Boothby, Fanny and Johnnie Cradock – befriended me, inviting me to their homes. I thought then it was because I was such excellent company. I realise now it was simply because I was young.

Over thirty-five years I have interviewed scores of remarkable people. Of course, many remarkable people are not necessarily famous, and some famous people are quite unremarkable. That said, in my experience people who sustain their celebrity – whether it is Liberace or Tom Stoppard – do have something unique about them, beyond their fame. Usually it is a matter of talent: they play the piano better, or write better plays, than the rest of us. Often, too, the fact that they are famous raises our expectation and, possibly, their game. We want stars to shine, so they do. When you meet a prime minister, the fact that he is prime minister affects you, and him, and those around him. The office adds something. When George Bush Sr was President of the United States it was exciting to meet him: by virtue of his experience, he was interesting; by virtue of his office the encounter became memorable. In or out of office, meeting Bill Clinton is extraordinary. He has an intelligence, charm and energy that need to be experienced to be believed. And that's the point. That's why, after all these years, I still get a thrill when I come face to face with fame.

That's probably why I remember my seven years at TV-am with such affection. It was nice to be earning good money before breakfast, but the real bonus was meeting so many intriguing people. In the 1980s 'everybody who was anybody' touched base with the TV-am sofa. Sylvester Stallone was shorter than I expected, Joan Collins gentler and prettier. Peter Ustinov was wonderfully droll (at 7.15 a.m.!), Anthony Hopkins was even funnier (but not on the sofa, in the canteen afterwards, doing the best Olivier impressions I've heard). There was a palpable aura about Billy Graham (truly) and a menacing posse around Jesse Jackson (just security men, but they kept their man encircled at all times. It was the same with Eddie Murphy: to have a conversation you had to shout across a human barricade of guards.) We met heroes and superstars, some humble, some less so. Willy Brandt was delightfully unassuming for a former West German Chancellor: 'Just call me Willy.' I sat down on the sofa next to Charlton Heston and put my mug of tea on the table in front of us. Immediately he picked it up and began sipping from it. When you are a star you take it for granted that any refreshment brought into your presence will be for you.

When you meet them, you find that some well-known people are just as you had expected. Others aren't. The Queen and Glenda Jackson are much jollier than you might suppose. The former Conservative Home Secretary

Michael Howard is a charmer. Anthea Turner is a doll. But being good company does not automatically make you a good – or easy – subject for interview. At home, in his kitchen, the actor Edward Fox is funny, racy, gloriously articulate. On the TV-am sofa, one memorable morning in 1990, he was at his most taciturn. Rex Harrison had died the night before, and since Edward Fox had recently been appearing with him in *The Admirable Crichton*, Anne Diamond turned to him for some appropriate actor-laddie reminiscences.

Anne: Did you know Rex Harrison?

Edward: Yes.

Anne: Did you like him?

Edward: Yes. Ver' much.

Anne: What was he like?

Edward: Erm . . . er . . . a genius.

Anne: What kind of genius?

Edward: (PAUSE) A genius.

Anne: But how did the genius manifest itself?

Edward: (LONGER PAUSE) Either the sun shines or it doesn't.

Anne: He was very much a stage actor?

Edward: (PAUSE) Yes.

Anne: And films?

Edward: (LONGEST PAUSE YET) Yes.

Interviewees who say very little are not easy. Interviewees who say too much can be a challenge as well. I interviewed the film actor Christopher Lee for the radio recently. We met in a small room on the ground floor of a discreet hotel near Knightsbridge. Coffee was served and, just on 11.10 a.m., I asked my first question. An hour and a half later, Mr Lee was still answering it.

The worst to interview are those who have done it a thousand times and those who don't want to be doing it at all. The endlessly interviewed have a set repertoire of standard stories and, understandably, speak to you on automatic pilot. If you have only got an hour with them, most of it can be taken up with them cheerfully recycling familiar material. These days, I try to get around this problem at the outset of the interview by signalling to the interviewee the stories of theirs that I already know and love.

As an interviewer, I have many faults. The worst is that I talk when I should be listening. (At the end of a radio interview with Kenneth Branagh, he said, 'That was fun, Gyles, but I thought I was supposed to be the one answering the questions.') Alan Whicker, a pioneer of the friendly-but-revealing television interview, advised me not to be frightened of silence during an interview. I know it is sound advice, but I find it nearly impossible to take. Because I want to be loved, I want my interviewee to feel comfortable. I hate awkward moments. I cannot bear to let silence fall and consequently, all too often, I start burbling at the very moment when my subject is about to say something of heart-wrenching significance.

Even after so many years in the game, my technique is all over the place. I still cannot decide whether to record my interviews or simply take notes. The disadvantage of relying on notes is that you are scribbling furiously when you should be observing your subject's body language. The risk of relying on a recording is that your equipment fails you or, more likely in my case, you fail your equipment. When I mentioned this at the beginning of my interview with Sir Richard Branson recently he said, rather tartly, 'Why don't you bring two recording machines?'

There are those who really don't want to give interviews, but are compelled to do so because the publicist (or the contract) for their novel or movie or what-have-you requires it. These interviews are hell because you and the interviewee are likely to be at odds from the start: they want to mouth some platitudes about the work in hand and you want to get beneath their skin (or at least their shades) and begin exploring the darker side of their torrid love life/childhood/past. In my experience, the best way to handle this sort of interview is to come clean up front: 'I know this is a nightmare for you. Let's cut to the chase. We'll have fifteen minutes on the movie, then fifteen minutes of what I think the readers want, then fifteen minutes on what you'd like to see in the interview, then I'll leave you in peace. I promise.'

In many ways one of the most enjoyable, and certainly by far the easiest person to interview was the late Dame Barbara Cartland. When I first visited her at her home, Camfield Place, near Hatfield, she was just completing her one hundredth novel, *The Prude and the Prodigal* (or was it her two hundredth, *The Goddess and the Gaiety Girl*?). Anyway, she looked a picture, a mature sugar plum fairy decked from neck to calf in a sparkling confection of pink tulle. 'She looks like a Christmas tree,' muttered the sound engineer who was with me. 'And don't we all love Christmas?' trilled Dame Barbara as she led us into the drawing room where she sat bolt upright in a high-backed armchair and was lit by her own special theatrical lamps that successfully accentuated her natural rosy hue.

'I'm afraid it's only a radio interview,' I ventured. 'I know, my dear,' she purred, 'but I always like to look my best. It's simply a matter of courtesy.'

Barbara Cartland was the personification of politesse – and professionalism. Through the interview she twinkled and sparkled and gurgled (and plugged her books and her vitamins and her honey), and on the stroke of four marched us to the dining room for a proper tea (including mouth-melting meringues). She left us briefly at one stage during the afternoon and, as we departed, we discovered why. Each member of the crew was presented with one of her books, personally inscribed, and individually wrapped up with pink ribbon. 'A little souvenir, lest you forget . . .'.

Lest we forget! Once met, Cartland was not likely to be forgotten. Her self-invented branding was strong, her niche market carefully carved out, her curious success deserved and sustained. The last time I saw her was in 1996, when she came to the House of Commons to have dinner with her friends (and mine), Neil and Christine Hamilton. There were ten of us in the party, in the Members' Dining Room, her son at one end of the table, Dame Barbara at the other. I sat on her left. She was as ridiculous and glorious as ever: white-powdered face, the giraffe's eyelashes, the eight remaining strands of hair spun into an extraordinary candy-floss confection, flowing pink tulle everywhere. She seemed to have come dressed as the fairy queen in a Victorian pantomime. She didn't draw breath. Out the stories tumbled: Noël Coward, Beaverbrook, Churchill – names worth dropping. 'Darling Dickie,' she said, coming back to Earl Mountbatten of Burma yet again. 'No one knew him as I did. He was quite extraordinary. He was the most fascinating man in the world, so ahead of his time.'

According to Dame Barbara, Mountbatten pioneered the zip fastener instead of fly buttons and persuaded the then Prince of Wales (later Edward VIII) to follow suit. 'But it all went terribly wrong one evening at a very smart supper in Biarritz. The Prince went to the cloakroom, but, poor lamb, didn't dare emerge because the zip got stuck! He had to slip out by the back door. He was furious, had all the zips taken out of his trousers.' She was full of concern for the plight of the current Prince and Princess of Wales (Charles and Diana). 'It's so sad for them both. It's heartbreaking. Of course, you know where it all went wrong? She wouldn't do oral sex, she just wouldn't. It's as simple as that. Of course it all went wrong.'

I think I try to portray people honestly, but, on the whole, I hope, in a favourable light. For me, the test is not so much whether the subjects of my interviews are happy with the outcome (though I am conscious that whoever I write about I may one day want to meet again), as whether their friends and those who know them well recognise them in the piece I have written. The subjects themselves react in different ways.

On the morning that my interview with Lord Snowdon appeared in the *Sunday Telegraph*, the telephone rang just as I was setting out for lunch. It was Snowdon. He didn't say who he was (he doesn't), but I recognised the silence. 'Hello,' I said 'Was it all right?' There was a long, eerie pause, then this rasping voice hissed down the line: 'You have made me out to be a drunk and a faggot . . .' My stomach lurched, then I heard him laugh, 'But I love you. Everyone says it's marvellous.' Whatever he may have thought of the piece, his friends had reassured him, so all was well.

My last piece about Lord Archer was less well received. It was written, against the clock, as the news broke of his enforced withdrawal from the race to become the Conservative candidate for Mayor of London. On the day the article appeared, I wrote privately to Jeffrey, expressing my regret at the sad way his political ambitions had turned to dust. A few days later, I got a brief reply from the Old Vicarage, Grantchester: 'Dear Gyles, You can either hunt with the pack or sympathise with the prey. You cannot do both. Yours sincerely, Mary Archer.'

Once you allow yourself to be interviewed you are inviting an intruder into your life. I try to play fair: I try to ask the difficult (i.e. most impertinent and intrusive) questions openly. As a rule, I don't do as some interviewers do (I know: I have been a victim too) and slip the key question in nonchalantly, on the doorstep, just as I'm saying goodbye. And if you invite me into your home, I try to behave as one hopes a guest would. (Yes, I snoop about a bit, but, as a rule, don't open cupboards or drawers. Sometimes they get opened for me. Gordon Brown, not long after becoming Chancellor of the Exchequer, showed me around his flat at 10 Downing Street and, when we were in the bedroom, opened the cupboards – I felt a little ostentatiously – to reveal the dresses of his then girlfriend, Sarah. I wasn't sure why. I confess I broke my own no-prying rule recently when I was the guest of another politician I rather like and admire. Interviewing Charles Kennedy, the Liberal Democrat leader, in the run-up to the 2001 general election, I spent an hour or so with him in his Westminster flat. Among other issues, I wanted to ask him about his drinking. I wanted to suggest that his fondness for alcohol was a weakness. He convinced me – completely – that it wasn't. But, prior to asking the question, I thought it would be useful to have evidence, so, whenever he left the sitting room to take a telephone call or visit the loo, I nipped into the kitchen and started frantically opening cupboards and bins and the fridge in the hope of finding incriminating evidence. I found nothing.)

Being interviewed is a risky business. Be wary. At Christmas 2000, I went to see Jim Davidson in his dressing room between performances of his pantomime. I found him curled up on the sofa, thumb in mouth, fast asleep. When I woke him, I asked how he was feeling. 'Grim' he said, 'I was interviewed by the *Observer* and they did me over, the bastards.'

'I'm sorry,' I said.

'I'm an idiot,' he said. 'Joan Littlewood told me, "Never let yourself be interviewed by a newspaper you don't read yourself."'

To be honest, whoever you are, my advice would be: never let yourself be interviewed at all. But, if you do, please let it be me.

Acknowledgements

My principal debt of gratitude, of course, is to the range of remarkable people I have met and who have allowed me to write about them over the years. Without them, my life would have been a lot less interesting and there would have been no book.

Some of what follows has not appeared in print before. Of the rest, the vast majority was first published in the pages of the *Sunday Telegraph*, to whose editor, Dominic Lawson, I am enormously grateful for the encouragement, employment, lunches, guidance and friendship he has given me. I have learnt much from a raft of colleagues at the *Sunday Telegraph* – Matthew D'Ancona, Con Coughlin, Mark Law, Andrew Alderson, Miriam Gross – and I am especially indebted to the team on the *Sunday Telegraph Review*: my friend Sandy Mitchell (editor of the *Review* when most of these pieces appeared), Anna Murphy, his successor, Charlotte Eager, Emma Gosnell, Jean Huckfield, Bridget Guymer, Sacha Lehrfreund and the matchless sub-editors (the unsung heroes and heroines of journalism) led by John Morgan and Ginny Hampton.

Over a period of thirty-three years I have written for a wide variety of newspapers and magazines. I began, in 1968, writing the 'Luke Jarvis' column in *Honey* magazine. I graduated to a column of my own in the *Manchester Evening News*, under the editorship of Brian Redhead: 'Gyles Brandreth for the young in heart – every Tuesday'. My career as a youthful columnist came to a climax when, aged 24, I joined *Woman* magazine as successor to the legendary Godfrey Winn, who, according to Lord Beaverbrook, 'shook hands with readers' hearts'. My column ('Gyles Brandreth is as modern as tomorrow – with a lot of time for yesterday') was not a success. Mr Winn knew what he was doing. I did not. I have since written for an eclectic mix of publications (the *Observer, Daily Mirror, Daily Mail, Daily Telegraph, Spectator, Dogs Today*) and if I have learnt anything along the way it is thanks to the counsel, example and practical help given to me by colleagues. I must single out Magnus Linklater and Michael Wynn-Jones, who thirty years ago sponsored me for membership of the National Union of Journalists (journalism was a closed shop in those days) and a quartet of life-long journalist friends: Michael Coveney, Anthony Holden, Tim Heald and Christopher Hudson.

Final and special thanks go to Iain Dale and John Simmons, founders of Politico's Bookshop and Politico's Publishing. They suggested the idea of this book to me and it has been a pleasure working with them and their colleagues Sean Magee and John Berry. If you have not visited Politico's Bookshop, you must. If you have not visited the Politico's website, you must. It is www.politicos.co.uk . If you have not heard Iain Dale on the radio, please tune in to the programme I present for ITN Radio every Sunday afternoon from 4.00 p.m. on LBC 1152 AM. He is a regular contributor, as witty as he is wise.

This book is dedicated to my mother, Alice Brandreth, and to the memories of my father Charles Brandreth (1910–82), and of his cousin, one of my role models, the writer George R. Sims (1847–1922), whose assorted claims to fame included writing the ballad 'Christmas Day in the Workhouse', pantomimes for Drury Lane, his 'Mustard and Cress' newspaper column every Sunday for forty-five years (without missing a single week), and being the highest-earning journalist of his day.

Gyles Brandreth
May 2001

Politics

Tony Blair at the WI

At London's Wembley Arena, on 7 June 2000 – a year to the day before the 2001 general election – Tony Blair, three years in to his first term as prime minister, gave the least successful speech of his career.

As chance would have it, I was there.

'Name-dropping,' as Prince Philip once said to me,' is vulgar and best avoided.' He is right, of course, and the truth is I can't claim close acquaintance with the prime minister, but I have met him, I do like him, and this week we shared a notable platform. On Wednesday last Tony Blair and I addressed the Triennial General Meeting of the National Federation of Women's Institutes at Wembley Arena. Mine's the speech you didn't hear about. I am relieved to report it went down fairly well. And – this is the point – the occasion could have, should have worked for Tony too.

As I stood waiting in the wings, registering his failure, peering round the curtain at the sea of stony, hostile faces, I didn't feel in the least bit smug. My heart pounded with his. As he blanched and laughed nervously at the distant rumble of discontent, my stomach also churned. If you have stood in front of an audience (of twenty or two hundred, never mind the 10,000 plus gathered this week at Wembley), and somehow failed to connect, you will know the feeling. It is the bleakest sensation in the world.

Apart from the obvious – the ladies felt exploited and patronised: they sensed that the Downing Street machine had hijacked their conference for base political gain – what went wrong? The pundits may now be writing this up as New Labour's defining hour – 'Blair's Ceausescu moment' – but on Wednesday morning, with Tony dying out front, and me on next, it seemed as clear as crystal what the problem was. The room was a nightmare and the poor fellow got off to a rocky start.

For a speech to work well, you need a receptive audience who are sitting comfortably and can hear you without straining. The Wembley Arena is a barn of a venue. The platform is yards away from the front row. Making eye contact with your audience is just not on: the bulk of them are the length of a football pitch away. They can see you on giant TV screens, but you can't see them at all. The acoustic is terrible. Not everyone can hear you clearly and it is next-to-impossible on the platform to judge how what you are saying is being received. Make a joke and it is moments before you hear a laugh – and, disconcertingly, a laugh sounds no different from a jeer.

Mr Blair was the opening attraction. There were wearisome queues to get in and the hall itself was chilly. Even before the prime minister opened his mouth, his audience was not in a particularly jolly frame of mind. I was luckier because I spoke just after lunch. The ladies were in a mellower mood and the room was a good deal warmer. They knew I wasn't going to be political and had nothing on my agenda except a desire to give them an entertaining time. Before Mr Blair started it was clear it wasn't going to be a doddle and when he got going he made four fatal mistakes. I recognised them at once only because I have made them too frequently myself.

1. He tried to speak to more than one audience at the same time and fell, heavily, between the stools. In a hall as vast as Wembley, you can't hold

an audience with the power of your personality. You have to be saying something that engages them. If he had simply spoken on issues that concerned the WI, if he had spoken entirely to them and for them, they'd have stayed with him all the way.

2. He was lumbered with a set text. Having heard Mr Blair's speech, I spent most of lunchtime modifying mine. I spoke from notes and, as my speech progressed, decided to include some passages and drop others. Mr Blair didn't have this luxury. Because his speech had already been distributed to the press, he had no choice but to stick to it. As one of the ladies said to me over lunch, 'When the going got rough he should have torn up his script and simply said, "Here I am, what would you like to ask me?"' but he couldn't. The speech had been 'delivered', printed and spun, before he'd uttered a word.

3. He got rattled. He did what it's so easy to do (I've been there, I know): when the barracking started he quickened the pace when he should have slowed down. He was unnerved and he let it show. (Even the most seasoned public speakers suffer from nerves: when I was in the House of Commons I marvelled at how Michael Heseltine's hands would shake when he was barnstorming at the dispatch box; listen to Michael Portillo: when his nerve begins to go, his voice momentarily leaps an octave.)

4. He outstayed his welcome. You can't beat the old rule: stand up, speak up, shut up. Mr Blair arrived with too much to say. This is a politician's besetting sin. They're determined to cover all the bases, but a speech isn't an essay or an article. It's an opportunity for human contact, a chance to convey a mood, a feeling and, at most, one message or two.

As soon as Mr Blair had spoken he was whisked back to Westminster for prime minister's Questions. As soon as I'd done my turn, I slipped away too.

I travelled back into London by underground and, on the train, found myself seated behind two hatchet-faced WI ladies of riper years. One of them (she was wearing a maroon beret) said with some relish, 'Tony Blair was a disgrace. I'm glad we gave him the slow hand-clap. I voted for Ken Livingstone for the same reason. I'll do as I please, not as I'm told.' Her friend nodded and then said, not knowing I was there, 'But wasn't Gyles Brandreth wonderful?' 'Yes,' said the maroon beret, 'He was very good, but then he's a failure, isn't he? When Mr Blair's lost the election we'll have him back and we'll love him to bits.' And the pair of them laughed like drains.

William Hague

I know William Hague as a friend (we are both ex-Presidents of the Oxford Union: I first met him at Oxford in the 1970s) and as a former parliamentary colleague. When I interviewed him, in the run-up to the 1999 Conservative Party Conference, he had been Leader of the Opposition for just over two years.

A couple of days before I made my appointment to interview William Hague, I happened to find myself in the rolling Sussex hills, in Denis Healey's handsome mock-Lutyens sun lounge, enjoying coffee and ginger cake with the former Chancellor of the Exchequer and Grand Old Man of Labour's Centre Right. We were talking about leadership. Lord Healey had been weighing Clement Attlee and Margaret Thatcher in the scales when, suddenly, the name of the Leader of the Opposition cropped up. 'William Hague?' snorted Healey. 'William Hague? He's a twerp. A twerp. There's nothing more to be said. Forget him, forget it. Move on.'

I know William Hague. We were Parliamentary Private Secretaries together at the Treasury. (William was Norman Lamont's bag-carrier, I was Stephen Dorrell's.) I like and admire him, but I have to accept that the

Healey view is not confined to the Labour Party. This week I have conducted my own straw poll among journalists, broadcasters, friends and Conservative activists (in London, Birmingham and Chester) and, quite simply, people don't rate William Hague. Those that have met him like him, but none believes he will be prime minister.

I went to see him at Central Office in Smith Square. The foyer is now New Conservative: colour scheme by Gap, Sky News on the TV, the *Independent* the one newspaper on the coffee table. The only vestige of William's predecessors is a small bust of Winston Churchill, the last bald leader of the party. Beneath a huge portrait of a purposive Master Hague, finger pointing to the future, is a yellow flyer inviting the faithful to sign up for a seminar at which 'leading professional consultants' will provide 'an excellent opportunity to perfect your skills in three key areas: presentation, personal development, interview technique'. (A four-hour session: £10 including lunch.)

As far as interview technique goes, I know my man. He is a safe pair of hands. (When I was in the Whips' Office there was no higher accolade.) Hague doesn't drop catches, which is why I am surprised to find that, for the interview, we are not alone. Amanda Platell (41, Australian, beady eyes, vivid lips, lately editor of the *Sunday Express*, now the Conservatives' Head of Media) perches on the sofa, Sebastian Coe (43, William's judo partner, close friend and private secretary) sits at the far end of the table.

The Leader is looking good: relaxed, slim, fit, lightly tanned. I begin by saying, both because I believe it and because I want to coax him off automatic pilot, 'I know you're flawless, William, but the danger of never putting a foot wrong is that you are so guarded you don't give enough. What I'm wanting is a bit of warmth, and remember, sometimes vulnerability can be a strength.' He smiles. I have been granted the pre-conference interview. He will certainly be watching his words. As I switch on my tape recorder, I wonder if anything he says will surprise me. Probably not. But will some of it move or inspire me? That would be nice.

Given his background in management consultancy (five years with McKinsey & Co in his mid-twenties), I suggest we kick off with a SWOT analysis, a quick overview of his position: the strengths, weaknesses, opportunities and threats. 'Let's begin with your strengths. I think you're bold, brave, decisive.'

He laughs. 'You want me to say that I'm bold, brave, decisive?'

'No,' I'm laughing now. 'I'll say that. The way you seized the moment to go for the leadership is an example. At first, I thought you wanted to be Michael Howard's deputy.'

'It was a difficult decision to make in a short time. I had hoped John Major would carry on for a time and tried to persuade him to do so – in this room – there – right there, by that window. However, I respected his decision to stand down right away. Then, within minutes, Ken Clarke announced he was standing. I remember I went out for a walk to think about it. When I got back there were 32 messages saying "You've got to stand". I did think about teaming up with Michael Howard, we didn't finalise anything, we didn't shake hands on it. You have to take an opportunity when it comes and I thought, "Here is a party that needs to move on a generation and we don't have many people if we are going to move on a generation," so I thought it was right. Of course, it was a complication that I had just got engaged and I'd said to Ffion, "After the election we're going to have a lot more time, and a more peaceful time." However, we decided to do it, we decided together.'

'Ffion is one of your strengths.'

'Yes, in many ways. To me she is a strength because she is a wonderful person, wife, and she's a strong person in herself.'

'Is she liking it?'

'Yes, yes, enormously. She found it hard to get used to initially, but now she really does like it.' (I have my doubts about this, but what else can he say? For the time being we are not going to discover more: Ffion is not giving interviews.)

'People say, "We should see a lot more of your wife," even though she did a hundred public engagements last year, they want to see more of her. I say, "Wait a minute, she has got a career of her own." We're very content with the life we lead, much more so than people might imagine. People say, "You must hardly ever see each other." Actually, that's not the case at all. Compared to a lot of professional couples, we see a lot of each other.'

Ffion is a strength, and William confirms she will continue to feature in photo opportunities, but he is aware of the risks involved in over-playing the wife card. I raise the case of the infamous £ sign pendant, sported by Ffion at a Tory Party fund-raiser, apparently a love token from her husband. My wife is of the view that no normal man would buy his wife a £-shaped anything as a personal gift and no normal woman would be particularly pleased to receive one. I say, 'So Amanda bought the pendant?'

'No, I bought the pendant—' He's laughing. I think he's blushing. 'Well, I paid for the pendant. I chose the pendant.'

I get the impression a lesson has been learnt.

'Another strength: you're intelligent. Are you brighter than Tony Blair?'

'Yes,' hisses Seb from his end of the table. 'That's for others to decide,' says William with becoming modesty.

'You have a First?'

'Yes.'

'Mr Blair doesn't.'

'Doesn't he?' Clearly, William is not going to be drawn into any unstatesmanlike banter.

'You're cool under fire. You're a star in the Commons. How long does it take you to prepare for prime minister's Questions?'

'It varies a lot, a few hours normally. Quite a bit of the preparation involves deciding which topic to tackle. I think about that the night before, commission any research that might be needed, then give it quite a few hours on the Wednesday. I enjoy it hugely and, as I've gone along, I've made it more spontaneous, rather than have it all written out and sticking to the script.

'I do enjoy speaking in the House of Commons. I like being in the House of Commons, though it's a less lively, less interesting place nowadays, with a vast majority of automatons. It has lost individuals and originality. I like the idea of senior politicians who stay on, like Ted Heath. They contribute an enormous amount by staying in the Commons instead of going off to the Lords.

'I believe in the House of Commons, its importance. I want to revive its importance in the British constitution. I want to do that in the early days of a new government. I want to strengthen the role of parliament. I thought it was too easy when I was a minister actually to get things through. The minister was always the expert, the civil servants were the experts, and the MPs were nothing. A lot of this needs changing.'

'Does Blair still wear make-up for Questions?'

'You'll have to analyse the film. I try to look away.'

'You don't wear make-up?'

'No.'

'We used to say: the mood of the country is set in the Commons and percolates out. That's not the case any more, is it? What happens in the chamber doesn't count for much.'

'True, but I think it's been important for us in these first two years of opposition. Imagine the scene in 1997: 400 of them, 160 of us. The fact that we could hold our own in parliament and win almost every debate was almost all we had, was the only thing we had to begin with.

'And Question Time, in effect, is the time when the Party Leader gives his MPs the message of the day, the line to take. And parliament will come back into its own when there is a government with a smaller majority and when there is a government that pays greater respect to parliament and doesn't try to diminish it all the time. It would be a foolish politician who said, "I'm not going to bother with treating the House of Commons seriously."'

Denis Healey would say this is just whistling in the dark. 'Hague has a certain Oxford Union debater's flair. He scores at Westminster. So what? No one's listening, no one's watching. It's how you come over on TV and radio that count.'

I say to William, 'Would you accept that Blair is more television-friendly than you are?'

'Not if you watched BBC *Question Time* with both of us in July. I think he's more experienced and has been doing it longer, but it was interesting being in America in August. They've just shown those two programmes on C-Span there and Americans came up to me and said, "You are far better on the TV because you were really meaning what you said."'

'Can we turn to your weaknesses now? Let's start with appearance and manner. The problem is that, fairly or not, once people get a picture of a politician it's difficult to shift. Michael Foot in that donkey jacket, Neil Kinnock with wispy red hair falling into the sea, David Steel sitting in David Owen's breast pocket, Mr Major "nice but grey". How do you think you're seen at present?'

'I think it varies hugely. It depends what people see me doing, whether or not they've met me. I'm well aware that a lot of them have constantly played back to them the picture of me in a baseball cap. The thing that always strikes me when I meet people is they say, "You're a lot taller than I expected", from which one forms the impression that people think you're a bit small. I'm 5' 11". They've seen the cartoon of the schoolboy in cap and shorts and that's what they expect.'

'What can you do about it?'

'The main thing you can do is be yourself. What other solution is there?'

'We hear that Amanda and Ffion have produced a list of things to be done.'

He laughs. 'They have not produced a list. The only thing that Amanda and Ffion tell me to do is to be myself. I don't think there is a better answer than that.'

'Are clothes important? Who chooses your clothes?'

'I choose my clothes.'

'Where do you buy them?'

'A variety of places to which I don't wish to send the media in a pack, so I think I'll keep that to myself.'

I persist with this, not because I want to be gratuitously rude, but because William's appearance is something the activists do talk about. I say to him, 'The unkind ones picture you as a foetus in a baseball cap – others see you as an old man in a young man's body, an odd-looking political nerd reading *Hansard* at the age of seven.'

'If there is some kind of difficulty like that, which there obviously is, the only thing to do is reach beyond it, to go above it if you like, because the answer to discussion on those sorts of things is to show the substance and to actually lay out what you would do for the country. I find that when I give a speech to an audience about what I really believe it never occurs to them for a minute to think about a baseball cap or a cartoon.'

'But if you take people like Ken Clarke or Ann Widdecombe who, let's face it, are not necessarily the most physically alluring creatures, somehow people accept their appearance because they sense that they are comfortable with themselves, comfortable in their own skins.'

'Mm.'

'Are you comfortable in your skin – compared with Widdecombe or Clarke?'

'I think the answer comes when you say what you think and believe.

'We've now got to a stage when I'm setting out what I believe. I certainly don't have a better answer than that. There's no point in trying to set up an image of something you're not. That's always seen through in the end, like it will be with Tony Blair.

'I have taken a conscious decision about my next task. We've reorganised the party, we've got the European election right, we've got the European policy where it ought to be; my next task is to communicate the policy the Conservative government would follow. Everything else is subordinate.'

'But look at the polls, William. You're nowhere.'

'What we've done and said on Europe is a model of how to proceed on other issues. We had to settle Europe. It was our Achilles heel. We had to turn a weakness into a strength. Three months before the European elections, the polls said we would get 17%, the pro-Europe Conservative Party 14% and Labour 45%. We went on to win with thirty-six times as many votes as the Pro-Europe Conservative Party. So I think after that I don't have to be run by opinion polls.'

'Okay, opportunities now. Do you think Europe is a very big opportunity for you?'

'It is. Just to speak up for the country is a big opportunity across a whole range of subjects – to speak up for the country on issues where they almost began to think that politicians, that all politicians, were no use. The country has a strong gut instinct we should not give any more rights and powers away from this country to the European Union. They don't want to pull out of Europe, but they think it's time to draw a line. They think there are things that can be done about crime and law and order on their estates where it is still a number one issue on a lot of doorsteps. And they say, "Why hasn't anyone done something about it?" because what they've heard from around the rest of the world is you can do something about it. Over the next few weeks we will be setting out of a whole range of law and order policies. Welfare state. Labour campaign on doing something about that. People know we have to do something about that. We can't spend billions more on the welfare state. Now's our opportunity to show how it can be done. So that is our great opportunity.'

'If Ken Clarke was ready to come back onto the front bench, would you enthusiastically grab him?'

'Well, anybody who comes onto the front bench has to support the policy on Europe, so the question doesn't arise because he has a difficulty with our policy. We don't have many other differences. He and I get on together extremely well and I've no doubt had we agreed on Europe we'd have been able to set out from the very beginning after the general election both on the front bench. It doesn't arise because he honourably disagrees. I'm not saying that no one can disagree. I'm saying everybody on the front bench has to agree, without exception.'

'Another opportunity is that you're young, you're new, but you'll hear the criticism that you haven't got enough "grown-ups" on board.'

'You can see from the three reshuffles I've had that I've now changed the entire shadow cabinet, except for me and George Young, there's only two of us left from the day after the general election. I've consciously decided to risk people saying "Who are these new people?" rather than "Why are you surrounded by all these old faces?"'

'And do you have "grown-ups" here at Central Office?'

'I've got some very grown-up people here. [Sniggering from Seb and Amanda.] My closest politician colleague in this building is Michael Ancram, who has been active in politics for twenty-five years, has been chairman of the party in Scotland, has been a minister, is hardly lacking in experience. I know this is a line that's peddled, but I've always thought it was ridiculous. I've read "William Hague is surrounded by all these young, single people", and I've looked around, across at the Chief Whip who is married with four kids; at my PPS until a couple of months ago, David Lidington, married with four kids; then I look at my private secretary with four kids. I have all these people bringing up their families with immensely diverse experience of life.'

(This, I think, is a weak answer. I know these chaps. Fecund they may be, immensely diverse they are not. They are very much of a type: gents, decent, delightful, conscientious, committed. Ancram is a wily bird, but Arbuthnot, Lidington and Coe are good eggs, not political heavyweights. In Hague's immediate entourage, who is doing the thinking, where's the intellectual grit going to come from?)

'Now the threats. Because you're mired in the polls, the press go on with leadership speculation. You'd accept that in the government there are two distinct camps, Blairites and Brownites?'

'Yes.'

'And now there are Hagueites and Portilloites in the Conservative Party. Yes?'

'Yes. I think all senior politicians have some kind of following otherwise they can't be a senior politician. Yes, they always have their groups of friends within a party. I approach this with a particular attitude. I don't spend my time being insecure about what I'm doing. I have actively promoted new people, many of whom could one day be the leader of the party. I think you do a great disservice to your party if you sit there and say, "Oh no, I mustn't have that so-and-so because they might one day be the leader." One day you'll want someone else to be the leader, you've got to provide for a succession, you've got to provide for a lot of people who are fit to do that. I never have any hesitation about promoting people in the shadow cabinet who are going to do really well, encouraging Michael Portillo back into the House of Commons, encouraging Chris Patten. Chris Patten decided to do something else, but I had a go at persuading him to come back to the House of Commons. You can't do a job like this properly if you spend all your time looking over your shoulder.'

'The consensus is that Portillo is the one to fear. He's reinvented himself, he's charismatic, even Denis Healey rates him. Do you think it was right for him to make his statement about his homosexual past?'

'Only he knows if it's right.'

'But don't you have an opinion?'

'No, I think it's entirely up to him. He could have chosen to say that, he could have chosen not to say that. But I don't think it should be held against him or should affect his future career.'

'As you know, people have said the same of you, that there are skeletons in your cupboard.'

'Every senior figure has had all sorts of things said about them. I once heard rumours that I had been secretly married and had kids I'd not owned up to. I've had every kind of rumour. You learn to live with that.'

'Given what Michael has chosen to do, and given that in the last parliament it was certainly openly said, by MPs and by journalists, that you had a homosexual past, though it may sound impertinent to ask it I am going to . . .'

'Impertinence has never stopped you doing anything.'

'Is it untrue in your case?'

'Yes.'

I manage to look him in the eye. He is smiling.

'Yes, yes, absolutely, but so are a lot of things said about a lot of people.'

'Does it worry you that people say it?'

'Not remotely.'

'On the age of consent, you voted for equality at sixteen, but I read somewhere that you would endorse gay marriage?'

'That was reported erroneously.'

'Would you mind if one of your children was gay?'

Pause. Momentary splutter. 'I'd better get to the stage of having the children first.'

'I don't think Ann Widdecombe would have any difficulty answering that. I don't think Ken Clarke would have any difficulty either. I think one can take caution too far, William. You're just being so cautious.'

'Well, I think these are . . . um . . . er . . . I haven't yet thought about the sex of the children, never mind the sexual orientation. I would want my kids, I would hope my kids would all grow up to be married and have kids of their own, but I would also want them to be free to live their lives however they wished. I say it's good for the country if people on the whole live in families bringing up children, but I also say that doesn't mean we have to insist that one hundred per cent of people live like that.'

'Would you encourage others to be open about their sexuality, to be themselves?'

'Yes, I would.'

'If somebody chose to say they were homosexual in the modern

Conservative Party that should not be a bar to them standing for election?'

'Absolutely not.'

'Going to constituency events, meeting the activists who will be gathering this week in Blackpool, I get the impression that your supporters respect you, find you likeable, thoroughly competent. They've no specific complaint, but they feel something's missing. There was that story about focus groups no longer being asked what one single thing could be done to improve the standing of the Tory Pary because the answer was always the same . . .'

'That was complete rubbish, total rubbish.'

'So what do you do?'

'You have to recognise what we've already done. The Conservative Party after the last election could have imploded, divided, could have gone down a lot further – which is what usually happens to parties when they go into opposition. But actually we've had the biggest reorganisation of the party since Disraeli, that has made it democratic. It's a huge change, a cultural revolution in the party. When I was elected I had 164 people deciding who was the leader. If I walked under the Smith Square omnibus this afternoon a third of a million people would decide. We have nearly two thousand more elected Conservatives in local government and in Europe. We have addressed that European issue. That means we've stabilised the party, we've started to renew the party.

'But you do only make the big strides forward when you show what you would do as an alternative government and that is the next stage. Some people have been impatient for that stage, but if we'd started out on that a year ago, eighteen months ago, nobody would have been listening, nobody wanted to hear from the Conservative Party. I would be disappointed if the people who have said what you say they say – which I entirely understand and agree that's what they say – if they were still saying that in six months' time, I would be disappointed.'

'Can we do some of the human stuff now? Do you have a favourite book?'

'The book I'm reading at the moment is so good: Andrew Roberts's brilliant biography of Salisbury, a great Tory leader.'

'Do you read fiction?'

'Yes, I do. I'm very fond of Patrick O'Brian.'

'When did you last go to the theatre?'

'A long time ago. I go to the cinema more than the theatre, but I don't think I've been this year. I buy jazz CDs. Ffion is educating me about jazz. And I like paintings. I particularly like the paintings of my local artist, Mackenzie Thorpe. [He created Hague's last Christmas card: a lonely shepherd with a motley flock of black-faced sheep.] I like Georgia O'Keefe. I'm very fond of Georgia O'Keefe.'

This is a surprise. O'Keefe is famous for her brilliantly-coloured evocations of exotic flora, paintings regarded by some as supercharged symbols of female sexuality. Alas, lack of time prevents further analysis. I simply say to William, 'When you do In the Psychiatrist's Chair I'd choose a different artist.' He laughs obligingly and we move on to more predictable ground.

'How do you unwind?'

'We walk a lot, we walk in the Yorkshire Dales a lot, that's what we were doing last Sunday. We have some great holidays. Our unwinding is often concentrated in a week at a time. We went sailing in the summer. We go cross-country skiing, so it's usually activity.'

'Do you have supper on your knees in front of the television?'

'No, not really. We always have Sunday lunch on our own. We have a proper lunch, prepared by Ffion, with her helper. That's me. We hardly ever go out for Sunday lunch. A lot of kind people invite us and can never understand why we're never able to go. We don't need anything to watch, we just like spending time together, we talk. I'm not one who has to find a lot of entertainment elsewhere.'

'Do you watch television recreationally?'

'Not very much. My favourite programme is *Frasier*.'

'Do you have a spiritual life?'

'I am a Christian, but I don't go to church every Sunday.'

'You're probably like me, when I go I enjoy the hymns, the ritual, the familiarity of the traditions.'

'Yes, exactly, that's exactly what I would say. I don't kneel at the end of the bed and say my prayers.'

'Do you sometimes lie in bed and talk to God?'

'I feel I am a Christian and believe in God, but not in that tangible way that He's there all the time and you can have a conversation.'

'Do you have political heroes?'

'William Pitt. I've got a portrait of him in my office at the Commons and above the shadow cabinet table. He also went into politics young, far younger than me, and led the Tory Party, and led the nation, very successfully.'

'Among contemporary politicians?'

'They are too contemporary to qualify as heroes.'

'What do you think you can learn from Blair? He's obviously doing something right. He's sustaining his position in the polls. And so are you.'

'I think we can all learn from him that he can communicate something by saying it time after time. The difficulty, of course, comes when the well-constructed image runs into harsh reality. The politician who can supply both the substance, who can do something for the country, and can communicate it consistently as well, that would be a devastating combination. With Blair, we've got half that, we've got the image half.'

'If you become prime minister, how will Britain be different five years on?'

'It will be clear about where it stands with Europe, that it's in it but it's not going to be taken over by it; it will be more law-abiding, people will be worried about breaking the law much more than they are today; it will have a stronger sense that people who do the right thing and their best for their families are rewarded for it and get to keep the rewards, that it's good to save, that it's good to provide for the long term, and that you're not in some ways penalised. It will have a strong sense of the uniqueness of being British in the world and the importance of continuing that, instead of trying to submerge our country into something else. We will have recovered our sense of being different, being able to get on with everybody but being different from them.'

'If you don't become prime minister, what will you do?'

'Carry on trying.'

Ah, an unexpected answer. I didn't think he would allow himself to be heard admitting the possibility of defeat. But he's not a fool. He knows it may take more than one haul for the Conservatives to regain office and he's in it for the long term.

My hour is up. The audience is over. I ask William if he has a favourite maxim.

'I think Willie Whitelaw said, I think he actually said to me, "Nothing is ever so good or so bad as it first seems in politics," which is very true.'

Sebastian Coe says his boss is 'the most qualified man who ever wanted to be prime minister,' and adds (and means it), 'I'd die in the ditch for that man.' Denis Healey says he's a twerp. I reckon the Whitelaw maxim may be nearer the mark. Hague is thirty-eight, a considerable achiever, likeable, clear-headed, quick-witted, rational, reasonable, intelligent, articulate, thoughtful, shrewd. But something's still missing. I was impressed, I wasn't moved. I was charmed, but not inspired. In theatrical terms, Hague is a first-class leading man: he knows the lines, he won't bump into the furniture, he'll never miss a performance. But, as yet, he isn't a star. And, right or wrong, these days that's what the punters want.

Edward Heath

Sir Edward Heath KG MBE was prime minister 1970–74 and retired, after fifty-one years in parliament, at the 2001 general election. I first met him when he was Leader of the Opposition in the late 1960s. I was not very well at the time and, just as we shook hands, I threw up. I interviewed him, in happier circumstances, at his home in Salisbury in the autumn of 1999.

S ir Edward Heath has known them all. Presidents, premiers, princes, pontiffs, from Jack Kennedy to Pope John XXIII, from Charles de Gaulle to Saddam Hussein, he's hobnobbed with every world figure of our time. The pride of his orchid house is a 'particularly virile specimen', a personal present from Fidel Castro.

The Member for Old Bexley & Sidcup lives in Salisbury, in an achingly enviable Queen Anne house in the Cathedral Close. 'When Roy Jenkins came to lunch he looked out of the drawing-room window and said, "Ted, this must be one of the ten finest views in Britain." I said, "Oh really, which do you think are the other nine?"'

The shoulders heave, the face lights up, the watery eyes twinkle, the nation's longest-serving MP is in mellow mood. When I was in the government Whips' Office we had our reservations about Ted: always complacent, often curmudgeonly, now and again downright unhelpful. Today I sense I am going to be charmed by the old monster.

He leads me through the house. It is his pride and joy. 'It's thirteenth-century in origin, built as a home for a canon of the Cathedral.' He shows off his treasures: the dish that once belonged to Disraeli, the Richard Strauss manuscript ('the concluding bars of the first act of *Der Rosenkavalier*'), the Churchill paintings. 'This is the one I prefer. It's got two signatures. Winston signed it when he painted it and then signed it again when he gave it to me.' I am particularly taken with the figure of a Chinese horse. 'You like it?' He is evidently delighted.

'It's beautiful,' I say. 'I won't touch.'

'Good. It's T'ang dynasty, well over a thousand years old, and in perfect condition.' He is beaming from ear to ear. 'What will you have? Tea, gin, whisky, champagne?' It is four o'clock. We settle for tea. With a little difficulty (he is eighty three and has not treated his body as a temple) he settles back into the sofa and, suddenly, assumes the appearance of one of the mighty Chinese leaders – Mao, Chou En-Lai, Deng Xiaoping – with whom he has had discourse down the years.

He nods at me. The interview can begin. He was leader of the Conservative Party for ten years and prime minister for four. I ask, 'What do you think are the qualities required for successful political leadership?'

Silence. Another nod. 'You suggest some and I'll respond.'

'Energy,' I venture.

'Yes.'

'Stamina.'

'Yes.'

'An ability to perceive reality efficiently and tolerate uncertainty.'

'Hmm. Yes.'

'An ability to inspire loyalty and maintain discipline.'

'Yes, but it depends how it's done. Political leadership is different from military leadership. In politics you can't just lay down the law and expect people to follow it. We see an attempt being made to operate in that way in the Conservative Party now. Hague says, "I'll do it my way!" That's not political leadership. It's an attempt to impose a particular point of view.'

'But come on, Ted, you know all about trying to maintain discipline within a party. You were Chief Whip, after all.'

'I once tried to explain my function as Chief Whip to Khrushchev and Bulganin when the Soviets visited London [in 1956]. Anthony Eden [the prime minister] introduced me to them and said, "This is my Chief Whip". This was translated and the Russians looked profoundly puzzled. Eden went on, "His job is to persuade members of our party to support its leaders by voting in the House of Commons." The pair looked even more non-plussed. "How do you mean, persuade them to support you?" asked Khrushchev. "Surely you just tell them to do so." In my day, we had differences within the party, of course, but we never withdrew the whip from anyone, we never for a moment thought of expelling people from the party. True political leadership is about persuasion, and about listening to and taking account of others.'

'But also about having a clear personal vision, knowing where you want to go?'

'Yes.'

'And to that end you have to be determined, single-minded, to have what Napoleon admired, the mental power "*de fixer les objets longtemps sans être fatigue*"?'

'Yes, yes, absolutely.' (I knew I'd score with that one.) 'The great leaders will always concentrate on the big picture, not get too bogged down in the day-to-day.'

'But that's easier said than done these days. The pace of modern government is incredible. It was very different when you started, wasn't it? Is it true that Attlee always made time to finish the crossword and Macmillan regularly read Trollope after lunch?'

'Oh yes. I remember, in the middle of one crisis [in 1958] – three ministers, including the Chancellor of the Exchequer, had just resigned – I went to see Macmillan in his room at Number 10 to talk to him about the timing of the announcement of their replacements. I found him sitting in his armchair with his feet up on a stool, reading in front of the fire. He agreed to what I proposed and then said, "But please don't worry me any more. Can't you see that I'm trying to finish *Dombey and Son* before I go off on this foreign tour tomorrow morning?"'

'Would that approach be possible today?'

'Yes, perfectly. It was that approach that allowed me my music, my concerts; it allowed me my sailing in the spring and the summer. It's a question of how you handle the job. I didn't interfere with departmental ministers just for the sake of it. I only became involved if something appeared to be going wrong.'

'When did that style of government begin to change?'

'With Harold Wilson. He was a workaholic. He had a small group around him and they met constantly, working into the early hours. They say Wilson was a great operator, but to what effect? There's nothing left of Wilson now.'

'And, of course, Mrs Thatcher only needed five hours' sleep and never stopped.'

'Hmm, yes, well. One saw the consequences.'

I am not expecting Margaret Thatcher to feature on Edward Heath's list of the top three British prime ministers of our time. I have given him notice of this question. Who does he choose?

'Churchill, naturally. His greatness as a political leader was at a time of war. The circumstances suited his temperament and talents. He was never at his best in peacetime. In peacetime, the British on the whole prefer a quieter style of leadership.

'Next, I'd choose Macmillan, who has been much maligned by the present right-wing generation. He was a true One Nation Tory. And he had enormous style. We had dinner together on the night he became prime minister. He wanted to go to the Grill Room at the Savoy, but I suggested somewhere less public. We settled on the Turf Club, off Piccadilly. Downing Street was packed with crowds and press and people from the television and the radio, but we managed to scramble into the car and get to the club without anyone catching up with us. We strolled into the bar, sat down on two stools and ordered drinks. There was only one other man there. He was reading the *Evening Standard* which carried the huge headline "Macmillan prime minister". The man looked up, saw the prime minister and then asked, rather casually, "Have you had any good shooting recently?" "No," said Macmillan. "What a pity," said the man. We finished our drinks and made our way to the dining room. As the prime minister was going out, the fellow looked up and said, "Oh, by the way, congratulations." After we'd had our oysters, steak, coffee, cognac, the manager of the club approached our table, bowing every few steps, before stopping to say, "Excuse me, sir, but I have arranged for you to leave by the back door." Macmillan said, "How very kind, but I think it is perfectly all right for me to leave by the front door. I am not ashamed of being prime minister, you know." As we left, a girl reporter pushed forward and asked the prime minister what we had been discussing, "Oh, just the future," he said with a wave of his hand.'

'And who comes third?'

'Well, if we're talking cross-party it has to be Attlee, no question. But if you're looking for a third Conservative . . .'

'Yes?'

'You're obviously waiting for Thatcher—'

'No, I—'

'Well, strange though it may seem—'

For an extraordinary nanosecond I think he is going to pick the nation's first woman prime minister after all . . . but no:

'Strange though it may seem, Alec Douglas-Home did a remarkable job in under a year to get us within three seats of an election victory [in 1964].

He is not to be underestimated. He had real leadership qualities. He is always represented as being the innocent, unambitious, stalking, shooting figure. Not at all. The motions he went through, which I saw at first hand, to get the leadership, they were impressive. He wasn't just sitting there, waiting patiently in case it came his way. Far from it.'

'I don't think Sir Alec is going to feature on many people's lists, Ted.'

A shrug of the shoulders. 'Possibly not.'

'I suspect that if you did a survey of public opinion, asking people who they regard as the great political leaders of the post-war years, Thatcher and Reagan would come close to the top. Why do you think that is?'

There is a long pause. 'I don't think I can answer that. I could, but I won't.'

'Reagan, of course, is credited with ending the Cold War.'

'Yes, well, that certainly isn't the case.'

'Do you think Reagan had much of a grip—'

'No, he hadn't. He is called "the great communicator" because of his capacity for presentation which came from his whole career as an actor. I have met all the American presidents since Eisenhower.'

'And who do you rate?'

'My top three? Eisenhower—'

I interrupt because this seems to me a surprising first choice: 'If we think of him at all now, it's as the general who played golf.'

'Yes, he got the balance right. The American people respected him as a soldier and loved him as a man. Jack Kennedy. He was wonderfully glamorous, but he was also very practical. He was a realist. And Nixon. Nixon was never very happy on internal, economic affairs, but on foreign affairs he was superb. I worked with him when he was President and saw quite a bit of him afterwards. I never had the nerve to ask him why he behaved as he did [over Watergate]. Why didn't he just sack those two [Haldeman and Ehrlichman]? Everyone would have accepted it and he could have carried on as normal.'

And on the wider stage, beyond the United Kingdom and the United States, who is Heath going to pick for his leadership hall of fame?

'Chairman Mao, Marshal Tito, General de Gaulle. Remarkable personalities, with one feature in common: they were all thinking in big terms.'

'Was Mao charismatic?'

'Very much so. He had presence, enhanced of course by the respect he was paid. When you meet with the Chinese leaders, they always have other high-level figures present. And when the great man speaks they sit back, listening respectfully. They have heard it all before. But if the leader says anything new or unexpected, you know at once, because suddenly they all sit forward.

'Tito was very interesting. You could see how he inspired fierce loyalty. He stayed with me at Chequers and was good company. He would only drink Scotch whisky, Chivas Regal. I sent him a case every year on his birthday. He believed he had bound the constituent parts of Yugoslavia together so tightly they would never come apart. Of course, he couldn't foresee the collapse of communism and, when it came, we could certainly have handled the break-up of Yugoslavia differently. Our people seem to have forgotten that the Serbs supported us in the First World War, supported us in the Second. Tito supported us. There's an ignorance of history which is lamentable.

'People say that when de Gaulle first became prominent, at the time of the evacuation of France, he was not impressive. He was tall, thin, made no great impact. But later, he became more substantial and, when he was President, he was very impressive. He was one of those who could sort out the great issues from the small and who, by their character, could dominate events. Adenauer too made a great impact, even though he was well into his eighties. He knew how to handle ministers and situations so that he was the dominant feature. From our point of view, of course, the problem was he always gave way to de Gaulle.'

'Again, Ted, if there was to be a poll I'm not sure any of your candidates would top it. I expect Nelson Mandela would come first.'

'I expect he would. But I look at these things in a very hard way. If you compare what Mao did or Chou En-Lai or Adenauer – they transformed their countries. Mandela's achievement has been very largely presentational. I've been down there twice since the change. And what I found worrying is that the people expected so much and have got so little. All the time Mandela was there it was all right, but now he's given up, how is their disappointment going to show? I'm afraid they are going to be in for a very rough time.'

To my surprise, Sir Edward is rather more optimistic about the prospects for Cuba. It turns out he is something of an admirer of Fidel Castro. 'He certainly knows how to make an entrance: the screeching of brakes, the hooting of horns and suddenly he's there, one hand on hip, the other in the air, shouting "Welcome, welcome!" Castro's got character and style, but he's also done an enormous amount for that island. I've been over a number of times. The agriculture is now very good. They've raised the standard of education, they've raised the standard of living and the rate of life expectancy. And he has some good people working for him.'

Reading this you may be thinking that a man who has barely concealed contempt for Margaret Thatcher and an almost gung-ho enthusiasm for Fidel Castro is simply preposterous, but sit with him for an hour, read his autobiography (*The Course of My Life*), and there is something compelling, impressive, moving even, about his certainty, his unshakeable belief that he has got it right.

As I get up to go, he expresses satisfaction that this interview will be appearing on Remembrance Sunday. His commitment to European union has its roots in the twentieth century's two world wars. In 1940, when he was twenty four, just down from Oxford and about to join the army, he wrote to a friend, 'This rock on which Hitler will break himself is the rock on which Europe will have to be rebuilt afterwards, and this time we shall not throw away that chance.'

For sixty years he has seen Britain's future at the heart of a united Europe.

You can hoot with derision, snort in disgust, or say (as John Major once said to me), 'Surely nobody takes Ted seriously any more?' He doesn't care. He knows he's right. And whatever Thatcher did or Blair might do (we can forget Master Hague altogether), it is neither here nor there. Heath signed the Treaty of Accession in Brussels on 24 January 1972. And there's no turning back. 'It was the proudest moment of my life.' His place in history is assured.

Ann Widdecombe

*I interviewed Ann Widdecombe, Conservative MP for Maidstone since 1987,
and at the time Shadow Home Secretary, for Mothering Sunday 2000.*

I have known Ann Widdecombe a long time. Thirty-two years ago we were contemporaries at Oxford, fellow officers at the Union. In the 1990s I was a government whip when she was minister of state at the Home Office. She is an oddity (always was), but, as a political animal, I rate her, and, as a person, I like her a lot. Writing honestly about a friend is a risky proposition. From the outset I know this interview isn't going to be easy, but the way it goes awry takes me wholly by surprise. About half-way through our allotted hour in her office at the House of Commons I register that my brand-new digital recorder isn't working. I have pressed the wrong buttons. 'And,' squawks Ann, pushing back her chair and hooting with derision, 'you haven't taken any notes, not one.'

As I sit, head in hands, muttering 'I'm sorry, I'm so, so sorry', the Shadow Home Secretary (a pint-sized bundle of energy: Danny de Vito meets Margaret Rutherford: Mrs Tiggywinkle on speed) jumps to her feet and beetles through to her secretary's room next door. A moment later she is back, chortling, triumphant, brandishing a dictaphone above her head. 'I'll recap on this.' She resumes her place at the table. 'This is Gyles Brandreth's Mothering Sunday interview with Ann Widdecombe.'

Pathetically I bleat, 'Edited highlights will do.'

'Drink your coffee. Leave it to me.' Ann fixes the machine with a mildly manic stare and in three minutes flat summarises the past half hour. 'I began by saying that Mothering Sunday is wonderful, important and worthwhile because it teaches us to think about all that we owe to our mothers, and how particularly nice it is for me this year because I am going to be able to hand over the flowers to my mother in person instead of having them sent round. My mother, who is eighty eight, has come to live with me and I couldn't be happier. People say, "How do you cope?" as though it's some sort of burden. I can't imagine anything nicer or more natural. My parents were married for 62 years. They were engaged for five years and knew each for five years before that, so they were together for literally a lifetime. When my father died last year, I invited my mother to come and live with me. We've installed a Stannah lift and it's been a total success. And, no, sharing a bathroom isn't a problem. We're in there at different times!

'My mother is accustomed to moving house. My father was with the admiralty (he ended up as director general of naval supplies and transport) so my mother spent years on the move, from Bath to Singapore and back again, twenty-four different homes in all. She was a traditional mother who stayed at home to look after her family. Her life has been dedicated to others, given over to caring for my father and my grandmother, and her two children. My brother Malcolm is ten years older than me, we're pre- and post-war babies, but she treated us exactly the same. Am I like her? I think I've inherited traits from both my parents. My father was very ambitious. Is my mother interested in politics? Not at all. She hates arguments of any kind. She feels sorry for absolutely everybody. I try to keep the worst things that are written about me away from her. She'd find them far too hurtful.

She is very soft and gentle.

'Gyles asked me if I found anything about my mother irritating. I said if I did I wouldn't be prepared to share it with the press, but I added that the one thing I do find strange about living with somebody else for the first time is that they interrupt your train of thought without realising it. One thinks invisibly, which is a problem. Then Gyles asked if my mother finds anything about me irritating and I said I was sure there were lots of things about me that are irritating, but she wouldn't be sharing them with the press either. Gyles asked if I would be cooking lunch for my mother and if I liked cooking and I said no I didn't like cooking, still less shopping, but that my mother would like the lunch that I prepared for her because her chief characteristic is kindness.

'Then Gyles asked, "Do we still value mothers?" and I said, "Plainly we don't, but we should." I was part of an extended family that included my grandmother as well as my mother. I regret the disappearance of extended families, never mind the break-up of nuclear families which we are seeing now. Let's face it, we are not a happier society as a result of the liberalisation of the seventies. We have record rates of divorce, record rates of suicide, record rates of teenage pregnancy, record rates of youth crime, record rates of underage sex. We should invite people to recognise that the Great Experiment has failed. You cannot have happiness without restraint. We should invite people to consider too that self-restraint is more than its own reward. Nowadays we seek quick-fix solutions, but in fact if you take time, trouble and effort you may get a rather better result. For example, instead of reaching immediately for the divorce lawyer you should work through a difficult patch in your marriage. It will be better for you, your children, everybody concerned.' She puts down the dictating machine and takes a sip of water (the only fluid to pass her lips during Lent). 'I think that's about where we'd got to. Shall I carry on, or do you want to say something?'

I am taken with the idea of Ann Widdecombe dictating her entire interview to me without pause (evidently she is too), but given that what she has just said has reminded me all too vividly of poor Mr Major and the disaster that was 'Back to Basics', I throw in the thought that politicians pontificating on moral issues can be dangerous.

'Shouldn't be, mustn't be. The alternative is just to surrender to what's going on. What is risky is to imply that there's some magic wand, some government edict that can change everything. There isn't. What we need is the sort of social revolution that caused all the problems in the first place.'

'Do you see any signs of this social revolution?'

'Not yet, but I am ever hopeful.' She chuckles.

'You say marriage is a good thing, but you have no experience of it.'

She gives me a withering look. 'No, but you can look at a picture and know that it's good without being able to paint anything at all.'

'Forty per cent of today's babies are born out of wedlock. You wouldn't have any children unless you were in a marriage?'

'Certainly not.' (The very idea!)

'Do you feel unfulfilled as a woman through not having children?'

'Oh, that's just tripe, that really is the most incredible tripe. That is the first time that question has been put to me so bluntly and I notice it is put to me, not by a woman, but by a man. Really, Gyles, what utter tripe. But the answer, since you ask, is "No". If you think of Gladys Aylward, Florence Nightingale, Mother Teresa, all these women have done things which are utterly fulfilling, but they haven't got married and had children. You've got other women, plain, unremarkable women, who have had very happy marriages, albeit childless.'

'You say it's tripe—'

'Real tripe.'

'But I know women in their thirties and forties who tell me that they are very conscious of the biological clock ticking away. You're telling me that's not something that ever occurred to you at that age?'

'Genuinely not.' Clearly the suggestion is preposterous.

'Look me in the eye.'

'Hand on the book, if you like. It wasn't something I set my face against. I didn't say I am never going to get married, I am never going to have children, but it was never a priority for me, it was never something I went and looked for. Gyles, if you go round with women maundering on at you about their biological clocks, I really feel quite sorry for you, you poor beleaguered male.'

I believe these apparently impertinent questions of mine are legitimate because what's triggered this interview is Ann's emergence as the latest celebrity novelist (a two-book deal, £100,000 advance, 20,000 copy first print-run) and her fiction debut is a story that revolves around small children (several of whom die during the course of it), opening with the words 'The christening party was assembled on the lawn' and closing with a wife in bed, asleep, 'stirring and gently moaning, as the child within her moved, proclaiming its life.'

While the author insists that the book is neither autobiography nor tract, several of the key themes – responsibility, faith, society's attitude to the severely disabled, euthanasia – are ones she cares about passionately. As a companion, Ann is generally rather jolly, but her novel is dark. Does it reflect her underlying view of the world?

'Obviously we do live in a vale of tears, that's an observed fact, but it wasn't what was behind the book. I was simply trying to explore human reactions to a given situation. A speeding sports car knocks down a four-year-old boy and leaves him severely brain-damaged. What happens to his family and those around him? A few generations ago we had a more enlightened view and then someone in Jeremy's position would have been looked after by the entire village. There would have been an immense rallying round. Now it's different. You are kind enough to say the book is thoughtful and thought-provoking. If it makes people think then I've achieved quite a lot.'

What sort of fiction does she read? 'Detective novels, Ruth Rendell, P. D. James. I like novels of the Pamela Hansford Johnson type, not very fashionable these days. I suppose now it would be school of Joanna Trollope.'

'Have you read any of Edwina's?'

Ann pulls her Disgusted-of-Maidstone face and speaks directly into the dictaphone. 'Never. I don't read that sort of stuff. Everybody knows I don't like excessive sex.'

Edwina Currie, Ann and I were born within a year of one another. 'People of our age do still think about sex, Ann. I think about it. Steve Norris, of course, does something about it.'

She laughs, 'Well, I don't.'

'But you do think about it now and again, don't you?'

'The answer is no, not from one day to the next.'

'Do you ever wonder if you're missing out on something?'

'No, I don't. And I wish everybody would stop patronising me by assuming I'm missing out on something. I am missing out on nothing. If you are true to yourself, and you have confidence in what you are doing, and you are happy in what you are, you are missing out on nothing, Gyles, nothing.'

At Oxford, Ann had a boyfriend, Colin Maltby, now a banker. They were a quaint couple, doll-like, awkward, rather earnest. I remember them always holding hands and I think I assumed that because they were keen Christians they spent tortured hours agonising over sex and then got down to it like ferrets. Clearly, I was wrong. Their chaste liaison fizzled out after three years.

Ann once revealed to me her romantic ideal: Rudolph Rassendyll, dashing hero of *The Prisoner of Zenda*, Anthony Hope's cloak-and-dagger Ruritanian romance. Her own next novel will be set in Second World War France, the tale of a convent girl who falls in love with a married German officer. Rather than discuss with Ann her subliminal preoccupation with impossible love and be told I'm talking tripe (or codswallop, another of her favourite words), I ask her whether becoming a popular novelist will help or hinder her prospects as a politician.

'What I say is this: Ted Heath had his sailing and his music, John Major had his cricket, why the heck can't I write? It's always been an ambition of mine. I want to have a series of works published and have them judged on their own merits.'

The instant analogy with two former Conservative prime ministers is significant. She won't admit it, but she knows she could be the next leader of the Tory Party. Unlike Edwina, who was generally despised by her colleagues at Westminster, Ann is liked. She is respected too. As a minister, she was highly rated in the Whips' Office: competent, clear-headed, conscientious (incredibly so: she visited all 131 of the prisons in England and Wales, mostly in her own time), doesn't drop catches (the ultimate accolade), 'a safe pair of hands'. She is no intellectual (she got a Third) and some think her just too eccentric, but the generality of her opinions is more mainstream than you'd imagine and, as with Ken Clarke, people tend to accept her as they find her because she's manifestly true to herself and easy in her own skin. The party faithful find her more exciting than Mr Hague. Put her up against Michael Portillo (Catholic virgin v. born-again heterosexual) and it will be a close-run thing.

Her dictaphone has whirred and clicked. We've run through both sides of the tape. She hands it over. 'Your interview, Mr B. Anything else?'

'What about the Seven Deadly Sins? I think we've established that lust isn't one of yours, so what is?'

She hoots with laughter, pushes back her chair and displays her ample girth. 'Gluttony. I eat too much. I like my food.'

'What about pride?'

'Oh yes, I'm enjoying this period of popularity. It's been positively miraculous what's happened to me recently, but my head is screwed on. I know it won't last. The one lesson I have learnt is simply to do what you believe is right and leave the rest to Almighty God. Carpe diem. Cheerio.'

Jeffrey Archer

In the late summer of 1999 Lord Archer of Weston-super-Mare had high hopes that he might become the first elected mayor of London. It seems incredible now. It seemed almost possible then.

Here is a question I have been pondering for nearly thirty years: when he is so ridiculous, why is Jeffrey Archer so much more successful than I am?

Jeffrey – whom I know quite well and like a lot – is a bizarre phenomenon. Brash, boastful, bombastic, engaging, amusing, generous, this lower-middle-class lad from Weston-super-Mare is now a peer of the realm, a multi-millionaire, world famous (big in the States, enormous in Japan), one of the most successful authors of all time. How has he done it?

And having done it, having won the freedom that wealth brings, why on earth does he want to shackle himself to the political treadmill campaigning to be mayor of London?

In search of answers I went to have breakfast with him in his penthouse apartment on the Albert Embankment. From the outside the block is unexceptional, sixties' banal; but from Jeffrey's vast L-shaped drawing room (deep luxury: large Lowrys, fabulous fresh flowers, lovely bits of statuary, framed photographs of wife Mary, the boys, Jeffrey with Diana, Princess of Wales) the view across the Thames to the Houses of Parliament is breathtaking. And, of course, adjacent to the panoramic window Jeffrey has one of Claude Monet's paintings of the same scene.

We are not alone. It is 8.20 a.m. and already, up in the gallery, Jeffrey's PA is fielding phone calls. Joseph, the butler (of middle European extraction and riper years, straight from Central Casting), pads discreetly in and out. While Jeffrey and I tuck in (for the master, a boiled egg, timed to the second; for me, crunchy brown toast and the crispest bacon), two of the mayoral campaign team sit quietly in attendance.

How many books has he sold?

'120 million worldwide is what Eddie Bell [Chairman of HarperCollins, his publishers] is saying at the moment.'

And how much money has he got?

'I don't know.' He frowns. 'I don't know. I don't care. I have enough.' (Guesstimates vary, but it could be £50 million. Or more.)

And what is the secret? 'I think I have boundless energy, determination and, when I see something, I go for it. Longfellow said, "The heights that great men reached and kept were not attained by sudden flight, but they, while their companions slept, toiled ever upward through the night."' The lines roll effortlessly off the tongue. Clearly it is a favourite quotation. (Later he offers me another gem: 'Energy plus talent, you'll be a king; energy and no talent, you'll be a prince; talent and no energy, you'll be a pauper.')

What fuelled his ambition?

'I didn't do very well at school. I failed completely. I was a disaster. I remember canvassing in Edinburgh with Malcolm Rifkind. We passed his old school and I said "I bet you were a prefect." He said, "No, I wasn't actually," and then he told me how, for fun, he had done a test on the Cabinet and three-quarters of the Cabinet had failed to become prefects too. I've often thought failure to succeed at school drives you to want to succeed afterwards. It's ironic how few school captains appear to go on to do anything else. It's almost as if they've achieved what they want to achieve. I still want to achieve.'

I mention a line of Aristotle Onassis: 'I must keep aiming higher and higher – even though I know how silly it is.'

Jeffrey chuckles, 'That's good. The line I love of Aristotle Onassis is, "If you can count it you haven't got any."'

It was 1961, when I was at school (and, alas, a prefect), that I first came across Jeffrey. He was twenty-one and teaching games at Dover College, a minor public school in Kent. I was thirteen, a pupil at a nearby prep school, and Jeffrey helped out with the athletics coaching. My headmaster said Jeffrey was the best athletics coach he had ever come across.

Jeffrey is not especially forthcoming about the years between leaving his own minor public school (Wellington, near Taunton, in Somerset) and arriving at Dover. He had spells in the army and the Metropolitan Police, he spent some time in America. 'I experimented and failed at lots of things.' Some still wonder how he got the teaching job and felt able to sport a graduate gown on Speech Day – did he allow a certificate from a body-building course (a diploma from the 'International Federation of Physical Culture' off Kingsway) to be mistaken for some kind of American academic qualification? – but what is not in dispute is that he was a fine sprinter and an inspirational coach who got remarkable results from the boys, both at my school and at Dover College.

'What happened at Dover was the headmaster said, "You've been a complete fool, Jeffrey. You should have had a proper education. You could still go to Oxford." I said, "Not with my examination results." He said, "I think we could convince Alec Peterson, the head of the Department of Education, that you should do a Diploma of Education", and Alec Peterson interviewed me and agreed to take me on. That was pretty tough because all the others doing it were graduates. I knew I would have to work pretty hard.'

He worked hard, he ran hard (he ran for his country in Stockholm in 1966), he became President of the University Athletics Club, he developed an interest in politics. 'I joined the Oxford Union and became a very close friend of Michael Beloff's, only because Michael was nuts about athletics. Michael's dream is to win an Olympic gold medal. It's not to be head of Trinity [College, Oxford, which he now is] or Lord Chancellor or any of those things which he assumes will come to him in time. Michael came down to the track and I went to the Union. What struck me about politics is, however much energy you had, you couldn't succeed, you couldn't get everything done – whereas in many other areas in life you can. You set a goal and you can achieve it.'

Jeffrey's early goals were to make a name for himself and make money. He did both. He first hit the headlines when he persuaded the Beatles to back a fund-raising campaign for Oxfam. Then he booked Bob Hope and Frank Sinatra to perform in a charity benefit for Lord Mountbatten's United World Colleges. He went on to become a professional fund-raiser, working for the Birthday Trust, the United Nations Association, the European Movement. He had flair, nerve, and a percentage of what he raised. He fizzed and crackled with energy and ambition. In 1967 he was elected to the Greater London Council. In 1969 he became MP for Louth.

He was an MP and I was in my early twenties, when our paths crossed again. He was gregarious, enthusiastic but quite unreal. He seemed to be playing a character in a drama of his own invention. I recall standing with him outside his office at the top of Whitehall and him giving me his various phone numbers. 'Call me, any time, day or night. Any time.' 'Day or night?' I repeated. He looked me straight in the eye: 'Day or night. Night or day. I never sleep.'

Over breakfast, I asked him what he had read as a child. 'I was nuts about *Just William*, and then I moved on to *Swallows and Amazons*, and adventure stories. I quickly fell in love with Buchan. I just thought his books were wonderful. I read the whole of Buchan in a week. And then I turned to

Fleming and read the whole of Fleming in a week.' That's it. He saw himself as Richard Hannay or James Bond. (On his first date with Mary at Oxford he took her to see *Dr No*. His telephone number still features the digits 007.) To me, he seemed more like one of my own childhood favourites, Toad of Toad Hall, still a hero, still charismatic, but unreliable, and absurd as well as engaging.

We were having lunch once in a little Italian restaurant on the corner of Sloane Square. I was early and seated at a window table. I saw Jeffrey's car drive into the square, but, instead of stopping, it drove round the square, once, twice, three times. When, eventually, Jeffrey stepped out of the car and joined me at the table, I said, 'What on earth was all that about? Why were you driving round and round the square?' Jeffrey pointed at his watch. It was one o'clock exactly. 'I am never late. I am never early.'

Like Toad, Jeffrey has a capacity for bouncing back, for brushing off disaster as if it had never befallen him. Unlike Toad, Jeffrey is anything but lazy. When, in 1974, a naïve investment in a Canadian mining scam brought him close to financial ruin, he resigned as an MP ('I can't expect people to have trust and respect for a man who behaved so stupidly') and immediately set about rebuilding his fortune. That he should turn to story-telling is not surprising. He is a natural spinner of yarns, and a brilliant one. He has had plenty of editorial help (readily acknowledged), but the books are all his. He conceived them, wrote them, marketed them with relentless gusto. He deserves the credit, he has earned the millions.

He has always been generous. One Christmas in the mid-eighties, over lunch at Le Caprice (a favourite Archer watering-hole), near the Ritz Hotel, off Piccadilly, I outlined a business idea of mine to him. When we'd eaten he invited me to walk up the road with him. We went into the Ritz and Jeffrey led me to the hotel restaurant where he summoned the maître d' and, none-too-discreetly, pressed a £50 note into his palm. 'Merry Christmas,' said Jeffrey. 'That's the way to get the right table. Now about your little venture, Gyles.' He paused by a telephone in the lobby, lifted the receiver, dialled and said to whoever answered. 'Mr Brandreth has a scheme. How much can I put in? £30,000? £30,000 it is then.' He turned to me, 'Merry Christmas, Gyles.'

When my scheme failed and I went to tell Jeffrey that I had lost all his money, he said simply, 'Bad luck. At least you tried,' and never referred to it again.

There is much in Jeffrey's colourful career that he would prefer not to have referred to again. Determined Archer-watchers have plenty of questions they want to ask, about his qualifications, about the row over expenses when he worked for the United Nations Association, about the time he walked out of a store in Toronto with three suits (he was released without charge: it was a simple misunderstanding). I ask Jeffrey what he would like to bury from his past. He laughs: 'So many things that I'd be burying all day. To think of one thing that's worse than all the others, that's tough.' Asking around in recent days, it seems that it is the episode involving the prostitute Monica Coghlan that lingers in the public imagination. She maintained they had a relationship, he stoutly denied it, but sent a friend to give her cash to help her leave the country. In the consequent libel action against the *Star*, the judge, famously, was bowled over by Mary's appearance in the witness box ('Your vision of her will probably never disappear. Has she elegance? Has she fragrance?') and the jury duly awarded Jeffrey a record £500,000.

I know prominent Conservatives who have consorted with prostitutes, but Jeffrey isn't one of them. I don't think that I (or any of his friends) believed the libel, but we could all picture Jeffrey, man of action, man of means, naïvely thinking he could solve it all at a stroke by sending an emissary with upturned collar, armed with booty, to a tryst at Victoria Station.

Jeffrey would acknowledge that he is a Romantic and I think is now ready to accept that he has been a fantasist. That's the worst I can say of him. He has a long history of embroidering, exaggerating, wiping out failure and enhancing success. When he was earning £2,000 he claimed it was £4,000; when he had made a million, he made it out to be five; when he had won an American 'Somerset Maugham Award' for his short stories he left me to think it was the more prestigious British Somerset Maugham Award for his first novel. When he was elected as one of the youngest MPs at Westminster, he had to claim he was the youngest. Why?

It is not unheard of for politicians to exaggerate. The great F. E. Smith, youngest Lord Chancellor this century, regaled audiences with tales of his exploits in Egypt as a boy. He would tell how he sailed through the Mediterranean, stayed at Shepherd's Hotel in Cairo, even rode a primitive bicycle from the city to the pyramids – to the wonderment of the Egyptians. When John Campbell came to write F. E. 's biography, he investigated the stories and found them to be a complete fiction. F. E. Smith never left Birkenhead as a boy. Even saintly Tony Blair was once tempted to turn a half-remembered childhood incident into an amazing tale of derring-do ('How I became an airline stowaway') only to find the story blowing up in his face when his dad emerged from the undergrowth to tell the world he had no recollection of any of it.

Mary Archer has spoken of her husband's gift for 'inaccurate precis'. My wife has accused me of having a tendency in the same direction. She calls it 'arrested development'. I telephoned a psychologist friend at Great Ormond Street and (naming no names) described the symptoms. 'Habitual lying? A compulsion to exaggerate? It's not uncommon. It comes from a lack of confidence in your own achievements. Whatever you've done, however remarkable, isn't good enough. In the jargon, you have a warped "internal model" of yourself. It's all to do with your early years, the way your parents react to you, consequently the way you see yourself. You can grow out of it, but usually you need a third party to help you – therapy, a partner, a friend. Essentially it's down to your parents, the model you form of them, then the model you form of yourself.'

At our breakfast, I asked Jeffrey about his parents.

'My father died when I was young. I was only eleven. I don't really remember him that well. He and my mother ran a small publishing business, which was pretty useless. My mother never talks about it, but when he died I think we were minus about £500 which in those days was a lot of money. She struggled on, God bless her, because she is a struggler, she is a fighter. She's eighty six now. She nearly died the year before last. They actually told me "We are taking the respirator off. We're going to let her die tonight. There's no purpose in her living." My son William sat with her all night and the doctor said, "You can keep saying goodbye to her, that's all right, because she can hear you, but she won't be able to respond. She will die during the night." He refused to believe it. He went on talking to her: "You'll be up tomorrow, Gran, we'll have breakfast together." She woke up the next morning and she had breakfast. And she's still here. She's not in great shape, but she's still alive.'

During our conversation I mentioned that I owned, but hadn't read, *Stranger than Fiction*, Michael Crick's biography of Jeffrey. As I was leaving, one of the campaign team, Stephan Shakespeare (former Lambeth teacher, policy adviser to Jeffrey since 1997), came down with me in the lift and said, 'It's a pity Jeffrey won't open up more about his childhood. I think it explains a lot. He was bullied at school. They called him "puny". That's why he took up body-building. You should read Crick's book. It's fascinating.'

I have just finished it. It's mesmerising. It turns out that Jeffrey's father (born 1875, died 1956, when Jeffrey was fifteen, not eleven) was a character worthy of one of his son's novels (if not one of Dickens's): rogue, Romeo, fraudster, convicted felon – and sometime Conservative councillor. He met Jeffrey's mother in the early 1930s, shortly after she had given birth to an illegitimate baby girl quickly put up for adoption. Jeffrey's parents had a son out of wedlock in 1934 (the first 'Jeffrey Archer'), but he too was adopted (and changed his name), and the couple did not marry until 1939, the year before the second Jeffrey was born.

Jeffrey acknowledges his brother ('It was much later in life that I discovered I had this brother I didn't know about. He is a very nice chap and when my mother was ill was a tremendous help, very kind and very good') but I imagine he chooses not to talk about his father because he knows that there will be those who want to visit the sins of one generation on the next.

When I had phoned Jeffrey to ask if I could interview him, he said, 'Okay. Come for breakfast. I trust you. But it's going well. I don't want to spoil it.' Jeffrey doesn't want anything to go wrong now. 'I don't feel that I've achieved anything politically and I don't really want to leave this earth having been a dilettante on the sidelines.' His stump speech used to contain the line, 'When I was three I wanted to be four. When I was four I wanted to be prime minister.' Now he wants to be Mayor.

Over breakfast I asked him why he thought he hadn't achieved office before. He spent years on the rubber-chicken circuit, booming at Conservative activists. He was an indefatigable Tory cheer-leader, first for Margaret Thatcher, then for John Major, who ennobled him in 1992 and, in 1994, was considering him either as a Minister of State at the Department of National Heritage or even as Party Chairman. Why didn't it happen?

'I think Anglia came at exactly the wrong time. I'd been led clearly to believe that something was going to happen, then Anglia came and I had to live through that. Bernard Ingham said to me, "You'll have to wait another two or three years now". I waited another two or three years and we lost the election.'

Was Anglia one of his famous 'lapses of judgement'?

He stares bleakly into his empty eggshell. 'Yes. Oh, yes.'

Anglia was so serious because he had no one else to blame. This wasn't tittle-tattle dredged up from his student days or a tawdry scam cooked up by the tabloid press. This was all his own doing. He helped a friend buy shares in Anglia Television in the run-up to a take-over when his wife was a director of the company. The DTI investigated and decided to take no further action, but Jeffrey had left himself open to the charge of insider dealing and profoundly embarrassed Mary.

What happened next?

'Mary said, "You're going to have to change. You're going to have to be very different." I was aware a change was necessary.'

An eerie silence falls.

'And?'

Suddenly Jeffrey moves the story on three years, from the DTI investigation in 1994 to his decision to run for Mayor in 1997. 'I sat down with Mary, James and William and said, "There's going to be a Mayor of London, the first Mayor of London, the person who sets the trend, the person who fixes the agenda, the person who has a small part in history. If I go for it, we're all going to have to face the past." To my shock, Mary backed me one hundred per cent. James said, "They're going to throw everything at you, but if you're willing to take that, Good Luck." William didn't want me to do it. And Mary said, "You're going to have to be very different. You're going to have to be serious. You're going to have to show people you can do the job. Just being an orator and a strong personality will not be enough, and if you're not willing to give that dedication then don't bother." I said to her, "I'll go for a year flat out. I'll pretend I'm Mayor for a year. I'll get up every morning as Mayor and I'll go to bed every night as Mayor and then, at the end of it, if I'm either bored, tired, or fed up with the attacks, I'll sign a new contract with Eddie Bell.'

Is he qualified for the job? At least Ken Livingstone ran the GLC. At least Steve Norris was transport minister for London.

'My experience is limited – in terms of not having held high office. But I have had the privilege of working quite closely with two prime ministers. You're quite right, I've never had to make the decisions, I've never had the responsibility, and this'll be the first big opportunity to do that. In many ways it's why I want the job, because I've played the game of working with the leader. I'd now like to have a crack at it myself. I want to get things done.

That's the story of my life, the story of my life.' He is banging the table now. The quality silver is bouncing up and down.

I say, 'You know what the charge is, don't you? The charge is that you're a political lightweight with a track record of lapses of judgement.'

'You can't prove you're a political heavyweight until you get a proper job. I always say to anyone who tells me they want to write a book, "Write the damn thing and find out if you can." And recently, over the last two and a half years, when I've been under the scrutiny of radio, television and the interviewer every single day, you will not find one line that they can repeat showing a lack of judgement. I think I have matured in that way. I think I have disciplined myself.' (This is said within hours of him landing in the soup over comments that thirty years ago black women in Britain were overweight and badly dressed.)

John Major and Margaret Thatcher have unreservedly endorsed the Archer campaign, but Conservative Central Office is keeping its distance. On the whole, Hague's men would have preferred anyone to Jeffrey. One of them said to me, 'London votes Labour so we're going to lose anyway. Let's lose quietly and with dignity – that means without Jeffrey.' Archer is undaunted. He has worked the patch (over five hundred formal meetings with every kind of London organisation), mastered the brief, produced a raft of detailed policies. He has vim, vigour, ideas, commitment. He believes he can win. But does he have the stuff of greatness?

He told me that Thomas Jefferson heads his list of heroes, so, as Joseph cleared away the breakfast things, I thought I'd finish up by running Jeffrey through Abraham Maslow's 'Jefferson Test'. Maslow, distinguished post-war psychologist, studied the lives of a group of great achievers (Jefferson, Abraham Lincoln, Albert Einstein, Eleanor Roosevelt, and the like), individuals who made extraordinary use of their potential, and listed the characteristics they had in common. These people all worked hard; assumed responsibility; tried something new rather than sticking to secure and safe ways; were prepared to be unpopular if their views didn't coincide with those of the majority; were concerned for the welfare of humanity; were spontaneous in thought and behaviour; were highly creative; had a good sense of humour. So far, Jeffrey scored rather well, but then we got to trickier territory.

I said, 'Maslow's people "perceive reality efficiently". Do you?'

'Nowadays, yes.'

'"Accept themselves and others for what they are"?'

'Very bad at that in the past. I look back and realise I don't have the right to want everybody to climb mountains.'

'"Are problem-centred rather than self-centred"?'

'Yes.'

'Are you sure?'

'Yes.'

'"Experience life as a child does."'

Jeffrey laughs. 'I remember Mary getting quite cross with me. We were at the Los Angeles Olympics, with Frank Marshall and Steven Spielberg. England had just won the 100 metres or something and I was like a four-year-old, because I love my countrymen to do well, and Mary said, "Stop behaving like a child," to which Mr Spielberg said, "Join my team, you can do it every day." He has that childlike quality and its value is not to be underestimated.'

'"Are honest, avoid pretences and game playing." This is the problem area, isn't it?'

'Yes.'

'This is what your enemies want to hold against you?'

'Yes.'

'And you say you've dealt with it and moved on?'

'And they'll never allow it to be the case. Never.' For a moment, he looks quite haunted.

'I'm nearly through. "Establish deep, satisfying personal relationships with a few, rather than many, people."'

'Oh, yes.' He rallies. 'I have a few very close friends and I always think when people judge me, perhaps they should look at my friends and decide why my half-dozen closest friends are my friends. Why will Michael Beloff go on holiday with me? Why did Malcolm Rifkind go on holiday with me last year? Why is Mary Archer married to me?'

Of course, Toad had good friends too, none better, but he was still Toad. And Jeffrey is still Jeffrey. At a meeting of young London business people he was asked, if he became mayor, how he would know if he had succeeded. 'If I come into this room in four years' time and you're chatting among yourselves, I've failed. If I walk in the room and everyone stands, I've done it.'

He can still sound a bit ridiculous at times. But something is different about him. He is easier, more relaxed, happier. He barks less and listens more. He seems more normal, more real. He isn't pretending any longer. Mary, I have noticed, is different too. Less the chilly ice maiden. 'Oh, yes,' says Jeffrey, 'she's softened, you're right. She's softened a lot.'

I don't think I've been conned. I've known him, off and on, for nearly forty years. I think he's changed. He's got my vote. Toad for Mayor!   Poop-poop.

Postscript

In the event, of course, I never got the chance to vote for Jeffrey. On 20 November 1999, his dream collapsed. 'Jeffrey Archer destroyed' ran the headline in the following morning's *Sunday Telegraph*. On page one the paper's political editor, Joe Murphy, reported, 'Lord Archer resigned in disgrace from the London mayoral race yesterday after being dramatically exposed as a liar who was prepared to commit perjury. He could now face criminal charges after admitting that he persuaded a friend to lie for him before the famous libel action in which he denied sleeping with a prostitute in 1986.'

On page three, I contributed a piece that began: 'So Jeffrey Archer may have conspired to pervert the course of justice. Are you surprised? Possibly not. I am.' I ran through Jeffrey's chequered and extraordinary career once more, but came to the same conclusion as I had done at the end of my recent interview with him. I felt he had changed. I still believed that in the aftermath of the embarrassment over the Anglia shares, Mary had made him confront the truth about himself and that, since then, he had been a different person. After I had filed my copy (at about 7.00 p.m.) my wife reminded me of something that the psychiatrist Anthony Clare had recently said to me: 'As a rule, people don't change.' At about 9.00 p.m., I decided to file an additional paragraph: 'Perhaps I am still being naïve. Perhaps he has self-delusion stamped all the way through him like a stick of rock. Perhaps it's in the genes: his father was a womaniser, a fraudster, a convicted felon – and a Conservative councillor. Either way, changed or not, it's too late now. All Jeffrey's dreams have turned out to be fantasies, after all.'

Go, Ken, go!

When the election for the first mayor of London came round in May 2000 the Conservative candidate was the former MP and junior transport minister, Steve Norris, the Labour candidate was the former Secretary of State for Health Frank Dobson, the Liberal Democrat was Susan Kramer, and the favourite, and ultimate winner, was Ken Livingstone, Labour MP for Brent East. For the first time in my life, I was uncertain about which way to vote.

Conservative women are something of a speciality of mine. As an MP and grass-roots activist, I have addressed them by the thousand. I have measured out my life in coffee mornings, balls and bunfights organised by them. I have spent hundreds of hours in their company. I know they are the backbone of the Tory Party. I respect, admire, value and (now and again) fancy them. I even live with one.

It is therefore with some authority that I report the following, based not on whimsy but on quite careful soundings taken over recent weeks: in the mayoral election on 4 May, if given the chance, the Conservative women of London will vote for Ken Livingstone en masse.

They won't vote Conservative because there's no point. London votes Labour, overwhelmingly so. Steve Norris doesn't stand a chance. Besides, this election is about personalities, not policies, and Mr Norris ('Nobber' to his chums) is not to their taste. They feel (and I quote one of them) he has 'the manner of a barrow boy and the morals of a tramp'. Doreen Miller (Baroness Miller of Hendon, President of the Greater London Area Conservative Associations) understands Conservative women: that's why, when a group of Mr Norris's former constituency supporters almost succeeded in scuppering his chances, she offered herself as a more wholesome alternative. She knew she couldn't win, but she would have lost with dignity.

My women won't vote Lib-Dem, not only because Conservatives despise Liberals, but more because Susan Kramer (although intelligent, articulate and persuasive) is a woman and, on the whole, Conservative women (especially older ones) still have a problem voting for women. (The reason there are so few female Tory MPs is that the constituency selection panels are dominated by women who opt for men.)

Most certainly, on 4 May Conservative women won't vote for the official Labour candidate. Frank Dobson has nothing to offer them. He looks like a moth-eaten Santa Claus. He sounds like a fumbly-bumbly North Country vet. As Health Secretary he made no impact whatsoever. In the eyes of my women, he has neither beauty nor brains. He lacks style, sex-appeal, commitment. We all know he never wanted the job. And now he protests he does, he is so strident nobody believes him.

Ken Livingstone, by contrast, wants the job passionately and women know that passion and commitment are important in a relationship. Dobbo is dull. Ken is cool. Ken is charming. They like his manner. They like his manners. Tell him that there are blue-rinse Tories rooting for him, not for his politics, but for his understated courtesy and he accepts the compliment. 'Yes, I understand that. Us working-class boys were taught to be polite because we knew our place. Even now, I find it almost impossible to interrupt if someone else is speaking. It is something the people campaigning against me do not understand and is one of the reasons their attacks have backfired.'

Conservative women know that Ken is the man who drove the old GLC into debt and disaster, who provided a London platform for Sinn Fein and epitomised many of the worst excesses of the loony Left; but they don't care. That was then, this is now. Ken has matured, they say. And if you ask them about his opposition to hunting with hounds or the detail of his plans for the underground, they change the subject. This is an instinctual thing: quite simply, women like the look of the fellow; the nasal twang is oddly attractive; the enthusiasm for newts curiously endearing; they trust him; they believe he is faithful to his long-term girlfriend, Kate. When they heard last Sunday afternoon that in the immediate wake of his narrow defeat at the hands of Frank Dobson, Ken took Kate to the cinema, they thought, 'Yes, that's the man for us.'

Of course, Conservative women aren't fools. They didn't want a London mayor in the first place, but if they are to be lumbered with one, they are adamant the choice will be theirs not Tony Blair's. The prime minister's implacable and cackhanded opposition to Ken is a major reason they find the boy from Brent so attractive. If Daddy is so against the suitor, he must have something going for him. (Tory women no longer find Blair remotely attractive: his patronising attitude annoys them, his messianic zeal is embarrassing. And, Cherie, of course, just grates.)

My women have made up their minds. They're saying 'Up yours, Tony' and 'Go, Ken, go.' They have decided that a fling with Mr Livingstone could be fun. And it's safe sex. The mayor has no tax-raising powers: no serious harm can come of the adventure.

My wife tells me that in this (as in everything else) I must follow her lead. I have to say I am tempted. How about you?

Jim Davidson

In October 2000 the entertainer Jim Davidson addressed the Conservative Party Conference in Bournemouth.

I have broken bread with some impressive Tory charmers in my time (Harold Macmillan, the Duke of Devonshire, Willie Whitelaw), but, to date, I have met none more likeable, and few more persuasive, than Jim Davidson.

'Fuck me, Gyles, is that right, mate?'

The cheerful Cockney comic, self-confessed alcoholic and noted womaniser is the new darling of the Conservative Party and, on Friday, when he addresses the massed ranks of the faithful at their conference in Bournemouth, I predict he will receive a standing ovation more heartfelt and sustained than those accorded to either Jeffrey Archer or Michael Heseltine in their prime.

Davidson, forty six, is one of Britain's highest-earning entertainers. He produces family pantomimes (nine this Christmas); he appears in adult cabaret (£25,000 a shot); he has just signed a £3.5 million contract to carry on hosting *The Generation Game* and *Big Break* for BBC TV. His money, his drinking, his marriages (four have failed so far), his taste in girlfriends ('Generation Jim's Old Flame on the Game as £500 Vice Girl' says the *Sunday Mirror*), have long made him a favourite with tabloid editors.

In search of the man behind the lurid headlines, I went to see him at his home, a rambling farmhouse set in fifteen acres on the outskirts of Dorking, Surrey, where he lives with two of his five children, housekeeper Annie, assorted dogs, horses and a £100,000 newly created lakeful of costly koi carp. 'Bit of a rock star's house, innit, Gyles?' Certainly, it has the attributes: indoor swimming pool, baronial dining hall, private cinema, state-of-the-art recording studio in one of the barns. The property once belonged to Oliver Reed ('On the night Ollie died, the plants round the pool wilted. Spooky or what?'), but Jim has made it very much his own. His enthusiasm for all things military is evident everywhere. In his den he has created a miniature sergeants' mess, complete with portrait of the Queen above the bar. The one surprise is his study: there's Mozart on the sound system and the walls are lined with well-thumbed hardback books: religion, history, biography, politics. Jim Davidson appears to be one of the select band who have read Norman Lamont's memoirs.

Why is he interested in politics?

'Because it's fucking important, Gyles. Everyone realises this country isn't great any more. It could be, it should be, it isn't.'

'Can you be specific?'

'Yeah. I'll give you an example. We have a navy that doesn't have the fuel to do the job. They can't go above 14 knots. I was on HMS *Gloucester* in Dubai and they hadn't switched their main engines on. The other night HMS *Invincible* was overtaken by the Isle of Wight ferry in the Solent. That's not a joke, it's a fact. In our entire armed forces we have fewer than a dozen people qualified to land a Harrier on an aircraft-carrier at night. I mentioned this at a polo do the other day and two Argies left to 'phone their military attaché. You're laughing, Gyles. I want to cry.'

Why is he a Conservative?

'I've always been a Conservative. Both my parents are dead. They died in the house I was born in. It was a council house. Thanks to the Tories, I was able to buy it for them. My father started out as an ordinary soldier and died a landowner with a famous son.

'The Conservative values – independence, hard work, a belief in your country – they're my values. One more turn of this lot and we'll be throwing Britain away. We've lost the pint, we've lost the Royal Tournament, we're going to lose the pound. Soon you'll arrive at Heathrow and it'll say, "Welcome to London, twinned with Antwerp". Vote for William Hague and he'll give you back the country you deserve. Shoulders back, head held high. Let's inject ourselves with pride.'

He says this with a directness and simplicity that are affecting. He believes the Conservatives can win the general election. 'I'm putting money on it. Hague listens. This government isn't listening. The fuel crisis proved that. They're finished. Doomed. Done for.'

I am not so sure, but in the presence of such certainty it seems lily-livered to admit as much. Instead, I say, 'The opinion polls seem to be sending out mixed signals.'

Jim chuckles and lights a Churchillian cigar. 'Forget the opinion polls, Gyles. The Old Labour lot can't stand Blair. When the day comes, they'll stay at home, like they did for the European elections. Our lot will turn out in force. We've had time to see through Blair. Blair is a bumbling idiot who makes it up as he goes along. I had a girlfriend just like him. She was called Debra. She gave me every version of the story until she came up with one that got her out of the poo. When I was in the drinks clinic I learnt all about the likes of Blair. He's got a co-dependency problem. He's a people-pleaser. He wants to be liked. He's horrified if people don't love him. You may not like Gerry Adams, but you accept that he's totally passionate in his beliefs. What does Blair believe in? Anything, everything, nothing. If you believe – if you really, really believe in something – you win in the end. Look at

Churchill, look at Mrs T. Tony Blair's a wanker. And he can't drink fourteen pints like our bloke.' Jim snickers happily and throws in, as an aside, 'Once I drank thirty-two pints in a day. It's quite do-able.'

Currently celibate and confining himself to the occasional glass of port, does Jim worry that his birds-and-booze reputation might make him something of a political liability?

'No, not at all. Ordinary working people, they know me. I've made the same mistakes in life they have. I've drunk too much, I've buggered up my marriages, I've been nicked for speeding. But I don't pretend to be anything that I'm not and I don't patronise anybody. I'm not one of those two bob socialist comics in cardigans: (a) they're not funny and (b), they're so fucking patronising.'

The only other Conservative I know with a barrack-room vocabulary to rival Jim's is Nicholas Soames, grandson of Sir Winston Churchill, bosom buddy of the Prince of Wales and Armed Forces Minister in the last Conservative Government. I can see Jim (seriously) in the same job in the next Conservative Government. In Whips' Office terms, there's no downside (we already know the worst about Jim) and the upside is considerable: he's popular, articulate, intelligent, can learn a script / absorb a brief / deliver a line, and he has a passionate, demonstrable commitment to the armed services. Since the time of the Falklands conflict, he has been travelling the world entertaining the troops.

'When I was sixteen, I wanted to join the Navy. I thought, it's the senior service, it's the one for me. You can eat all the chips you like, they've got indoor toilets and when the commanding officer says "Charge!" he's got to come with you. When I applied they kept me waiting for a month, then I had the medical and the doctor looked up my backside with a torch. I thought "Oi, oi, what's happening here? I'm not having this every morning." I should've done it. It's my one regret.'

In the next twelve months he is committing himself to one hundred Conservative Party events. Would he like to go into politics full-time? 'I could have some fun at the dispatch box, couldn't I? But I've got to sort out my finances first, got to stop living beyond my means. Look at today's post, Gyles. Bills, bills, parking ticket, tax demand. I'm paying £300,000 in tax this year. I'm too honest, that's my problem. I've never got any money in my pockets. It all goes to my wives and children, (a) because that's the way I like it, and (b) because a judge says that's the way it's going to be.'

Jim makes me laugh a lot. He has a nice line in jokes at Michael Portillo's expense ('The House isn't sitting at the moment, but when Michael turns up it will be', etc) but there's no malice in his humour and his lack of political correctness is positively heartwarming.

I ask him to respond to the charge that some of his material is racist. 'Rubbish, isn't now, never has been. But I've learnt things along the way, I admit that. Do you remember Norman Tebbit saying the test of whether or not an immigrant is fully integrated comes down to the cricket team he supports? At the time I thought Tebbit was right. Now I think he was wrong. You can be British, but you don't have to give up your identity, your roots. My dad was born Scottish, so I support a Scottish football team, but I live in England and I'm British.'

Jim comes over as patriotic, not jingoistic. There's a warmth and generosity of spirit about him that other showbusiness Tories (Paul Daniels, Bob Monkhouse, Bernard Manning) fail to get across. In three hours of conversation he dropped no catches. He won't be drawn into territory he knows nothing about. Effortlessly, without embarrassment, he mouths the Party line on 'the common sense revolution'. He deflects personal criticism with self-deprecation. 'I know my weaknesses. If baby isn't the centre of attention, teddy gets thrown out of the pram.'

Jim concedes he has an addictive personality. I am surprised he is not a member of Alcoholics Anonymous, but perhaps he does not need to be because he has found an alternative life-support system: freemasonry. He larks around, he rolls up his trouser leg, he offers me a funny handshake, but clearly he takes it very seriously. Recently he has become Worshipful

Master of his lodge. 'It was the ideals of freemasonry that stopped me killing myself with drink. I need rules to live by. I like the discipline, I like the fellowship, I like the way Catholic sits down with Protestant, black with white, Millwall supporter with Charlton supporter. I am reading a lot about religion right now. I am a gnostic Christian. I've got the King James Version on the computer, for instant access.'

Rudyard Kipling is another of Jim's enthusiasms. Next to his desk, alongside a picture of the SAS in action and the poster for one of Jim's adult pantos (*Boobs in the Wood*) is a framed copy of 'Mandalay'. 'Kipling was a mason, you know. "I'm Sir on the parade ground, but I'm Brother in the lodge". Great line.'

I imagine Kipling would have liked Jim enormously. These days he walks with kings ('Prince Charles has called me here, John Major's called me here, amazing innit?') and, for certain, has not lost the common touch ('Fuck me, I hope not.' Eight million tune into *The Generation Game* each Saturday).

The Prince of Wales is patron of the British Forces Foundation, a charity set up by Jim to fund and supply quality entertainment for British troops. 'I love Prince Charles. I don't swear in his presence, unless it's part of the act. The other day he invited me to speak at the Beaufort Hunt Ball. I did my usual stuff. Poor bugger, he sat there with his head in his hands. He said to me afterwards, "Thank God you were funny."

'I stayed at Highgrove. Nice place. You should have seen us at breakfast. I had eggs and bacon. Charles hand-picked his own muesli, bless him. The boys were there. I wish the public could have seen them. They were all over each other. He's a fantastic dad. His sons adore him, you can tell. I love Camilla too.'

'She's not really your type, is she, Jim?'

'I don't know. She's a lot prettier than that ghastly picture of her they keep printing in the papers. She's lovely. And she's so kind. And she's great for Charles. The boys can see that. I tell you, eventually the country will love her for loving him. If they want to, they should get married. Of course they should.'

I can see what a superpatriot and traditionalist like Jim gets out of hobnobbing with Prince Charles, but what does the Prince of Wales get out of Jim?

'A bloke who isn't pretending to be anything but what he is. What you see is what you get.'

Conference diary

In October 2000, I attended the Conservative Party Conference in Bournemouth. I went to meet up with old friends, to appear on the Conference platform with a motley band of 'celebrity Tories', to sell copies of my Westminster Diaries: Breaking the Code, *at the Politico's Conference Bookshop, and to hear – and cheer – the speeches of Jim Davidson and William Hague.*

Tuesday

10.45 a.m.

This is a nightmare. I set off from London SW13 at the crack of dawn to get to Bournemouth in good time for William Hague's unscripted question-and-answer session and here I am, four hours later, stuck on the M3 listening to *Woman's Hour*. There's been a bomb scare. On the motorway the traffic is moving at a snail's pace. On the radio a feisty young lesbian is telling Martha Kearney that the Conservative Party needs to be more inclusive or it is doomed. Hear, hear.

1.30 p.m., Highcliff Hotel, Bournemouth

I may be late, but I have not gone unrewarded. Incredibly, as I arrived, the very first person to greet me was the feisty young lesbian. She's called Karen Gillard. She wants me to come to the Tory Campaign for Homosexual Equality bash, hosted by Steve Norris (natch). 'It's up the other end of town, near the gay guest houses, you'll like it.' I certainly like her. And she says she likes me. (My wife often says I'm a lesbian's idea of a real man.) Next chance encounter, in the corridor, outside my room, Michael Portillo. 'Gyles, my friend,' he says. 'Michael, my hero,' I respond. He is looking sensational: full tan, full lips, full head of hair. How he makes it stand up and wave like that we'll never know. He's out to wow 'em, without notes, 'from the heart'. He's on a roll. It can't go wrong.

7.30 p.m.

Amazing afternoon. Michael triumphed. In the press room the hacks shook their heads in wonder. 'It's incredible how he's changed' is their line. I don't think he's changed at all. He's abandoned his hectoring style of speaking, he seems happier with himself since sharing his secret past with the wider world, but fundamentally he's the same man. People don't change. But they do grow older. Ted Heath gave me the sweetest smile and shook his shoulders in greeting, but he's not looking good. Wisely they had him on the platform for the Health Debate: Liam Fox, our Health spokesman, is a former GP.

At 4.00 p.m. I made my way to the VIP Room behind the stage to join the gathering gaggle of 'Celebrities for a Conservative Victory'. It was exactly like being in the green room before recording a daytime game show for the BBC at Pebble Mill. 'Darling, you look wonderful. Isn't Anthony Andrews looking fantastic? How old is he now? Where's Dana?' 'She couldn't make it. We've got Ed Stewart instead.' 'Stewpot? Stupendous. Crackerjack!' We were happy to see one another, but listening to a couple of Party workers whispering over the tea urn was not encouraging. 'Who's that?' 'I don't know.' 'And that?' 'I'm not sure. I think it's Ruth Madoc.' 'Ruth who?' 'You know, from *Hi-de-Hi*.' 'Actually, I'm Nicky Stevens from

Brotherhood of Man. 'Of course, thank you for being here.'

At 4.40 we were lined up to make our way on to the stage for the Culture, Media and Sport Debate. I was supposed to be between Tim Rice and Anthony Worral-Thompson ('What about you and Delia Smith then?' 'Not a barrel-load of laughs, is she?' 'She's the Mary Archer of home cooking.'), but at the last moment a distinguished-looking old boy joined the line next to me. I assumed he was our culture spokesman in the House of Lords and made appropriate small-talk. The poor man looked quite bemused. 'He's David Shepherd,' Tim hissed at me. 'The bishop? I thought he was dead.' 'No, world-famous artist. Paints elephants. Makes a fortune.' 'Ah.'

I know the press will mock our line-up, but the hall was full, the mood was good and those they recognised the crowd seemed pleased to see. Mike Yarwood and Bob Champion got the loudest cheers. Patti Boulaye opened the proceedings. We are lucky to have her. She's black and beautiful – not attributes with which the Conservative Party is overendowed.

1.00 a.m.

Quite an evening. The celebs dinner was very jolly, with Jim Davidson in cracking form. He's going to be the warm-up act before the Leader's big speech on Thursday. 'I'm going to come on wearing a blue shirt and open my jacket and it'll be drenched – just like Blair's. What d'ya think, Gyles? Fucking great idea, ain't it?' 'Fucking great, Jim.' 'The Tory Party's changing, Gyles.' It certainly is. I have agreed to be Patron of the 'Lesbians for William' campaign. (They really wanted Virginia Bottomley, but I think she demurred.)

At 10.00 p.m. we were herded onto a bus and driven across town to the Bournemouth Pavilion for the Conference Ball. Traditionally, this is a grim affair, peopled by elderly activists jitterbugging sedately to over-amplified music they neither recognise nor enjoy. Tonight it was different. Jim took command of the proceedings. 'Did you hear about the Brad Pitt Lookalike Contest? (PAUSE) Robin Cook came second. (LONGER PAUSE.) Lenny

Henry won.' Tim Rice and Michael Ancram did Buddy Holly duets. Jim introduced Tim as the man who has written a musical about the prime minister called 'The Lying King'. 'Actually,' said Tim, 'it's called Superstar – Jesus Christ!'

When William and Ffion appeared on stage the room went berserk. We stamped our feet. We hollered. The girl standing next to me said, 'I love him, I love that man.' I must say I've got the hots for Ffion. She is looking so good. And she's relaxed into it. William is a sensational performer. On that stage he was as strong, as sharp, as funny as Jim Davidson. 'And look,' he said, 'no sweat.'

When the Hagues departed Faith Brown took to the stage and gave us an impression of Mrs Thatcher crossed with Vera Duckworth (which we loved) followed by a joke about Jeffrey Archer that we didn't want to hear. (Jeffrey is now a non-person. This time last year we were all over him. Tonight we don't even want to hear his name.) Faith (old trouper) fought back with a selection of Abba hits and then went into the title song from *The Full Monty*. For an alarming moment, it looked as if Jim was going to strip for us. He didn't, of course. He gets pretty close to the wire (there was a story about a suppository and the weight of the doctor's hands on his shoulders that left my neighbour a little confused), but he knows his audience and played us to perfection.

Around midnight, I left with Faith and Diana Moran, the Green Goddess. We couldn't find a cab, but a young man offered the girls a lift. 'I've only got room for two.' 'You'll be quite safe,' said the doorman. 'He's a friend of Michael Portillo's.'

I walked back across the park. It is a beautiful night. It has been a good day. The Conservative Party seems more at ease with itself than I have known it in ten years. As I climbed the hill to the hotel I noticed a couple with their arms around each other in the car park. They were kissing. It was Penny and John Gummer. I shall keep eating the hamburgers.

Wednesday

Lunchtime

At the signing session for my *Diaries* at the conference bookstall this morning a little old lady, with twinkly blue-grey eyes and perm to match, held out her copy and said, 'Will you put "To Auntie Marje"?' 'And whose Auntie are you?' I asked. 'William's, of course. And this is William's Dad, and this is William's Mum, and these are William's sisters.' One of the sisters has an American accent. She is wanting to buy 'William and Ffion mugs' to take back to the US. The Hagues are surprisingly small and they've all got a full head of hair. Mr Hague explained to me, 'William's baldness is a throwback to an earlier generation, but it suits him, don't you think?' They are so proud of their boy it is touching. 'He hasn't done badly, has he? And he's hardly started, believe me.'

The Hagues were stocking up on copies of the new biography of William to send out as Christmas presents. The book was piled up alongside Michael Heseltine's autobiography. 'Will you be buying Mr Heseltine's book?' I asked. Auntie Marje pulled a naughty face. The bookstall has sold hundreds of books in the past seventy-two hours, but so far not one of Mr Heseltine's has gone. To spare the great man's blushes, they are wondering whether they should cancel his scheduled signing session.

At 10.30 I tried to get into the hall to hear Ann Widdecombe. It was packed to the rafters. I watched her on one of the giant TV screens by the cafeteria. Another ex-MP came up to say hello. 'Shh,' snapped the elderly lady standing in front of us, 'Keep quiet you two.' The ex-MP muttered, 'It's only a speech.' The elderly lady turned round and glared at us. 'No it's not,' she said without a trace of a smile, 'It's a religious experience.'

Ann came off the stage, out of the hall and, by chance, straight into my arms. I kissed her. 'Happy birthday. You were brilliant.' 'Was I?' I looked into her eyes. Already I think she knows she's blown it.

Midnight

I have been to seventeen parties tonight. No pot to be seen, but plenty of pot-bellies and enough champagne to sink the *Titanic*. (Champagne is our recreational drug of choice.) The activists are euphoric: they believe we can win! The leadership is encouraged: it knows the truth. We may not win, but we will do better than anyone dared hope three months ago, William will survive, and thrive, and four years from now we could be back in government. It's beginning to feel good again.

At the Yorkshire TV party Ffion was in another shimmering outfit (saying little, smiling a lot, we don't ask for more) and William was in his element. He seems to have grown taller and (alarmingly) his head appears to have got considerably larger too. He looks like a blanched version of the Green Mekon, but when he's with you there's electricity in the air. At the ITN party, by contrast, Michael Heseltine is looking his age. Loss of power diminishes a man even more dramatically than a heart attack. Once Tarzan stood head and shoulders above the crowd. Now, he is leaning forward, cupping his ear, trying to catch what John Serjeant has got to say. The media may still be fascinated by the big beasts of yesteryear, but the troops here have lost interest in the old guard. They really have.

At the celebs dinner, Jan Leeming reveals that she might quite like to be an MP, Mike Read tells me he has rewritten *A Midsummer Night's Dream* as a rock musical to be called *O Puck* (Jim will like the title), and William Roache is anything but boring. He has been Ken Barlow in *Coronation Street* for forty years, but his nerves are all a jangle. On 8 December, to mark the programme's ruby jubilee, they are doing an episode 'live'.

The *Daily Mirror* has had a field day sending the celebs up rotten, but I tell them that they've been good and brave and there are always risks when you nail your colours to the mast. 'Remember the famous last words of General Sedgwick as he put his head over the parapet at the Battle of Spotsylvania: "They couldn't kill an elephant at this dist—."'

Thursday

4.00 p.m.

Jim's warm-up was a triumph, so hilarious that the laughter and applause drowned out the BBC interview with Hezza in the commentary booth. William's speech raised the roof. We knew it would. He is our best orator in a generation. In the press room, the verdict was that this has been our best conference in years. I rounded on one of the hacks: 'I hope you'll say so.' 'I will – except no one will notice.' 'Why not?' He pointed at the television screen. 'It seems there's a revolution in Yugoslavia. I'm afraid your friend William is going to be wiped off the front pages. He'll be lucky to make page six.' The man from the *Guardian* chuckled. 'That's politics.'

Theatre

Celia Johnson

Given that I have borrowed the title of this collection from Noël Coward's cele-
brated film (directed by David Lean, 1946), it seems fitting that this section
should begin with my own brief encounters with the stars of Brief Encounter,
Dame Celia Johnson (1908–82) and Trevor Howard (1916–88). Howard I met
at the lunch to mark Sir John Gielgud's eightieth birthday. He had a gloriously
leathery lived-in drinker's face, with gravelly voice and irascible manner to
match: 'I've been number two in films for donkey's years'. Celia Johnson I got
to know in my early twenties, when I first worked in the theatre and set out to
meet – and employ – some of the leading theatrical luminaries of the day.

I t was my friend Noel Davis, actor turned casting director, who introduced me to chutzpah, not as the Yiddish equivalent of cheek,
effrontery and gall, but when I said, in passing one day, that there were
no sympathetic Jewish characters in Shakespeare.

'Nonsense,' said Noel, 'think of *Henry IV.*'

'Who's Jewish in *Henry IV?*'

'Chutzpah, of course,' said Noel, 'Harry Chutzpah!'

Noel also introduced me to the Chinese waiter in *King Lear.* He appears only fleetingly. Lear calls him on in Act I Scene 3: 'Come hither, Ho!'

Then there was the story of the old actor, a prima donna of the bull-queen variety, who when told there wasn't a part to suit his temperament or style in *King Lear*, flourished his copy of the New Arden Shakespeare in front of the director triumphantly and declared (kindly assume a Kenneth Williams voice for this bit): 'There is! There is! Look at the list of characters. What does it say on the bottom line? "A camp near Dover"!'

Naturally, it's the way he tells them. Nobody tells them better and nobody has more of them to tell. Noel is funny (outrageously, consistently, tremendously funny), thoughtful, courteous, camp (though these days more James Robertson Justice than Graham Norton), a wonderful worker and the best of friends. Together we ran the Oxford Theatre Festival between 1974 and 1976 and put on eight plays, seven one-man shows, four concerts, six fringe companies, ten lunchtime lectures, five tours, three West End transfers and one *Evening Standard* Play of the Year. It wasn't all plain sailing, but when it was at its worst Noel was at his best. On one of our darkest nights he took us both off to the Elizabeth Restaurant in St Aldates. ('One would not want to eat there too often – who could afford to? – but it is always an excitement to go there, and the proprietor and waiters know it.' *Good Food Guide*, 1973.) Noel ordered a magnum of the Château Latour '49 at £26 (that was a week's salary for most in 1974) and, as we charged and clinked our glasses, he defied the gods, 'Fuck 'em, darling, fuck 'em!'

The Oxford Theatre Festival came about because I wanted to put on plays and the Oxford Playhouse, having wilfully rid itself of Frank Hauser's (justly) acclaimed Meadow Players, needed some middle-brow fare that would put bums on seats and restore some of the lustre that had been lost with Frank (whose leading artistes had included Judi Dench, Leo McKern, Alan Badel).

Over lunch at the Tackley in the High Street (where they used to flambé your dish at your table: veal with brandy, cream, mushrooms and a pleasant aroma of lighter fuel; unthinkable now, delicious then), the formidable lady who ran the Playhouse put her hand on mine and said, 'If you can find the plays, and you can find the stars, and you can find the money, you can have the theatre.'

I told her I could and I would. And I did. Age twenty five, if you think you can you will, so long as you've got the chutzpah, a current edition of the *Spotlight* casting directory, a typewriter and a handful of first class stamps.

My first letter went to Rita Tushingham, a considerable film star in the sixties, from *A Taste of Honey* to *Doctor Zhivago* via *Girl with Green Eyes* and *The Knack*. Would she care to play the title role in Bernard Shaw's *Saint Joan* at the 1974 Oxford Theatre Festival? She replied at once. She thought she might. We met. She thought she would. I wrote to Sir John Clements, who had just completed his last season as director of the Chichester Festival Theatre. How did he feel about playing the Earl of Warwick? He felt he was too old, but if I hadn't yet settled on a director for the piece, could he be considered? And what did I think of his stepson, John Standing, as the Dauphin? Excellent. Excellent.

I wrote to Ian Carmichael. What would he say to a stage version of Oscar Wilde's *Lord Arthur Savile's Crime*? He'd say No, but if I'd care to trundle up to Mill Hill on the jolly old tube he'd meet me at the station in the Roller and we could chinwag over other possibilities and have a spot of lunch. He wanted to revive Benn Levy's *Springtime for Henry*, a high comedy and Barbara Murray would be the ideal leading lady. Done.

I wrote to Sir Ralph Richardson and made a pilgrimage to his house in Regent's Park. Number One Chester Terrace was a house in the grand manner. Sir Ralph had a play, a new play, a ver' strange, ver' cu-rious new play, deah boy. Patrick Garland had found it for him. Ralph was to be a missionary in the piece. The rest of the cast were animals. Anna Massey would make a ver' clever giraffe, don't you think? Sets in the style of Douanier Rousseau. Heigh-ho, cocky, if you do *The Missionary* I'm going to be working for you this summer . . .

I was finding the plays, I was finding the stars. What about the money? I bought *Who's Who*. I needed someone entrepreneurial, someone different, someone with money. I worked through the As. The first person I wrote to was Jeffrey Archer. He was the youngest MP in the Commons, apparently, the member for Louth, and best known for having reunited the Beatles for an Oxfam benefit.

Yes, said Jeffrey, intriguing. Some good names. Sir Ralph is extraordinary, extraordinary. Jeffrey's favourite actress was Celia Johnson. So talented. So under-rated. Why oh why wasn't she a dame? He'd spoken to Ted about it. Get Celia Johnson, Gyles, and you've got your money.

John Cadell, a distinguished agent (and father of my friend Simon Cadell), suggested that James Bridie's play *Daphne Laureola* (in which Dame Edith Evans had first triumphed) might be an attractive vehicle for Miss Johnson. I wrote to her. I found her address in *Who's Who*. A postcard came back from Mrs Peter Fleming, Merrimoles House, Nettlebed, Near Oxford. Yes, she'd love to.

Before I could get back to Jeffrey, who had given me a range of telephone numbers, in the Boltons, in Whitehall, in Louth, and told me to contact him at any time, day or night, any time, I received a letter from Ray Cooney, arch-farceur with ambitions to go legit. Was I looking for a partner? If so, I'd found one.

Ray was bald and slight and energetic and, thanks to *Move Over Mrs Markham*, *Don't Stay for Breakfast* and sundry other classics of the genre, rich. He was also determined to present Ralph Richardson and Celia Johnson in the West End, especially Celia, because nobody could get Celia to say yes to anything, but I had, so if I was interested we could do a deal. He'd bank-roll the Oxford Theatre Festival in return for any West End transfers.

I'd get a share of the profits. (This was the moment in my life when I learnt the golden rule never take a share of the profits. There won't be any. In the world of entertainment, the only share that has meaning is a share of the gross.)

I got more than a deal from Ray. I got an 'assistant'. To keep a close eye on this theatrical *wunderkind* (I was twenty five) and an even closer eye on the accounts (we were set to spend £100,000) Ray produced Noel, a forty-something actor-turned-producer and walking *Spotlight*. From start to finish Noel was Ray's man, but from the first moment we set eyes on one another I knew he was my ally.

And I needed an ally because no sooner had the deal been done than everything began to go wrong. We were working out of my wife's and my basement flat at Clarence Gate Gardens, off Baker Street. (T. S. Eliot had once lived there. The hall porter would occasionally show American students around. 'And this is where the celebrated poet, G. H. Elliott, used to reside . . .') The telephone rang. 'Hello. It's Celia Fleming here.' She seemed to be telephoning from a garden. You could hear birds in the background. I could picture the trug over her arm and the gardening gloves and the secateurs in the hand that wasn't holding the 'phone. 'I'm frightfully sorry, Mr Brandreth, but I don't think it'll do.'

My mouth was already dry. 'What won't do?'

'The play. It really won't do. I read it again last night. And it's so dated. I'm sure Edith was marvellous, but Edith's Edith. It just won't do.'

'But –'

'I am sorry.' A lawnmower had started up. 'The trouble is no one's writing my kind of plays any more. Why can't people write like Noël and Terry nowadays? Willie's the only one who comes anywhere near. I am so – very – sorry. Do read the play again. I'm sure you'll agree. It just won't do.'

'Who's Willie?' I wondered. 'William Douglas-Home,' said Noel, my Noël. (Noël Coward had died in 1973; Terence Rattigan was to die in 1977.) I reached for *Who's Who*. I wrote to Douglas-Home that night. Did he have a play that might suit Celia Johnson? It arrived by return post. The title seemed ominous. It was called *In the Red*. It was a light comedy about the travails of a bank manager and his stockbroker-belt wife. It went to Nettlebed by special delivery.

'Celia Fleming here.' She was indoors. Did she have a gin in her hand? Could I hear ice? Was she about to play Bridge? 'I've read Willie's piece. It's very funny. I think we'll do it, don't you? What about the bank manager? Is John Clements too old? What about Michael Hordern? He'd be perfect.'

Having been to school with his daughter I had kept Sir Michael Hordern's home address in my book for more than a decade against this very eventuality. I dropped the script, with covering note, through his letter box at about midnight. For seventy-two hours we heard nothing. Then the telephone rang.

'Celia Fleming here.' She was in the hallway now. Or was she in the drawing room, standing by the piano, gazing out over the lawn, watching her daughter Lucy set up the croquet things? 'Look, I'm frightfully sorry. Michael Hordern's just been on to me. He thinks it's a dreadful play. He says it's crude and obvious.' The bastard. 'I'm so very sorry Mr Brandreth. He's adamant he won't do it. And he thinks I shouldn't do it either. He's probably right. I hope you'll understand.'

I understood. Willie understood. My wife and I went to East Meon and stayed the night. We arrived late. He offered us bread and cheese and shambled around the kitchen, affecting to be totally lost. He attempted to slice the bread using the blunt edge of the bread-knife. My wife saw through the ploy, but took over all the same. William and I went to his study and flicked through his unperformed works. There was nothing that was right. We munched our bread and cheese, drained our glasses, and went up to bed. As his bedside reading William took with him a biography of Sybil Hathaway, the Dame of Sark, who throughout the German occupation of her island stayed valiant, defiant and heartwarmingly British.

At breakfast, he said, 'There might be something in this.' He set to work that morning and five and a half days after writing, 'The drawing room of the Seigneurie on Sark' he penned the words 'The Curtain Falls' in time to catch the start of the two o'clock race at Newbury. The script reached me on Monday. I got it to Celia on Tuesday. She said yes on Wednesday. We issued a press announcement on Thursday and that was that. Celia Johnson as the Dame of Sark, with Tony Britton, perfect as the professional-soldier-with-a-tender-heart-despite-the-Nazi-uniform, played to capacity in Oxford, transferred to Wyndham's and then to the Duke of York's (where Anna Neagle took over). We had a hit.

I don't believe we'd have had a hit with *The Missionary*, with or without Sir Ralph, though I'm damned sure Anna Massey would have been the best bloody giraffe to grace the West End stage since Michael Saint-Denis presented André Obey's *Noah* with John Gielgud and friends at the New Theatre in 1935. Sir Ralph was right to have misgivings about *The Missionary*. He was equally well advised to decline the role of Goya in an epic that came my way (via Peter Coe, I think) and featured the great artist towards the end of his life when he had gone blind. It was a powerful piece, but, as I recall, it required the audience to shut their eyes whenever Goya himself was on stage to fully share the sensation of his blindness. Sir Ralph twigged that the more conscientious members of the audience would consequently miss much of his performance.

We replaced Sir Ralph with Geraldine McEwan in a revival of *The Little Hut*, Andre Roussin's desert island high comedy ('neither comedy nor farce – tricky'). This was Ray Cooney's idea and allowed Noel to invite every black actor in London and under thirty to come to our basement and take his clothes off. 'The native is a loin-cloth part,' explained Noel, 'I'm sure you understand.' Happily, the actors did (even if our neighbours didn't) and eventually we cast Olu Jacobs, a fine actor and equally fine figure of a man, in the role.

We had been looking for a middle-brow season. It seemed to be verging on the lightweight now, so, between the high comedies, I was allowed to squeeze in *Waiting for Godot*. It was the first revival since Peter Hall's original production in 1955. I looked up Samuel Beckett's address in *Who's Who* and wrote to him. He wrote back saying yes, particularly if Patrick Magee would direct. He would. And did. Brilliantly.

We appeared to be back on track and then Rita Tushingham pulled out. She had been offered a movie in Israel. We'd have to release her. She was sorry. She knew we'd understand. We understood all right. We released her and scrawled offensive remarks all over her entry in *Spotlight*.

'We will never, ever, ever, EVER use that cow again,' I bawled.

'Until we need her,' said Noel.

Saint Joan without Tush was *Hamlet* without the Prince, especially as we'd lined up Sir John and John Standing and James Villiers and Noel Willman and Charles Dance and heaven knows who else entirely on the strength of her name. We told Ray. And we also told him our solution. We had enough stars for one season. Let's just go for a good actress, unknown but absolutely right: Frances de la Tour.

'Good God,' spluttered Ray, 'I'm not putting on George Bernard Shaw's *Saint Joan* with Frances de la Number Three Tour. I want a name, a canopy name.'

We trawled *Spotlight*. Eileen Atkins, not available. Diana Rigg, not available. Maggie Smith, not available. Anna Massey.

'We're looking for a martyr, not a giraffe.'

'She's good.'

'I know, but . . .'

Janet Suzman, not available. Susan Hampshire, not available. Jane Asher, not available. Anna Calder-Marshall.

'Who?'

'Never mind . . . Billie Whitelaw. How about Billie Whitelaw?'

I called Miss Whitelaw's agent. I called Miss Whitelaw. I was a friend of Samuel Beckett. (Well, a pen-friend.) Sir John Clements wanted her above all others. (Actually I hadn't yet broken the news to him about Tush's flight to Israel, but that was to be my next call.) Could she sleep on it?

In her sleep, she must have heard voices. They told her to say Yes.

'Sir John, I have bad news and good news. The bad news is that we've lost Rita Tushingham. The good—'

'Get on a train at once,' he barked, 'at once. Bring *Spotlight*. We'll sort it out today.'

'But Sir John . . .'

'At once!'

It was a Sunday morning at ten. By noon I was perched on the little balcony of the Clements' flat on the front at Brighton. Sir John was fixing us sclerosis-sized gins and tonic and his dear frail wife, Kay Hammond, was trying slowly and painfully to explain to me that she had been something of a star herself before she had her stroke. 'I know,' I said, 'I loved *Genevieve*.' (That was Kay Kendall, you fool. Kay Hammond, *Blithe Spirit*. Remember?)

'Lunch first,' said Sir John, 'then work.' Lunch was served in a small room off the drawing room and brought in by an elderly servant in an improbable wig who was summoned by an electric bell whose button was discreetly positioned by Miss Hammond's place at table. Unfortunately, while the bell made a dreadful racket all over the flat, the servant in the kitchen couldn't hear it and Sir John had to go and fetch her between every course.

Over coffee, I broke the good news.

'I've secured Billie Whitelaw.'

'But you can't have.' He was open-jawed.

'I have.'

'No, no, no. You haven't.' He was wild-eyed.

'I have.'

'But you cannot have recast the title part without consulting the director.'

I had. It was wrong. It was a mistake. And even now, more than a quarter of a century after the event, my palms go damp as I think back to the call I made to explain to Miss Whitelaw and her agent that I had failed to consult the director, that Sir John loved Miss Whitelaw, both as a person and as a performer, but that for him as *Saint Joan* she was wrong, all wrong, that the fault was mine, all mine, and that Miss Julia Foster, a younger actress, in Mr Cooney's eyes a film star (*Alfie*) and a canopy name following her West End triumph in Wedekind's *Lulu*, would be giving her *Saint Joan* at the Oxford Theatre Festival.

The production was not an unmitigated disaster. There were problems. My wife and I were still sizing the set at 3.00 a.m. on the day of the dress rehearsal, and the éclat of the first night when it arrived (forty-eight hours later than advertised) was clouded by the theatre management's insistence on showing advertisements on the safety curtain during the interval (including one featuring our Earl of Warwick as a chinless wonder smoking Benson & Hedges, or was it Craven A?). Sir John gave it his all. He rehearsed relentlessly and didn't seem to need to sleep. He and I and Noel sat up till six in the morning at the Randolph Hotel drinking port and doing card tricks. At ten on the morning of the press night, Sir John rang Noel's bedroom.

'Is that Noel Davis? Why aren't you down here?'

'Is that you, Sir John? Where are you? In the foyer?'

'No, you fool. I'm in the fucking theatre – where I belong.'

The notices turned out not to be too bad. It didn't look great, but it sounded well. Indeed, I got into the habit of saying it was possibly, no, it was probably, the best spoken *Saint Joan* since the War.

And, Noel said, by way of consolation, 'It was so much better than Celia's. When Celia played Saint Joan you felt sure she was going to pop into Peter Jones on her way to Rouen.'

John Gielgud

Sir John Gielgud OM CH, widely regarded as the finest Shakespearean actor of the twentieth century, was born on 14 April 1904 and died on 21 May 2000.

The first time I saw John Gielgud on stage the audience booed. It was 1963, the opening night of Thornton Wilder's *The Ides of March* at the Theatre Royal, Haymarket, with Sir John as a modern-dress Julius Caesar. It was not a success. When I first met the great actor, not long afterwards, (I was twenty, a star-struck undergraduate; he was sixty five, the acclaimed leader of his profession), he asked me what I had seen him in. I told him. 'Oh dear,' he sighed, 'Were you really there? I am so sorry. It was terrible, truly terrible. I went through a bad patch, you know. I've had one or two.' Not many.

I know the highs and lows of his career pretty well. I wrote his biography, twice, and, over thirty years, spent many memorable hours sitting, notebook in hand, gazing at that noble countenance, listening to the famous Gielgud voice – all cello and woodwind – as, effortlessly, and at an alarming pace, he rattled off anecdote after anecdote. He could talk for an hour without pause. As I scribbled I looked up at him, but he rarely looked at me. As a story reached its pay-off – every tale appeared beautifully crafted – his eyes would slide to one side and he'd glance my way to see that I was suitably amused – or moved. (Alongside a waspish sense of humour, he had a profoundly sentimental streak. Famously, he could cry at will. 'It's rather a cheap effect. I know I shouldn't do it. If the actor cries, the audience doesn't.') Always immaculately turned out, with ramrod back and Turkish cigarette permanently in hand, he was an odd mix of Edwardian dandy and Roman emperor, gossip and grandee. He performed his stories not to me, I felt, but to an invisible audience somewhere in the middle distance.

To get on with Sir John, to understand him at all, you had to share his love of the theatre. It was his life. The writer Beverly Nichols told me the story of the house party that he and Gielgud attended during the darkest days of the Second World War. It was Sunday morning and Nichols came down to breakfast to find Gielgud, looking like death, surrounded by the Sunday papers, headlines double-decked with grim news from the front. 'What on earth has happened?' asked Nichols. 'The worst,' wailed Gielgud, shaking his head in despair. 'Gladys [Cooper] has had the most terrible notices.'

A few weeks ago, Sir John confessed to me, 'I have lost all interest in the London mayoral race now that Glenda [Jackson] is out of the running. She was a wonderful Cleopatra, you know. She'd have been a splendid Lady Mayoress.'

All I ever heard him talk about was the world of entertainment. 'You must understand that cast adrift in the ordinary world I am a timid, shy, cowardly man, but once I go into the theatre I have great authority and I get great respect and love from all the people working in it – from the stage-hands, the costumers, my fellow actors. It is where I belong.'

Had there ever been a prospect of him doing something else? 'No. My parents hoped I might become an architect, but I was besotted with the theatre as far back as I can remember. As a boy, I took lessons from Lady

Benson. She said I walked "like a cat with rickets", but I persisted. I went to RADA. There really wasn't anything else I wanted to do. Or could.' As with the other 'greats' of his vintage – Olivier, Richardson, Ashcroft, Redgrave – it was to the formidable Lillian Bayliss, manager of Sadler's Wells and the Old Vic, that he owed the break that established him as a classical actor of the first rank. 'She could be rather fierce, you know. She was terribly devout. And utterly determined. She was found on her knees once, praying out loud, "Dear God, send me a good Hamlet, but make him cheap."

'I must say she kept us on our toes.' At the Old Vic, between 1929 and 1931, in a period of just twenty months, Gielgud's roles included Romeo, Richard II, Oberon, Mark Antony, Orlando, Macbeth, Hotspur, Prospero, Antony, Malvolio, Benedick, King Lear, and the first of his celebrated Hamlets. 'I was very young. I simply threw myself at the part like a man learning to swim and I found the text would hold me up if I sought the truth in it.'

When I last saw Sir John I asked him to name a favourite performance. He simply shook his head and closed his eyes. I know he had a particular place in his heart for Gordon Daviot's *Richard of Bordeaux*, 1932 ('My first "smash hit". There were queues around the block. I said to myself, "I'm a star!"') and for the successes he enjoyed in the 1970s with Ralph Richardson ('Dear Ralph. Dear, dear Ralph.') Outside Shakespeare, he had a special fondness for Jack Worthing in *The Importance of Being Earnest* and Sir Joseph Surface in *The School for Scandal*.

Sir John said (in a way Olivier might not have done): 'I am lacking in ambition for power, large sums of money or a passionate desire to convince other people that they are wrong or I am right, but I have a violent and sincere wish to be a good craftsman and to understand what I try to do in the theatre, so as to be able to convince the people I work with.'

Rightly, this week's obituaries have celebrated Gielgud as the great interpreter of Shakespeare, but to people of my generation it is in modern work that he will best be remembered.

In 1958 he was asked to play in the British premiere of Samuel Beckett's *Endgame*. He told me he turned the offer down because he hated the play: 'I thought it's no good pretending for pretension's sake. The play nauseates me. I won't do it. And yet I longed to be in something as avant-garde as that.'

The sense of being out of touch ('I was old hat for quite a while, you know'), unable to relate to the writers of his time, lasted for several unnerving years until in 1968, age sixty four, he accepted the part of the Headmaster in Alan Bennett's play-cum-revue *Forty Years On*. 'It was hardly avant-garde, it was a nostalgic pastiche', but it was the vehicle that brought him back into the vanguard and led him to the Royal Court and to playing with Ralph Richardson in David Storey's *Home* and Harold Pinter's *No Man's Land* – for many the definitive modern Gielgud performances.

Gielgud was making silent pictures in the twenties. (He told me, without much conviction, that there had once been the possibility of his marrying Lillian Gish.) Half a century later he emerged as one of the world's most sought-after movie actors. He won his first Oscar for *Arthur* at the age of 78 and then appeared in dozens of films – many of them 'dreadful, quite appalling,' he would say, his face wreathed in smiles, 'but it's good to work and the money's nice.' He particularly enjoyed recounting the tale of his appearance in the notorious *Caligula*, produced by Bob Guccione of *Penthouse* magazine. 'They offered me the part of the Emperor Tiberius and I turned it down saying, "This is pure pornography". Gore Vidal, who wrote the original script, then wrote me a terrifically rude letter, saying how impertinent it was of me to refuse it and that if I knew what Tennessee Williams and Edward Albee said about me, I wouldn't be so grand. Terrible vituperation. Then they offered me another smaller part that wasn't so dirty, and I rather shamefacedly took it. I played a whole scene in a bath of tepid water. It took three days to shoot and every two hours some terrible hags dragged me out, rubbed me down and put me back in the water again. Most extraordinary proceedings.'

On his eightieth birthday, I organised a party in his honour at the Old Vic. Christopher Reeve brought on the birthday cake. 'Oh,' cooed Sir John, 'Superman. Thank you, Gyles. You really have thought of everything.' I got the impression that Sir John was quite comfortable with his own homosexuality. In 1953, shortly after receiving his knighthood, he had been publicly humiliated when he was arrested and fined £10 for 'persistently importuning male persons for an immoral purpose'. Years later, when, with his companion Martin Hensler, he was happily established in his Palladian villa in Buckinghamshire, he said to me, 'I wished I had settled down and moved to the country years ago. I am not sure that living in Cowley Street [Westminster] was a good idea, too many temptations. You know when Oscar Wilde was cross-examined about that part of town – it was quite notorious in his day – he said, "I don't know about it being a disreputable neighbourhood. I do know it is near the Houses of Parliament."'

In April 1994, when I was an MP, I invited Sir John to join me and my wife and Glenda Jackson for lunch at the House of Commons to celebrate his ninetieth birthday. He arrived in Central Lobby at one, on the dot, twinkling and cherubic, amazingly upright and steady.

'It's a great honour that you should join us, Sir John,' I said.

'Oh, I'm delighted to have been asked,' he murmured. 'You see, all my real friends are dead.'

(He had a legendary capacity for the accidental insult. When rehearsing Maggie Smith in *Private Lives*, he interrupted a scene: 'Oh, don't do it like that Maggie, don't screw your face up. You look like that terrible old woman you played in that dreadful film . . . Oh no, I didn't mean *Travels with My Aunt*.')

That day (actually, every day) the stories just poured out of him. He had known everybody. He had seen them all, from Sarah Bernhardt to Ralph Fiennes. (While the best of his stories came from the past, he took pride in being fully up to speed on the latest plays, films, performances.) We talked about his times in New York. 'Marlene [Dietrich] invited me to hear her new record. We gathered round the gramophone, and when we were settled the record was put on. It was simply an audience applauding her! We sat through the entire first side and then we listened to the other side: more of the same!'

He talked about his famous production of *The Importance of Being Earnest*. 'When we went to America, Margaret [Rutherford] moved up to play Lady Bracknell instead of Edith [Evans].'

'Why didn't Dame Edith play the part in New York?'

'She was introduced to a blind devotee of the theatre who heard her speak and said to her, "You are much too beautiful to play Lady Bracknell", and that was that. Edith was very much concerned about her beauty, you know. Margaret agreed to move up from Miss Prism to play Lady Bracknell on condition she could model her performance entirely on Edith's. It was typically modest of her.' (Pause. Sip of wine. Twinkle.) 'Of course, Margaret's Lady Bracknell was very much the Lady Mayoress to Edith's Queen Mary.'

Had he known Queen Mary? 'Indeed. Queen Mary enjoyed the theatre. King George enjoyed his playgoing at the back of the box, chatting about racing with Sir Edward Elgar. They came to a matinee of *Hamlet* at the Haymarket and the Queen enquired at what time the performance was due to end. "You see, the King always has to have his tea punctually, and he is so anxious not to miss the girl with straws in her hair."'

Sir John loved a wicked story. He had a wicked sense of humour. David Hemmings appeared with him in *The Charge of The Light Brigade* in the 1960s: 'Sir John was so charming and so funny. There was a wholly inaccurate rumour that the film's director, Tony Richardson, was having an affair with our leading lady, Jill Bennett. We were on location, filming in the Anatolian plain. Jill was in her tent while the rest of us, Sir John included, were standing around the coffee urns waiting for the next set-up. Tied up near the tent was a Russian dancing bear that somehow managed to free itself and, before any of us could do anything about it, went lumbering towards Jill's tent and got tangled up in the guy ropes. Poor Jill came rushing out of the tent, pursued by this enormous bear. Sir John looked up and cried, "Oh, Mr Richardson, how could you! And in your motoring-coat too!"'

At the ninetieth birthday lunch Sir John's conversational cast list included Orson Welles, Michael MacLiammoir (was it MacLiammoir or Welles who kept a flashlight up his sleeve so he could illuminate his face on the darkened stage? I can't remember), Kenneth Branagh ('so clever and so delightful'), Peter Brook ('so very clever – but oh dear . . .'), Donald Wolfit ('He hated me, hated me. The feeling was entirely mutual').

He was extraordinary – and he was ninety. I said to him, 'After lunch, would you like to come to prime minister's Questions?'

He grinned. 'I've been before. As I recall, last time Mr Bonar Law was answering the questions.'

'Do come again. I know the prime minister [John Major] is hoping to pay a small tribute to you.'

'Oh, no, no,' he looked quite alarmed. 'I think I might find that a little embarrassing. I'll just slip away quietly, if you don't mind. I don't want any fuss. I think a clean exit is so important, don't you?' As we were walking back across Central Lobby, he paused and smiled and fluted gently, 'This has been great fun. Thank you. I have had a very lucky life.'

I rather think we were the lucky ones.

Noël Coward

Encounter any actor of a certain vintage – John Gielgud, Celia Johnson, Michael Redgrave, John Mills – and within minutes, without fail, one name would crop up: Noël Coward. Noël knew everybody and everybody knew Noël. He was born on 16 December 1899 and died on 26 March 1973. In 1999, to mark the centenary of Coward's birth, I went to Switzerland, to the mountains above Montreux, to meet his partner and friend, Graham Payn.

I've been to a marvellous party. They were all there – Marlene, Tallulah, Nureyev and Fonteyn, Dickie Mountbatten, Larry and Viv – a star-studded array, in silver frames on top of the piano. And across the room, on the mantelpiece, on her own, in pride of place, looking lovelier than ever, the dear, darling Queen Mother.

I am standing in the drawing room of Chalet Coward, the Swiss home of Sir Noël Coward, the self-styled Master, playboy of the West End world, the twentieth century's foremost theatrical entertainer. And I'm gobsmacked. Signed photographs apart, it is all so – well – ordinary. Yes, the house is half-way up a mountain, with breathtaking views across Lake Montreux, and cow bells are clinking in the distance, and Dame Joan Sutherland lives next door, so the setting is theatrical enough, but the house – and its architecture, furnishings, feel – are (dare I say it?) positively mundane.

I am here to meet Graham Payn, Coward's lover, companion and friend, the last living link with the legend. Graham is eighty one, spry, bright-eyed, charmingly self-deprecating, and, like the house, quite unexpected: cosy, comfortable, friendly, unpretentious, as ungrand as you can imagine.

'We weren't grand, not in the least. It's hard for people to believe what a simple life we led. Some people don't want to believe there was a domestic side to Noël Coward, but there you are. I am sorry to shatter the illusion, but the cigarette holder and the Sulka dressing gowns were just props. Noël's standard wardrobe was modest, off the peg. All that brittle, sophisticated stuff was just a cover. Professionally, he was tough as old boots. Personally, he was quite vulnerable.'

When did Graham and Noël first meet?

'At some ungodly hour one winter morning early in 1932 on the stage of the Adelphi Theatre, London. Noël, of course, was enormously famous. He'd already done *Hay Fever*, *Private Lives*, *Cavalcade*. He was auditioning for his new revue, *Words and Music*. I was fourteen. I had come over from South Africa with my mother.'

'Destined to be a child star?'

'Not quite. I was a boy soprano in an Eton suit. My mother knew I wouldn't get very long to show my paces, so she said, "You'd better sing and dance at the same time," so I did. I sang "Nearer My God to Thee" while doing a tap dance. And when I'd finished I saw this elegant figure in the stalls get to his feet, turn to his colleagues and say, in those unmistakable clipped tones, "We have to have that kid in the show." And that's how I met Noël Coward. Wasn't I lucky?' Graham sits back and beams. 'My first job, £5 a week, in the show that launched "Mad Dogs and Englishmen" and "Mad About the Boy."'

'Did you have a lot to do?'

'Not very much – and less by the time Noël had finished with me. I played a beggar boy singing to a cinema queue and I really threw myself into it. I did a wonderful dance, I was a miniature whirling dervish, until after a few rehearsals Noël came up, wagging his finger at me, and said, "Graham, we know what a good little artist you are, but this boy, the character you're playing, he wouldn't know what you know. He'd stand quite still and just sing." So stand still I did. Like a rock. Noël was a great finger wagger, all his life.

'After *Words and Music* I didn't see him again until towards the end of the war. I was in my mid-twenties and beginning to make a bit of a name for myself. I rather thought I was hitting my stride so I sent him a couple of first-night tickets for a revival of *The Lilac Domino*. After the show, he came storming into my dressing room, finger already raised, "I have never seen anybody learn so many bad tricks in so short a time. It's disgraceful." He was probably right, but he must have seen something in me because, not long after, he asked me to be in his new revue, *Sigh No More*. That's when he wrote "Matelot" for me. Wasn't I lucky?'

He is still beaming. 'That was 1945. And it was during *Sigh No More* that Noël invited me to move in. There was a spare room. It seemed the most natural thing in the world. I somehow never moved out. I joined the family.'

Understanding 'the family' is key to understanding the domestic life of Noël Coward. In public he consorted with the stars. In private, he surrounded himself with a small coterie of like-minded souls – not courtiers, chums, friends between whom there were 'no pretences and lots of laughs'. At the family's heart were four women – Lorn Loraine (Lornie, Coward's personal assistant), Gladys Calthrop (designer), Joyce Carey (actress), Clemence Dane (novelist, playwright, artist, sculptress) – and two men: Cole Lesley (Coley; initially, in 1936, Coward's dresser, ultimately his secretary and right-hand man) and Graham. 'Neither Coley nor I ever had a real family. Gladys and Lornie were widows, and Joycie never married. The "family" was our support system. And we were family. Not your conventional Victorian family, granted, but in many respects something better, more alive, because we chose each other. We got together and stayed together because we wanted to be together. Each of us was vulnerable in our own way. We'd had to pick ourselves up early in life and make what we could of the hand we'd been dealt. We sensed that quality in each other. It brought us together and kept us together in a cocoon that kept the world out.'

I can't help noticing, as Graham escorts me to the lunch table, that there appear to be rather more pictures of the Royal Family than Noël's 'family' on display. 'Ah, yes, well, I'm afraid where royalty was concerned, Noël was a snob. It was his one weakness, but remember he was an ordinary boy from Teddington and then, when he became a big star in the twenties, he found himself mixing in this exalted company. I think we can forgive him. And he always preferred the Yorks, long before there was any thought they might be King and Queen. He used to visit them quite often, much to the irritation of Queen Mary who felt her eldest [the Prince of Wales, later Edward VIII and Duke of Windsor] was being upstaged. Let's face it, the Windsors were not exactly joy unconfined. The Duchess was a lot quicker and wittier than her husband. The Duke, to be honest, was an extremely dull man. Noël said he even danced a boring Charleston, which is no mean feat.

'One evening Wallis said to Noël, "You know I don't understand why the British dislike me so much." There was a terrible pause before Noël replied, "Well, because you stole their Prince Charming." She rather liked that. On social occasions, the Duke rarely spoke, not because his mind was pre-occupied, but simply because he had nothing to say. Noël used to say, "he had the charm of the world with nothing to back it up."'

'What about the younger brother, the Duke of Kent?'

'The one who died in the war?'

'Yes. Wasn't Noël supposed to have had a fling with him?' Even as I make the suggestion, I feel a little ashamed. My host is 81, I only met him an hour ago, and here I am tucking into the caviar and sour cream starter while prying pruriently into the private life of the man I've come to celebrate. I need not have worried.

'Oh no. That story about Noël and the Duke of Kent, it wasn't true. We can put the record straight on that. I asked Noël about it and he was quite clear. "We did not get over-friendly."'

Coward was discreet about his homosexuality. 'He was neither proud nor ashamed of it. He firmly believed that his private business was not for public discussion.' Twenty-six years after his friend's death, Graham can be more open. 'I loved the man totally. At first I only saw the public Noël, fascinating but distant. But I grew to love him as I got to know him, saw the compassion behind the wit, sensed the vulnerability . . . I realised I wanted nothing more than to share my life with this remarkable man, to help protect him as best I could.'

Was Coward promiscuous?

'He was vulnerable to the temptations of a brief infatuation, but his pleasure was always outweighed by the irritation he felt at losing control of his emotions. It didn't happen often, and it made no difference to our relationship, that's really all there is to say.'

In one of his last interviews, Coward told the New York Times, 'One's real inside self is a private place and should always stay like that . . . I have taken a lot of trouble with my public face.' To his diary, he admitted, 'I am no good at love.' Being 'in love' bothered him. 'How idiotic people are when they are in love. What an age-old devastating disease . . . To me, passionate love has always been like a tight shoe rubbing blisters on my Achilles heel.'

Coward's grand passion in the late 1920s and 1930s was a handsome young American, Jack Wilson. Rather to my surprise, Graham mentions his name before I do. 'Now Jack was promiscuous. He hurt Noël with his affairs. He hurt Noël a good deal. For a while they were inseparable, but they parted when Jack got married, long before I came on the scene. Jack carried on looking after Noël's interests in America, but, I'm afraid, he couldn't be trusted. Jack loathed me on sight. He saw in me a younger version of himself. Noël was very trusting. He wanted to believe the best in people he loved, but

Jack really was a hopeless case. He was a self-destructive alcoholic. Booze destroyed him before the Great Producer finally stepped in.'

Graham gave up alcohol three years ago. Coward was not especially abstemious ('A gin and tonic before lunch, a dry martini before dinner; in later years he'd nurse a diluted brandy and ginger') but he detested the idea of 'losing control' himself and was appalled to see friends consumed by alcohol. Hugh 'Binkie' Beaumont, the impresario, who, between the 1930s and the 1960s, was the undisputed ruler of the West End, died not long before Noël in 1973. 'During Noël's last days, the most difficult task Coley and I had was to distract Noël from the fact of Binkie's death. Noël kept

Masterpieces

'Wit is like caviar. It should be served in small, elegant portions and not splodged around like marmalade.'

'You ask my advice about acting? Speak clearly, don't bump into the furniture and, if you must have motivation, think of your pay packet on Friday.'

'The most important ingredients of a play are life, death, food, sex and money – but not necessarily in that order.'

'She stopped the show, but then, the show wasn't really travelling very fast.'

'I have always been very fond of theatre critics. I think it so frightfully clever of them to go night after night to the theatre and know so little about it.'

'I love criticism, just so long as it is unqualified praise.'

saying, "I can't get Binkie out of my mind." Poor Binkie. At his own parties in the later years he would have a couple of young men waiting in the wings. When he was too drunk to stand, they'd pick him up and cart him off to bed. My last sight of him was being carried unconscious from the room.'

Self-control and discipline were important to Coward. 'Once he'd set to work, he was totally single-minded. His routine never varied: an early morning start, a light breakfast, and no interruptions except coffee until lunchtime. In the afternoon he might revise the morning's work and, if the mood was right, he'd keep going. If not, he'd put the work aside and do some painting. He was never idle. He wasn't traditionally well-educated, but he had this amazing vocabulary. He soaked up information like a sponge. Trollope, Dickens, Polynesian circumcision rites, you name it, Noël knew about it. He was a voracious reader. E. Nesbit was his all-time favourite.'

Noël admired talent and hard work. 'He longed for me to be a success. He kept hoping I'd break through, that I'd become a star. I had a number of near-misses, but I didn't make it because, let's face it, I wasn't a star. I didn't have "it", whatever it is. I remember once in Jamaica [Coward acquired his homes in Jamaica and Switzerland when he went into tax exile in the 1950s], we were messing around by the swimming pool, and I was feeling rather pleased with life so I did a little song-and-dance routine, which prompted some crack from Noël. I said, rather grandly, "I'll have you know, people have paid good money to see me sing and dance." Noël shot back at once, "Yes, but not very many and not for very long!" And with that he plunged into the pool.'

'Could he be cruel?'

'Oh no, never. He was sharp. He was intolerant over little things. "Has this whisky enjoyed more than a tentative flirtation with soda?" "Must we have this Alpine tornado raging through the room?" But I never saw him – ever – try to destroy anyone with a crack. He was a kind and generous man. And very funny. A lot of his humour simply involved using an unexpected word: "There is less to this than meets the eye . . . Let me be the eighth to congratulate you.' And, of course, it was his extraordinary clipped way of speaking, and the way he bared his teeth, that made whatever he said seem amusing.'

Lunch is being served by Jean-Rene, who came to Chalet Coward thirty-one years ago as Noël's masseur. 'It turned out his real forte was as a chef.

We've eaten wonderfully ever since. Jean-Rene looks after everything. And what he doesn't do, his wife does.' As the fillet of beef makes way for the homemade strawberry and raspberry ice cream, I ask Graham if he has a favourite 'Noël Coward story'.

He looks quite thrown. 'Oh goodness, I'm not sure that I do.' He is anxious to please. I can see he is racking his brain to come up with a gem. Feeling guilty, I offer one of my own. 1955, the first night of *Titus Andronicus* at Stratford. Olivier in the title role, Vivien Leigh as Lavinia. She has been cruelly ravished, her hands cut off and her tongue cut out so she cannot name her attackers. She enters and, holding a stick between her wrists, scrawls the names of her assailants in the sand. Unfortunately, as she comes on, the stick slips and clatters noisily onto the stage. After the performance, Noël sweeps into Vivien's dressing room, finger wagging, 'Tut-tut, butter-stumps!'

'Oh, that's wonderful,' Graham is chortling courteously, 'that's lovely, I've never heard that. And you do the voice. Oh, do another.'

This is absurd. I am sitting at Noël Coward's dining table with Noël Coward's lover telling Noël Coward stories in a Noël Coward voice – and my charming host is chuckling and nodding and assuring me he hasn't heard any of them.

Graham, of course, is drinking water. Jean-René keeps refilling my glass with the delicious local wine. I say, 'Now this one you will know and you can tell me if it's true or not. Noël goes to a clinic, a sort of health farm for the stars, where their most famous treatment is a rejuvenating serum taken from sheep's glands. As Noël drives up to the clinic, he passes a field full of sheep and, right in the middle of the flock, he spies a single black sheep. Noël points to it and says, "Ah, I see Paul Robeson is here already."'

'Oh, that's wonderful. I've never heard that one, I really haven't. But Noël certainly went to the clinic. It's over at Vevey. He didn't like getting older, he didn't like looking older. They all went to that clinic, Marlene, Vivien . . . I'm not sure about Paul Robeson. It cost a bomb.' A little giggle. 'I don't think it did much good.'

Coward found no consolation in the ageing process. He had always prided himself on being word-perfect from the first rehearsal. The only time I saw him on stage, in his final West End appearance in 1966, he was having trouble with his lines. 'I have been increasingly worried lately about my memory,' he wrote at the time. 'Not my far-away memory. I can still remember accurately plays and events of 1909. But my immediate memory, which has been behaving in a disconcerting manner. A sort of curtain descends in my mind veiling what happened last week.' In 1969 he stopped keeping his diary. He was diagnosed as having a form of arterio-sclerosis, but the recommended exercise routine was not to his taste and giving up his beloved cigarettes (two packs a day, usually Player's tipped) out of the question. 'When [in 1970] he knelt to receive his knighthood,' Graham remembers, 'there was no question of going down on one knee. It was both or nothing.'

Coward died in Jamaica on 26 March 1973. 'His last evening was like any other, with Coley and me, drinks and chat and lots of laughs. As we took our leave, he said, "Goodnight, my darlings. See you in the morning." We left him sitting in his chair on the terrace, his wire-rimmed glasses perched on the end of his nose and a copy of E. Nesbit's *The Enchanted Castle* propped up in front of him, with *The Would-Be-Goods* close by.

'After he died they came to take his body to Kingston. But after they'd taken the coffin away, they had to come back. There'd been some muddle, so they had to return and then set off all over again. So Noël did two exits – absolutely typical.'

Coward is buried in Jamaica, 'on the spot where we would sit with our drinks, gazing down on the Spanish Main.' Graham and Coley returned to Switzerland. 'Coley died here in January 1980. The family's all gone now. I'm the only one left. I run the estate. They're performing Noël's plays all over the world. They have stood the test of time. Somerset Maugham's plays seem dated. Noël's don't. He's very big in Norway and Sweden. You wouldn't think the Scandinavians would have a great sense of humour, would you? And they do him a lot in Japan. Can you imagine "Very flat, Norfolk" in Japanese? I have to keep an eye on things, especially in America, stop them doing an all-male *Private Lives*, that sort of nonsense. I've learnt to be tough. I told one producer who wanted to haggle about royalties, "This is the Coward Estate, we're Cartier, you know, not Berwick Street." I think Noël would rather have liked that. In fact, I think he'd be quite pleased to see how busy I am: "Doing something at last, lazy little sod."'

'Do you miss him?'

'All the time. Most of all I miss the laughter. If he'd had to write his own epitaph, Noël claimed it would read: "He was much loved because he made people laugh and cry." If mine reads "Friend of Noël Coward" that will suit me fine.'

Postscript: leading ladies

Graham took me on a guided tour of the house. 'I've changed very little since Noël died. This is the guest room. The ladies who've slept in this bed ... Merle [Oberon], Marlene [Dietrich], Vivien [Leigh].

Graham's manner is dapper, unflamboyant. He is modest about his own achievements, quick to acknowledge the opportunities that came his way because of his friendship with Coward. In 1948 he toured the US with Gertrude Lawrence in *Tonight at 8.30*. 'Working with Gertie was daunting but a privilege. I met some extraordinary ladies through Noël. Many of his closest friends were women.'

Gertrude Lawrence: 'Of all the people Noël loved throughout his life, Gertie was undoubtedly first among equals. Were they ever lovers? Noël kept mum on the subject. There may have been an early attempt on her part to goad Noël into trying "it" simply for the sake of knowing what "it" was all about, but their love transcended sex. The picture of them standing on the balcony in *Private Lives*, together yet apart, eternally elegant, forever sums them up for anyone who ever saw them.'

Marlene Dietrich: 'Noël and Marlene were founding members of the Self-Invention Society. Each of them had worked out every detail of how they wanted their public to perceive them: dress, speech, deportment, all scrupulously tailored to fit the image. Each of them admired the elegant machinery at work in the other. The difference between them was that Noël never took himself too seriously. Conversation with Marlene was almost exclusively about Marlene. It was Marlene's phone bills after a visit to us in Switzerland that caused Noël to have the phones removed from the guest rooms. "Doesn't the dear girl know anybody who doesn't live eight thousand miles away?"'

Vivien Leigh: 'Viv? Such ups and downs. Sadly, the downs won out. I adored her. We were friends independent of the "family". Some people made me welcome only when I was with Noël, but Vivien wasn't like that. Towards the end it was sad beyond belief. One evening we got a call from Jack Merivale [with whom she lived after her marriage to Laurence Olivier ended], begging us to come over right away. We arrived to find Vivien standing naked over a flight of stairs, convinced she could fly. It took all of Noël's considerable love and skill to talk her back to safety. It was a long way from Scarlett O'Hara.'

Queen Elizabeth the Queen Mother: 'Of all the Royals the Queen Mother was by far his favourite. When she came to lunch with us in Jamaica, Noël decided he would prepare the meal himself: curry in coconuts, fish mousse and rum cream pie. He rather overdid the garlic and the curry powder, and the fish mousse took on a texture Noël described as "akin to an ordinary Slazenger tennis ball". Rising above it, Noël whipped up an iced soup, just as the royal party crossed the threshold. Crème de Queen Mum certainly saved the day, though God knows what went into it. Years later, when the Queen Mother unveiled the memorial stone to Noël at Westminster Abbey, I mumbled my thanks to her for coming. She smiled that amazing smile of hers and said, "Not at all. We were very great friends." She meant it.'

Michael Redgrave

Sir Michael Redgrave, husband of Rachel Kempson, father of Vanessa, Corin and Lynn, and grandfather to a third generation of notable actors, was born on 20 March 1908 and died on 21 March 1985.

I first met Michael Redgrave a little over thirty years ago, when I was twenty and an undergraduate at Oxford, and he was sixty and a major star of stage and screen. I found his address in *Who's Who* and wrote to him out of the blue, telling him he was 'my kind of hero' (well, I was only twenty) and inviting him to come to Oxford to perform the prologue to the student pantomime I was producing at the Oxford Playhouse. Forty-eight hours later I received a telegram: WHAT FUN. ACCEPT WITH GREAT PLEASURE. REDGRAVE.

When the great day came, I went to Oxford Station to meet him. His train was late and crowded. The passengers poured out of the carriages and surged past the ticket barrier where I was waiting. There was no sign of my hero. The last passenger handed in his ticket and the platform was bare. The Playhouse curtain was going up within the hour and where was my star? I peered down the platform and there I saw him, in the far distance, a huge frame in a dishevelled raincoat, carrying a little battered suitcase and looking about him with a puzzled, vacant air. I ran towards him. He shuffled towards me.

'Sir Michael?'

'Yes?'

'Sir Michael!'

'Yes. Are you, er—'

'Yes.'

'Oh good,' and his large, old face broke into a sweet smile. He had a wonderful smile.

'How are you, Sir Michael?'

'Not well,' he sighed. 'Not at all well.'

Slowly, painfully slowly, we made our way to the waiting taxi. Sir Michael explained that he felt unsteady, 'strange', and that his voice had gone, 'completely gone'. At the stage door, he said he thought a glass of port might help. Michele, my girlfriend, ran into the Gloucester Arms and bought a bottle. He wouldn't use a dressing room. He preferred to stand in the wings.

He took a glass of port, gargled with it and swallowed it down. He took another. And another. And one more. The orchestra had finished the overture. An expectant hush had fallen over the auditorium.

'You're on now, Sir Michael,' I whispered.

'I don't think I can do it,' he said.

'You're on!'

And the stooped, shambling figure stepped from the wings onto the stage, and into the spotlight, and was transformed. Tall, erect, formidable. 'Ladies and gentlemen, good evening!' the voice boomed, the audience cheered, the magic happened.

That night he found the energy. Over the next fifteen years, as Parkinson's Disease took a firmer grip of him, finding the energy became increasingly difficult. At first no one realised what was wrong. One day (a year or so later) we were having lunch at the old Empress Restaurant in

Grosvenor Square and his head simply fell forward onto the table. He seemed drunk, but he wasn't. He invited me and my girlfriend to lunch at his new house in Lower Belgrave Street and, showing us round, flopped down onto the stairs. He was bewildered. 'What is happening?'

He had long had a dread of first nights. In 1971, at the Mermaid Theatre, we witnessed the worst of them. It was a play by William Trevor, *The Old Boys*, with Michael in the lead, and because, by the dress rehearsal, he still didn't have a grasp of his lines, for the first night the management equipped him with a hearing aid through which he could be prompted. Unhappily, in the audience we could hear the prompter better than Michael could. We reckoned we could also hear the local minicab service. We certainly heard a cacophony of electric squawks and squeals and burrs and when, suddenly, the apparatus fell from Michael's ear and disintegrated and scattered in pieces around him, it seemed to symbolise the heartrending end of a glorious career.

It wasn't the end, but the beginning of the end, and at least it got him to the Hospital for Nervous Diseases and a correct diagnosis. At last he knew what was wrong, even if he didn't like it. He described this period of his life as 'a grey expanse, with intermittent shafts of light'. When we met (in Oxford, in London, off and on, over about ten years) his mind would come and go. He would talk of the early days, of his time as a schoolmaster, teaching modern languages at Cranleigh, of how he abandoned respectability 'to fulfil my destiny' and joined the Liverpool Playhouse where, in the summer of 1935, he met and married Rachel Kempson ('Dear Rachel, she puts up with such a lot you know'), of his daughter Vanessa and her politics ('It gives strength to her acting, it doesn't detract'), of Edith Evans. He always came back to Edith Evans. 'If you are going to play Orlando, you must love your Rosalind! You know, I made love to Edith on the night Vanessa was born.' Acting with Edith, he said, 'was like being in your mother's arms, like knowing how to swim, like riding a bicycle. You're safe . . . For the first time in my acting life, I felt completely unselfconscious. Acting with her made me feel, oh, it's so easy. You don't start acting, she told me, until you stop trying to act. It doesn't leave the ground until you don't have to think about it . . . For the first time, on stage or off, I felt completely free.'

Orlando to Edith Evans's Rosalind was in 1936, Redgrave's first Old Vic season, when he also played Horner in *The Country Wife* and Laertes to Laurence Olivier's Hamlet and the three of them, as the season's leading players, were each paid £20 a week. From then, for thirty years, Michael enjoyed an extraordinary career. He made his first film in 1939, Hitchcock's *The Lady Vanishes*, and his last, of note, in 1971, Joseph Losey's *The Go-Between*. In between he starred in fifty pictures and worked with fine directors: Carol Reed, Anthony Asquith, Fritz Lang, Basil Dearden, Orson Welles, Joseph Mankiewicz, Lewis Gilbert. On stage, he climbed the peaks: Hamlet, Macbeth, Antony, Lear. The critical consensus of the time was that 'of all the modern Lears – and there have been many fine ones,' his was the finest. 'Lear is a labyrinthine citadel, all but impregnable,' wrote the young Kenneth Tynan, 'and it needed a Redgrave to assault it.'

Michael was up there with the giants, but, in most minds, he remained in third place when it came to assessing the great triumvirate. Famously, Tynan conjured up the mighty gulf fixed between good and great performances: 'Olivier pole-vaults over in a single animal leap; Gielgud, seizing a parasol, crosses by tightrope; Redgrave alone must battle it out with the current.'

Michael died on 21 March 1985, the day after his seventy-seventh birthday, and somehow now, thirteen years later, he still seems to be struggling. This week I asked a pair of theatre-aware Oxford students what the name Michael Redgrave meant to them and one said, 'He founded the dynasty, didn't he?' and the other asked, 'Wasn't he Noël Coward's boyfriend?'

Redgrave was immensely proud of his children and grandchildren, but he laid no claims to founding any dynasty. He was glad to be part of a long line of troupers going back several generations. His mother, Daisy Scudamore, was a not unsuccessful provincial actress in her mid-twenties, when she met Roy Redgrave in a theatrical stock company at Brighton in the summer of 1907. Roy was a popular barnstorming player of the old school (the self-styled 'Dramatic cock o' the north', 'so long the favourite of the Britannia Theatre, Hoxton'), a legendary drinker, a ladies, man who seduced Daisy (ten years his junior), married her (probably bigamously), and set off for Australia within a year of Michael's birth. Daisy pursued her lover to Australia, but to no avail. He was not the domestic type. He died of drink in Sydney in 1922. That Michael was given the benefits of a comfortable middle-class upbringing – public school, Cambridge, a nice house off Belgrave Square – was thanks to his stepfather, a sometime tea and rubber planter who encountered Daisy and her baby son on the P & O liner that brought them back from Australia in 1911.

Michael was bisexual. All his adult life he had affairs, occasionally with women, principally with men. He hinted at his bisexuality in the autobiography his son Corin coaxed out of him, with infinite patience and love, in the early 1980s: 'Always it returns to this question of a split personality, and I cannot believe it would be right – even if I had the will-power, which I have not – to cut off or starve the other side of my nature.' There were one-night stands – a succession of evenings when he would return home, half-full of remorse, to find Rachel, bereft, in floods of tears – and at least four or five long-term relationships, two of which involved his lover living in a studio at the end of the garden. How or why his beautiful wife put up with this I am not sure. Understanding one's own marriage isn't easy. Understanding someone else's is next to impossible. It was clear to me, seeing them together, that they were in many ways a happy couple, well-suited, devoted even, mutually necessary. According to Rachel, Michael made no attempt to hide his nature from her. Perhaps, when they married, she believed she could change him. Later, perhaps she simply felt she had made her bed and so must lie on it. She had her own affairs, but

Michael's behaviour hurt her. At the beginning of the war, on the eve of his call-up to join the navy, Michael spent the night with Noël Coward. 'I would have liked Michael to spend his last evening with me,' said Rachel. Years later, Coward apologised, but he couldn't help it, he explained, he had found Michael 'so irresistibly charming'. Rachel said, 'I couldn't but agree with him.'

Redgrave was charming. And selfish. And, in many ways, hopeless. He was hopeless with money. He got into financial difficulties time and again. He was hopeless with his children: as a father frequently absent, as a dominating force ever-present – even after death. I imagine Vanessa, the most successful, the one of which he was the most admiring, to whom he was most obviously devoted, is the one most at ease with his memory. Corin recently published a touching and revealing memoir of his father, which will have helped him, even if it must have ruffled a few feathers among family and friends. Lynn, the youngest, now fifty five, still seems to be wrestling with the ghost.

Michael Redgrave was selfish, self-indulgent, flawed, but he was also extraordinary – honest, intelligent, fastidious, delightful – both as an actor and as a person. On stage and off, he was brave too. He had a lifelong tendency to hypochondria (especially when confronted with something he didn't want to do), but he faced his decline with Miltonic fortitude. Talking about it, he seemed to date the beginning of his troubles to his time at the National. Sometimes I felt he held Olivier in some way personally responsible.

In 1963 Sir Laurence invited Redgrave to join him for the opening season of Britain's newly formed National Theatre Company at the Old Vic. Michael was Claudius to Peter O'Toole's Hamlet under Olivier's direction. Redgrave appeared in *Hamlet* seven times. He loved the play, but as Claudius he couldn't make it happen. In rehearsal Olivier admonished him, 'When you came on as Macbeth, it was as if you were saying, "Fuck you, I am Macbeth". As Claudius you are dim.'

In that initial National season he also played Hobson in *Hobson's Choice* and hated it (how he hated it!) and Solness in *The Master Builder*. The Ibsen was well-received, but Michael wasn't happy. He knew something was wrong and, though there were still good things to come (an assured Rakitin in *A Month in the Country* with Ingrid Bergman, a touching blind old man in John Mortimer's *Voyage Round My Father*), he sensed the best was behind him.

It would be sad – and wrong – if this great actor was remembered for his bisexuality, his family and his decline. I remember him for his flawless portrayal of the unbending, scholarly schoolmaster in *The Browning Version* and for his Uncle Vanya, the best performance by any actor I ever saw. Harold Hobson called the production at Chichester in 1962 'the admitted master achievement in British twentieth-century theatre'. The company included Olivier, Joan Plowright, Rosemary Harris, Max Adrian, Fay Compton, Sybil Thorndike, Lewis Casson. 'But the greatest of these,' wrote Bernard Levin, 'is Sir Michael Redgrave . . . I do not think he has ever done anything better – not even his Prospero. Foolish and laughing at one moment, tragic and pitiable at the next, and both together at the one after, Sir Michael dominates the play without – it is his greatest achievement – ever unbalancing it.'

I have the record of *Uncle Vanya*, four LPs, and I defy you to listen to them without laughing, crying and cheering out loud. Michael gave me several records. He was specially fond of his own readings of the stories of Hans Andersen, translated by his old housemaster from Clifton. I have just been listening to his Macbeth (recorded in the late 1950s) and in my head I can still hear his Hamlet. Once, in the deserted debating chamber of the Oxford Union (of all places), he recited 'To be or not to be' just for me. It was our fifth or sixth meeting. I was twenty-one and he was forty years my senior, but he had the most beautiful voice in the world and the sweetest way with him.

I didn't think about it then, but perhaps it was flirtation-by-Shakespeare-soliloquy. If so, there are worse kinds and I know I loved it, was flattered, touched and honoured by it. I know, too, I am grateful for the memory of it. He was my kind of hero.

Vanessa and Corin Redgrave

In November 1999 Michael Redgrave's elder daughter and son, Vanessa (born 1937) and Corin (born 1939) appeared together in a revival of Noël Coward's last full-length play, A Song at Twilight. I went to interview them – to talk about Noël Coward, and their parents and their younger sister, Lynn (born 1943) – in their adjoining dressing rooms at the Gielgud Theatre in Shaftesbury Avenue.

On the first Sunday in November 1969, at the Elizabeth Restaurant in Oxford, I had supper with Sir Michael Redgrave. I keep a diary, so I can tell you what we ate (carréd'agneau dauphinoise, £1.50 for two) and drank (a 1964 Beaune – 'wonderful') and how animated the great actor became when I asked him about his famous daughter. His eyes shone. 'Vanessa? She is beautiful, extraordinary. I love her very much. You must meet her.'

Thirty years later, I have. Last week I found myself in her dressing room at the Gielgud Theatre on Shaftesbury Avenue. She *is* beautiful. And extraordinary. She glows. She is about to appear in *A Song at Twilight*, Noël Coward's last work, playing – for the first time – opposite her younger brother, Corin. Because they know I knew their father, because I admired him and he was kind to me, they have each granted me a rare interview.

Coward's play is about a celebrated writer (Corin) who is a closet homosexual. At the height of his fame he publishes a self-serving and dishonest autobiography and then is forced to confront his past – and his true nature – by the two women central to his life: his long-suffering wife (played by Corin's own wife Kika Markham) and an actress with whom he had an affair years ago (Vanessa).

As I begin to say, 'The play is obviously about Somerset Maugham', Vanessa interrupts: 'I don't know anything about Maugham. Maugham means nothing to me. The play is about the people in the play. It's about the tragic result of the way that society has forced the central character into conflict both with himself – with his own talent, which is a very great one – and with all his personal relationships.'

When I talk to Vanessa, she looks straight at me. Her gaze is wide-eyed, steady, intimate, a touch unnerving. Corin hardly looks at me at all. For forty minutes or so he keeps his eyes firmly on his coffee cup and his sandwich. This (I guess) isn't so much because he is shy (he may be: his father was, painfully so) as because he is concentrating on what he wants to say. He is fastidious, determined to get it right. 'In this play Coward chose to write about a man who, unlike himself, could never come to terms with his own homosexuality. He is hurt by it, rather as Richard III says of himself, "scarce half made up and that so lamely". He feels he carries some sort of unhappy torment. What you see in the piece – and it's both very painful and very wonderful – is a man liberated to the extent that he starts to be able to acknowledge his own feelings.'

Did Vanessa know Noël Coward?

'Oh yes, I met him quite a lot. He used to come to my parents' house. He once gave me the greatest compliment of my life as an actress. I'm not going to tell you what he said, but I hold it as the greatest compliment of my life.'

This is not untypical of Vanessa's answers: tantalising, but incomplete.

She could not be sweeter or more friendly, she doesn't talk politics, she laughs, she squeezes my hand, she responds to every question, but, time and again, she starts a thought and then, suddenly, leaves it hanging in the air and her penetrating stare and seraphic smile suggest there's no point in pressing further.

Corin is more forthcoming. 'I think Coward was blessed with a fairly direct approach to his feelings and his temperament. The man in the play is not like Coward, who seems to me to have been a kind man – he could be sharp no doubt, but not vindictive, not malicious. The role I play seems to have been deliberately taken from Coward's understanding of what Somerset Maugham had become. Coward admired Maugham hugely as a writer and was deeply distressed with the way Maugham's late autobiography was so vicious about his wife Syrie and utterly dismissive of Gerald Haxton, the great love of his life. Maugham is a self-hating gay – he loathed himself for being gay. Coward was much more mature, much more wise, and his play is about the withering effect upon a human being, and a creative human being at that, of having been forced, obliged, as he thinks, to live all his adult life under a cloak of concealment.'

'Are there echoes here of your father?'

Corin looks up at me. 'There are echoes. I don't use them in the piece, but they are there. Oh yes.'

'Your father and Coward were very close?' I try to say it delicately.

Vanessa is gazing at me intently. Her smile broadens. 'I should think they were very, very close.'

Corin is more robust: 'Oh, yes, they were lovers.'

According to Rachel, Michael made no attempt to hide his nature from her. Perhaps, when they met and married in the summer of 1935, when Rachel was 25 and he was 27, she believed she could change him. Later, perhaps she simply felt she had made her bed and so must lie on it. She had her own affairs, but Michael's behaviour undoubtedly hurt her. At the beginning of the war, on the eve of his call-up to join the Navy, Michael spent the night with Coward. 'I would have liked Michael to spend his last evening with me,' said Rachel. Years later, Coward apologised to her, but he couldn't help it, he explained, he had found Michael 'so irresistibly charming'. Rachel said, 'I couldn't but agree with him.'

Corin is contemplating his sandwich: 'Frith Banbury [the veteran director], who didn't like my father very much, told me something very interesting about him. He told me he was once very moved when Michael said to him, "Thank God none of my children is queer." Frith was pleased that Michael was able to say that about himself, but I would only half be pleased because if you are thanking God that your children are in quotes "normal" – and one must put quotes there – then what does that mean you think about yourself? I found it very touching and moving, but I couldn't be happy for him that he said that.'

Later, when we are alone together, I ask Vanessa if she feels that she is at all like her father.

'That's a hard one. I'm not as shy as he was. I have been able to be free about who I am, what I am, in a way he couldn't be, thanks to all the people who have been very brave about who they were, what they were. That's the enormous change that's happened in my lifetime. It's a major, major thing. For men and women to be able to say, "I'm this, I'm not that."'

When, once, I asked Sir Michael who was his favourite actress, he said, without hesitation, 'Vanessa, Vanessa,' and then, with a shy smile, added, 'But if family is to be excluded, then, of course, it must be Edith.' He always came back to Edith Evans. He told me, more than once, 'If you are going to play Orlando, you must love your Rosalind! You know, I made love to Edith on the night Vanessa was born.'

Corin prods his sandwich: 'Yes, Edith.' A pause. 'You're right. I don't think he got that quite sorted out.' Another pause. 'As a rule, he was very undeceptive. That doesn't mean to say it was easy for Rachel – it wasn't – but on the whole he was undeceptive about who he was seeing or who he was fond of or who he wanted to spend more time with. I think the only person he probably did deceive her with was Edith, and it was a big shock to Rachel when she found out. A big shock. Also, because Rachel had been terribly fond of Edith and thought of her as an older sister figure. Needless to say, Rachel has totally forgiven now, utterly.'

Later, I begin to say to Vanessa, 'Nobody can understand anybody else's marriage.'

She interrupts with a big, throaty laugh. 'I can't understand any marriage!' She goes on laughing. It's disconcerting. I want to ask her about her own love-life, about her marriage to Tony Richardson (another bisexual), about her relationships with the actors Franco Nero and Timothy Dalton, but I don't think I will get very far. I decide to stick with her parents.

'In an odd sort of way, their marriage worked, didn't it?'

The laughter stops. 'I don't know that it did, I don't know that it did work. But the remarkable thing is what they did do for each other, as well as not for each other. It's quite a wonderful thing to see two people who know that they are destructive of each other, and yet . . .' She stops, and smiles, and starts on a new tack. 'Because Michael got his fame very hard and high very early on, it was difficult for her. Everything was concentrated on him. There was no interest in her at all. It was all him . . . It was understandable, but . . . But, anyway, she is a wonderfully loyal person. You know, I am living with Rachel now. I am so grateful that I am. I love living with her, I really do. She will be 90 in May. She is extraordinary. We do a Chekhov programme together. We've just done it with Lynny in Los Angeles, the three of us. It was wonderful.'

'Is the news of Lynn good?' (Vanessa's younger sister, now an American citizen, is divorcing her husband of thirty-two years. Last November, while she was preparing the turkey for the family's Thanksgiving dinner, he confessed to her that he had been 'a naughty boy'. Some years ago, unknown to his wife, he fathered a child by a woman – his personal assistant – who subsequently married his and Lynn's only son.)

'Yes. The news of Lynn is good. But I don't want to talk about her husband. We call him "The Unmentionable", so don't let's mention him.' Another loud, throaty laugh. 'I adore Lynn. I always have.'

The sisters have had their ups and downs over the years. On politics they don't see eye to eye. In 1991, at the time of the Gulf War, Vanessa attacked the United States for intervening. Lynn retaliated in print. 'I had been living in America for almost twenty years and I needed to make it clear that when they wrote "Redgrave says . . ." it wasn't me.'

Lynn too was conscious that both Vanessa and Corin had been closer to their father. There was an almost farcical dispute over the final resting place for Michael's ashes. Corin (for £600) had bought a plot for them in Highgate Cemetery. Lynn wrote to her brother, 'I quite understand that you would like to bury Dad's ashes near Karl Marx. I should have preferred St Paul's, the actors' church in Covent Garden, and so would Mum I think. But your choice means more to you than ours would to us, so you should go ahead.' He didn't. For almost nine years the matter lay unresolved: Sir Michael's ashes remained unclaimed at Mortlake crematorium. Eventually, Corin collected them and, for several weeks, they kept him company in the boot of his car. 'Strange as it might seem, I felt comforted by them. After a while I began to wonder how I had ever managed without them. Alone in my car . . . I would play music to them, and even sing to them. Sometimes they would sing back, a distant, clear, pure baritone – "every valley shall be exalted". Once, when Radio 3 was playing Haydn's "Miracle" symphony, I could hear them laughing. It couldn't last, of course, and it didn't.' Eventually Rachel said, 'I must take Michael's ashes to St Paul's, I've promised Lynn I would.' And that's where they now are.

I ask Corin about Lynn.

He looks up again and smiles. 'She's very happy. She's sorted out her life.'

'Is she happy with you?'

'Completely happy now. Looking back – I don't know whether this is off the record . . . I don't know whether it's off or on . . . oh, let it be on – looking back, thinking about it, it's clear that we get on so much better because a lot of the troubles, the misunderstandings that occurred, were stoked up by her soon-to-be ex-husband. His betrayal of her . . . it was bizarre, so dreadful.'

'So you're one great big happy family.'

'A very happy family. Mind you, I should say that Vanessa and Lynn, even though they may have had arguments from time to time, they always managed to be very close. I did too really, but it was difficult sometimes. One sees a lot now that one didn't see at the time.'

I ask Vanessa what it's like working with her brother.

'As a matter of fact, this may sound really odd to you, but to me it's not primarily about acting with my brother at all, it's about acting with a really fine actor who I know well, but is also full of surprises.'

Corin beams: 'Working with Vanessa? It's lovely, lovely. It doesn't feel like the first time. That's partly because I know her and I feel I know and like and understand her attitudes and her ideas and her way of working.'

'Have you always been friends?'

Vanessa: 'Yes, yes. As children we were very much thrown on each other's company, much more than children now would be. We would delight in doing things together . . .'

Corin: 'We were thrown together because of the time when we were born. I was born just as the war began, she the year before, so fairly soon, anyway by the time the Blitz began, we were evacuated together to an elderly cousin on my mother's side, and we spent most of the war there, with Lucy Kempson and a nanny. And even when we came back, because both Rachel and Michael were in the theatre, sometimes acting together, and once going off for quite a long time to Hollywood, we spent a lot of time in one another's company. We shared lessons together at home. We tried to go to a local school. We got teased and singled out because Michael was so famous at that time as a film star. You felt you were some sort of exhibit.'

'Was Vanessa always remarkable as an actress?'

'Oh yes. When I saw her at school play Saint Joan – she would have been about fourteen or fifteen – I could see she was quite wonderful.'

Vanessa has always been acclaimed. Ever since she made her London debut, in 1958, playing opposite her father in N. C. Hunter's *A Touch of the Sun*, she has been recognised as an extraordinary talent. Some (well, most of us, frankly) may have reservations about her political views (loopy but big-hearted is the kindly verdict), but the quality of her work has never been in doubt. Since 1961 she has received more than thirty major national and international awards, including an Oscar (for *Julia* in 1977). She is at the height of her powers. (If you doubt me, see her recent performance in *Mrs Dalloway*, just out on video.)

It has taken Corin longer to gain recognition. A leading casting director said to me this week, 'All that Workers' Revolutionary Party nonsense was a terrible distraction. Corin is a very fine actor. And he gets better all the time.'

He was nominated for a Tony on Broadway earlier this year.

I say to him, 'When you were younger, did you feel you were in Michael's shadow?'

He doesn't look up. 'I must have done. At the time I didn't, I really didn't. And you couldn't imagine a more generous and less over-shadowing father. He was absolutely wonderful in that respect.' He pauses. I know when he speaks he wants to be scrupulously honest. He measures everything he says. 'I think, psychologically, there is a great problem for sons about being better than their fathers. If you surpass your father, in a way you kill him. I know that I consciously never took on, if I could avoid it, any part he had made his own – not because I was afraid of not living up to him, but because, deep down, there was a subconscious feeling that I might do it better – which sounds boastful, but you know what I mean. I think it's a problem that all sons who have fathers in any walk of life who shine will understand. You destroy your father if you do something better, so it's only when he's gone you no longer have that problem.'

Corin has published a touching and beautifully written memoir of his father. 'I think about Michael a lot, a huge amount, more and more. I know you won't make it sound as if I'm obsessed by him. I'm not. He is a point of reference: I think how he would have been amused by this, how he would have liked that, what he would have said . . . I think it's a good thing to think about the dead, and be able to think about the dead.'

Because I have tried to ask each of them the same questions, I say to Vanessa, 'Do you think about Michael much?'

Her eyes are shining now. 'Oh, yes, all the time. All the time. I'm so grateful for his memory. I am happy with it. I have such happiness now. Lynny's fine and Corin's here. I'm in an extraordinary play with extraordinary actors, and when the show is over I go home and my mother, aged 89, has made supper for me. Yes, supper on a tray, all ready. Who could want anything more?'

Donald Sinden

I have known Sir Donald Sinden (born 1923), his wife Diana, and their two sons, since I was about fourteen, when they visited Bedales School in Hampshire, where I was a pupil, and I was detailed to show them round. I interviewed Sir Donald, two years after he received his knighthood, in the summer of 1999.

I f theatrical anecdotes, well-honed, fruitily told, are not your bag, kindly leave the page. I mean it. Move on, now. Please. This is an interview with Sir Donald Sinden.

I spent a couple of hours in the great man's dressing room this week, during which he smoked nine cigarettes and recounted fifty-three separate stories. (No exaggeration: I've checked the tape). I laughed a lot and, right at the outset of the encounter, I even made him laugh too. He is on tour in a new play by Ronald Harwood (capacity houses, standing ovations, opening in the West End shortly) and I caught up with it in Norwich. I told Sir Donald how, during the interval, I had overheard two elderly ladies discussing him. One of them, the one with the violet rinse (yes, in 1999, in Norwich), said, 'He's what you'd call a proper theatrical knight, isn't he?'

'Oh, yes,' cooed her friend. 'He's the real thing.'

Sir Donald beamed, gurgled, chuckled softly. 'Oh, I like that. That's rather good, isn't it?'

'Wait,' I said, 'I haven't finished. The lady with the violet rinse then added, "I always thought a knighthood was rather wasted on Derek Jacobi."'

Sinden exploded with pleasure. 'Oh – ah – ee!' Cigarette ash, which he had been gathering in an old envelope, sprayed around the room. His face performed a five-second arabesque of gleeful mock-scandalised tics and twitches. 'Oh, no, you can't say that.' He was hooting with happiness. 'It's wicked. You mustn't.' As the cachinnation subsided, scooping the ash off the dressing table back into the envelope, he narrowed his eyes, puckered his lips, leant forward conspiratorially and confided, 'Actors are not always as generous towards one another as they should be. Did I ever tell you about the television programme I did years ago with Edith Evans and John Gielgud? We were shown clips of the great players of yesteryear and asked for our reactions. During the bit of Ellen Terry, Edith nodded off – nodded off during Ellen Terry! And when they showed a bit of Olivier's Othello and asked Gielgud what he made of it, John didn't know what to do: "Oh, no, no, no, no, no, no." That was all he could say.'

Donald Sinden has measured out his life in anecdotes. You ask him a question and he tells you a story. He offers an account of the day he heard about his knighthood. It's a simple enough tale. The letter comes. He can't believe it. He has to reply. He won't trust the post. He drives to Downing Street to hand-deliver his acceptance. He gets home and panics. Did he tick the wrong box? He discovers Number 10 is in the phone book. He calls. All's well. That's it, but he transforms it into an eight-minute music-hall routine.

Sinden has been a household name since he started in films in the early 1950s: *The Cruel Sea*, *Doctor in the House*, *Mogambo* with Clark Gable, directed by John Ford ('He was a monster, a professional Irishman who blamed me personally for all of Ireland's troubles.') He is now (I'd argue) our most versatile actor: Sheridan, Shaw, Chekhov, Wilde, TV sitcom, Ray

Cooney farce, King Lear, he's scored with them all. He has earned his 'K'. And the Norwich matrons are right: it suits him. I tell him (sincerely: I have known his family since I was a schoolboy) that it hasn't spoilt him either. Another gurgle, another story. 'A dear friend of Donald Wolfit's wrote to him to congratulate him on his knighthood and added, facetiously, "I do hope I'm still going to be able to call you Donald." Wolfit replied, "My dear fellow, we've known each other for forty-five years, you must certainly continue to call me Donald. [Pause.] Of course, I cannot answer for Lady Wolfit."'

Why is he like this? Where did it begin?

'My first job, in the early 1940s, when I was still in my teens, was entertaining the troops with an outfit called MESA [Mobile Entertainments, Southern Area] run by a fellow named Charles F. Smith, one of the unsung heroes of the British stage. He'd started going to the theatre in the days of Henry Irving, the great Victorian actor-manager, and he knew everybody. During the war, most of the London theatres were closed, so actors were continuously on tour and they'd all come through Brighton, where we were. Every Sunday Charles would have a party in his flat and we young ones were invited to meet these astonishing luminaries of an earlier era. John Martin-Harvey, Marie Tempest, Irene Vanburgh – I sat at their feet and heard them talk about the people they had seen. I was hearing stories about Irving and George Alexander and Beerbohm-Tree. I fell under their spell. And I learnt so much.'

'Who taught you most?'

'I learnt from all of them. The first master comedian I learnt from was Laurence O'Madden – forgotten now, but, oh, his timing! [Sinden's eyes are full of tears.] He'd be beside me on stage and under his breath he'd say, "Wait for it, w-a-i-t for it, wait – for – it . . . Now!" A laugh is like the roof of a house. It starts under the eaves and works its way to the top and then rolls down the other side. You wait till it's half-way down the far side before you move on. It was Balliol Holloway who taught me how to do asides.

Gave me a master-class. Who remembers Ba Holloway now? And Newton Blick? Do you know about his routine with the apple? [This is a four-minute story. If ever you see Sinden emerging from the Garrick Club, stop him and get him to tell it to you. It's a gem.] I am fascinated by the craft, by how it works. It was Ralph [Richardson] who told me, "You've got to have at least five consonants in a tag line. You can't get a laugh on a vowel." I once asked John Gielgud, "What are the most essential things about acting?" With hardly a pause he replied, "Feeling and timing," and then, head erect, his eyes twinkled to the side, as he added, "I understand it is the same in many walks of life."'

Has Sinden, in his turn, passed on what he has learnt to younger actors? 'I'm not sure that many of them are interested. You see, mine is the last generation that did rep. I'm told on good authority that for students leaving drama school today, of the work they get eighty-five per cent of it will be in television. So they don't have to learn how to play it like a chessboard, they don't have to know how to be heard in the back row. Good grief, there's Trevor [Nunn] introducing amplification to the National!' He shakes his mane and exhales like a carthorse. 'When we went to New York with *London Assurance*, we played at the Palace. It's like the Palladium, 2800 seats. The stage staff said, "Don't worry, guys. We amplify you." We said, 'We are the Royal Shakespeare Company. We do not need amplification." And we didn't.'

Sinden collects artefacts as well as anecdotes. 'I always try to wear or carry something in any production that an old actor once wore or carried. When I was playing Benedick in *Much Ado*, I wore the ring that Irving had worn. When I played *The Scarlet Pimpernel* at Chichester, I used the very spy-glass that Fred Terry had worn in the original production. And in this one I'm carrying Ralph Richardson's stick.'

'This one' is *Quartet*, a four-hander set in a musicians' retirement home. Sinden plays a priapic old baritone. Were the Puritans right? Are theatricals more promiscuous than most? 'More open, freer, more accepting of one another, more immediately intimate. We share our vulnerability. In what other business are you invited to kiss a perfect stranger full on the lips? You know the story of the young actor who was set to play Hamlet and, wanting to understand the full psychology of the part, asked an older actor if he thought that Hamlet had actually slept with Ophelia? "I don't know about the West End, laddie, but we always did on tour."'

Sir Donald will be 76 in October. Does he think about death? 'No,' he says emphatically, convincingly. 'We've all got to drop off the perch one day, but not yet, I hope.' He smacks his lips. 'This is a lovely story. A man of 89 was talking to a small child who asked him how old he was. "I'm 89," said the old boy. "I don't want to be 89," said the child. "You will when you're 88."'

At this point in the process of writing up the interview – wondering how I was going to fit in the story about Mrs Patrick Campbell, Sarah Bernhardt and the goldfish – I got a call from a journalist friend. 'What are you up to?' he asked. I told him. 'Oh God,' he said, 'the old ham! I've interviewed him – all those stories!' 'I like them,' I said. 'They're funny.' 'Some of them are, but they're his protective coating, aren't they? They're how he keeps the world at bay. You've got to get beyond the stories to find the inner man.' 'I think the stories reflect the inner man,' I said. My friend snorted, 'No, they're all part of his life-lie.' 'I don't think so,' I persisted. 'They're his life force.' 'Hmm. Did you ask about his son?'

Three years ago Sir Donald's elder son, Jeremy, also an actor, died of cancer, age 45. 'When I interviewed Sinden,' said my friend on the telephone, 'he told me what a tragedy it was that his son died just when he was reaching the age to get the right parts, how he could have inherited the mantle of Charles Laughton or Robert Morley. He wouldn't talk about their relationship. He talked about the memorial service, how it was packed. I got nowhere.' I said, 'You got everywhere. He's an actor. Jeremy was an actor. That's what these people are. I went to the memorial service. It was wonderful. There were trumpets, an all-star cast, standing room only, people queuing round the block. And Donald was amazing. His heart was breaking and at the same time it swelled with pride.'

There was a pause. 'Well,' said the journo, 'did you ask him about his son?' 'Yes,' I said, 'I asked him if he brooded about Jeremy.' 'And what did he say?' 'He said, softly and quite slowly, "No, no, not at all. 'If it be now, 'tis not to come; if it be not to come, it will be now; if it be not now, yet it will come: the readiness is all.'"'

'Christ almighty, you ask him about the death of his son and he quotes William bloody Shakespeare.'

'Of course,' I said. 'He's an actor.'

If you don't understand that, you won't understand him. He is an actor to his fingertips. It is said of Laurence Olivier that he was only himself on stage. I do not think that its true of Donald Sinden. He may be most alive, most intensely happy, when he is on stage, but he is not acting when he's off it. He is stagey, fruity, over-the-top, but not as a pose or a mask or as a cop-out. That's how he is. Because he loves an anecdote and lives and breathes the theatre, that does not make him shallow. He is theatrical, but profoundly so. The way to his heart is through his stories.

'This play I'm doing, it's an affirmation of life. We're here, now, we'd better get on with it.' He's not finished by a long way. What about Falstaff? 'Yes, yes, Falstaff. That might be rather fun. Or a farce. I enjoy a farce. I need to do a farce every five years to keep my hand in. It's the most demanding of all styles. Garrick said, "Any fool can play Hamlet. Comedy is a very serious business."' He is proud of his versatility. 'I was once ring-master in a circus. I've done pantomime, opera. I loved doing *An Enemy of the People*, Ibsen. And Beckett. I haven't done ballet. But now I've got these two new hips, who knows?'

As I gathered up my notepad and tape recorder, I said, 'How shall we end the piece?' 'Hold on,' he said, 'Don't go. I've got to feed the meter.' When he came back, out of breath, wheezing slightly, he said, 'I'd like to say something about Diana [Lady Sinden]. I owe everything to Diana. I rely on Diana. She comes to see everything, more than once, bless her heart. She has seen everything I have done over fifty-two years and tells me the truth.'

His eyes are shining. 'Or John and Gill [his oldest friends: John Cadell was his agent for thirty years]. John understood me completely.' He looks at me for reassurance. 'No? Leave them smiling, that's it. The ink-well story? What d'you think?

'A young actor in weekly rep hated his leading man. He kept a diary and in it he confided the details of his obsession. "Tonight, HE killed my exit round.' 'Tonight, HE ruined my finest scene." Then came, "Monday, 6.15 p.m. Dear Diary, Tonight I believe I am going to get the better of HIM. We open a new play and I have a speech ten minutes long. Downstage. In the light. Facing out front. And HE is upstage, seated at a desk, with his back to the audience. I think I must win . . ." Later, a slightly drunken hand added, "11.45 p.m. HE DRANK THE INK!"'

Michael Gambon

I interviewed Sir Michael Gambon (born 1940) in his dressing room at the Albery Theatre in April 2000.

Sir Michael Gambon has a new woman in his life. At 38, she is twenty-one years his junior. At almost 6 feet 1 inch she is his equal in height. She is an African princess, granddaughter of the chief of the Kalanga tribe of Botswana. According to her lover, 'Her conversation is limited, but between the sheets she is extraordinary, quite frightening really. I've never known anything like it.'

More of this excitement anon. First things first. We are here to talk about acting. To general acclaim 'The Great Gambon' (so nicknamed by Sir Ralph Richardson – 'I think he meant it in the circus sense') has just opened in a new play at the Albery Theatre, London. It's a drama (with laughs) about a real man, one John Shank, a seventeenth-century actor whose speciality was schooling the boy players who took the women's roles on the Jacobean stage. Sir Michael gives a big, fruity, physical performance – engaging, energetic, enjoyably eccentric – which may explain why, when I find him in his dressing room, he looks exhausted. His thinning, wispy hair is all over the place, the bags under his eyes are hanging down in pleats. He has the haunted look of a defeated bloodhound. He is famous for his dislike of interviews, but today – perhaps because we have friends in common – he has decided not to show it. He plays both good-hearted bloke's bloke and self-deprecating charmer (Jack-the-lad meets Jack Buchanan) and, when I switch on my recorder, weary-but-willing, without complaint, he does the business.

'Testing, testing. Hello, hello. Golf Alpha Tango Juliet Echo, approaching from the South East, 2000 feet.' (His private passions include flying single-engine aircraft, making and mending clocks, collecting and restoring antique firearms.)

Why is he an actor?

'It's a compulsion. It's display, it's showing off, it's wanting, needing, to be someone else.'

Was he destined for the stage?

'God, no. I'm Camden Town Irish. My parents came over from Dublin when I was eight. Father an engineer, mother a housewife. I went to St Aloysius School for Boys in Somers Town and left at fifteen, pig ignorant, with no qualifications, nothing.' A rueful smile. 'That's not quite true. I could play the cello. I played at the Royal Albert Hall in the Catholic Schools Festival and got told off for combing my hair as we came on. My teacher, Mrs Baker, wrote to my dad and said, "You have to buy Michael a cello because he shows great promise". And my dad took me down to the Charing Cross Road, into all the music shops, and he asked, "How much do cello players earn?" and they told him, "Not much", so my dad said, "I don't think we'll get you a cello then."' Sir Michael gives a wheezy laugh and lights another cigarette. 'Terrible, isn't it?

'So I became an engineering apprentice at Vickers Armstrong and did seven years. I like all that mechanical stuff, mending things, tinkering with machines. But I got distracted, started going to the pictures, saw Marlon Brando, got hooked on James Dean. I thought, "That's who I want to be, that's what I want to do."

'I joined the Unity Theatre in Camden, the old socialist amateur theatre, and helped build the sets and started to act in plays. When I was 21 my dad said, "Why don't you go to Ireland? They like actors there, you'll get a job easier." So I wrote to Michael MacLiammoir at the Gate in Dublin – just because I'd heard of him – and he gave me a part walking on, a few lines, that's all. It was 1962, he was playing Iago. He had an extraordinary quality, an amazing voice. He could whisper in a great barn of a theatre and you'd hear every word. And he used his whole body in his acting. He'd play an entire scene with his arm crossed over his chest, his right hand resting on his left shoulder. He did odd things that made you look at him. Clever.

'He wore make-up in the street and an absurd wig. We took the production on a European tour and I remember walking round the edge of Lake Geneva with him in the sweltering sunshine. He was beautifully dressed – immaculate suit, collar, silk tie – with his toupet curling up in the heat and his make-up running down his face, just like Dirk Bogarde in *Death in Venice*.

'When I got back to England I was twenty-two, frightened, unemployed. Then I landed my first London role in the Christmas show at the Mermaid: *Rockets in Ursa Major*. I've never talked about this before. I played a spaceman.' More wheezy laughter: Gambon likes the absurdity of it. 'After that I did my first stint in the West End, as Assistant Stage Manager and understudy in a play with Spike Milligan. He was quite mad, stood behind me in the wings making farting noises. It was 1963. Laurence Olivier was launching the National Theatre. They wanted six six-foot blokes as spear carriers. I went along, did the audition and that was it. I've never done anything else for a living since.'

What was Olivier like?

'He wore beautiful suits, Savile Row, with sharply dropping shoulders. He wore his watch loosely, so that it fell down over his wrist. He walked with rolling hips. I thought, "God, I want to be like that." In the day, if he looked at you just once you remembered it – for ever. If he spoke to you, you would not be able to utter a word. I am not exaggerating. I remember the time he asked Anthony Hopkins where he came from, and Tony, in his native Welsh accent, stammered "Dundee". Olivier said, "How the f— can you be from Dundee?" Tony whimpered, "I'm not". That was the effect he had on us. He threw you completely. We were utterly in awe of him.

'Olivier came from a grand tradition that's completely disappeared. His Othello was brilliant. People knock it now, but they've got no right to. When I did Othello not long after at the Birmingham Rep, I simply copied him – the voice, the walk, the lot. Ridiculous, but it seemed to work. Actually, as an actor you do copy. You turn what you see into you.'

Since his breakthrough at the National in 1980 (when Peter Hall cast him as Galileo: 'Michael was unsentimental, dangerous, immensely powerful, the performance turned him into a star') and his first TV triumph in *The Singing Detective* (1986) Gambon has scaled most of the heights and won all the big awards. Is he satisfied with his work? 'Not really. Not at all.' Who is the actor he would most like to be now?

'Robert De Niro, no question. Last year, when I was filming *The Insider* with Al Pacino, I told him I really, really wanted to meet De Niro. Al said, rather pathetically, "Aren't I good enough?"'

Increasingly Gambon is appearing in movies, but he isn't yet a film star. 'I'm not recognised in the street – well, perhaps for a week or two after a telly like *Longitude* or *Wives and Daughters*. Olivier wasn't recognised in the street either. We were in Birmingham with the National and I remember standing in New Street with Sir Laurence looking for the Kardomah cafe. I thought, "I can't believe this, I'm here with Olivier – some of his glory is going to rub off on me." But he was wearing his hat and his glasses and nobody noticed him, not a soul.'

In the new play, Gambon's character gives a spell-binding master-class on the actor's craft. Has he ever taken acting lessons himself?

'Yes, in the early sixties at the Royal Court. That's where I learnt that I didn't like improvisation. I thought it was nonsense. They'd give you a football, and another actor had to go up and get the football off you by persuasion. Load of bollocks.'

If he had to give young actors just three bits of advice what would they be?

'On stage? Use the voice. Give it plenty of energy. Fill the auditorium. Make it big. I hear they're using mikes at the National now – for Christ's sake. What is the point of live theatre? Anyone can come on and mumble. Use the space. Be aware of what the third eye is seeing. Think about movement. Be conscious of how you stand, how you plant your feet on the stage. Let the audience feel your presence.'

Gambon is an interesting mix of old darling and gruff artisan. He is admired by his peers. 'Massive talent, massive ego,' is the general verdict. 'Likeable, but fundamentally unknowable. Like Ralph Richardson, he hides behind his eccentricity. I doubt you'll find a fellow actor who has ever been invited into his home.' I tell Sir Michael I have done a ring-round to discover his faults and flaws.

He starts giggling and pulling silly faces. 'Tee-hee. What have they said?'

'Not much to worry you. They say that when you've been in a run for a while your interest goes, your concentration slips.'

'Oh God.' He pleads guilty. 'I get bored and then I muck about. Olivier would muck about too, you know. As Othello, he'd walk on in the Senate scene and, under his breath, assume the voice of a West Indian bus conductor and hiss at us, "Any more fares, please. No standing on the top deck."'

'I'm told you're overly interested in money.'

This he resents. He looks quite hurt. 'I wouldn't be in the theatre if all I cared about was money. Of course, I like money. Who doesn't?'

'And some say you're still chippy about your working-class background.'

'Oh, no, not at all. I've joined the middle classes now. I've accepted a knighthood. I'm a member of the Garrick Club, for God's sake. And my son, Fergus, he's a smooth-talking gent if ever you met one, number two in the ceramics department at Phillips. What do you say to that?'

I am surprised that Sir Michael mentions his son. He is notoriously reluctant to mention his wife.

'What wife?' he says when I ask about her.

Her name is Anne Miller. They were married in 1962. For all I know, they may be married still. I tell him she's included in his entry in *Who's Who*.' I don't think so,' he says slowly, furrowing his brow, shaking his head, twitching his nose.

'She used to be.'

'Really?' He looks at me with a wicked charmer's smile and, with his tongue, makes his cigarette slowly wobble from side to side.

Why is he so cagey about his private life?

'The less people know about you the better. Ideally an actor should be a blank canvas. Otherwise you walk on as King Lear and the fellow in the front row whispers to his missus, "You know he collects antique guns, he's got hundreds of them." What does it matter what we get up to off stage, off screen?

'I shouldn't do interviews because I don't believe in them and I can't be trusted. Years ago, when I did Oscar Wilde on the telly, a lad from the *Birmingham Post* asked me if I found it difficult playing the part of a homosexual. "No," I said, "it comes to me quite easily. I used to be one." The boy said, "Oh, really?" And I said, "Yes, but I was forced to give it up." He didn't look at me. He just scribbled away. Eventually, he said, "May I ask why?" And I said, "Well, it made my eyes water." He didn't get the joke. He didn't know it was a joke.'

I tell Sir Michael that keeping his domestic arrangements under wraps is not a risk-free option. I overheard a couple in the audience discussing him during the interval. The woman said, 'His private life is very dark and difficult, you know.' The Great Gambon rumbles with delight. 'Oh, God, I like that. Put that in. That must go in.' He is breathing hard now, banging the dressing table. 'In fact, go for it. Put in anything you like.

Let's have some fun. Boys' games. If you haven't got what you want, make it up. Okay, Gyles?' Okay, Michael, willco. Anything to oblige. Roger, over and out.

Peter Hall

I interviewed Sir Peter Hall (born 1930) in the spring of 2000, in the week that he set off for the United States to direct John Barton's ten-play cycle, Tantalus.

Sir Peter Hall has upped and left the country. He departed these shores yesterday morning, taking his fourth wife and his sixth child with him. 'I am going to Denver in the Rocky Mountains to direct this huge epic, ten new plays by John Barton based on the Greek legends and the Trojan War. I wanted to do it here with the Royal Shakespeare Company. They would have done it, but they haven't got any money. It drives me mad this country because of its stupidity. The arts are starved of cash. Chris Smith [the Culture Secretary] is nice enough, but he's got no clout. And Blair doesn't care. He's indifferent to the arts. He isn't remotely interested.

'The greatest artist of all time was British. Shakespeare and his fellow dramatists created the richest theatrical culture in history. Thirty years after Shakespeare's death, the theatres were torn down and the dramatists sent into exile. The Puritans triumphed. They seem to be triumphing again in the person of New Labour. And I voted for them. Of course, we're all going to be voting for Ken Livingstone now. At least he seems to care.'

Sir Peter ('Don't make me sound like a cross old bugger') is not leaving us for ever, but after six months in Denver he has some Shakespeare to attend to in Los Angeles and an opera in Chicago, so he may be away some time. I am sorry to see him go, not only because he is a beguiling creature (intelligent, articulate, determined, charming, disarming), but also because it seems odd – and wrong – that the man who, arguably, has been the single greatest contributor to British theatre in the past fifty years (he ushered in a whole new world when he directed *Waiting for Godot* in 1954; he founded the RSC in 1960; he established the National Theatre in the 1970s) can no longer find the berth to do what he wants to do in his own country. 'I can't complain about the opportunities I've had, but I'd rather be working where I grew up with the people I grew up with than having to go abroad.'

I am giving him a valedictory lunch at a fish restaurant of his choice around the corner from his beloved Old Vic ('That's what I wanted. My own small company at the Old Vic. I needed a half-million guarantee from the Arts Council, but I wasn't to have it. That's why I'm leaving.') He is 69, but seems ten years younger. He is a big man (tall, bulky) with a beady eye and a soft voice. He has a healthy appetite, for life, for work, for food.

As we tuck in (moules with salmon and Pernod for starters; then Dover sole, with rocket and parmesan cheese salad on the side; a couple of glasses of an unpretentious Chablis) I suggest we conjure up a farewell party for him. Of all those he has known, worked with, loved, who would he have on the quayside to wave him off?

Given he sees the essence of his life's work as 'unlocking texts', I suggest he starts with writers. The waitress is mopping up the Pernod sauce that's cascading down his beard and jacket, but he doesn't hesitate.

'Samuel Beckett, a good man to have a glass of Guinness with, a man of grace, elegance, generosity of spirit. Sam's face is one of the icons of the twentieth century. We all know the gaunt bones and the ravaged cheeks. Prone to melancholic fits, but wonderfully funny. *Waiting for Godot* changed my life. I was 24, the East Anglian railwayman's son just down from

Cambridge, directing at the Arts Theatre Club. I got sent the play because nobody else would do it. I can't pretend that I thought it was the seminal play of the mid twentieth century – which I now do – but I knew it had something. It made waiting dramatic. *Look Back in Anger* won't last, it feels dated already, but *Godot* will go marching on. It's a metaphor for life. And its language is extraordinary: it's poetic speech that sounds real. Pinter wouldn't be Pinter without Beckett.'

'Will you have Pinter on the quayside?'

'Yes,' he laughs. 'I suppose so. We did a lot together.'

'Are you two reconciled?'

'I never fell out with Harold. Harold fell out with me. He took exception to my diaries when they were first published. I wrote about him leaving Vivien [Merchant, the actress, who later committed suicide] and his affair with Antonia Fraser, and he wrote me a letter full of hurt and sorrow and didn't speak to me for eight years. Then he sent me a postcard saying "Life's too short". He was right.'

'Harold takes himself seriously?'

Another laugh. 'Oh yes. You know the lovely story about Harold and the Comedy Theatre, don't you? There was a thought that a theatre might be renamed in his honour, and since several of his plays had been put on there Harold had hopes it might be the Comedy. Tom Stoppard got wind of this and said to Harold, "You've got the wrong end of the stick. It's not the theatre that's going to change its name, it's you. It's not going to be the Pinter Playhouse, you're going to be Harold Comedy."'

'What about Tennessee Williams?'

'Yes, I'd like him there. It was again through *Godot* that I met him. He just rang up. "Halooo, this is Tennessee. Would you like to direct my new piece?" He was wonderful in his prime, but, oh, the sad and awful end of it all when he would come reeling into my office at the National with yet another terrible play.'

'Who are the actors you want to see on the quayside?'

'Judi Dench, Peggy Ashcroft, John Gielgud, of course. And Ralph Richardson. He had an extraordinary quality. In rehearsals most actors describe to you what they plan to do in performance, talk about it and around it, begin to sketch it out. Ralph simply did it. Edith Evans was the same. From a standing start, they just got up and gave you the complete performance.

'Ralph was like a father to me. About six weeks before he had his stroke and died, we were having lunch. He was 81. He said – imagine the voice – "Are you religious? I am. I've tried to lead a good life, but when I die and go up to the pearly gates, will St Peter come and open them and say 'Hello, Richardson, come in, old boy'? You know, I don't think he will. I don't think there'll be anyone there at all." I miss Ralph very much.'

What about Olivier, Hall's predecessor at the National?

'No, no, thank you. I don't have a good memory for pain. Larry is a tragic and heroic figure. He was a medieval monarch, inspiring, awesome, wilful, sometimes giving favours, sometimes withdrawing them. He never believed he would stop, retire or die. He thought he was immortal. He had genius, but he was hell to work with towards the end. It was like the last days of Stalin.

'Larry did not make it easy for me. One of the things I'm most proud of is the way I laid the ground for my successors at the RSC and the National. I'd want Trevor Nunn and Richard Eyre there to see me off. And Peter Brook, of course.'

'Any members of your family?'

'My parents, not simply out of sentimentality, but out of reparation. I was the cliché an only child, the scholarship boy, the working-class lad who turned himself into a phoney member of the middle classes. I was not as generous or grateful to them as I should have been.'

'What about your wives? Will you have any of them to see you off?'

'All of them, please. I have loved them all.'

Talking to Hall's friends, talking to him, reading his patently honest and beautifully written autobiography, it is clear that women, love and sex, have been central to his life for virtually all of his near-seventy years.

'My parents were very physical and tactile. This surprises me now because their attitudes and morality were essentially Victorian. They were very correct, very respectable, but there was nothing prudish about my upbringing. I was cuddled and caressed. On Sunday mornings I would creep into my parents' bed and luxuriate in the sense of being physically at one with somebody else. This sense of recognition, of being seen by somebody else's eyes, of being appreciated and touched by another's hands, is the happiest sensation for a child. Out of it come the first stirrings of a healthy sensuality. When I was three or four, I had a recurring erotic dream in which our next-door neighbour, her children and I all danced naked.'

He remembers falling in love for the first time. 'She was a fragile-looking blonde with blue eyes called Monica. I watched her all day in my class at school. I kissed her during Postman's Knock at a party. She seemed to find me absurd, and I suppose I was. She giggled at my intensity.'

During the war, when he was twelve or thirteen, a family of evacuees, bombed out in London, moved into the house directly opposite the Halls in Cambridge. 'Edith was the daughter of the family and I fell passionately in love with her. I kissed and kissed her in the darkness of the autumn garden. She tired of the activity, but I wanted to go on and on. Sexual passion is agony before we have the means to assuage it.'

He met the first real love of his life after the war, when he was doing National Service in Germany. 'Her name was Jill and she was a porcelain-faced member of the WRAF in which she was intending to make her career. She was private and shy, and as young and virginal as I was. We cuddled and I groped feverishly. This, remember, was the pre-Pill age when how far you could go with a girl was a clear indication of her morality. I masturbated lustily in my bed and dreamt of making love to Jill. Being a romantic, I took the whole thing terribly seriously – much more, I suspect, than she did. Just before I was demobilised, we became engaged.'

Soon after, at a hotel in Leamington Spa, they went to bed together. 'How and why our love-making worked, I cannot imagine. My knowledge of sex and of a woman's body was confined to chatter and gossip, my avid reading of Penguin sex education books, and a great deal of D. H. Lawrence, whose rhapsodic descriptions were, at best, rather unclear.

'Sex is the great mystery, as great as death. Yet we commercialise it and destroy it with fear, prudery and envy. It is the expression of our love, and the means by which nature ensures our future. It gives the greatest pleasure and the greatest pain. At nineteen, I had been given no education, no counselling and no help in this crucial part of life. Is it really much better for young people now? Knowing how to give pleasure to a woman is the nearest most men get to being an artist. It is something that should be helped and cherished.'

His relationship with Jill foundered 'because of the extent to which my ambitions consumed me – a taste of terrible things to come.' Hall has been married four times and had two other serious long-term commitments which were marriages in all but name. 'I don't wonder that people doubt me when I say that I believe passionately in marriage, but I do. I am senti-mentally uxorious. It was through *Godot* again that I met my first wife, Leslie Caron. I was asked to direct *Gigi* as a play. I was twenty-five. We fell in love, we married, but she was a star who needed to be in Hollywood, when I needed and wanted to go to Stratford. Leslie begged me not to, but I had to. After Jill, after Leslie, there were many attempts to get it right. Until Nicki [Frei, a press officer at the National, whom he married in 1990] they all ended in pain.

'The other day my youngest daughter, Emma – she's seven – asked me, "Papa, why do you split up with all your wives?" I said, "Darling, for me, if it isn't all right, somehow it is all wrong."'

I suspect there's more to it than a search for perfection. I reckon there's an element too of 'what Peter wants, Peter gets'. When he was six he badgered his Auntie Vera into giving him a brass band of toy soldiers that was almost certainly beyond her means. When he was thirty he cajoled

Leslie Caron into giving him a vintage Rolls-Royce. Toys, girls, performances: once he has seen the potential, it must be realised. This must be part
of why he is so frustrated now. He wanted his own company at the Old Vic
and a stupid government wouldn't let him have it.

The coffee has arrived. We are resisting further alcohol, because Sir Peter
has to return to the rehearsal room and then go on to give a talk at the
National Theatre and then go home to pack. He works all the time. His
energy, his commitment, his achievement are extraordinary: two hundred
productions over five decades, many of them true landmarks. I say to him,
'This is going to be a celebratory piece, because I think you are one of the
great men of our time.'

'Thank you.' He looks genuinely pleased. He blushes.

'I think perhaps too that you are a narcissist.'

He looks perplexed. He frowns. 'What do you mean?'

'I am sorry. I don't mean to be rude. I am probably one myself. As my
wife would say, "Most men are". I just mean that everything revolves around
you, always has, always will. You see everything in relation to yourself, as a
reflection of yourself. When you said a moment ago that Nicki was clever,
for a moment I thought you meant she was intellectually bright.'

'She is.'

'Yes, of course, but what you meant is that she is clever at handling you.'

'Yes, that is what I meant.'

'It's all about you, about what you want. Your work, your ambition have
always come first. Your wives have had to accept that.'

'Yes. In the beginning they always say they understand, they won't mind,
they can manage. But is it bad to be a workaholic? Is it wrong? Isn't it a great
blessing to know what you want to do and to have the passion that makes
you do it? I don't want to pause. I want to keep moving. I have always
striven to be booked up so I can go briskly from one job to the next. I am a
director: each day I want to direct, not wait for the phone to ring or
meditate on my failings.'

'But people say you do too much, that you take on more work than you should because you need the money. Unlike some of the other directors from the subsidised theatre, like Trevor Nunn, you haven't had a big commercial success, you haven't hit the jackpot.'

'I suppose the nearest I've come to a jackpot has been *Amadeus.* I've earned quite nicely out of that. But I don't do things for money. I don't think I've ever done anything I shouldn't have done for the money, except perhaps once. I've done all right, but it has all gone on divorces and school fees.' (He may be a lifelong Labour voter, but four of his children went to Bedales; the fifth is currently head girl at Roedean.) 'I am going to be seventy in November. I enter my old age with a pension and a house and nothing more.'

For a moment he looks exhausted. Beached on his banquette in our fish restaurant in SE17, Sir Peter suddenly, fleetingly, puts me in mind of the rejected Sir John Falstaff, as he appears at the end of the two *Henry IV*s, Hall's favourite plays.

'I have always been prone to black depressions, but they have been much less frequent since the coming of Nicki. I have achieved the marriage I dreamed of, but the happiness is not unalloyed. There is thirty years' difference between us, so an in-built sadness, the sense of the shortage of time. I have a daughter of seven who I shall be lucky to see grown-up. I have five other talented children and five grandchildren who I shall be heartbroken to leave. I know that I am a better director now than I have ever been. And that is a further sadness, because I don't have a theatre or a company. You say I've always got what I wanted, Gyles. Well, I'll tell you what I want now. I want more time. A few more years. Please. I mean it.'

Jerry Hall

January 2001.

'They're small, but perfectly formed, don't you agree?' I am in Jerry Hall's dressing room at the Gielgud Theatre in London's Shaftesbury Avenue and the forty-four-year-old model-turned-actress is showing me her breasts. 'Look at them, Gyles, what do you say?'

'They're charming,' I mumble nervously. I have seen them before, of course, but at a distance. For the past five months Jerry has been playing Mrs Robinson, the mature seductress in the smash-hit stage adaptation of *The Graduate* and, consequently, eight times a week, West End audiences have been getting a fleeting glimpse of the statuesque Texan beauty in the altogether – 'tastefully lit, because the part demands it,' she insists. 'I never go topless on the beach. I don't wear thongs. I don't like those things.' The critics were ungracious about Hall in the buff. 'Two fried eggs in the gloaming,' said one. 'So mean, so cruel,' drawls Jerry, eyes wide, eyebrows arched, waving a cigarette in one hand and a David Bailey close-up of her bare torso in the other. 'So wrong,' I mutter, taking a closer look.

'Why, thank you,' she offers me a curtsey like a proper Southern belle.

She is going to make me a present of the photograph. 'And, since you ask – which no one has before – I take a 34A size cup, but I always wear a padded bra. Height, 5 foot ten and three quarters; weight, 135 lbs; dress size, 10; shoe size, European 42, I think that's an English 9. I'm not a natural blonde, I redo the roots all the time. IQ 146, but I have dyslexia. Figure, 36-24-36. When the show opened I think I was too skinny. I've put on a little here.' Slowly she caresses her stomach and her hips. 'It feels kinda right right now.'

Jerry is at ease with her body. Jerry is at ease with herself. The bitter-sweet Mick Jagger years are behind her. For two decades the priapic rock star and the long-legged, long-suffering model were an item. She loved him 'deep and hard'. She bore him four children. She endured his wayward ways. There was hurt: Carla Bruni – Mick's fling while Jerry was giving birth to their third baby – has larger breasts and, reputedly, nipples that stand up to order. But last year there was closure: a formal separation following the birth of Mick's 'love-child', Lucas, by Brazilian bombshell Luciana Morad. Now there is only friendship. 'Mick, great guy, lousy husband. I saw Prince Andrew the other night and there was a real fellow feeling between us. He said, "Nobody else seems to understand Sarah and me, but, Jerry, you know exactly how you can be friends after the marriage is over. To have your ex as your best mate is just fantastic."'

The Duke and Duchess of York are divorced but still share a home. Jerry and her children live in the family mansion in Richmond and Mick has bought a flat immediately next door. 'It's been fine while I've been in the play and he's been able to help look after the children, but I've told Mick, it can't go on, it's not a good long-term set-up. It kinda cramps your style.'

Jerry is beautiful, rich and famous. She is also a free woman, once more. What does she look for in a man? 'Looks are not top of my list. Age is irrel-evant. They don't need to be rich, but they've got to make me laugh. And I'd never, ever, knowingly go out with a married man. That's my number one rule.' (When Mick and Jerry met, he was still married to Bianca, but

Mick gave Jerry to understand otherwise.)

I say, suddenly fixated by the alarmingly realistic erect phallus dangling from her silver bracelet, 'If you had to give me any advice on how to seduce you, what would it be?'

She tosses her mane and laughs. 'Don't let fear or insecurity into the picture. People do and that's a mistake. If I meet someone and they ask me out, I say "yes". It's as simple as that. If I like someone, I say "Why don't we have a meal?" You don't have to jump into bed with them.'

'Don't you?'

'No.' Jerry looks quite scandalised. 'When you go out with a man, you should have no expectations. Just go with the flow, just see what happens.'

'And has anything happened to you?'

'Well . . .' She hesitates. She rearranges her legs. She plays with her silver phallus. I have impressed on her that I want my interview to contain as much as possible that has never appeared in print before and I lean forward, sensing an unexpected exclusive coming my way. 'Okay, Gyles, here goes. I am going out with someone. He's in America, in Hollywood, he's a film producer with Paramount. His name is George Ward.' She takes a deep breath, 'And, wait for it, he is only thirty-three.' She whoops with glee and claps her hands. 'He is way, way, way too young for me, but there it is. Go with the flow. He's gorgeous. He's smart. He's single. And he thinks he isn't good-looking, which makes him all the more attractive.'

'Are you going steady?'

'In my book, you aren't going steady until you're engaged. We're not engaged. But we're happy.'

Jerry gives me a sassy grin, settles herself on her cushion, smooths out her new Vivienne Westwood skirt and lights another cigarette. To me, across the footlights, and in magazine photographs, she looks a bit like a horse. Up close, I have to admit she's pretty cute: peachy skin, naughty eyes, beguiling manner. 'The happier you are the more attractive you are,' she says. 'Happiness is something you have to develop in yourself.'

She is a bundle of energy and a powerhouse of positive thinking. Everything in her life is 'so so good right now'. Her twin sister, who has had breast cancer, is fully recovered. 'She's quite well. Thank you for asking. Do you want another exclusive? No one's heard this. My sister has been looking into our family tree and guess what she's discovered? We're part Dutch, part Jewish, part Cherokee Indian, part Afro-American.' Jerry leans back and laughs. 'When my mother heard, she was very upset.' (Mrs Hall is 74, a retired medical record librarian, celebrated as the originator of Jerry's most memorable quip: 'A wife should be a maid in the parlour, a cook in the kitchen and a whore in the bedroom.' Jerry's father is now dead. Regularly described in the press cuttings as 'a gambling Texan truck driver' his daughter prefers to say 'he drove explosive chemicals cross-country and was General Patton's Master-Sergeant. He won a stack of decorations.')

Jerry's children are thriving. The two little ones (Georgia May, eight; Gabriel, three) are at home; James is rising sixteen and 'doing brilliantly' at Stowe; and Elizabeth is seventeen and in New York, following in mommy's footsteps, modelling and going to drama school. 'She got good GCSEs, but she's dyslexic too. They all are. And she wanted to start acting. You can't stand in their way.'

'Who is looking after her?'

'She's in Mick's house in New York. There are people there who look after her. But she earns her own money. She's independent.'

'How do you prevent them from being spoiled?'

'You teach them good manners, and that the reason for good manners is the need to show consideration for other people. You teach them that Christmas is about more than presents, it's about sharing with others.' Jerry, by upbringing, is a Baptist, 'but the children are C of E and we go to church in Richmond. It's important.'

'How do you explain to them their father's sex addiction?'

'Sexual promiscuity just leads to chaos, we all know that. But I never say anything bad about their father at home. Never. That's another of my rules.'

Jerry has no money worries. 'My legal agreement with Mick means I can't talk to you about money,' but the buzz is that, at the parting of the ways, she hoped for £30 million, settled for £10 million (including £3,000,000 in trust for the children), plus the £5 million house in Richmond. 'I've also got a place in Texas, to be near my family, and a beach house in the South of France. And a flat in Kensington. I let it out as an investment. Seems sensible. I am Cancerian. I love home-making. I love my two dogs, my nine cats, my organic vegetables. But I also love parties. I love clothes and jewelry and I adore going out.'

As we speak, Jerry has everything she wants. She has friends ('So many – all the Rolling Stones' wives, for a start'), she has hobbies ('Complicated jigsaws are a speciality, but science is my real hobby. I get the *New York Times Science Supplement* every week, and *New Scientist*, and *Scientific American* – and, guess what, Gyles, I read them!'). Best of all she has a new beau, and a brilliant, blossoming, bedazzling new career. 'I am an actress,' she says breathily, with pride. And it's true. The critics came to mock, the audience stayed to cheer. She believes she has earned her spurs and to prove it she now unveils her third exclusive. 'No one has been told this but you, Gyles, no one. Are you ready?'

'Yes.'

She shuts her eyes tight and spits it out: 'Steven Berkoff – yes, the Steven Berkoff – has asked me to appear with him in a revival of his play *Decadence*.'

'Fully clothed?'

'Fully clothed and with two accents. One upper-class British – fabulous, sweetie – one cockney. I've got a voice coach. I don't want to sound like Dick Van Dyke. Later this year, Jerry Hall and Steven Berkoff together in the West End. What do you say?'

'Wow.'

'Exactly.' She is so excited it's quite touching. 'And then there's the movie. I'm going to be in the new Merchant-Ivory picture, with a proper part.

There's no money, but plenty of class. And I've been asked to go to the Gate in Dublin to do a season of American plays. And they'd like me to do *The Graduate* in Paris – in French. And my friend Tom Stoppard, who is a genius, says he's going to write a part for me. Truly. And, guess what? At the Old Vic I may be guesting in *The Vagina Monologues*. What do you say to that?'

'Did you catch *Puppetry of the Penis* while it was on?'

'No.' She shakes her head and runs her fingers through her hair. 'God, I wanted to see that show. I wanted to see it so, so much. By all accounts the two guys were very well endowed.'

As she kisses me goodbye, she puts her hand to my head and I see the silver phallus jangling out of the corner of my eye. 'Thank you, Gyles, for not dwelling on the past. I am so fed up with the past. I want what's hot and fresh and new. I love now. I love the future. I love acting. I adore acting. Now I have discovered what it's about I want to do it more and more. I'm hooked on it. There's some kind of chemistry that happens with the audience. Every night. Without fail.' She wrinkles up her nose at me. 'Yes, it's better than sex. You can do it eight times a week and still you don't get pregnant.'

Simon Cadell

The actor Simon Cadell (1950–96) was my oldest friend. He won an Olivier award for his last stage appearance, in Travels With My Aunt, *but was best known for his work in television comedy, ranging from* Blott on the Landscape *to* Hi-de-Hi. *I wrote this open letter to him to mark what would have been his fiftieth birthday on 19 July 2000.*

Dear Simon,

How are you? Stupid question, of course. You're dead. All the same, I wanted to write, both to mark what would have been your fiftieth birthday on 19 July and to think through why – more than four years after your death – I still miss you as much as I do.

You will be pleased to know that you have not been entirely forgotten by the wider public. Predictably, it's not for your stage work that they remember you: your Mercutio, your Hamlet, Oswald in *Ghosts*, that archetypal silly-ass in *Tons of Money* at the National, Elyot in *Private Lives* (those would be my top five), not even for your award-winning performance in *Travels With My Aunt*. No, your immortality, such as it is, seems to rest on your portrayal of the holiday camp manager in the TV sit-com *Hi de Hi*. It could be worse. When Sir John Gielgud died the other day, one tabloid ran the headline: 'Dudley Moore's Butler Dead at 96'.

Because for so long you were one of the masters of the commercial voice-over – at your peak earning a quarter of a million a year at the craft – you still crop up in unexpected places. The other morning I stepped out of the London Underground at Bank Station and, suddenly, over the loud-speaker system, I heard you booming at me: 'Mind the gap!' It's not much of a line, but I must say you do it brilliantly. (Stanislavski: 'There are no small parts, only small actors.')

I stood on the station platform and let three trains come and go just to listen to you. I could picture you in the recording studio: a small cigar in your right hand, left hand cupped behind your ear, your lopsided mouth close to the microphone, taking such pleasure in pitching it so perfectly. It was good to hear that voice again (crisp, energetic, fruity, lived-in), a voice I heard most days, off and on, for thirty-five years. You were my best friend.

You will recall that we met at Bedales, the 'progressive' coeducational boarding school in Hampshire, where, as a rule, it is the parents (from Oscar Wilde to Laurence Olivier), rather than the children, who turn out to be the achievers. I was fourteen and you were twelve. On your third day at the school, I sought you out. My settled lifeplan was to run the newly created National Theatre before going into politics, becoming prime minister and running the country, and I had heard that your father was a theatrical agent (star client: Donald Sinden), your grandmother was an actress (Jean Cadell), and that you had been the all-singing all-dancing sticks-out-a-mile star at every play, performance and Christmas concert at the junior school. I nabbed you for the lead in my end-of-term production of *The Adventures of Sherlock Holmes*. It was love at first sight.

This was the early 1960s, the dawning of the age of the Beatles and the Rolling Stones, but you and I (bless us) were living in another world. Our heroes were Gerald du Maurier and Jack Buchanan. I played you my Noël Coward records: you played me your Flanagan and Allen. We spoke of Sir

Ralph and Sir John, Sir Michael and Dame Peggy as though we knew them – and, as it happens, one day we would. We took that for granted.

I see now what a quaint couple we must have seemed: an absurd pair of prematurely middle-aged teenagers who thought they knew it all. In fact, while I had long sensed (at least since I was seven) that I understood everything – absolutely and completely – when I met you I had to concede that, in terms of sophistication and a thorough understanding of the ways of the world and the pleasures of the flesh, you were the undoubted master.

At thirteen you could blow perfect smoke rings (at that stage you preferred Gitanes to Gauloises); at fourteen you could tell the difference between a Chablis and a Montrachet at a hundred paces; at fifteen, girls would do things for you that the rest of adolescent Britain could only dream of. (Do you remember that brief dalliance I had with the nurse in the sanatorium? I suppose I was seventeen and she was 23. It seemed to me to be the most thrilling thing that had happened in the long history of desire – until I gave you the graphic details and you explained to me, quite kindly, that, by your standards, my tentative kissing and cuddling was very thin beer indeed.)

Why did our friendship work?

We had common interests and shared values. We were equally narcissistic, self-absorbed, ambitious, but never in competition with one another. We were never critical of one another either. In time, our wives might tell us to spend less, drink less, improve our posture, hold our stomachs in, but we simply accepted each other, exactly as we were, without qualification, without question. Neither of us was ever judgemental. If you had reservations about my politics (which you did) you never said so. If I had reservations about your women (and the assortment was varied) I never spoke a word.

Our friendship may have been profound, but our conversation wasn't. We avoided introspection. We didn't discuss our feelings, ever, not even when you were dying, possibly because we were middle-class Englishmen of a certain vintage, but perhaps, too, because, instinctively, each knew how the other felt and there really wasn't any need. We never had a cross word – not once in thirty-five years.

Our relationship was totally secure and wonderfully uncomplicated. There was no jealousy, no envy, no confusing desire. That's the joy of friendship: sex never gets in the way. A love affair is fun, thrilling (the highs so high), but it's unsettling, dangerous, exhausting too; and, if you've been around the block, you know it always ends in tears. Marriage (I think I understood this better than you) is magnificent – fundamental, essential, and, when it works (thank you, Lord), a blessing like none other – but it isn't easy. Living a lifetime with your lover/husband/wife calls for energy, staying power, infinite care, eternal compromise. Ours was an altogether easier lot. A friendship that begins in childhood is simply a favourite cardigan: you don't need to keep it in good repair, you simply need to slip it on.

We were good companions, you and I. We made each other laugh (without fail), telling the same stories in the same funny voices, year after year. We had awarded ourselves a special licence (irrevocable) to quaff (the best champagne), to scoff (the finest caviare), to gossip until dawn.

We both went along with the Noël Coward line that 'on the whole work is more fun than fun'. That doesn't mean to say that we didn't take our pleasures where we found them. (Do you remember the *menu gourmand* at the Hotel du Cap at Antibes? Our wives said, 'Eleven courses and a different wine with every course? You can't!' We did.) But, essentially, we were defined by our work rather than by our family lives or our relationships. Our careers came first. Yours was more satisfactory, of course, because you never had any doubt about what you wanted to do. Being an actor was your life: you were most alive in a studio or on a stage. You relished and understood your craft. (You were also very ready to share your experience. When I was an MP and a government whip, you and I discussed John Major's distracting way with words, his curious sing-song speaking voice and his annoying way of saying 'want' as 'wunt'. You suggested I suggest to the PM that you give him some help with his pronunciation. Did I tell you that I did? Mr Major was not amused.)

There was an unspoken conspiracy between us, wasn't there? It was our world and whatever we wanted of it could be, would be, must be ours. Do you remember one summer turning up in the South of France at the villa your parents had rented and finding the sky hopelessly overcast? You opened a bottle of champagne and stood there, glass in hand, glaring at the heavens, commanding the clouds to part. Of course, they were happy – they were honoured – to oblige.

We thought we were invincible and then, one day, we had our come-uppance. On the morning of Saturday 11 September 1993 I was standing in the kitchen at home, squeezing the breakfast orange juice, when the telephone rang. 'You are going to have to be brave,' you said. 'I'm in the Harley Street Clinic. It's not good news. I'm riddled with cancer. It could be just a matter of days. I'll want you to do the address at the service. We must talk about that. And the music. I think a combination of Charles Trenet and the Battle Hymn of the Republic, don't you?'

In the event, you struggled on for two and a half years, with such grace and style and indomitable *joie de vivre*. John Wells (who appeared with you in *Travels With My Aunt* and then followed you all too quickly to the grave) put it perfectly: 'Simon showed us how to live and then taught us how to die.' You were very funny to the last. A young nurse (she was very pretty) whipped back the bedclothes to give you an injection. 'Just a little prick,' she said. You looked at her indignantly: 'Darling, there's no need to be insulting.'

Four years on, what's the news at this end? Not much: Tony Blair is prime minister now (but it won't last: quite suddenly he's lost his sheen); Norman Wisdom is a knight and Elizabeth Taylor and Julie Andrews are dames (I kid you not); and, apart from *Frasier* and repeats of *Inspector Morse*, there's still nothing worth watching on the box.

On the domestic front, the big news is that your wife has a new man. Don't worry. He's okay. In fact, he's lovely. She often says you must have sent him. He's younger than you, taller, better-looking, better-read, calmer, easier-to-live-with. (He isn't an actor, so he must be. Actors are impossible. We know that.) I like him a lot now, but at first I found it difficult to be in the room with him. It was nothing personal. He's intelligent, thoughtful and kind. I just couldn't bear to see him sitting in your chair, drinking from your glass.

He is wonderful with your sons. He does those dad-like things with them (watching football, playing games) that you (and I) were never very good at. The boys seem happy: the tension that was in the air during the years when you were dying has gradually disappeared. They are 12 and 14 now, looking good, growing tall, winning prizes. You've got plenty to be proud of.

Your mother is pretty perky too. In truth, she's the one I feel for. I can imagine nothing worse in all the world than losing your child. At her house in France, she created a glorious sundial in your memory. You'd love it, and you'd be proud too if you could see the way she soldiers on. No doubt, in the still watches of the night she feels quite bleak, but she's British and she's brave and she doesn't let it show.

And how am I? I'm fine. I lost my seat at the general election (a relief really). I'm a hack now: doing radio, TV, journalism. It's quite fun. I'm well paid. I travel the world meeting interesting people. I've lost weight. I drink less. The curse of cholesterol means I've given up the pâté de foie gras. It's all okay. It's really very good. I want for nothing and I surround myself with famous, funny and delightful people. Oh yes, there's still laughter at my end of the table – but, old friend, let's face it: without you it isn't quite the same.

Yours ever,

Gyles

A touch
of class

The Duke of Edinburgh

May 1999.

The other evening some friends came to supper, professional people, in their thirties and forties, fair-minded representatives of middle England. I asked them what they thought of the Duke of Edinburgh. I wanted instant judgements, immediate responses. I got them. 'Bit of a reactionary.' 'Short-tempered.' 'Rude.' 'Selfish.' 'Doesn't like his son.' 'Traditionalist.' 'Bully.' 'Looks good.' 'Loyal to Queen.'

He is certainly good-looking and, for a man who will be 78 next month, remarkably fit and trim. And it's something that at least one of my kitchen table pundits registered his unswerving loyalty to the sovereign. But the rest of it? Is that the general perception? Is that the verdict of Blair's Britain? If it is, they've got him wrong.

I am an admirer of the Duke of Edinburgh. I first met him in the 1970s when I became involved in one of his pet charities (the National Playing Fields Association) and over twenty years I have seen him in action at close quarters. I like and respect him. I like his style, his sense of humour, his hands-on approach, his ability to make a difference while others, mostly, only make a noise. I envy his energy. I admire his achievement. I think he deserves to be better understood.

With this in mind I contacted Prince Philip's office explaining that I wanted to write an article about him and wondering whether he would consider giving me a brief interview as part of the piece. Word came back that His Royal Highness would be happy to grant me an interview.

We met in his library at Buckingham Palace. It is a large room with a workmanlike feel, airy, ordered, user-friendly, serviceable not cosy. There are some 10,650 books on the shelves, all carefully arranged and catalogued. (The collection is both predictable and surprising: over a thousand books on wildlife and conservation, 494 on sport, a complete run of cartoon annuals by Giles; more than 200 volumes of poetry, 990 books on art.)

I explained to the Duke that my aim was to write something celebratory, saluting his achievements over half a century of public service and challenging one or two of the myths that have grown up over the years. He looked at me a little doubtfully and said nothing.

We were alone. We sat on firm sofas facing one another. I produced my notebook. 'How do you think you're seen?'

He frowned. 'I don't know.' Pause. 'Refugee husband, I suppose.' Yes, the Greek who married the Queen. 'And your achievements?' I asked. He snorted. He spread his hands across the sofa and sighed. Stupid question. Where do you begin? The man is Colonel or Colonel-in-Chief, Field Marshal, Admiral, Air Commodore, forty-two times over. He is founder, fellow, patron, president, chairman, member of at least 837 organisations. The first achievement is simply to have endured, to have survived – to have put up with – fifty-two years of royal flummery, official mumbo-jumbo, parades, processions, receiving lines, receptions, lunches, dinners, upwards of 20,000 official engagements. He has measured out his life in handshakes and small-talk. And to keep his sanity, alongside all the surface stuff (necessary, unavoidable), he has got stuck in to a range of particular projects where in-depth involvement has (I hope) given him the satisfaction of a worthwhile job well done.

Having a natural conversation with a senior member of the royal family is next to impossible. ('When royalty leaves the room,' said Joyce Grenfell's mother, 'it is like getting a seed out of your tooth.') I said to the Duke, to set the ball rolling, 'I've made a list of achievements – and myths – half a dozen of each.'

I read out my list of 'achievements'.

1. *Supporting the Queen.* A good start. He smiled. That's what it's all been about. 'Absolutely.'

2. *The Duke of Edinburgh's Award Scheme.* Started from scratch in 1956, the concept has spread to fifty countries. Some two and a half million young people have taken part. In my book (and in terms of a legacy) this is the Great Achievement, both because of its impact and because the qualities the Award encourages – self-reliance, compassion, fitness, skill, endeavour – are among those Prince Philip values most. (The night after our interview I watched an episode of *Hornblower* on television and there were the virtues heroically exemplified: decency, daring, courtesy, comradeship, kindness, loyalty, courage. There are not many novelists represented on the Duke's shelves, but C. S. Forester is one of them.)

3. *The International Equestrian Federation.* Outside the horsey world, this means nothing, but I put it on the list because the Duke was the active (some felt hyper-active) President for 22 years. He introduced international rules for carriage driving, long-distance riding and vaulting, he added international competitions for pony, juniors and young riders; he steered the veterinary committee; he ran the show. (600 books on matters equestrian, including two by HRH.)

4. *The World Wide Fund for Nature.* Ornithology has been a life-long enthusiasm (781 books on birds), but his involvement with WWF (UK

President since 1961, International President from 1981, President Emeritus since 1996) has seen his interest in wildlife broaden from a commitment to the conservation of natural habitats to a passionate and tireless championing of global environmental issues.

5. *The Commonwealth Study Conferences.* The Duke initiated these. They happen every six years. The first was in 1956: a three-week international conference on work and the changing demands of industrial society. Each Conference is an opportunity to take a big issue, examine it, worry it, look at it in depth and from different perspectives. Last year it was in Canada: two weeks on the impact of technology in a global 'infodustrial' society.

6. *Fund-raiser, fire-fighter, problem-solver.* Having chaired one of his charities, and seen him at work with others (the National Maritime Museum, the RSA, the English Speaking Union, Shakespeare's Globe at Southwark, the Central Council for Physical Recreation) I know him to be an unrivalled fund-raiser (focused and fearless) and a persuasive leader with an unnerving eye for detail (and for flimflam and flannel) who is at his best when given a problem to solve, a difficult meeting to chair, an internal row requiring resolution. (He likes to be given something specific to do. He welcomes detail. I accompanied him to the opening of a youth centre on Merseyside. His lengthy debriefing note to me was devoted to how best to relocate the lavatories and showers so as to maximise the space available for the sports facilities.)

Having read out my short-list of 'achievements', I hoped he might add to it, put me right in certain areas, prioritise. He didn't. He was anxious to give credit to others (John Hunt as the first director of the Award Scheme, Prince Bernhard of The Netherlands for getting him on board at WWF), evidently pleased that the Commonwealth Study Conferences were on the list, ready to concede that the Award Scheme was probably the achievement that had widest impact, but not willing to be drawn on the area that had given him greatest personal satisfaction. 'That would be invidious.' (Later, when I asked him about the most impressive people he had met, he began, 'Oh goodness . . . Bob Menzies [Australian prime minister, 1939–41, 1949–66], Vincent Massey, the Governor-General of Canada [1952–59] . . .' then he stopped: 'No, no, a list would be invidious.' He has to watch what he says because there's always a come-back. I asked him if there were countries he hadn't visited that he'd like to. 'If I name them, they might invite me and then, if I couldn't make it, there'd be trouble.')

Achievements listed, silence fell. His eyes narrowed. 'What about these myths then?'

I looked at my notebook. 'First, that it's been a life of frustration, that you've always regretted that you weren't able to pursue your naval career . . .'

Now he interrupts. 'In 1947 [the year of his marriage] I thought I was going to have a career in the Navy, but it became obvious there was no hope. The Royal Family then was just the King and the Queen and the two Princesses. The only other male member was the Duke of Gloucester. There was no choice. It just happened.'

'In at the deep end?'

'Yes.' He laughs. 'The first ten years I don't remember much about.'

His friend Lord Lewin (First Sea Lord in 1977, Chief of the Defence Staff at the time of the Falklands) used to say that if the Duke had stayed in the Navy he'd have gone right to the top.

'No,' says the Duke, firmly. 'Given the way of the British press, I wouldn't have got very far. Every promotion would have been seen as me being treated as a special case.'

He has fond – and vivid – memories of his time in the service: as a midshipman with Lewin on HMS *Valiant* during the war; as First Lieutenant of HMS *Chequers*, the Leader of the 1st Destroyer Flotilla in the Mediterranean Fleet at Malta in the late 1940s; ultimately, 1950–1, 'two very satisfying years', in command of the frigate *Magpie* (the men called their captain 'Dukey'). 'The late King died in February 1952 and that effectively brought my naval career to an end.' But he won't accept that he's disappointed. 'You have to make compromises. That's life. I accepted it. I tried to make the best of it.'

'When King George died, did you know what to expect?'

'No. There were plenty of people telling me what not to do. "You mustn't interfere with this." "Keep out." I had to try to support the Queen as best I could, without getting in the way. The difficulty was to find things that might be useful.'

'But there was the example of the Prince Consort, you'd read biographies . . .'

'Oh, yes.' A slightly exasperated sigh. 'The Prince Consort . . . The Prince Consort's position was quite different. Queen Victoria was an executive sovereign, following in a long line of executive sovereigns. The Prince Consort was effectively Victoria's private secretary. But after Victoria the monarchy changed. It became an institution. I had to fit into the institution. I had to avoid getting at cross-purposes, usurping others' authority. In most cases that was no problem. I did my own thing. Got involved in organisations where I thought I could be useful. The Federation of London Boys' Clubs, the Royal Yachting Association, the MCC. Of course, as long as they were going all right, there wasn't much for me to do. But if an organisation was going bankrupt or had some crisis, then I'd help. The fund-raising never stops.'

'Has much of it been fun?'

A puzzled look. 'I don't think I think very much about "fun". The Variety Club events were fun. The cricket matches for the Playing Fields were fun. The polo was entirely fun!'

I said, 'The second myth is that you're a stick-in-the mud, old-fashioned. In fact, I think you're a moderniser—'

A more explosive interruption. 'No, no, not for the sake of modernising, not for the sake of buggering about with things. I'm anxious to get things done.'

'Weren't you the first member of the Royal Family to use a helicopter?'

'Yes, in the run-up to the Coronation. It was just more practical, but it caused a ruckus. I didn't go through the proper channels. There was a lot of pettifogging bureaucracy.'

How had he got on with the old guard at the Palace in the 1950s? A wry smile. 'I introduced a Footman Training Programme. The old boys here hadn't had anything quite like it before. They expected the footmen just to keep on coming. We had an Organisation and Methods Review. I tried to make improvements – without unhinging things.'

Was he the prime mover behind the Way Ahead Group, the regular planning/policy get-together of senior members of the family? 'No, but it's sensible, necessary. We've got to think about what's going to happen next: the millennium, the impact of devolution, the Queen's jubilee in 2002. And we have to coordinate. Don't forget, at the beginning of the Queen's reign there were just one or two of us doing things, but then the children grew up and instead of one of two we had ten or twelve. People were tripping over one another. We got them to specialise in their interests. Charles went off to the arts, Anne went off to prisons. It's about an efficient use of resources.'

He does not say so, but I imagine he takes a special pride in having a noticeably lean and cost-effective private office. He takes a professional interest in science and technology (the creation of the National Fellowship in Engineering is another unacknowledged achievement), and what he espouses in public he carries through in private. He pioneered the use of IT at the Palace (and introduced an eco-friendly electric taxi to the royal car pool), he was the first in the Family Firm to take to producing his own correspondence on his own word processor; he understands the Internet, its potential and its dangers.

The next myth, I suggest, is that he's curmudgeonly.

He looks quite hurt. 'I don't think I have ever got up to make a speech of any kind, anywhere, ever, and not made the audience laugh at least once. You arrive somewhere and you go down that receiving line. I get two or three of them to laugh. Always.'

This is true. I have seen it happen, time and again. Meeting royalty isn't easy. For most people, it's an awkward moment, unreal, exciting but oddly nerve-racking. Prince Philip makes a crack to break the ice. Nobody does it better. But Michael Seward, canon treasurer at St Paul's Cathedral, complains about the Duke's manner: 'You never know if it will be a snort, a snub or a merry laugh.' The canon misunderstands. It's only ever banter. The Duke has no desire to hurt. He merely wants to please, but he knows he has to say something – always – because if he stays silent that will be interpreted as him being surly. He can't win.

From my limited experience as a member of parliament I'd say that one of the most wearisome aspects of public life is having to be genial all the time. If you are the Queen's consort you will not remember everyone you meet, but everybody you meet will remember you, and how you seem, and what you say. 'Occasionally I get fed up, going to visit a factory, when I'm being shown round by the chairman who clearly hasn't got a clue, and I try to get hold of the factory manager but I can't because the chairman wants to make sure he's the one in all the photographs.'

I please the Duke (I think) by saying what I believe: 'You've got a reputation for not suffering fools gladly, but in fact you've been suffering fools willingly for over fifty years.'

He is grinning broadly now. 'I have suffered fools . . . with . . . patience.'

This reputation for curmudgeonliness also comes about because, in conversation, he is deliberately challenging. He questions, he argues, he plays devil's advocate, he answers back. He does it to show an interest and (I believe) to maintain his own interest. When you meet scores of people in a day (and some days he meets hundreds) it would be very easy to let everything that's said wash over you. However briefly, the Duke tries to become engaged in whatever he is doing. He has an enquiring mind. 'I haven't looked at it before, but yes, I suppose I challenge things to stimulate myself and to be stimulating. You don't have to agree with everyone all the time.'

I think his manner with people is delightful and the more ordinary the people the friendlier he is. I suggest to him that long before Diana had come onto the scene as the unstuffy tactile people-friendly princess, he had been the true pioneer of royal informality. I remember, years ago, coming down the back stairs with him after some lunchtime function in the West End. We passed the kitchen. He stopped, turned back and marched in, unannounced, to meet the chefs and dish-washers. There was laughter, back-slapping, joshing, a peerless display of people skills and unselfconscious charm.

He smiles. 'Yes, yes, but . . . You won't remember this, but in the first years of the Queen's reign, the level of adulation – you wouldn't believe it. You really wouldn't. It could have been corroding. It would have been very easy to play to the gallery, but I took a conscious decision not to do that. Safer not to be too popular. You can't fall too far.'

He is suddenly full of energy, leaning forward, peering over my notebook. 'What's next? "Tactless overseas"? Is that on your list?'

I glance down at my notes and see the words 'Slitty eyes'.

On 16 October 1986, in Beijing, when the Queen and the Duke were on a state visit to China, Prince Philip met a group of British students studying at the North West University in Xian. The Duke was particularly interested in the students because they came from Edinburgh University (he has been Chancellor of four universities: Edinburgh since 1952) and chatting to them informally (with neither Chinese nor press present) he expressed surprise when he discovered that they were spending a whole year in China – long enough 'to go native and come home slit-eyed'. It was a joke, a bit of badinage, but because one of the students later gave a friendly account of the conversation to a journalist an inconsequential private aside was turned into banner headlines around the world. 'The great wally of China' said the *Mirror*; 'The Duke gets it wrong' said the *Sun*. As well as depicting the Duke as accident-prone, there was the unpleasant implication that he was some kind of closet racist. (He may not be a disciple of all that is politically correct, but there is not an ounce of racism in him. I was once with him at a private party where I overheard him stopping someone mid-sentence because they were attempting to tell a joke with racial overtones.)

Since 1952, on behalf of the United Kingdom, the Commonwealth and the range of causes he supports, he has taken part in 586 overseas visits to 137 different countries. Looking through the newspaper cuttings, and having had access to some of the obituaries ready-and-waiting on file, it is the two or three alleged gaffes – in China, in Brunei, most recently apparently nodding off at a state banquet in South Korea – that command the coverage. 'Now,' he says wearily, 'I am desperate if I find there are British press on a foreign visit. I know they'll wreck the thing if they possibly can.'

It is not a myth to say that he has reservations about certain sections of the media. What exasperates him is that 'so much coverage is so unremittingly negative'. When did it all start to go wrong? 'After Murdoch bought the *Today* newspaper founded by Eddie Shah. Day after day there was a derogatory story about one member of the family or another.'

Clearly it rankles. I also think it hurts. We don't discuss this, but I know that, over the years, he has been distressed by stories of his allegedly colourful love life. Newspapers and magazines around the globe repeat unsubstantiated tittle-tattle and get away with it because what, realistically, can he do about it? Suing isn't the answer: it's ponderous, expensive, and gives more coverage to the libel. I think he sees one solution as some form of complaints tribunal: authors would be required to satisfy the tribunal that there was sufficient acceptable evidence to prove the truth of their statements.

To the outside world, he shrugs it off: being gossiped about is the price paid for life in the limelight. Privately, I believe he finds it frustrating and upsetting. (And, of course, he is aware that he is not the only victim. As I write I am looking at the cover of a best-selling Australian magazine that I know he has seen too. It boasts the low-down on 'Philip's torrid sex-life'. Inside are nine pages of fantasy presented as fact: 'Philip's affair with Katie Boyle was very steamy. They had the most extraordinary times together.' Because I know Katie Boyle, I call her. 'Yes, I've met Prince Philip several times. I think he's the most fantastic man. I love his dryness. But an affair? It's ludicrous, pure fabrication. When it appears in print, people believe it. You can't take legal action because it fans the flames, so you just have to accept people telling complete lies about you. It's hateful.')

Prince Philip has no special fondness for tabloid journalists, but he claims it's a myth that he's unfriendly towards photographers. 'I go out of my way to line people up for the photographers, to make sure everyone in the group is in the picture, to make sure the photographers have got the shot they need.' A laugh. 'Of course, they always want one more. They're never satisfied.'

I suggest that some of the problems with the press are of his making. He was the one who first spoke to the press, who made the first TV programme, who gave the first interview. 'Yes, I made a conscious decision to talk to the media – but not about me, only about what I'm doing, what I'm supporting.'

'The trouble is,' I venture, 'talk about the Commonwealth Study Conferences and after three lines people are yawning. They want what's sexy, they want personalities.'

'The press have turned us into a soap opera.'

There is something despairing about his laugh. He glances at my notebook. 'Any more?'

'Diana.' I stare down at the pad. 'The public view, for what it's worth, is of a grouchy old man, unsympathetic to his daughter-in-law.' I pause and look up. 'But I happen to know – not from you, but I know it – that when things were difficult you wrote to Diana – kind letters, concerned, fatherly, loving, caring letters from Pa, explaining how you knew, first hand, the difficulties involved in marrying into the Royal Family.'

He smiles. I say, 'The impression the public have got is unfair.'

He shrugs. 'I've just got to live with it. It happens to a lot of people.'

'And Sarah? There's a knee-jerk reaction out there that if the Duchess of York isn't being treated generously, somehow you're behind it.'

He shakes his head. 'I try to keep out of these things as much as possible.' He pulls a face. 'Her behaviour was a bit odd.' A sigh. 'But I'm not vindictive. I am not vindictive . . . I don't see her because I don't see much point. But the children come and stay. Our children come and stay. The atmosphere is very happy. We are a happy family.'

'And what about being at odds with Prince Charles? People say how different you are. I think you are remarkably similar, in mannerisms, in interests—'

A final interruption. 'Yes, but with one great difference.' Pause. 'He's a Romantic – and I'm a pragmatist. That means we do see things differently.' Another pause. 'And because I don't see things as a Romantic would, I'm unfeeling.' Another laugh. Another shrug.

The Duke of Edinburgh is far from unfeeling. He cares about his children and his grandchildren. He cares about his wife. He cares for her. (A friend said to me, 'I was quite touched to overhear the Queen and Prince Philip calling one another "darling".') He has given over his life to supporting her in the role destiny threw her way. When on parade as consort he doesn't put a foot wrong. (He knows all the verses of the National Anthem.)

From those who know him and work with him, the Duke of Edinburgh inspires loyalty and love. Perhaps he has mellowed in his sixties and seventies, but I just don't recognise him in the commonly accepted caricature. He is tolerant, kindly, amusing, amused. He is in several ways a man's man of his generation. He is straightforward, unsentimental, scrupulously honest. He mixes a matchless gin and tonic and I imagine his list of personal achievements would include his 6,000 hours of pilot's flying time. He is practical. The conversion of the chapel to the picture gallery at

Buckingham Palace is his doing. He has built log cabins at Sandringham and demolished the dry-rotten Victorian addition to Abergeldie Castle at Balmoral. But he is also creative. He has planted avenues of trees, created water gardens, laid out borders and beds. He loves painting. He reads poetry. He is fascinated by nature and by religion. (634 books on religion on his shelves. 'Yes, I take an interest in comparative religion, but if I talk about it I'm labelled a religious crank.' And he is a pragmatist: he has used his relationship with religious leaders around the world to recruit them to the cause of conservation.)

To me he seems to be a quite remarkable man, dealt a bizarre hand which he has played pretty flawlessly. 'I am not going to write an autobiography,' he says. 'I don't spend a lot of time looking back.' What does he think the future holds? Where does he see the monarchy fifty years down the road? 'I'm not going to be drawn into speculating on that. All I'll say is that I've tried to help keep it going while I've been here.'

Lord Snowdon

February 2000

It is 11.30 on Tuesday morning and I am writing this on a London bus, a number 9, travelling along Kensington High Street, on my way to meet the Earl of Snowdon, celebrated snapper and sometime husband to Princess Margaret. I am apprehensive because, while we are meeting with a common purpose – he is giving selected interviews in the run-up to his seventieth birthday on 7 March – we will be working from different agendas. I will be there feverishly attempting to get something new, surprising and gossipy out of a man who notoriously gives nothing away, and he will be there, all buttoned-up professional charm, simply wanting to tell me about the giant retrospective of his work which is about to open at the National Portrait Gallery.

It is now 5.30 p.m. and I am back on the bus, half-drunk and more than a little in love. I have been seduced (metaphorically but comprehensively) by a sixty-nine-year-old photographer with a gammy leg. I don't just mean charmed: I mean wowed, bowled over, blown out of the water. I have met some experts in this line in my time (Bill Clinton, John Profumo, Hugh

Grant), but Snowdon is something else. He is the Grand Master.

This is what happened.

12.25 p.m. I arrive at his house, a handsome Victorian villa in a leafy Kensington backwater, where Catherine (Snowdon's new PA, twenty-something, jolly, pretty, friendly) lets me in through the everyday entrance, a side door leading straight into a kitchen-cum-scullery. Catherine is making me coffee when her boss appears. He is not tall, a little stocky, his face reminds me instantly of Ronnie Corbett. He is much frailer than I expected. The limp is severe. He shuffles in. He is looking weary, but happy. He doesn't greet me at all. He treats me as if I've been standing there all morning and we've known each other for years.

'Oh, lovely, you're here. You couldn't have timed it better. The book has just arrived, literally just now, the ink's still wet.' This is the book of the show: *Photographs by Snowdon 1950–2000*. 'Catherine, he's not having coffee. We're having white wine. We are going to celebrate.'

I follow him along the narrow corridor that leads to his study. It is small and inviting, crowded with prints and files and attractive bits and pieces. (My favourite is The House of Mystery, a penny-in-the-slot machine, once a feature on Brighton Pier.) The new book is laid out on the coffee table. We sit side by side on two of the chairs he designed with his friend Carl Toms for the Investiture of the Prince of Wales at Caernarvon Castle in 1969.

'The Ministry of Works were such snobs. They wanted the VIPs to have grand chairs and the riffraff, as they called them, to sit on planks on the scaffolding. We weren't having it. So we made 4,000 chairs like this and they were sold at the end of the day, for £12 each. I bought six.'

'Was the Investiture fun?'

'It was important. I was proud to do it. It was hilarious too. We had to go to pompous meetings at St James's Palace, to get our plans approved by the Garter King of Arms. You had to call him "Garter". His actual name was Sir Anthony Wagner, so you can imagine our nickname for him. There was a frightful row about the dragons we wanted to put on the banners. Carl said,

"The dragons must have a knot in their tails: all dragons have knots in their tails." Garter wouldn't have it. Garter stood his ground. Eventually I said to him, "Oh, come on, Garter darling, can't you be a bit more elastic?"'

This story makes me laugh. Indeed, every one of the dozens of stories Lord Snowdon tells me over the next four hours makes me laugh. He sets out to entertain and he succeeds. Quickly, he discovers my fondness for camp theatrical anecdotes and in his repertoire there are many. He does wonderful impressions for me too: Marlene Dietrich, Hermione Gingold, Ralph Richardson and, because he knows I know him, the Duke of Edinburgh: 'Now, yes, Brandreth, what are we going to do about these ruddy playing fields?' (It is uncannily accurate, but clearly affectionate. To my surprise, the clutter of framed photographs on his desk includes a solo portrait of Prince Philip.)

We clink our glasses of chilled white wine and gaze down lovingly at the book. It is very handsome. I do all the right things. I caress the jacket, admire the spine, suggest we smell the binding. I coo (sincerely) over the endpapers: they are beautiful, Chinese red, just like the chairs for the Investiture.

'I do a book because it's something permanent. The exhibition will come to an end. Photographs in a magazine or a newspaper, they're just journalism. This lasts. That's why I love the aviary [the one he designed with Cedric Price and Frank Newby for Regent's Park Zoo, now Grade II listed]. It needs love and attention, but it's still there.'

'Have you been to the Dome?'

'God no. I don't want to. Ghastly. Soulless. Pointless. I'm not going, thank you. Actually, I was very naughty. I was sent two tickets by BT for a boat trip up to Greenwich and a visit to the Dome. I gave them to Catherine. She took a child. I understand they loved the boat trip.' He pulls his have-I-said-something-wicked? face. 'I felt so sorry for the Queen on Millennium night. Nothing seemed to work. And as for *Auld Lang Syne* . . .' He lapses into a pantomime of Her Majesty holding hands with the prime minister.

It's nearly half past one. 'Lunch? We'll take the book. Look, it comes with its own bag.' Lord Snowdon proudly flourishes the National Portrait Gallery's see-through plastic carrier bag and suddenly, possibly sensing it's all of thirty seconds since I last laughed, puts it on his head and wears it like a bishop's mitre. Then, alarmingly, he pulls it right down over his face. He is giggling, so am I. But now he is spluttering, 'I can't breathe. Help, this could kill you.' He yanks it off his head. He is looking a lot younger than he did an hour ago.

1.45 p.m. The Launceston Place restaurant, his local. We are shown to a tiny corner table. 'You can never have too small a table or too low a ceiling. Never have a party in a high-ceilinged room. It kills it.' Lord Snowdon is clearly the master of instant intimacy, and, I imagine, pretty good at parties too.

The manager arrives with more white wine and the news that the chicken with the bread sauce is off. Snowdon pulls a few supplicatory faces and, hey presto, the chicken with the bread sauce is back on. 'I am a connoisseur of bread sauce. You have to make it with slightly stale bread and an onion stuffed with cloves. I live on bread sauce and Marmite. Did you know if you pat Marmite with a knife it goes white?'

'I love Marmite on toast.'

'Try Marmite soup. And Marmite's wonderful in milk. Really. I always take Marmite to India. You never get ill. I hate curry, I don't eat rice. Actually, all I want in life is Marmite and bread sauce.'

When the avocados have been cleared away and the red wine and the chicken with bread sauce have arrived and we have exchanged stories about the Aga Khan in Sardinia, Kenneth Branagh on his sun bed and a Companion of Honour arrested in the gents, I wave my notepad in the air and say, 'Look, I've got a piece to write.'

'Forget the interview, let's just have fun.'

'No. I must write my article and you must help me. You've taken pictures of all these famous people. What do you try to achieve?'

'If it's a portrait, I want a reflection of the person. I don't want a clever photograph. I want my pictures to make ordinary people react – to laugh, to cry, to see something they hadn't taken in before. But not to wince. Kenneth Clark said of Leonardo, "He was an inquisitive man". Inquisitive, but not intrusive. I'm anti-intrusion. That said, I have to admit I rather admire some of the paparazzi, people like Richard Young. Arguably their work provides a better record of the 1970s and 1980s than the sort of artificial thing I do. Photography should be recording a split second. Paparazzi do that. The kind of photos that end up in frames on the piano are simply a cheap form of painting. I am a photographer because I couldn't paint and I failed my architecture exams.'

'So my challenge is to give my readers a flavour of you.'

'Oh, forget the article. Let's just have lunch.'

'No. I've talked to people who know you, who've worked with you and I'm going to run through what they've said and you can tell me if you agree or disagree. Okay?' He smiles. 'I'm starting with the nice stuff. You're a professional, but you're not easy.'

'Well, I do like things to be right. And I do like people to behave properly. I am old-fashioned in that sense.'

'You're an enthusiast. You like a project.'

'Yes, I waste hours and hours on projects that end up nowhere.'

'You're funny.' He pulls a face. 'You're very funny. And you're ungrand.'

'Oh, I don't know. I managed to get the bread sauce.'

'You manage to get the best of both worlds. You are a Bohemian and yet you're an establishment figure.'

'I always feel very sorry for those people from Bohemia.'

'You know what I'm trying to say. You want to live the sort of life Augustus John might have led and at the same time you rather like being Constable of Caernarvon Castle. People say you're eccentric.'

'I'm never sure what that means.'

'It may be the way you manage to do whatever you want. I can't decide if it's true eccentricity in your case, or a convenient mask, so you can slip into eccentric mode whenever you don't want to face up to something or won't answer the question.'

'I like having idiot time – looking for shells on the Lido at Venice because there are no shells. And I like magic. I like illusion. I like defying gravity.'

'You're a flirt.'

'With men or with women?'

'With both.' He smiles. 'You do it all the time, fall in love, instantly, wham bam—'

'It's enthusiasm. It's to do with energy. I feel terribly close to people. I've been with you for two and a half hours and I feel very close to you.'

'Look,' I say, rather too loudly, 'you've won, don't worry. I'm going to say the book is brilliant, the exhibition will be amazing, you're lovely. It's all right. I'm seduced.'

'It doesn't have to be physical.'

'Of course not.'

'But I take it you had homosexual experiences at school?' A smile. A pause. 'And after?'

At this point I try to pull myself together and remember who is supposed to be interviewing whom and why.

I look at my notes. 'You'll like this. From all sides I've been told you are a good father.'

Of course, he likes it. 'I do have a close relationship with my children. I ring them up all the time and we talk about projects. David is married to a spiffing girl. I've dedicated the book to their baby, my grandson, Charles.'

I interrupt: 'Tell me if this story's true. It's set in the 1960s. You and Princess Margaret are with Laurence Olivier and Joan Plowright talking about your little boys. Joan says proudly, "Our Richard's just said his first word: 'Dada.'" And Princess Margaret says, "We can beat that. Our David's just said his first word: 'Chandelier.'" Is it true?'

Snowdon laughs. 'It might be. It could be. I know I used to call Sarah

"YaYa" because that's how she pronounced her name. When she was, I don't know, eight, no maybe twelve, we started something called the YaYa Club. It was a chance for me to get her into the real world to meet designers, artists, different people. We always began the lunches by saying, "I swear to obey all YaYa rules and regulations – but there are no rules and regulations." Sarah's lovely. She's painting now.'

'And Frances?' Frances is 20, Snowdon's daughter from his marriage to Lucy Lindsay-Hogg.

'Frances is in Paris. I talked to her this morning. She's got a job with French *Vogue*. I go to Paris on the train to see her. I take my tool box with me and do what I can. I've converted her bathroom. And made her shutters.'

'What's happened to Frances's mother?'

He looks at me blankly.

I say, 'Come on, this is not a trick question. Do you see her still? Are you divorced? Say something.'

He won't. I push my face right into his. 'Look, I've told you you are a good father and we talked about that. Can we accept you are a bad husband?'

He smiles. I have my right hand on his shoulder. He won't say anything. Why should he? As a human drama it may be fascinating – man marries king's daughter, divorces her, marries again, second marriage apparently founders when, age 67, he fathers a child by a young mistress who, it seems, may be one of several unconventional and ultimately unhappy alliances: along the way one girl commits suicide – but, truly, it's none of my business. Or yours. But moments later something strikes me and I realise there may be more to this silence than commendable discretion. I am showing Lord Snowdon a 1970 photograph of his that is featured in the current issue of *Vogue*. It's black and white, an inner city street scene, there's a little girl in the foreground and, in the background, a mother and child standing in a doorway. Snowdon taps the picture. 'It's very annoying. They got that print from an agency, not from me. The two figures in the doorway shouldn't be there. I took them out of the picture. I believe in retouching if I want to.'

He can airbrush what he wants from his pictures. Does he airbrush what he doesn't want out of his life?

With the blue cheese and more white wine and the double espressos we get out the book again. This is safer territory. Pictures prompt stories. A picture of Noël Coward in Covent Garden prompts singing. It is four o'clock in the afternoon and, nose to nose, the Earl of Snowdon and I sing 'London Pride' together. The Great Seducer is back on track.

I say to him, 'Your seventieth birthday is coming up.' He pulls a face. 'Let's play a game. See if I can portray you as a reflection of the company you enjoy. There's going to be a party in your honour. Who do you want to see come in to the room first?'

'You.'

5.00 pm. We're back home. When we arrive we find Nettie, a sweet, bent, elderly, Scottish Mrs Tiggywinkle sitting in the scullery perched over the ironing board. 'Nettie, darling, could you do us some coffee? And two glasses of white wine?' We return to the study to finish leafing through the pictures.

At last we reach one of Princess Margaret, taken in 1967, looking dazzling. I say, 'Won't you give me one line on Princess Margaret?' He looks away. 'How is she?' He hesitates. 'Please.'

'I spoke to her just the other day. She's much better. She's much better. She had a horrid, horrid experience. I have tremendous admiration for her, tremendous.'

That's it. More wine, more banter. The last picture in the book is a portrait of Stephen Fry, laughing. Says Snowdon, laughing too: 'He's sending the whole thing up.'

'I must go.'

'We'll do it again, Gyles. Soon. Promise. And next time I'll have the notebook.'

Postscript

It is seventy-two hours later and what is my sober assessment? The man is immensely gifted, a more versatile photographer than I realised, and he has made a considerable contribution to British public life. I had a wonderful afternoon with him and if you get the chance to meet him, grab it. And, yes, flirt with him by all means. You'll have a lot of fun. But don't fall in love. That way madness lies.

Sarah, Duchess of York

Mothering Sunday, March 2001.

'What have you done to her, Gyles? She's crying.' Kate Waddington, friend and public relations adviser to Sarah, Duchess of York, has come into the room – a modest suite on the third floor of the Berkeley Hotel, Knightsbridge – to find me cooing over her gently blubbing client.

Kate raises an eyebrow and shakes her head. She decides it is not safe to leave us on our own and settles herself discreetly in a far corner of the room. Sarah looks at me. Her face is grey, her eyes are puffy, her famous red hair seems suddenly to have lost its bounce and sheen. 'I have given you my heart,' she says.

I have come to talk to her about motherhood. Whatever the follies and indiscretions of her twenties and thirties (toe-curling toe-sucking with an American money-man in the South of France, for example), I admire the way Sarah Ferguson, now 41, and five years divorced from the Queen's second son, has turned around her troubled finances (in the United States she is an A Grade celebrity with a reputation for delivering the goods and an income to match), and no one can doubt her devotion to her daughters, the Princesses Beatrice and Eugenie, now 12 and 11, and fifth and sixth in line to the throne. Sarah lives with them (and a new Norland nanny, Ellie, 22, 'our dragon-tamer', she calls her) at Sunninghill Park, Ascot, the home she shares with Prince Andrew, her former husband and 'bestest, bestest friend'.

'We're celebrating Mothering Sunday,' I explain at the start of our conversation, 'so can we talk about you as a mother? Shall we begin at the beginning?'

'Conception was the easy bit.' We laugh. She looks strained, she speaks quietly, but her manner still has something of the hectic gosh-golly Sloane Ranger of the 1980s about it.

'What about pregnancy?'

'Being pregnant?' she grins. 'I loved it. I liked lemon puff biscuits and smoked mackerel sandwiches from Marks & Spencers. I remember ballooning up to a great 14 stone 7 lbs.' (She is now a trim size 12 and earns much of her money as a spokeswoman for Weightwatchers International. While I tuck into the sandwiches, with her fingers she picks at small slivers of chicken breast.)

'What about their births?'

'Beatrice had to be induced. I was married to a naval husband, a serving officer who only got two weeks' shore leave for the baby. There was no special treatment. He was based in Hong Kong and came back for a fortnight and the baby had to be born then. I remember the day, the eighth of the eighth eighty-eight, walking through Windsor Park, all 14 stone 7 lbs of me, trying to get through a barbed wire fence to avoid the press. It took three men with great clodhopping boots to break the fence to let me through. Then I got into the car and went to the Portland Hospital in London. Andrew nearly fainted when he saw the epidural needle. He was holding my hand when I was having it done. He's a deeply sensitive person. He's so sweet. He's so kind.

'Anyway, Beatrice was born and she was fine. And Andrew did his two weeks with us, then he had to go back to sea. And I wanted to go with him. That's when the criticism started. I hadn't seen my husband for nine months. The last time he'd seen me I was 14 stone 7 lbs. I felt I needed to work on the marriage, so I left Beatrice in the hands of a wonderful nanny and went off to be with him. And the press thought that was not on. They said I should have taken my baby with me, but the Palace refused to let me take her. They said, "No, she must stay at home." That was very difficult for me. I had to make a choice between husband and child. I made the decision I felt was right.'

'What about Eugenie?'

'Just before touchdown with Eugenie – this was March, 1990, three weeks before she was due – I was called in front of three men from the Palace and was given a telling off for doing something wrong – yet again – using the wrong car at the wrong time in the wrong place.

'Eugenie was connected, ready to go for natural childbirth, head down and all that. I got such a fright. I hated it so much. I came out of that meeting, I came up the stairs and I felt Eugenie turn round. She didn't want to come out. She was frightened. I nearly fainted. She went into a breach and she turned round and they had to do a Caesarean section. There are really sad memories for me with all that, because it was so unnecessary to be so hard on me at a time when I was very emotional. When you've done your time and you're ready to have your baby, it's very sad not to have it naturally.'

'Were you any good at the domestic side of bringing up babies?'

'No, I was hopeless, hopeless. The maternity nurse, Esmee, aged sixty, came for six weeks and taught me things. "You don't put cold milk back in a jug that's been washed up with hot water. It has to be washed up with cold water." That was one of her rules. I thought, "Do I have to remember all this?" I didn't breast-feed.'

'Do you feel guilty about that?'

'No, no, no. Good heavens, no. I didn't do it because, quite frankly, I didn't want to. I wanted to get on, to get everything sorted. I am a perfectionist. I like everything neat and tidy. And breast-feeding . . . I'm not very patient and I like my sleep. They talk about breast-feeding and bonding – well, my girls are bonded to me at the hip. We are so close.'

'Would you like to have another child?'

'As long as it's a boy. I couldn't have another girl.'

'Do you think a lot about the way in which you are bringing up your daughters?'

'Yes. My mother brought me up never to look in the mirror because she said that was vain. She taught me never to cry, but to grin and bear it. She also taught me to believe that you shouldn't worry about yourself: you should see how others were doing. And that's how I looked on everything too, until one day, when I was in a hotel in New York, it was the Plaza Athene, and I saw Beatrice – she was about three – looking at herself in a mirror. Suddenly I heard myself saying, "Beatrice, don't be so vain," and then I thought, "I don't believe I said that."

'Later that same day I went to visit Mother Hale, this huge, wonderful Afro-Caribbean lady who runs a home for abandoned children in New York. I went into her house and all the way around I saw little mirrors at children's height. I said to Mother Hale, "What's all this about?" and she said, "It's so important for children to be given a sense of self-esteem, so that they know that in themselves they have the strength to achieve anything." From that day forward, I changed my approach with my children. I broke the pattern set by my mother and grandmother. And my children have blossomed. I say to them, "Aren't you pretty? Aren't you lovely? Aren't you special?"'

While Sarah takes a gulp of tea, I offer my own two cents' worth. 'Freud says somewhere that a mother's favourite child keeps for life the feeling of a conqueror, "that confidence of success that often induces real success".'

Sarah looks directly at me. 'Gyles, I promise you even to this day I walk into a room and think I'm ugly, fat and my hair is silly, red and curly. I have absolutely no confidence. I can stand up in front of a room of five thousand people and they tell me they're pleased to see me, but I think they're only saying it. I won't feel it because I haven't learnt it yet. I'm getting better. And my mother meant no harm. She loved me and she gave me other things. For example, she gave me her great Irish energy and her magic. The pixie dust. The belief that Tinkerbell does exist. And that *Alice in Wonderland* isn't just a story about a girl going down a rabbit hole. It's about how you can go into your mind and really see the Cheshire Cat. You can see magic anywhere if you look hard enough.'

I know exactly what the Duchess is getting at, but I would hazard a guess that Prince Philip, if he's got this far, has now thrown the *Sunday Telegraph* into the fireplace.

Sarah no longer believes in the virtues of the stiff upper lip. She reckons bottling up your feelings is positively harmful. 'My mother's generation said, "Don't speak. Don't say you're unhappy. Don't say you're angry." I think that's all wrong. I say to my girls, "Go on, tell me. Are you angry with me? Have I annoyed you?" We sit down and talk. "Was that a grubby day? Why was it a grubby day?" Or I'll make them stand in the middle of Sunninghill Park and scream – which is what I do.' Sarah suddenly goes 'Aargh!' for me. 'I make them scream. They say, "Mummy, we can't." I say, "Why not? Who's going to hear? Scream."'

Knowing that some readers may dismiss this as so much self-indulgent psychobabble (Sarah spends a lot of time in America these days), I ask her where she has learnt these ideas. 'From talking to therapists?'

'No, not therapists,' she says firmly. 'Talking to children, talking to wise people like Mother Hale. I'm lucky, I meet a lot of remarkable people. If I was asked to have a dinner party, who would I have to sit next to me? Rudyard Kipling. I carry that poem 'If–' with me wherever I go. It's in my handbag now. The philosophy expressed in that poem – that is what I think is right.'

We agree that Mr Kipling writes exceedingly good poetry. We exchange favourite lines, we laugh and move on. 'What, for you, have been the best moments so far in being a mother?' I ask.

'In a nutshell? Every single night – not so much now, but when they were small – at five o'clock, when I was able to shut the nursery door. I literally closed everybody out – my bank manager, my bad press, everybody – I went into that room with my children and that was it. No one could get me. We were safe. And I was playing. I had magic. I did colouring, we watched telly. I loved it because I could absorb myself totally with my children. And then at seven o'clock it was bath time and then at 7.30, every single night – come what may – we would pile into one or other daughter's bed and read three books. On a busy night, two books. Without fail.'

'What about the worst moments? The first time they were ill – do you remember that?'

'I do admire so much parents who cope with children who have leukemia or cancer. My children have a cold and it freaks me out. But when they're ill I get on and fix it as best I can.'

'When Beatrice went off to school for the first time, was that traumatic?'

'Not at all. I was very proud of this naughty little thing with her hat on, with her funny little walking shoes, with everything so sweet and so little, and her little tiny satchel. I just loved her, like a doll. I still call them my dolls. They are my dolls. They're just talking dolls. My children are talking dolls. I dress them, I brush their hair, every day.'

'You don't dress them in identical outfits any longer?'

'I did for ages. I got criticised for that. But Beatrice wanted to dress like her sister. When she said she didn't want to any more, I changed it. She loved it to a certain point.'

'Isn't one of the pleasures of motherhood going shopping with your daughter?'

'Yes. I wish my mum had taken me shopping and taught me her style. Mum had tremendous style and' – Sarah hesitates and pulls a quirky face –

'I obviously didn't quite inherit that at the beginning. I made some huge blunders. But the great thing with my girls is that we chat, we talk, we discuss. There's nothing taboo. And I'm not over-suffocating with them. I'm the opposite. I believe they are God's children and I'm just there to guide them in a certain way. I don't believe they're mine.'

'Are you an active believer then?'

'Yes, oh yes. Didn't you know?'

'You're a proper Christian, not just a spiritual person?'

'Yes.' She looks over to Kate. 'Can I say that?'

Kate is at the far end of the room, head down, staring into her coffee cup. I decide to move on. 'What about schools?'

'They're both going to be at day schools for the for seeable future, which is what I like and they like. If they want to board they can board – we're easy. I didn't like boarding school. I missed my mum. And I needed to be with my ponies. They were consistent and safe. The ponies understood me. That's another story.'

There is a silence. I look down at my list of questions. 'How do you keep your daughters real? You've had an unreal life in many ways—'

'Totally.'

'So how do you keep them normal?'

'They do sleepovers. They stay the night with friends. They know exactly how other people live. They also have a mother who works. If you want to be real: I am a single working mum with two girls who has to meet the budgets every month.'

'Do they get pocket money?'

'Yes, and they have to keep a little account of it. I do about £1 a week at the moment. It needs to go up a bit, but it's not just hand-outs when they need it. They really have a great sense of responsibility, especially Beatrice. She's much more responsible than I am.'

'Do they watch TV? Do you let them see *Friends*?'

'Yes. Andrew makes them watch the National Geographic Channel. With me they watch Disney.' She laughs.

'Do you have house rules?'

'Monday to Friday during term time we don't allow fizzy drinks and crisps, and we keep to lots of greens and good home cooking.'

'Do you cook?'

'No, don't cook, shan't cook, won't cook. And I don't have any qualms about it. I know what tastes good, but I just will not do it. Because we live at Sunninghill Park we have His Royal Highness [Prince Andrew]'s cook.

'We have three sets of table manners – this is very important. Table Manners A is for Granny – their granny in particular – the Boss.'

'The Queen? And what does that involve?'

'If we go to tea at Windsor or Balmoral, we do it properly. We have our little napkin. We offer granny the sandwiches first, before we take the whole lot onto our plate. We don't take the raisins out of the scones half-way through a conversation – or flick them across the table. We don't ask for ketchup when the Duke of Edinburgh is sitting there. We don't say, "Oh, the Ribena tastes old" which it probably is. We don't say, "We don't eat pâté sandwiches". We just shut up and eat what we're given. We can have fish fingers when we get home.'

'Speak when you're spoken to?'

'No, I encourage them to speak up actually – even on Table Manners A. It keeps the conversation going, and saves me having to do it.'

She rolls up another piece of chicken breast and takes a bite. 'I know this is for Mothering Sunday, but if we're voting for the best granny in the world I have to tell you the Boss is the best granny.'

'You're keen on Her Majesty as a granny?'

'And as a person. She's my icon. I look up to her. I think she's the finest woman I know.' Sarah's eyes are glistening. 'Don't make me blub again. HM has got a wonderful sense of humour. She loves to sing. She is the widest-read woman in the world and yet she has this wonderful compassion and total and utter understanding. She is very forgiving. She doesn't poke her nose in. She lets you have free rein, but she doesn't miss a trick.'

'Do you think she is better as a grandmother than as a mother?'

'My father is a much better grandfather than he was a father. I just think – I wrote this down before I came to talk to you – that 1945, the end of the war – I think it must be very difficult as a mother and father to have gone through that time bringing up children – everything was different, there was rationing, you didn't have television. We're different now. Not that she does [she is referring to the Queen here], but you might regard my behaviour as very extravagant and completely over-the-top because you're coming from that sort of look on life. So when you see this redhead, you think she's very greedy and over-the-top . . .'

She runs to a halt. The sentence trails away. She hasn't answered my question, but I don't press it because I sense she is trying to say something else that is important to her. She knows there are still those at Buckingham Palace – senior members of the Royal Family, courtiers of the old school – who regard her as beyond the pale. She wants me to know she understands where they are coming from. She only wishes they would try to understand her too.

At the far end of the room Kate stirs and Sarah gets back on track. 'Table Manners B is for in a restaurant, especially when you're being watched. You can have fun, but always remember people are looking at you. That will go for the future as well. I tell the girls always to smile because it costs so little and it means so much.

'Table Manners C is for at home, when it's just Andrew and me. We like to have lunch together always on a Sunday. It gets kinda funny. Anything goes.'

Famously Lord Charteris, for many years private secretary to the Queen, described the Duchess as 'vulgar, vulgar, vulgar'. Canny old bird that he was, in this instance I think he was wrong. Headstrong, impetuous, naive, worldly but not wise, eager-to-please but so often getting it not-quite-right, touchingly hungry for love, the v-word that first springs to mind when I think of Sarah is 'vulnerable'. I try to put the next question to her as kindly as I can. 'Do you feel when your marriage fails that you have also failed as a mother?'

She frowns and says, after a long pause, 'In my particular case, no, not at all. When we got divorced, the girls knew they had our total devotion, they felt the love of us both, in separate ways. Andrew and I communicated so well they didn't feel there was a loss because the sense of loss comes from antagonised talk or the terrible tear of going between one house and another. There was none of that with us. We just stepped into another room for a few years. Now we've stepped back into the same house again. The girls know exactly how mummy and papa are, how they talk to each other, how they hug each other, how they are very happy to be in the same room as each other.'

'You were twelve when your mother left home?' Sarah's mother, Susan Wright, married Major Ronald Ferguson in 1956. They were divorced in 1974.

'Yes. Mum fell in love with Hector [Barrantes, an Argentinian polo professional] and followed him to Argentina. It was an obsession. She couldn't stop herself. I was angry. I wanted to tell her I loved her and I missed her desperately, but I couldn't because I didn't want her to worry about me. She'd just found her love and I didn't want to hurt her because she was so happy, and I'd seen her unhappy, so I just ate my emotions. I ate my feelings – which is why I had weight problems from the age of twelve. I want to teach my girls not to have to hide from their feelings.'

Susan Barrantes was killed in a car crash in Argentina in September 1998. 'Now she is dead, are you still angry with her?'

'May I say it a different way? I look at Beatrice at the age of twelve – as she is now – and I think, "How could my mother have ever left me?" If I left Beatrice now . . . I couldn't, I couldn't, I couldn't. She's my world.'

'Do you miss your mum now?'

'I think of her every day. It's awful. I miss her energy. I miss the excitement of thinking she's going to arrive. She had a special necklace – it had a tiger's claw on it that she'd been given in India, and a coffee bean she'd been given in Brazil. She used to come clanking down the landing and you'd hear her coming with the sound of the necklace. I sort of wish she'd taken me with her to Argentina, but dad said I had to be schooled in Britain and he was right.'

'You were brought up largely by him?'

'And the housekeeper. And then he married Sue [Deptford], my wicked stepmother. I loved her with all my heart. She taught me about petticoats under skirts and the contraceptive pill and what I was to do when boys kissed me. Because my mum was out in Argentina and it was the Falklands war, I had three years without talking to her. I had Sue instead. She's the born mother. She's so loving and giving. She wouldn't harm a fly, so much so that you'd walk over her if you weren't careful. She just made magic for me, in her homely way.'

'So we should salute stepmothers as well as mothers on Mothering Sunday?'

'Oh yes. And mothers-in-law. I had the best mother-in-law. I always send her something on Mothering Sunday – a card and a little bunch of flowers.'

'And Her Majesty likes that?'

'I don't know, but I do it. I love her to bits.'

Kate is hovering. It's time to go.

'One last question. What is the single most important thing a mother has to do?'

Sarah looks at me. She shakes her hair. 'Okay, I'll tell you.' She brushes her skirt and stretches her arms out wide. 'The lap is always open and the arms are always there. All you need is that. And my mum had great difficulty in doing that.' The tears are tumbling down her cheeks.

Lord Longford

In June 2000, I went to talk to the Earl of Longford about his life-long commitment to prison visiting.

'Peter Sutcliffe, the Yorkshire Ripper, when I met him, he struck me as the most normal man I've ever seen. Dennis Nilsen was different. He's impressive. Tall, good-looking, quite strong. I suppose you have to be strong to strangle people.'

I am in the House of Lords, taking sherry and talking mass murderers, with an eccentric ninety-four-year-old, Knight of the Garter, former cabinet minister, peer of the realm. You may think Frank Longford is as daft as a brush, but I have spent several hours with him in recent weeks and I can tell you he's got all his marbles and those that know him well love him dearly.

Sitting with him on the red leather sofa is Maggie, one of the House of Lords' secretaries, who once worked for Lord Longford and clearly dotes on him still. Gently she is brushing back his wild and wispy strands of hair, dusting down his jacket (it is in urgent need of a dry-clean) and telling him how wonderful, how lovely, how special he is. He whispers to her, 'When I say my prayers tonight I shall begin, "Heavenly Father, I confess I took too many compliments today."'

When Frank has downed his sherry and Maggie has stroked and patted him once more, he struggles to his feet and, none too steadily, pushing his own wheelchair, leads me to the interview room he has reserved for our meeting. It is tiny (six foot by five at most), claustrophobic, uncomfortable, an appropriate setting for our conversation. I have come to talk to Lord Longford about his work as a prison visitor, the only aspect of his life, he claims, that has been in any sense worthwhile. 'When Saint Peter asks me, "What did you do down there?" I shall say, "I visited prisons for over fifty years."'

The first he visited was in Oxford in 1936. 'I was 31. I'd just become a Labour councillor for Cowley and I wanted to visit the poorest, the most deprived, the people in the worst situations. Inevitably I went to the local prison. I was a minor aristocrat, the second son of an earl, a don at Christchurch. Herbert Morrison [Labour minister and Peter Mandelson's grandfather] said to me years later, "You and I have moved in opposite directions, Frank. I've tried to move up and up and you've tried to move down and down." I became an official prison visitor just before the war.'

'Why did you do it?'

'It was my social work. The need was so obvious. It made such a difference to them. When I was in the Attlee government I let it slide, but I began actively again in 1951 and, apart from a short break when I was in the cabinet in the sixties, I've done it ever since.' Travelling in his own time and at his own expense, he has visited many hundreds of prisoners in every part of the country, some only once, others regularly over many years. 'Until I was injured in a fall recently I went about twice a week. I am hoping to start again soon.'

'What do you think the prisoners get out of meeting you?'

'Encouragement, hope, the strength to keep going. And practical help now and again.'

'And what do you get out of it?'

'Everything. These people are my friends.'

'Really?'

'Oh yes.' He is not looking at me (I think he can barely see), but he turns his head in my direction and offers a wonderfully engaging smile. 'Christopher Craig [who shot a policeman in 1952: Derek Bentley was hanged for his part in the murder] asked me to his wedding in 1965. I was Lord Privy Seal or Secretary of State for the Colonies and Harold Wilson was anxious I shouldn't go, so I didn't, but I gave Chris and his fiancée dinner the night before at the White Tower as a compromise. Shane O'Docherty, who was an IRA prisoner, when he was released I had him to a party here at the Lords. I knew the Krays too, of course.' Lord Longford is actually smacking his lips as he drops these names. 'I've seen Dennis Nilsen for several years. The authorities were anxious at first because he's got this reputation for taking people hostage, but we get on. We're good friends.'

Until the advent of Harold Shipman, Dennis Nilsen was Britain's most prolific serial killer. 'I said to him once, "Des, you seem rather arrogant." He said, "The world thinks I'm a bastard. I'm stuck here for life. If I wasn't arrogant I wouldn't survive."'

'I like Eddie Richardson. He is the younger brother of Charlie Richardson who had the gang. If Eddie had been in some other profession he'd have gone to the top. I first visited him thirty years ago somewhere in the Midlands. He came out once, but got into drug-dealing and then got a dreadfully long sentence. He's got wonderful daughters, high-class girls. You might think they'd both been at Oxford.

'Do you know Charlie Bronson?' This is not the actor, but a psychopath who has adopted his name. 'He is considered one of the most violent men on the prison circuit. They have to keep moving him around. He will go for a long while without being violent, then suddenly a rage will overtake him and he will attack the prison doctor or librarian or someone. He keeps very fit. He can do up to three thousand push-ups at a stretch. To show willing once, I got down and did some with him.'

'Do you find these people have a sort of bizarre star quality?'

'The ones we've mentioned certainly have, yes. They're all stars, but that isn't what appeals to me. I like to converse with them. I enjoy their company, their conversation. I don't only meet the famous ones. The prisoner I visit most often now is called Roger. He's doing fifteen years for buggery. He became a Catholic the other day with my hand on his shoulder.'

'What do the prison officers think of you?'

'God only knows. I have never been insulted, but they don't always make it easy. Sometimes they search me when I arrive, get me to stick out my tongue to show I'm not hiding drugs, make me take off my shoes. In the early days I always had a warder in the room, but I haven't had that for many years. You know when Michael Howard went to visit Jonathan Aitken he had two guards with him – not to protect Jonathan, but to protect Michael Howard. In fact, the prisoners were very pleased to see him. It was the prison officers who were hostile.'

'Do you ever talk to your prisoners about their crimes?'

'I don't try to explore their psychology very deeply. I don't go into it in a way that would make the relationship uncomfortable.'

I have spent the morning rereading the details of the Moors Murders, horrific beyond belief. I cannot envisage wanting a relationship of any kind with either Myra Hindley or Ian Brady. Lord Longford has known them both for more than thirty years.

'Myra wrote to me for help. It was two years after they'd both been sent to prison. She was still in love with Ian and wanted to be allowed to see him. I went to meet her. It must have been at Holloway. She was totally unlike that picture of her with blonde hair and staring eyes that appears in all the papers. She was a quiet, dark woman, I took to her at once. Many people have done terrible things. The point about Myra is that she was a good Catholic girl before she met Brady. He was brilliant, I mean brilliant. He was reading Dostoevsky by the time he was fifteen. He was an extraordinary man, with an interest in religion. He finished up as a strong atheist, but he read a lot of religious books. For a girl meeting him – she was 18, he was 22 – it was like meeting an amazing tutor. Bonkers but amazing. She got under his spell.'

'And together they committed the most terrible acts.'

'Awful. She herself would be the first to agree. She has become very religious, really religious, like Jonathan Aitken. These people are haunted by their own crimes. They don't cover them up to themselves. Myra has no doubt confessed her sins to priests many times. The priest who is now her spiritual adviser said to me, "She is a truly spiritual woman."'

'But she can be a truly spiritual woman in prison, can't she, Frank? We don't need to let her out.'

He smiles. 'Evelyn Waugh said that we'd all have been murdered in our beds if I'd been Home Secretary. But Myra should be released. She is quite harmless.'

'Do you think about the feelings of the parents of Hindley and Brady's victims? Having lost a child yourself, you know there is nothing worse.' Frank's daughter Catherine was killed in a car crash in 1969.

'Having a child murdered is worse, no doubt about it. But go back to St Augustine: "Hate the sin, love the sinner". Of course, it's very difficult to do, especially for the public who don't know the person. Once you do, you become very fond of them. I'd say I get more out of my friendship for Myra than she does out of her friendship for me.'

'There are people who say you are a saintly buffoon.'

'They don't usually say it to my face, Gyles.'

There is a long silence, a minute or more. Eventually, he says, 'I couldn't have done this without Elizabeth. We have been married for sixty-nine years. She has supported me, always. She is fond of Myra too. She has been to see her twice, fairly lately. Myra doesn't really want me to visit her now. She doesn't want me to come because of the publicity.'

The word 'publicity' prompts me to ask him about his besetting sin. Is it vainglory? Is it vanity?

'If you say so, I am ready to accept it.' Another silence. His eyes are tight shut. I can see he is concentrating, pondering what to say next. 'Do you want the truthful answer? Weakness is my besetting sin. You know, I failed in the army. I'm not nasty, I get angry occasionally, but I don't get any pleasure from hating anybody. I joined as a private, became a second lieutenant, collapsed and had a nervous breakdown. That will be marked on my tomb: "Nervous breakdown when he tried to be a soldier". All my family are military you see, so it was very disgraceful. If I saw a child being run over in the road I wouldn't be the first to rush over to it. I hope I would eventually summon up the guts, but I can't be sure.'

Our time is up. He has given me two hours and he is tired. As I manoeuvre him into the wheelchair, I say, 'It's odd, isn't it, when in your life you have achieved so much, that actually what you are going to have as your epitaph is "Friend of Myra Hindley"?'

'Do you think so? "Friend of the friendless". I'd be very happy with that.'

Going to Hell with Lord Longford

I had first met Lord Longford in 1968, when I was President of the Oxford Union, and invited him to speak in a debate on prison reform. I got to know him better in 1971 when he set up an independent commission of inquiry to investigate the issue of pornography in modern society and invited me to be one of the members of his team. These extracts come from the diary I kept at the time.

Thursday 13 May 1971

Telephone call from Lord Longford. He is setting up an independent commission of inquiry to look at the whole question of pornography. Is there a problem? If there is, what can be done about it? 'It's a high-powered group. We've got two bishops, an archbishop, a High Court judge and Malcolm Muggeridge. But we need some young blood. I thought of you and Cliff Richard. What do you say?' I said yes.

Tuesday 25 May 1971

To the Institute of Advanced Legal Studies, 25 Russell Square, where the

Porn Commission gathers for the first time. I sit with Cliff who is dressed in the most gorgeous nut-brown chamois-leather suit, with silken shirt and scarves to match. He must be ten years older than me [he was thirty; Brandreth was twenty three], but he looks so young and so, so wholesome. And, of course, he's goody-two-shoes nice.

The room is crowded: mostly distinguished old buffers, clerics, lawyers, retired civil servants, one or two senior journalists (I recognised Peregrine Worsthorne [then deputy editor of the *Sunday Telegraph*]), a couple of token women (middle-aged doctors, with heavy specs and low-slung bosoms: Cliff is the prettiest thing here by far.) We sat at long tables set in a square, pencils and paper to hand, earnest and eager, and at 4.30 sharp Lord L called us to order and welcomed us to 'the crusade'. (Crusade? I thought this was supposed to be an independent open-minded inquiry.) He told us he had worked with the late Lord Beveridge on the famous Beveridge Report that, thirty years ago, had formed the basis of the welfare state. He hoped, he prayed, that our work would prove as significant.

After the rallying cry and roll-call, we discussed aims and methods. It was all rather humdrum and platitudinous. I think I was expecting something more sparky from this gathering of the great and the good. Cliff and I kept stumm. Lord L did most of the talking. He is 65 and as nutty as a fruitcake, but the mad professor look and the fumbly-bumbly way of speaking make him oddly endearing. And because he's been around for ever, he knows everybody. He was a minister under Attlee and Wilson, but he started out as a Tory. When we were chatting over the pre-meeting cup of tea, he told me about his first encounter with Stanley Baldwin. In the early thirties Frank ('You must call me Frank') was a Conservative Party researcher and found himself at a country house party where Baldwin was guest of honour. After lunch, the prime minister invited young Frank to join him for a stroll. The conversation didn't exactly flow, but eventually Frank thought of something intelligent to ask the great man. 'Tell me, prime minister, who would you say has most influenced your political ideas?'

After an interminable pause, Baldwin replied, 'Sir Henry Maine.'

'And what did he say?'

'That whereas Rousseau argued all human progress was from contract to status, the real movement was from status to contract.' Baldwin halted in his tracks. His face darkened. 'Or was it the other way around?'

Tuesday 8 June 1971

First gathering of the Porn Commission TV Sub-committee. I put on my new flared turquoise trousers, but, sure enough, Cliff quite outdazzles me in a sumptuous plum velvet outfit, complete with medallions and silver and gold chains. His skin is pretty peachy too. The meeting is chaired by Malcolm Muggeridge, broadcaster and sage. Looking like an ancient dandified turtle, he gets away with not knowing who anybody is by calling everybody 'Dear boy'. He introduces me to Peregrine Worsthorne: 'Dear boy, you must meet this dear boy.' I get the impression from Perry that, once upon a time, Malcolm was a bit of a goer, a proper red-blooded ladies' man, but now that his libido has collapsed he's discovered the joys of chastity and vegetarianism.

Malcolm opened the meeting by reading out to us the BBC's original statement of intent, inscribed on the wall at the entrance to Broadcasting House: 'This temple of the arts and muses is dedicated to Almighty God by the first governors in the year 1931 . . . It is their prayer that good seed sown may bring forth a good harvest, that all things hostile to peace or purity may be banished from this house, and that the people, inclining their ears to whatsoever things are beautiful and honest and of good report, may tread the paths of wisdom and righteousness.'

We all agreed that, sadly, things ain't what they used to be – and Cliff declared that some of the dancing on *Top of the Pops* is undoubtedly designed to titillate – but, hand on heart, we couldn't say there was anything approaching what you'd call pornography to be seen on British TV. 'Mark my words,' said Malcolm, narrowing his eyes and smacking his lips, 'the rot's set in. If we don't do something now, within a generation nudity and profanity on the box will be commonplace, and rampant homosexuality will be offered to us by way of entertainment.'

Tuesday 15 June 1971

Lunch at the Garrick Club with Lord L. and the *Evening Standard* film critic, Alexander Walker. Lord L. was particularly mellow, fresh from yesterday's trip to Windsor where he was installed as a Knight of the Garter. He is devoted to the Queen: 'She is wonderful, beautiful and very funny. People don't realise how amusing she can be.'

I suddenly heard myself asking, 'Do you think the Queen enjoys sex?' Frank wasn't the least abashed. 'Of course, she does,' he enthused, raising his glass of Beaune to her. 'She's a healthy Christian woman. And she enjoys riding, as I do. She isn't a puritan, you know. And nor am I. People expect me to be teetotal, but I'm not. I love wine. And I enjoy sex greatly. After all, I've had eight children. I swim in the nude, regularly. There's nothing nicer. I doubt that the Queen swims in the nude. Prince Philip might. They've got a pool at Buckingham Palace, you know.'

Alexander Walker, his Cannes tan very much in evidence, then brought us back to earth with a crisp analysis of the current cinema scene. Forget what it says in the papers, old-fashioned romance is not making a come-back: ever more explicit sex and violence are on their way. Lord L sighed, 'This is bad news, Gyles. You and I are going to have to go and see some of it.'

Wednesday 30 June 1971

7.00 p.m. rendez-vous with Lord L in the Ladies' Annexe of the Athenaeum Club. We are having supper with a couple of girls before going on to a dirty movie. 'I've brought the tickets,' says Lord L, positively trembling with nervous excitement. I say, 'And I've brought the raincoats.' He doesn't get the joke. 'What are we going to see?' I ask. '*Catch-22*' he says. *Catch-22*? Ye gods! I try to explain to him that, whatever it is, *Catch-22* isn't pornography. It's a serious film based on a tremendous novel. Frank won't be deflected – 'I've been told it's quite disgusting' – so he takes his young lady (a trainee publisher, I think) to *Catch-22* and I take mine (a student nurse) to a double bill at a tiny cinema at the top end of Piccadilly: *Anybody's Body* and *Collective Marriage*. Naturally, my nurse had seen it all before, but (let's face it) I hadn't, and (Frank, forgive me!) I rather enjoyed it.

Thursday 22 July 1971

Frank tells me that today is the Feast of St Mary Magdalen. He also tells me that one of his daughters has invented a new dinner-party game. The idea is that for the length of the soup course all the guests must converse in words of one syllable; with the next course they are allowed two, and so it goes on through the meal, until you get to the brandy and liqueurs by which time antidisestablishmentarianism is the one topic on everybody's lips.

The meeting itself was useless. No Cliff, which was a bore because I'd splashed out on a special silver-buckled belt for the occasion. Instead I sat next to a charming, rather pretty peeress called Lady Masham. She is confined to a wheelchair and told me to watch what the men did the moment the meeting came to an end. I did and every man jack of them – except for Lord Longford – darted for the door without offering to help get her up the stairs. She told me that coming to London by train she has to travel in the goods van, even on a First Class ticket. We should be campaigning about that, shouldn't we? Instead, the meeting deliberated for ninety minutes and concluded that *Catch-22*, if not pornographic, is certainly obscene.

Tuesday 24 August 1971

I have come to Copenhagen with the Earl of Longford, KG, PC, to reap the alien porn. This is Sin City, advertised as 'the most permissive place on earth' and we're here till Thursday. There are six of us from the Commission and an accompanying posse of at least two dozen newshounds. I have not known a charabanc outing like it. On the plane I sat next to Lord L. From take-off to landing he read the Bible (Book of Proverbs), and didn't lift his eyes from the page once. 'I am preparing myself for the ordeal we are going to have to face.'

We arrived early evening and, over dinner at the hotel, were briefed by a British embassy official on where to find Denmark's hottest sex clubs. 'You seem remarkably well informed,' said Frank, brow furrowed. 'We try to be of service,' said the diplomat, with a smile. After we'd eaten, Frank gave us each £10 spending money. 'That should be more than enough,' said our man from the embassy. 'You can usually get live sex for around a fiver.' We decided to hunt in pairs and agreed to meet back at the hotel at midnight to compare notes.

I teamed up with Sue Pegden (twenty-one-year-old social psychologist and one of the Commission's official researchers) and Lord L went off with Dr Christine Saville (wise old bird and prison psychiatrist). Chaperoned by the *Daily Mirror* and the *News of the World*, Sue and I wandered somewhat sheepishly in and out of assorted sex shops and eventually ended up at the Private Club where (for £/) we had ringside seats. Stark naked hostesses offered us plastic beakers of beer and, frankly, anything else we wanted. The man from the *News of the World* couldn't resist a quick fumble and as a consequence one naked girl removed his spectacles and made them disappear about her person. When eventually they were returned, he was too self-conscious to wear them and so missed the rest of the performance. Sue and I missed quite a bit of it too. The press presence was inhibiting. During the most lurid moments, we simply grinned inanely at each other or gazed steadfastly at our knees.

When we got back to the hotel, Frank was looking positively wild-eyed. 'I feel exhausted, disgusted and degraded.' He had had a night to remember. The first club he had been to was 'small, crowded, no more than fifty in the audience'. When Frank arrived, he found a fat middle-aged man on stage with his trousers round his ankles being attended to by a naked dancer equipped with a battery-operated vibrator. To put it delicately, the girl was not getting much change from the fat man. Frank gazed on the scene aghast and then the penny dropped. The fat man was not part of the act: he was a visiting tourist. This was a club where audience participation was the order of the day. Hastily, Lord L got to his feet and, dragging Dr Saville with him, made for the exit as discreetly as he could. Unfortunately, the manager caught sight of him and, taking him for a disappointed customer, chased after him, 'But, sir, don't go, you haven't seen any intercourse yet. The intercourse here is excellent. I assure you it's next on the programme.'

Frank fled into the street. 'I wanted to come straight home, but, in fairness to Christine, I felt we should give another club a chance. It was even worse than the first. We were placed in the front row and, almost as soon as we arrived, a naked girl approached me with a whip. She used the whip to caress the top of my head and then looped it round my neck. She vibrated me for seconds that seemed like minutes. The next thing I knew she was sitting on my neighbour's lap caressing him indescribably. I realised what was about to happen. I could sense whose lap she was going to be landing on next. I had to get out, and I did. Don't think me faint-hearted, Gyles. I had seen enough for science and more than enough for enjoyment.'

Wednesday 25 August 1971

Copenhagen. A day of meetings. At the Ministry of Justice officials explain to us that Danish society now 'takes sex in its stride' and the essence of the law here is that anything goes, so long as you keep it out of the reach of children and don't impose it on the general public by littering the streets with it. They maintain that decriminalising porn has drastically reduced domestic consumption and coincided with a substantial drop in sex crimes.

This afternoon we met Jens Theander, 27, the man they call 'the pornographer royal'. For a moment, I think Lord L thought he might have been by appointment to the King and Queen. He isn't. He is simply the biggest noise in the Danish porn trade, a big teddy-bear of a man, twinkly and fun, difficult to resist. Lord L took him in his arms and embraced him warmly. (Frank is marvellous the way he lives his philosophy of loving the sinner while hating the sin.) Jens told us his business would collapse if countries like Germany, Japan and Britain didn't maintain strict censorship. The bulk of his business is exporting. Having almost won us over to his side, he then undid all the good he'd done by giving us a flavour of his merchandise. It was appalling. 'Surely, you don't use children?' asked Frank, voicing the general disgust. 'Of course not, Sir Longford. It is against the law. These are midgets.'

Thursday 26 August 1971

Last night we took in a blue movie. It could not have been more explicit. In the front row Lord L. and Peregrine Worsthorne perched on tubular chairs, eyes popping as they studied outsize genitalia thrusting to and fro on a scratchy screen. Quite soon, and quite loudly, they began to tell one another how desperately boring it was. 'Let's go,' said Perry. 'I can't,' said Frank, 'I walked out of the live show last night, I've got to sit this one out. You go first.' 'No, you're the leader,' hissed Perry. 'You must leave first.' In the end, a compromise was reached: we endured five minutes' more thrusting and then all left together.

Today Lord L. and I had lunch in the Tivoli Gardens with one of the press retinue. Frank pretends to be wary of the press, but, in truth, he can't get enough of them. This trip to Denmark has turned us all into ludicrous figures of fun, but he doesn't seem to mind. He loves the publicity. He told me a taxi driver had dropped him off the other day and said, 'I can never remember your other name. I know you're Lord Porn, of course, but your other name escapes me.'

He's even ready to accept that my favourite 'Longford story' may be true. In it, he is walking up Piccadilly and passes Hatchard's bookshop. He looks into the window for a moment and then, suddenly, storms inside demanding to see the manager. 'Where's my new book? It's only just out. Why isn't it on display?' 'I'm so sorry, Lord Longford,' mumbles the manager, 'I didn't know about it. What's it called?' '*Humility*, and you should have it in the window.'

He may be a vain old goat, but he's good company, patently sincere and his eccentricity is genuine. When we got up from lunch, he inadvertently put on my jacket, so I put on his. He really didn't notice. He walked back to the hotel wearing a jacket whose sleeves only reached his elbows.

Friday 27 August 1971

Our BEA Trident brought us safely back to Heathrow at 6.50 last night. As soon as we reached the customs hall Lord L. accosted a young man in uniform and thrust a thick blue folder into his hands. 'I want you to examine these magazines. Carefully. You may have heard of me. I am the Earl of Longford. I was a member of the last government. I have just returned from a fact-finding mission to Copenhagen . . .' The young man leafed through the sordid material, nodding appreciatively. At this point Lord L. realised he was not addressing a customs officer, but a courier for American Express. Eventually, Heathrow's Chief Customs Officer appeared and, having secured Frank's assurance that the magazines would remain in his 'personal control', allowed us back into the country.

It's been a funny few days. Frank is disappointed that the rest of us haven't been as horrified by what we have seen as he has been. He believes sex outside marriage is sinful and pornography is the devil's work. It's as simple as that. 'Sex should be something beautiful. What we've seen isn't beautiful. It's revolting. It is total degradation. Every instinct in me tells me that it ought not to be allowed.'

On the flight back I asked him, 'Are you sorry we came?'

'No, it has been necessary, dreadful but essential. Of course, I would rather have gone to Rome with Mary [Whitehouse]. You know she flew to Rome yesterday. She's gone to see the Pope. She wants to show him *The*

Little Red School Book. I said to her, "Mary, you are off to Heaven, while I am going to Hell." That's where we've been, Gyles. You do realise that, don't you? I have taken you on an excursion to Hell. Will you ever forgive me?'

Postscript

The Longford Report was published in September 1972 and made a range of recommendations for tightening the law, none of which was acted upon. At the time, both in my diary and in the press, I mocked the commission's activities. Nearly thirty years later, it is self-evident that most of what Lord Longford and Malcolm Muggeridge were predicting has come about. Were they right all along?

Lord Montagu of Beaulieu

In September 2000, Lord Montagu of Beaulieu gave his first-ever interview about the notorious 'Montagu case' of 1953.

'All my life I have been an emotional man, but all my life I have been nervous of revealing it.' Until now. In brilliant September sunshine Edward Montagu is giving me lunch by the swimming pool in the garden of Palace House, Beaulieu. The seventy-three-year-old peer, best known these days as the founder of the National Motor Museum, has pushed his plate of poached salmon to one side and is sobbing uncontrollably. His shoulders are heaving, his face is bright red, from behind his dark glasses tears are tumbling down his cheeks.

'I'm sorry,' he splutters, fumbling for his handkerchief, 'I am so sorry.'

'It doesn't matter,' I say. 'We can talk about something else.'

'No, let's go on. I have waited a long time for this.'

Later this month Lord Montagu is publishing his autobiography. It runs to three hundred pages, most of them dealing with his varied and impressive contribution to public life: as the first chairman of English Heritage, as the man behind the Historic Houses Association, as a tireless promoter of

British tourism. But the book also contains two brief chapters about the notorious 'Montagu case', the cause célèbre of 1953–54, when, in two separate trials, Edward Montagu, then in his late twenties, was charged with a variety of homosexual offences and sent to prison for one year.

Thanks to 45 years of dignified silence, the old scandal has almost been forgotten. Why, then, is he reopening the file, reawakening the public memory, putting himself through the mill like this?

'Because I want to tell my side of the story. I want the truth to be known.'

Lord Montagu has regained his composure. He is offering me an elfin smile and a second glass of chilled Beaulieu wine. 'It's light, but it isn't bad, is it?' (He is President of the UK Vineyards Association.)

'Can we talk about the trials?'

'Yes, we must.' He adjusts his Beaulieu baseball cap (he likes the sunshine but the sun isn't good for his skin) and leans towards me. He is friendly, likeable but not easy to know, a curious mix of shyness and vanity. 'Where shall we start?'

'If we begin with the incident involving the boy scouts – what happened?'

'Nothing happened, nothing at all. It was the August Bank Holiday. The scouts were camping here on the estate. It was a hot day. I suggested they might like to go for a swim. I had a friend staying and we went too. It was totally innocent, I promise you. Later, when I discovered that a camera had gone missing, I thought it might have been stolen by one of the scouts and I called the police. When they came to investigate, two of the scouts suddenly accused us of interfering with them. The police chose to believe the scouts not us, and decided to press charges.'

'Why do you think the police believed the boys and not you?'

'The Chief Constable of Hampshire then was a man called Colonel Lemon.' Lord Montagu skewers a new potato and smiles. 'Good name, isn't it? He was an old military type and someone suggested I'd rubbed him up the wrong way because I hadn't asked him over to go shooting.'

'Are you serious?'

'You've got to understand too that the climate of the time was violently anti-homosexual.'

'And you had a reputation as a homosexual?'

'I am bisexual.'

'And there would have been rumours about you because of the way of life you led?'

'I fell in love with another boy when I was at Eton. When I joined the Grenadier Guards in 1945 I found homosexuality was a fact of life. There were a number of notoriously gay officers and I went to their all-males parties and enjoyed them. By the time I got to Oxford in '48 I'd had affairs with men and with women. I saw nothing wrong with it. It seemed to me – it seems to me – entirely natural and healthy. In London at the beginning of the 1950s I was having a wonderful time. One night I was dancing with debs, the next I'd be at a gay club like the Rockingham.'

'But did you realise the terrible risks you were running?'

'Oh, yes. For some of us the danger was part of the excitement. I think it was Maurice Bowra, the Warden of Wadham, who said, "Once they make it legal, they'll spoil all the fun."'

But the charge of buggering a boy of fourteen was no fun at all. 'I felt like a character in a Kafka novel. I am bisexual. I am not a paedophile. I knew I was innocent. Fortunately, as the trial proceeded the original charges were dropped and a new charge was introduced.'

'What was that? It's not clear from your book.'

'Indecent assault.'

'And what happened?'

'The jury couldn't agree and a new trial was ordered. It never took place, of course, because almost as soon as I was released from the first case I was rearrested. The police were out to get me, and they did.'

In the second case, Montagu and two friends – the *Daily Mail* diplomatic correspondent, Peter Wildeblood, and a West Country landowner Michael

Pitt-Rivers – were accused of conspiring to incite two young airmen to commit acts of gross indecency. Montagu pleaded Not Guilty.

He still protests his innocence. 'Nothing happened.'

'Nothing?'

'We were in the beach house. We had some drinks, we danced, we kissed, that's all. But the airmen were adults, they knew what they were doing.'

'How old were they? Twenty-one?'

'No, they were younger than that, but they were self-confessed homosexuals. We didn't corrupt them. They were experienced. Peter had picked his one up at Piccadilly Circus. Of course, the police put all sorts of pressure on them. Their evidence was inconsistent and unconvincing, but the jury believed them and that was that.'

'The trial was a nightmare. My first night in prison I felt nothing but a sense of relief that it was over. In prison I remained celibate and continued to be in love with my fiancée, Anne. Understandably, she broke off our engagement. Poor girl. The publicity had been appalling.'

'Had she known you were bisexual when you became engaged?'

'Oh, yes.'

'Did you tell her?'

'Not in so many words, but I'm sure she knew. She accepted it. We had a vigorous physical relationship, so there were no complaints in that area.'

When he emerged from prison, what did he decide to do? 'A friend of my mother's, Major Goodwin, suggested I leave the country for a time, so that when I got back people could say, "I hear you've been to Africa" and not have to refer to the case at all. But I knew I had to come back to Beaulieu right away. It wasn't easy. I remember my first meal out in London after my release. Some friends took me to the Mirabelle in Mayfair. It was a lovely gesture, but not everyone in the restaurant approved of my presence. People started to make remarks and the atmosphere grew quite unpleasant. A few tables away Hugh Gaitskell was having lunch. He was the Leader of the Opposition then. I didn't know him at all, but he got up and came over to me and shook my hand and said, "How nice to see you back." It was a wonderfully generous thing to do. Many people were very kind. Down here in Hampshire, Lord Mountbatten went out on a limb for me. He was fantastic. And to this day, whenever we are at the same function, Prince Philip always makes a point of coming to say hello.'

What happened to his love life when he came out of prison?

'I got it into my head that I was now so notorious and undesirable no one would want to marry me. I embarked on a series of interesting love affairs, but none of them led anywhere. Unfortunately, I made one girl pregnant. It was in the days when abortions were illegal, but her father was a distinguished scientist and a fellow peer and he used his influence to secure an abortion for his daughter on the grounds that any child of mine would be bound to have bad blood in his veins.

'In 1958 I married a local girl, Belinda Crossley. We had two children, Ralph and Mary, and, at first, we were very happy, but, over time, we began to drift apart. I thought we could still make it work, but Belinda wanted a divorce. Later, in 1974, I married Fiona and she gave me a second son, Jonathan. I have dedicated my book to both my wives and my three children. We are all friends. We get on well together.'

I suggest to Lord Montagu that he cannot be easy to live with. 'I'm not. I'm restless. I have a short attention span.'

'You're bisexual. You do as you please.'

'Yes,' he says, quite bleakly. 'What do they get out of it? I wonder.'

I let a silence fall, hoping Lord Montagu might answer his own question. He doesn't. He is staring at his plate. My answer, I suppose, would be that they get to call themselves Lady (and, in some circles, that still counts for something), they meet interesting people and travel to unusual places and they have the companionship of a gifted and achieving man who, in his way, has done the state some service.

'I must admit that both wives sometimes found it extremely difficult to keep up with me and my various activities and interests, and both wives have found it necessary to get away from it all, from time to time – just as I enjoy the beach house by myself.'

Does he have any idea why he is bisexual?

'My father died in March 1929, when I was two and a half. He had five daughters, two by his first wife, two by his second and one by his personal assistant, Eleanor Thornton. She was the model for the Rolls-Royce mascot, Spirit of Ecstasy, you know. Until my mother remarried I was brought up in a house full of women. I'm not a psychiatrist, but that might have something to do with it. When I went to the Coronation of George VI in 1937 I was ten, the youngest peer in the kingdom, and I was dressed like Little Lord Fauntleroy. I was a sickly child and I had a strange adolescence. During the war, before I went to Eton, I was sent off to school in Canada where I felt quite isolated. I really can't explain it. Perhaps it's in the blood. In the 1930s my half-sister Elizabeth was certainly sexually ambivalent.'

Elizabeth will be 92 this month and, according to Montagu, will have no qualms about his book. Other members of the family are not so sanguine. His sister Anne feels that the publication will cast an unfortunate shadow over her forthcoming golden wedding celebrations. What do his children think? 'The younger two will be fine. I don't know about Ralph. He's reading it now.'

In his book Montagu pays repeated tribute to the forbearance of his family. I suspect he's a man (like so many) who does exactly as he chooses, regardless of convention, yet yearns for approval, reassurance and love at the same time. Because I have told him, truthfully, that I have enjoyed his book and found it honest and, at times, touching, he is eager for me to meet his wife to report my views to her. We finish our coffee and set off to find her. It is 2.30 p.m. The girl in the kitchen says her ladyship is in her bedroom. Lord Montagu knocks and enters. Fiona is in bed, she's resting, she doesn't wish to be disturbed.

Before I go (driven back to the station in Lord Montagu's handsome Daimler) there's time for a very quick tour of the public parts of the house.

With pride, he shows me John Ward's painting of the family, featuring his lordship, one car, one horse, five dogs, two wives, three children, and his beloved mother, who died in 1996, aged 101. With amusement, he shows me the place at the top of the stairs where there used to be a full-sized portrait of him. 'I once saw a woman pulling her offspring away from the painting, "Nasty man," she said, "come away," as though I might step out of the canvas and molest them.'

I ask him, when people have read his book, what he hopes they will come away feeling. He looks me in the eye and says, without hesitation, 'Respect.'

And a hundred years from now, what would he like to be remembered for?

'The National Motor Museum is important. The motor car is probably the most significant invention of the twentieth century.'

I say, 'You will have a place in history, too, because of the Montagu case. It led to the Wolfenden Report which recommended the decriminalisation of homosexual acts between consenting adults in private. It led to a change in the law that has made life easier and better for many people.'

'Yes, I know.' He hesitates. He smiles. 'I am very proud of that.'

'That's your memorial,' I say.

His eyes are full of tears again.

The Duke of Devonshire

23 April 2000.

Andrew Cavendish, 11th Duke of Devonshire, has all the credentials required of the quintessential English gentleman: silver spoon, stately home, Eton, Cambridge (Trinity College), the Guards, a good war (MC, 1944), Minister of State for Colonial Affairs (1963–4), Knight of the Garter (1996). More to the point, I know no one more blessed with the traditional English virtues: he is humorous, tolerant, self-deprecating, gently eccentric. He has an urbane manner, by turns languid and breathlessly enthusiastic, and an impressive wife. In celebration of St George's Day, over tea in his study at his London house (Mayfair, naturally), for my benefit and yours, he conjured up an idiosyncratic A to Z of the people, places, qualities, things that say something special to him about England and Englishness.

A 'A is for ancestors. I've got plenty, but I'm thinking of one in particular, the Marquess of Hartington who became 8th Duke, born 1833, died 1908. He had the best of all worlds: he was never prime minister, but held many of the high offices of state, and enjoyed a pretty raffish private life. It was said of him, "Lord Hartington is a decent gentleman who yawns in his own speeches and prizes the triumphs of the turf and the boudoir above those of the forum." Sounds about right, doesn't it? Family lore has it that when people – colleagues, civil servants – would come up with schemes, proposals, plans, he would dismiss them with the phrase, "Far better not." That seems rather a sensible approach to government.

B   'I have two for B. Beau Brummel once lived in this house. He came to a tragic end and died in a pauper's lunatic asylum in France, but in his heyday he was a friend of the Prince Regent and the epitome of elegance. I am a great believer in good manners and sartorial style. My other B is Capability Brown who laid out the park at Chatsworth, my home in Derbyshire. Is there anything lovelier than settled English parkland in the afternoon sunshine?

C   'C is for Cheltenham. I have to be careful here, because my son is the Queen's representative at Ascot, but, let's face it, Cheltenham is now socially the smartest race meeting and the Cheltenham Gold Cup the racing day of the year. The secret is that steeple-chasing is still a sport, whereas flat racing is now a business. Epsom, alas, is very déclassé.

D   'D is for Debo, my wife. We're both 80. We celebrated our 59th wedding anniversary this week. She is extremely tolerant. She runs Chatsworth beautifully. I have enormous respect for her judgement. We work well together: I am very good at spending money and she is very good at making it. She is on the bossy side, of course, but I've always liked that in a woman. And she's a Mitford. In their own way, the Mitford sisters are something of an English phenomenon. Did you see the musical about them? I called it "La Triviata".

E 'E is for Eton and Eastbourne. I was a horrible boy, lazy beyond belief, dirty, filthy, useless. This is no exaggeration. I wasted my education. Cambridge was a wash-out. Too near Newmarket. But I did enjoy Eton. If you wanted to work you could, but if you didn't no one forced you. That's changed, but when I go back now and then on a sentimental journey I find there's still something special about the ethos of Eton.

'The family developed Eastbourne as a resort in the nineteenth century. I go every year for the last week in July, stay at the Cavendish hotel, and feel completely and utterly free. I like everything about Eastbourne. I like the pier. I like the theatre. It puts on jolly shows like *A Bedful of Foreigners* and *Run for Your Wife*. You can take a boat trip round the lighthouse. There's a miniature railway and, best of all, on the front, really good military bands, morning and afternoon. You can't beat the English seaside and a really tiptop military band.

F 'F is for the fragrance of English flowers. The tube rose is lovely, but my favourite is the gardenia. I used to sport a buttonhole, but no longer. If I go to the Derby again I might wear one, but, as a rule, a buttonhole doesn't become old age.

G 'G is for the Guards. I can't tell you how much I'm looking forward to meeting the chap we've got at Northern Ireland – Peter Mandelson isn't it? – so that I can say to him, "You do realise you're speaking to a chinless wonder?"

'The key to my life was the army. It turned me from a filthy, useless boy into something vaguely approaching a man. The discipline wouldn't be allowed now. I remember at the end of my first day at Caterham barracks I bought an apple and was eating it crossing the parade ground. The Sergeant-Major's stick descended on my shoulder like a whip. He'd have been had up for GBH these days. It did me a power of good.

'The Brigade of Guards is like a family. My lot, the Coldstreams, are second to none. That's our motto: "nulli secundus". That said, if you are looking for the epitome of the English soldier it has to be a Grenadier.

H 'I think we can take the English sense of humour as read, so H is for hats. Having the right hat at the right time in the right place is important for an Englishman. I never wear a hat in London. I have a trilby to go racing, and I take my boater to Eastbourne. And I think a boater with a pale grey suit is appropriate for Goodwood, don't you?

I 'I is for indolence. All Cavendishes are lazy by nature and my entire life has been a battle against indolence. When you consider my advantages – there probably isn't anybody more fortunate in the world – I've achieved absolutely nothing. It's quite shaming. And I never forget, not for a moment, that if it wasn't for a German sniper's bullet in September 1944 I wouldn't be sitting here now. I'm the younger son. My brother, who should have become the 11th Duke, was killed in action. He was a better man than me in every way.

J 'J is for the Jockey Club. Racing is important to the English and it's open to all. As the saying goes, "On the turf, and under it, all men are equal." I like that.

K 'K is for KG. I know the Duke of Wellington said, "There's no damn merit in the thing", but the Garter is far and away the greatest honour I have received and it gives me real joy every hour of every day. I don't deserve it, but it is our oldest order of chivalry and I take the idea of English chivalry seriously. It's important. I know it makes one or two of them livid, but I like getting up and opening doors for a lady. I talk to taxi drivers – that's how I keep in touch – and they tell me that a polite passenger with a friendly smile transforms their day. Courtesy costs nothing and makes all the difference.

L 'L is for Lawn Tennis. I used to be President of the Lawn Tennis Association and the All England Club kindly let me have two tickets every day for Wimbledon. Around this time of year I start to get calls from people I hardly know saying, "Andrew, old boy, how are you?" I no longer play – I used to, very badly – but, if we're conjuring up a perfect English scene, can we do better than to sit out in the sunshine, drinking our squash, and watching the girls playing tennis on the lawn?

M 'M is for marmalade, Oxford marmalade on toast. One bite and you're eating a little bit of England.

N 'N can't be for nightcap because I no longer drink. That wasn't always the case. Now I'm a newsaholic. I sit up till three in the morning watching CNN, but that's not frightfully English, so perhaps N should be for nostalgia. I feel nostalgic for the House of Lords. I really miss it.

O 'We'll give O to Oscar Wilde. I remember my father, who died in 1950, talking to me about homosexuality. He said, "In my father's day, people like Wilde were put in prison. In my day, it was illegal, but we tried to turn a blind eye. However in your day, son, it may become compulsory, so watch out." I think promoting it is going too far, but a sympathetic understanding is important. Tolerance has always been an English virtue. I am proud to be English because this country is tolerant of everything except intolerance.

P 'P is for Pratt's, White's, Brooks's, the English gentlemen's clubs. The membership of Pratt's is Brigade of Guards, politicians, landowners. A friend of mine calls it "a grown-ups' nursery". In the fifties and sixties, White's was very agreeable. You met everyone there, from Evelyn Waugh to Harry Rosebery. Now I favour Brooks's. The days of fast women and slow horses are behind me. What I like to do now is sit in the hall at Brooks's watching the world go by. Actually, that wouldn't be a bad place to die. I shall be rather relieved when my time's up. I've lived beyond my shelf-life.

Q   'Q is for the Queen who, in half a century, hasn't put a foot wrong once. Her accumulated wisdom is extraordinary. Her charm is infinite. She is duty personified. And a sense of duty is an important English characteristic. If I was to give advice to my grandson, it would be, "Never don't do the things you don't want to do."

R   'R is for reading which I can't do any longer. My eyes have gone. But if you want to get to the heart of England, read Galsworthy, Kipling and Trollope.

S   'S is for the Cavendish family motto, "Secure by caution". It suits us admirably. We've never gone in for things we don't know about. On my mother's side I'm a Cecil and the Cecil motto is "Late but in earnest". You know the difference between the two families? The Cecils are High Church and convinced the aristocracy knows best, while the Cavendishes are very much in favour of improving the lot of the underprivileged – provided it doesn't interfere with their own wealth.

T   'T is for English tailoring, and afternoon tea, and the thrush, my favourite English bird.

U   'U is for Uncle Harold [Macmillan, the duke's uncle by marriage]. When he put me into his government it was the greatest act of nepotism ever. I think we'd given him some good shooting. He was a remarkable character. If he had been more happily married, he might have achieved less. He had the most beautiful manners. He was very bright. When he was Chancellor, some mandarin was lecturing him and Uncle Harold interrupted. "Look here," he said, "I'm very clever too." He was. And he was the most complete actor you ever met. He could have made a fortune on the boards.

'After Debo and the army, I owe everything to Uncle Harold. And to Messrs Currey & Co, my legal and financial advisers. I don't know what we'd have done without them.

V 'V is for my valet, Henry. He's been with me thirty-five years. He knows what I want before I do. If someone's coming who has given me something – a handkerchief, cufflinks – he puts them out for me to wear. He is a great friend. People who don't have servants don't realise that they are part of your family, they become your friends.

W 'W is for the great Duke of Wellington and for Winston [Churchill]. Winston's judgement was frequently faulty – think of Gallipoli, think of the Abdication crisis – but he was undoubtedly the greatest Englishman of my lifetime.

X 'X is what we censor. There's generally too much talk of sex nowadays. I know attitudes have changed and, thanks to the Pill, young unmarried ladies can sleep around in a way they simply didn't in my day. They're more relaxed, which is nice, but are they happier? English girls are the loveliest in the world and an Englishman should marry an Englishwoman, without a doubt. As to a dalliance? Well, the French have their strengths and the Italians are very agreeable, but if you want my advice stick to English women. They know the rules.

Y 'Yellow socks are a weakness of mine. They come from Turnbull & Asser and I have worn them for more than thirty years. I imagine I care so much about all things sartorial because my father was the worst-dressed man in the world. He wore paper collars and shoes that were half ordinary leather and half-suede.

Z 'Z is for zizz. I think it was Winston who said, "I don't take a nap after lunch, but sometimes a nap takes me." Snoozing is another great Cavendish characteristic. Get things done in the morning, then have a little zizz in the afternoon. Indeed, if good-hearted English people are kindly reading this after lunch, I think, with a clear conscience, they can nod off about now, don't you?'

Barbara Windsor

September 2000.

'Hello, darling, how are you, love?' Barbara Windsor is a national institution. According to a recent survey, after the Queen Mother, she is the most-loved woman in the land. I have known her a long while. We have appeared together in pantomime (she was the Fairy Godmother, I was Baron Hardup); we had a mutual friend in Kenneth Williams. Next week she publishes her autobiography – full of torrid tales of her estrangement from her father, her marriage to Ronnie Knight, once Britain's 'most wanted man', her affairs, her abortions, her triumphs and her heartache – but when we met up for lunch yesterday we talked about being English. I told her how earlier this year the Duke of Devonshire had conjured up for me his A to Z of Englishness. 'I'll have a go at that,' said Bar, with a throaty giggle. 'He gave you upper-class. I'll give you working-class.' He gave me the Cheltenham Gold Cup, Lawn Tennis and Oxford marmalade. She gave me the East End, Arsenal and spotted dick.

A 'A is for Anderson Shelter. I was born Barbara Ann Deeks in the East End of London on 6 August 1937, an only child, the daughter of a dressmaker and a bus conductor who didn't get on none too well. By 1940 we'd moved upmarket to Stoke Newington and when I think of the war I think of the Anderson Shelter in the garden, hiding in there with my cousins, watching them have their first cigarette. "Cor," I thought, "this is living."

B 'If it wasn't for Blackpool I wouldn't be Barbara Windsor, I wouldn't be on the stage. My mum sent me to Blackpool as an evacuee when I was five. I ended up with quite a posh family, middle class, and they wrote to my mum saying, "We send our Mary to dancing school, shall we send Barbara too?" I came back to London a year later with a thick Lancashire accent and a note saying I was a good little dancer. There was a magic about Blackpool in the old days: the theatres, lights, arcades, funfair. It was special and very English.

C 'C is for the *Carry Ons*, of course. No other country could make films like that! All the English types are there: the fat lady, the lech, the poofter, the bouncy blonde. The *Carry Ons* showed us how to laugh at ourselves. There was something comforting about them too. Whatever your problems, whatever was going wrong with the world, watching a *Carry On* you'd feel cocooned, cosy, completely safe. I was in just nine out of the twenty-nine. The most I got paid was £4,000, usually it was £2,500 a picture, with no repeat fees or anything. I moan about the money, but it paid the rent.

D 'D is for Danny La Rue. I know he was born in Ireland, but to me he's the best kind of English entertainer. He's got style, class, real star quality. He's a grafter. And he introduced me to Noël Coward – and you can't get more English than that.

E 'E has to be for East Enders, the real ones and the TV soap. I only spent two and a half years in the East End as a child, but I remember Angela Street where we lived. A hop, skip, jump and two little runs and I was across it. I can smell the Mansion polish on the doorstep, and when they tell you that they left the door on the latch and no child was ever left alone, it's true. I watched *EastEnders* for ten years before I joined the cast. I love it, but I don't know how like the real East End it is. We don't have any Bangladeshis on the show and these days it's the ethnic groups who are down there making things happen. The storylines are a bit grim, but the audiences seem to like the drama. It's encouraging to find that someone else's life is worse than your own.

F   'F is for football in general – I support Arsenal – and Sir Stanley Matthews in particular. He was a real English gentleman, so polite, so modest. He just went out there and did it.

G   'G is for gardens, not so much the grand, formal English gardens, as the pocket handkerchief gardens that I remember as a child, with holly-hocks and sunflowers in them, and mum chatting to our neighbour across the garden wall.

H   'H is for Hawtrey, Charles, my favourite performer in all the *Carry Ons*. He was so skilful. His timing was immaculate. I loved him in the Will Hay films as the typical English schoolboy with glasses. He was a little pasty-faced Englishman of a certain type. He lived in Deal, smoked Weights, and drank too much. He was great.

I   'I is for *ITMA* with Tommy Handley, *Dick Barton – Special Agent, Round the Horne* and all those classic radio shows from the 1940s and 1950s. Is there anything more English than Kenneth Horne playing it absolutely straight while Kenneth Williams and Hugh Paddick are camping it up as Julian and Sandy?

J   'J is for jam roly-poly, bread and butter pudding, bread pudding and spotted dick. I loved school dinners. Meat, potatoes and greens, what more could a girl ask for? Other kids didn't like their greens, but I loved mine. I loved everything about being at Church Street School. I felt I belonged.

K   'K is for Kenny Williams, my special friend. I can picture him now, in that overcoat of his, wearing his brown brogues, unmistakably English, with a self-taught command of the language that was simply fantastic. If I didn't know a word, I never used a dictionary. I just gave Kenny a call.

L   'L is for Marie Lloyd, the last of the great music-hall stars who died in 1952. She sang "My old man said follow the van". My grandad used to sit me on his knee and tell me all about Marie. She was small, five foot, with protruding teeth. As a little girl I used to stick my tongue behind my teeth, trying to push them forward so I could look like her. She was the real working-class star, the Madonna of her age.

M   'M is for Matron. I've met people in the health service who don't really approve of the way I played the busty, bubbly nurse in films like *Carry On Doctor*, but sometimes I think it wouldn't be a bad thing if the hospitals were still being run by Matrons like Hattie Jacques.

N   'The *News of the World* was the great English working-class paper. Of course, in the old days the revelations were all about vicars and scout-masters. It didn't touch showbusiness. They've written about me now and again. As a rule, it's best not to complain. Like Kenny Williams' stories, there's usually a grain of truth in it somewhere.

O   'O is for the Order of the British Empire. I became a member of it this year. Can you believe it? When I went to pick up my medal, this wonderful old policeman at the gate said, "This is the best thing that's happened since Charlie Chaplin came here." I'm in a business I love with a passion. When I feel low, I walk down the street and people call out, "Carry on, Bar". To have an MBE as well is amazing. I said to the Queen, "This is the cherry on top of the cake." She laughed, bless her.

P   'P is for the English postman. When I left home and moved to Stanmore, my mother, who always wanted us to better ourselves, said she couldn't bear the way I'd stand on the doorstep in my dressing gown talking to the postman or the milkman, but I love them. They keep you on the ground. They work hard, long hours. They're the best of British.

Q   'Q is for the Queen Vic, the pub in *EastEnders*. There are still traditional pubs like it and you can't beat 'em. When I joined the show, I felt I was floundering, but when they put me behind the bar at the Queen Vic, I knew I'd be all right. I felt completely at home. When I had a real pub, with my second husband, I was useless. I kept dropping the glasses.

R   'R is for royalty. I love the Queen Mum, I love Prince Charles – and, of course, I'm one of the family. When I started out in the business Deeks was not a good stage name. Aida Foster, who ran the theatre school I went to, said you've got to change it, either to Ellis, my mum's maiden name, or to Windsor, my Auntie Dolly's name. It was Coronation Year so that settled it.

S   'S is for Shakespeare. When I took my 11-plus I achieved the highest mark in North London. My parents were thrilled and I went to Our Lady's Convent in Stamford Hill. My mum wanted me to become a foreign language telephonist and go to college. I wanted to go on the stage. I took part in a charity concert at Stoke Newington Town Hall, doing a tap dance, singing "On the Sunny Side of the Street". An agent spotted me and I was offered a part in the pantomime at Wimbledon, but Reverend Mother wouldn't give me time off school. I rebelled. I became the worst-behaved girl in the school. As a punishment I was given one of Puck's speeches from *A Midsummer Night's Dream* to learn overnight. I had to perform it next day at Assembly. I did it faultlessly. Years later, when I played Maria in *Twelfth Night* at Chichester, I had real difficulty with the text until Bill Fraser, who was playing Sir Toby, said to me, "Don't treat it like Shakespeare." It was just a little note, but it worked.

T 'T has to be for Terry-Thomas, the quintessential English actor. I loved him – and Margaret Rutherford and Joyce Grenfell. Where have all the wonderful character actors like them disappeared to?

U 'U is for Uncle Alf, my godfather. He had a tailor's business and when I earned my first wages, he said to me, "Bar, never get into debt, and pay your taxes." When I was a child, we listened to our elders. It's a bit different now, isn't it?

V 'V has got to be for the English virtues. We've seen them on display this week: a sense of humour, a sense of fair play, a feeling for the underdog, a way of rallying around in a crisis. You can't beat it.

W 'This is the one choice that the Duke of Devonshire and I have in common. Winston Churchill was my hero, the greatest Englishman of the twentieth century.

X 'Do you remember the X-rated films in the 1950s? There wasn't sex in the cinema in those days. An X-rated film meant it was horror. At Warner's Leicester Square, I got in to see *House of Wax*. They said, "How old are you?" I was fifteen, so I lied about my age. I wish I hadn't. I was terrified.

Y   'Y is for Young Men, young Englishmen, of course. When I married my
    second husband, Stephen, he was twenty years younger than me and I
    think that's when the British Press started using the expression "toy
    boy". Scott, who I married in April, is the son of a schoolfriend of mine
    from the Convent. Yes, I had an affair with Sid James and he was South
    African, and I've been out with Americans and all sorts, but I could only
    marry an English bloke. Englishmen don't make a fuss.

Z   'Z is for Alfredo Zomparelli, "Italian Tony", who killed my first brother-
    in-law, David Knight, and was murdered himself in the Golden Goose
    Arcade in Soho. I know he wasn't English, but we had to get the
    gangsters in somewhere, didn't we? People expect it. I only met the Kray
    twins because they came round to my dressing room one night after a
    show. I went out with their elder brother, Charlie, a few times. He was
    everything I found attractive in a man: gentle, giggly, happy-go-lucky.
    But they were hardly romantic dates because, for some reason, Charlie
    always had a mate in tow – Limehouse Willy or Big Scotch Pat. I don't
    suppose the Duke of Devonshire had any gangsters on his list, but, let's
    face it, they're part of England too.'

Phenomena

Oscar Wilde

No, I didn't know Oscar Wilde – but I knew a man who did. I remembered them both at the end of November 2000, exactly a century after the death of the great Oscar Fingal O'Flahertie Wills Wilde.

Oscar Wilde – playwright, wit, convicted corrupter of young men – died at about 1.45 p.m. on 30 November 1900 in a small, dingy first-floor room at L'Hôtel d'Alsace, 13 rue des Beaux-Arts, Paris. He was just forty six. Last Thursday lunchtime, exactly one hundred years later, in the same hotel, in the same bedroom (now expensively refurbished), a band of devotees – twenty or so of us: English, Irish, French, American – gathered to honour the man whose greatest play, according to Frank Harris, was his own life: 'a five-act tragedy with Greek implications, and he was its most ardent spectator.'

At 1.45 p.m. on Thursday an Anglo-Catholic clergyman – a Canon of Christ Church, Oxford: he was tall and blond, called Beau and came from Cincinnati: Oscar would have approved – lit a candle and led us in prayer. There was a minute's silence and some tears and, later, as we toasted the shade of the great man in champagne (absinthe is now outlawed in France),

much laughter. We gazed in wonder at the huge turquoise peacocks deco-
rating the wall above the bed and recalled Oscar's last recorded quip: 'My
wallpaper and I are fighting a duel to the death. One or other of us has to go.'

Why were we there, this motley crew, clutching lilies and sporting green
carnations?

Sir Donald Sinden had come both as an actor who has appeared in
Wilde's plays (and has portrayed Wilde in a one-man show) and, signifi-
cantly, as a friend of Lord Alfred Douglas, Oscar's 'dear, darling Bosie',
whose relationship with Wilde triggered the first of the three calamitous
trials of 1895. At our impromptu service, Sir Donald read the (rather good)
poem Bosie wrote on hearing of the death of Oscar and, afterwards, showed
us Bosie's pocket watch and talked about Wilde's notorious young lover.
'Bosie died in 1945, aged 75. I was in my twenties when I knew him. He
wasn't always easy, but he was kind to me and I rather feel he has been
maligned. Bosie is blamed for ruining Oscar, but the truth is Oscar brought
the crisis upon himself, and, in terms of the relationship, the responsibility
lay with Oscar. Bosie was only twenty when they met. Oscar was 36. He was
very much the older man.'

Wilde was not imprisoned because of his love for Bosie. It was his
partiality for rentboys that landed him in Reading Gaol. One hundred years
on, Wilde, a social pariah at his death, is the great gay icon of the twenty-
first century. One of our party on Thursday, a middle-aged businessman
from Purley ('Don't mention my name: my parents read the *Sunday
Telegraph*. They know I'm gay, but their friends don't') was clear why he had
made the pilgrimage to Paris: 'When I was a boy in the 1950s, I first heard
about Oscar Wilde and it made me feel all right about my sexuality. To me
he was a martyr and a hero.'

Oscar is a hero to me too. In 1961 I was given the *Complete Works* and
read them from cover to cover – yes, all 1,118 pages. I can't have understood
much, but I relished the language and learnt by heart his *Phrases and
Philosophies for the Use of the Young*: 'Wickedness is a myth invented by

good people to account for the curious attractiveness of others.'

At school I felt close to Oscar too because I was a pupil at Bedales, where Cyril, the older of the Wildes' two sons, had been at school. The founder of Bedales, John Badley, was a friend of Wilde's, and still alive and living in the school grounds when I was a boy. Mr Badley told me (in 1965, at around the time of his hundredth birthday) that he believed much of Oscar's wit was 'studied'. He recalled staying at a house party in Cambridge with Oscar and travelling back with him to London by train. Assorted fellow guests came to the station to see them on their way. At the moment the train was due to pull out, Wilde delivered a valedictory quip, then the guard blew the whistle and waved his green flag, the admirers on the platform cheered, Wilde sank back into his seat and the train moved off. Unfortunately, it only moved a yard or two before juddering to a halt. The group on the platform gathered again outside the compartment occupied by Wilde and Badley. Oscar hid behind his newspaper and hissed at his companion, 'They've had my parting shot. I only prepared one.'

When I told this story on Thursday, Donald Sinden volunteered that Lord Alfred Douglas had told him too that much of Wilde's spontaneous wit was carefully worked out in advance. This revelation disappointed, even shocked, some of the company. But never mind how he did it, he did it. Bernard Shaw said, 'He was incomparably the greatest talker of his time – perhaps of all time.'

John Badley told me (when I was seventeen and he was 101: I recorded the conversation), 'Oscar Wilde could listen as well as talk. He put himself out to be entertaining. You know, he said, "Murder is always a mistake. One should never do anything that one cannot talk about after dinner." He was a delightful person, charming and brilliant, with the most perfect manners of any man I ever met. Because of his imprisonment and disgrace he is seen nowadays as a tragic figure. That should not be his lasting memorial. I knew him quite well. He was such fun.'

Postscript

On 3 December 2000, a hundred years after Wilde's burial at Bagneux Cemetery (his remains were moved to Père Lachaise in 1909), I interviewed Wilde's grandson, Merlin Holland, on the radio. Merlin showed me his uncle Cyril's school report for the Spring Term of 1895 and the letter to Constance Wilde from the headmaster of Bedales that had accompanied it. The letter was sent within a week of Wilde's arrest.

Dear Mrs Wilde,
    Enclosed are Cyril's Report and Term's account. I think you will find the Report satisfactory. His progress is not rapid, but it is well marked [his writing was 'greatly improved', his spelling 'very backward'].
    I am making enquiries as to schools in the French-speaking cantons of Switzerland, and will send you any particulars I may learn that may be useful.
    With kind regards, believe me,
    Sincerely yours,
    J.H. Badley

In Switzerland, where Mrs Wilde went with her sons to escape the scandal at home, she was asked to leave the hotel where they were staying because of the notoriety of her surname. It was this incident that prompted Constance to change her and her sons' name from Wilde to Holland. Merlin told me that out of loyalty to his father and grandmother, he had decided that he would retain the name of Holland during his own lifetime, 'but so that the name of Wilde does not disappear from the family altogether, on my death-bed I shall change my name to Wilde.'

Kenneth Williams

I wrote this recollection of the actor Kenneth Williams (1926–88) to mark the tenth anniversary of his death.

I was a friend of Kenneth Williams – not a best friend, but what he called 'a good chum' and, over several years, quite a close one: we collaborated on the books he wrote, spent hundreds of hours in one another's company, shared countless meals, train journeys, trips to the cinema – so when, ten years ago, on the night of 14 April 1988, he took his own life, I felt a sense of real loss and sadness. But I wasn't surprised.

Kenneth had told me that his father had committed suicide. 'When you get to the end of your rope, tie a knot and hang on. If you can. Charlie couldn't.'

Charlie Williams was a hairdresser, with a shop in Marchmont Street, Bloomsbury. According to Kenneth, the service Charlie offered his customers was unique. He did their hair his way or not at all. 'I'm not dyeing your hair. D'you want to look like a tart? Stick to your own colour. You can't improve on nature. You ought to know that. You're old enough and ugly enough.' Perhaps not surprisingly, Charlie's business didn't prosper. In time he ran out of customers and money, and when the Inland Revenue came down on him for years of back taxes, he went bust. The shop went, the house went, and Charlie drifted into desultory retirement. He lasted a year or two and then, one night in October 1962, 'took a concoction of cleaning fluid – carbon tetrachloride – and that was that.' The inquest returned a verdict of death by misadventure.

When Kenneth died from an overdose of barbiturates ('my hoard of poison') washed down with alcohol, the coroner brought in an open verdict. But the truth is that Kenneth Williams, at sixty two, was at the end of his tether. The final words in the journal he kept so conscientiously for more than forty years summed it up: ' – oh – what's the bloody point?'

He was in pain ('oh, this bloody ulcer and spastic colon'), he had given up smoking (a lifelong recreation), and he was waiting to go into hospital ('how I HATE those places') for an operation he dreaded. He was frightened. And he was fed up. He knew he had painted himself into a corner. Professionally and personally, he had nowhere left to go.

That he died a burden and a disappointment to himself is so sad, and wrong, because here we are, ten years after his death, and he seems as potent a presence as ever. The books, the tapes, the *Carry On*s, we buy, we listen, we watch them still. That extraordinary voice continues to resonate, one of the most distinctive English sounds of our times. If you can do it (and it's a tough one to imitate: Frankie Howerd is so much easier), there's good money to be earned in the voice-over market as a Kenneth Williams sound-alike. For the past couple of years, a young actor, who never met him, has been touring the country with a one-man show that provides an uncanny evocation of Kenneth, funny and touching, and the crowds go to it, knowing Kenneth is dead, but clearly wishing he wasn't. They loved Kenneth Williams. They would like him still to be here. 'I'm a cult,' he used to scream, 'a cult, d'you hear?' eyes narrowed, nostrils flaring. Well, now, perhaps he is.

John Gielgud – one of the pantheon of Kenneth's heroes, along with

Olivier, Coward, Orson Welles and Kenneth Horne – defines the attributes necessary to a star performer as 'energy, an athletic voice, a well-graced manner, some unusually fascinating originality of temperament; vitality, certainly, and an ability to convey an impression of beauty or ugliness as the part demands, as well as authority and a sense of style.' Kenneth had all the qualifications then, yet as the years went by the offers of work on stage and screen grew fewer and less interesting. By the end they had virtually dried up. The problem, of course, was that gradually the versatile character actor and consummate revue artiste of the 1950s and 1960s became a coarsened caricature of himself. He was frightened of failure (who isn't?) and often would say, 'oh, I can't be bothered, I can't be fagged' when really he meant, 'I don't want to, it might not work'. Increasingly, he fell back on the mannerisms and gags and routines he knew he could rely on, running round in ever-decreasing circles. He got less work because there was less he could do. He knew it. He knew, too, that he wasn't an easy ride. Some found him quite impossible.

We never fell out, but then I never crossed him. He could be sweet and sour, but when he came to my house he was only sweet. Yes, he was outrageous, waspish, wickedly funny, and often wicked simply to be funny. He would say terrible things about people, dreadful, hurtful, calumnious things, without necessarily meaning them, or, if meaning them, meaning them for the moment, or, if really meaning them, not meaning them to hurt. He would go as far as he needed – and frequently far beyond – to create an effect, to provoke a reaction, if necessary of shock, preferably of hysteria. One evening after dinner, when he already had the table in a roar, he got to his feet, spun round, dropped his trousers and his pants and cried, 'Look! Look! The bum – it's hanging down in pleats!'

He was funny and kind (when my father died he wrote me a wonderful letter of consolation, careful and caring) and, contrary to reputation, in my experience not in the least bit mean. He was careful with his money, but until the 1980s, his earnings had never been spectacular. The *Carry Ons* were regular, but they didn't pay a fortune. 'I never got more than £5,000 for any of them. None of us did.' In 1983, when London Weekend Television offered him £10,000 for *An Audience with Kenneth Williams*, he was amazed, and thrilled. 'Ten thou for one evening of my old tat!' he gasped. I said, 'Remember Whistler's line when asked how he dared demand two hundred guineas for a painting that hadn't taken more than a day to complete?' 'Oh, yes,' purred Kenneth, ' "I don't ask it for a day's work, I ask it for the experience of a lifetime!" Yes. Yes, that's it exactly.' With Kenneth, references to Whistler or Ruskin always went down well. He liked to talk about art and music and philosophy. He was self-taught and widely and well read, he had reams of poetry by heart, and enjoyed showing off his erudition. When he was writing his autobiography, he read it to me in draft, out loud, paragraph by paragraph, for approval, and the only time we nearly came to blows was when I forced him to leave out great chunks – pages and pages, thousands of words – about Hegel, Nietzsche, Schopenhauer. 'Oh, all right, have it your own way. If you think they want the same old rubbish, they can have it. I don't care.'

He did care, of course. When people he respected suggested he wasn't fulfilling his potential or upbraided him for excessive vulgarity, he snapped back defensively. 'Have you read *Twelfth Night*? "These be her very Cs, her Us, and her Ts, and thus does she make her great Ps." And that's the greatest poet the world has ever known. Don't talk to me about vulgarity!'

Kenneth knew he went too far too often. Once we had him to supper with the head of an Oxford college, a woman he professed himself eager to meet. He liked the idea of conversation with academics. First he charmed her, then, as the drink and the devil got to him, he appalled her with a stream of the crudest obscenities. He recognised that this outlandish behaviour drove friends away, but somehow he couldn't stop himself. One of his oldest chums was the film director John Schlesinger, who had been with Kenneth, and Stanley Baxter and Peter Nichols, in Combined Services Entertainments in the Far East in the 1940s, putting on those concert parties so brilliantly evoked in Nichols's *Privates on Parade*. John hadn't seen Kenneth for some years, so we invited them for a meal. John was apprehensive, fearing an evening of self-indulgent, self-centred queeniness. In the event, Kenneth was on his best behaviour, twinkling, nostalgic, affectionate, fun. John suggested a rematch at his house and, when it came, Kenneth was at his worst. He started loud and funny, but as the night wore on grew ever louder, more raucous and less amusing. The problem, I sensed, was that, at John's, Alan Bennett was part of the party and was so delightful, so gently droll, that Kenneth couldn't cope with the competition and couldn't bear himself for seeing it as competition. The evening was a flop and, I imagine, John and Kenneth, once such friends, never saw each other again.

His very brilliance as a raconteur added to his self-loathing. 'Most good talkers, when they have run down, are miserable,' said Cyril Connolly, 'they know that they have betrayed themselves, that they have taken material which should have a life of its own to dispense it in noises upon the air.'

Kenneth, full of contradictions, was angry with himself for letting his career be reduced to the chat-show circuit, yet recognised – and relished – his own skill in the genre. After recording one of his appearances on *Parkinson* early in the evening he would come on to our house to view the transmission, providing a running commentary on his own performance. 'That's good, that's very good. Don't I look a dish? Lovely tag to that story.'

Kenneth, of course, was a natural performer, but as a person I think he was probably happiest without an audience, one to one with one of the two or three amiable, tolerant, intelligent chums (usually not from the world of entertainment) who gave him time and uncomplaining, uncomplicated companionship. Kenneth liked to be what he called 'ordinary', to spend time with 'normal families'. He loved to be with the Scottish actor Gordon Jackson and his wife Rona and their children. With the Jacksons, probably more than anywhere, he felt secure.

Contrary to several opinions, I don't believe he was tortured by his sexuality. He was born in 1926, 41 years before the legalisation of homosexual acts between consenting adults. He belonged to a more discreet generation, as he said, 'before the love that dare not speak its name started shouting the odds from the rooftops.' Was he homosexual? 'Mentally yes, spiritually yes, physically no,' was his sober answer. In his cups, he would tell the tale of his exciting encounter with a young Sikh in Ceylon, in a coconut grove in Kurunegala. 'It was only fumbling, just the Barclays Bank.' Customarily, when ladies were present, he eschewed the rhyming slang and put on his Noël Coward voice to roll the word 'masturbatory' round his tongue.

He was ready to lend tacit support to the Campaign for Homosexual Equality – he told me he had been to a couple of their meetings – but he wasn't interested in 'gay rights', just 'the alleviation of suffering'. 'The sex urge is just an animal instinct,' he used to say, 'the bit left over in us from the apes. It is the human heart we should be concerned with, and its intense vulnerability.'

Kenneth was so brilliant, so gifted, so vulnerable. I felt guilty about his death because I knew that I was one (of several) of his friends who had given up on him. He was very demanding and we didn't have the time or the patience for our old chum.

Not long before he died I got a postcard from him, featuring what looked like a still from a *Carry On*, a picture of Kenneth peering into a periscope. On the card he had written: 'Are you still there?' I wasn't. And now I miss him.

Barry Humphries

In June 2000 Barry Humphries received Broadway's ultimate accolade: a Tony for his one-man show Dame Edna: The Royal Tour. *I was in New York and went to meet him and his unique creation.*

Scene 1

11.00 a.m. Upstairs at Sardi's, New York's fabled theatre restaurant on 44th Street and Broadway. Dame Edna Everage, housewife superstar, is giving a press conference to celebrate the raft of awards she has received for her one-woman show and to announce the national tour that will take her the length and breadth of America. 'I am doing this against the advice of the man whose counsel I value above that of any other – pause – my gynacologist. He is an adorable person. He happens to be Julio Iglesias's father. Of course, he is getting on in years. His hand shakes terribly (longer pause), not necessarily a bad thing in a gynacologist . . .' Dame Edna is incorrigible, outrageous, adored. For nine months in New York she has played to capacity business; she is the darling of the American TV chat show circuit; hardened hacks (who in their heads must know that she is, in truth, a sixty-six-year-old man dressed up in a fright frock) applaud her as she arrives for the press conference and line up to be photographed with her as she leaves.

Dame Edna, *la dame aux gladioli*, is an improbable creature: over six foot tall, with no bust to speak of, lilac hair ('I've reverted to my natural colour, possums'), double chins ('I've succumbed to plastic surgery – these chins used to be Elizabeth Taylor's love handles'), more pantomime dame than Nicole Kidman – except for her legs. Dame Edna has incredibly slim, shapely, sexy legs. And dainty feet. I am sitting in the front row, right by them. She catches my eye. She stares at me beadily. It is quite alarming. 'I know you,' she rasps. 'Tomorrow you're having lunch with my manager, Barry Humphries, aren't you? Take care. It grieves me to say it, but the man cannot be trusted.'

Scene 2

Twenty-four hours later, on East 54th Street, the spectacular penthouse apartment of Gillian Lynne, choreographer of *Cats*, Barry Humphries' New York base. The view over the East River is breathtaking. Barry, soft-spoken, elegantly suited, a little weary but effortlessly urbane, is at the picture window pointing out the local landmarks. 'Henry Kissinger lives over there. That's his bathroom. On a clear day you can see him flossing.'

Has Kissinger been to see the show?

Barry narrows his eyes and purrs. 'They've all been. Spielberg, Sondheim, Whoopi Goldberg. This time we're a hit. It's very nice.'

Last time was 1977. Edna had been a wow in London's West End, but was a major flop off Broadway. 'An Adelaide newspaper carried a banner headline recording the disaster: "BAZZA GOES DOWN IN NEW YORK LIKE A JAFFA DOWN THE LIFTWELL OF THE EMPIRE STATE". For its imaginative ingenuity, and as a classic illustration of Australian Schadenfreude, I was almost proud to have inspired it.'

Why does he think America has taken Edna to its heart this time around?

'They're no longer so worried about cross-dressing. It used to disturb something profound in the American nature. It was almost pathological. Now I'm no longer preaching to the unconverted. They've seen Edna on TV. And I'm following the success of *Benny Hill* and *Monty Python* and *Absolutely Fabulous*. A lot of Americans think I'm British.'

Humphries has a British wife, a London home, teenage sons at Stowe and Marlborough, but remains, quintessentially, Australian. He was born in a genteel suburb of Melbourne in February 1934. His father was a house-builder, his mother a housewife: they brought him up in the kind of respectable, aspirational milieu he has spent much of his adult life mocking. 'John Betjeman understood suburbia. He said Wembley was Australia and Wimbledon was New Zealand – even though he'd never been to New Zealand. My mother used to shake her head and say, "Not everyone thinks you're funny, Barry. The *Sun* didn't like you."' He tells the story of taking his baby son Oscar to meet her for the first time. 'When we arrived she was listening to a phone-in on the radio. By a macabre coincidence, the topic was me. The ladies of Melbourne were ringing in to agree with the host of the show that "Barry Humphries is selling Australia short overseas". My mother looked up and said mournfully, "You see Barry, that's what they think of you." I went into another room, found the phone book and called the radio station. "This is Dame Edna here. Put me on air." They did, right away. "Hello," I said, "I just want to say I adore your show, especially today. How I agree with all those wonderful women who are ringing you up. I know Barry Humphries better than anyone and he is dragging Australia through the mud as often as he can for base financial gain. The millions who laugh at his shows should be ashamed of themselves – and I happen to know that his mother agrees with me!" Trembling, I put down the phone and returned to the other room. My mother switched off the radio and shot me a dry smile. Then, as though nothing had happened, she held out her arms towards Oscar and said, "Don't just stand there, I want to see my grandson." She died soon after.'

Scene 3

1.30 p.m. at Gustavino's, Terence Conran's swish, spacious, clattery Upper East Side eaterie. Barry tucks in to chilled pea soup, steak and fries, with onions 'lightly tossed in oil' on the side, followed by a fabulous apple pie with a scoop of caramel ice cream. He doesn't finish any of it, but he likes the range of flavours. He drinks mineral water. He hasn't touched alcohol for many years. He drank to excess from an early age. Memorably, on his twenty-first birthday, a surfeit of rum and champagne caused him to crash his mother's car. 'I woke the next day with a terrible feeling of guilt, shame and impending doom. Thereafter whenever I drank I always felt exactly the same way, although strange to say it never discouraged me. I always believed it would be different next time, that I would conquer the problem and eliminate the side-effects.' In time, Edna would become the inebriate woman, taking 'fortifying nips' before the show, and Barry turned, in his own phrase, into 'a dissolute, guilt-ridden, self-obsessed boozer.' Not any more.

Today he strikes me as wonderfully sane, my kind of Renaissance man: he wears his learning lightly and he's ready to send himself up. He writes (a new volume of memoirs is on the way), he collects books, he paints landscapes in oils, he's a serious authority on surrealism. He goes to church. He shared with his friend (and alternative father figure) John Betjeman a love of the lost worlds of variety and music-hall. 'As a child on the wireless I listened to comics like Arthur Askey and Richard Murdoch, Sid Field, Mr Pastry, Jack Hulbert and Cicely Courtneidge. Cyril Fletcher, with his "Odd Odes", was a particular favourite. I feel part of that wonderful fellowship of the music-hall.'

In his own way, Barry has been 'working the halls' for forty years. He likes to talk about his craft.

'The first essential, of course, is that the audience likes you. You don't have to be likeable as a person, but the audience must warm to your persona. Terry-Thomas wasn't very nice, but audiences liked him. Jimmy Edwards was a difficult man, but the listeners loved him. In New York they like Edna. In Berlin they like Edna.'

I interrupt: 'Is that why all those Germans turned up at the press conference?'

'Yes. She's big in Germany. Her theme tune "Edna über Deutschland" has an encouraging march tempo.' He skewers some onions contentedly. 'Next, you've got to persuade the audience to play the game with you, enter the conspiracy, accept your character completely and without question. You do that by creating a world that, however absurd, is utterly believable. Detail is important. The audience enjoy seeing life through your eyes, being released for an hour or two from their own point of view. At all times you've got to maintain a mesmeric hold over them. If your concentration slips for a moment, they're aware that you've loosened the rein. You've got to be fearless. A fearful comic isn't going to be funny and the audience can smell fear instantly. At every performance you are walking a tightrope – without a safety net. Finally, whatever you do, make it memorable. Give them something they won't forget.'

Supplying the unforgettable has long been a Humphries trademark. As the camomile tea is served, I ask him about the street theatre that was once his speciality. 'You mean the Heinz Russian Salad routine?'

'Did you really do it?'

'Oh yes. Surreptitiously spilt and splashed in large quantities on the pavement, tinned Russian salad, consisting largely of diced potato in mayonnaise with a few peas and carrot chips thrown in, closely resembles human vomit. While disgusted pedestrians would give it a wide berth, I'd kneel down by one of the larger puddles, produce a spoon from my top pocket and enjoy several mouthfuls.'

'Why did you do it?'

'To provoke, to shock, to show off.' He chuckles happily at the memory.

At lunch the real surprise is to find how easy it is to talk to him about

Dame Edna. Reading old cuttings I had gained the impression that he would only talk about her as though she were a real person. Not so. She's a character, an act honed and developed over 44 years. She evolved in the back of a bus. When Barry dropped out of university and started out as a young actor, in 1956, age 22, he played Orsino in a touring production of *Twelfth Night.* 'It was mostly one-night stands on a variety of stages, in town halls, cinemas, assorted institutes. After the performance there was always a bun-fight provided by the local ladies with an inevitable speech from one of them thanking us for bringing culture to the township. As the tour progressed and we moved around Victoria from town to town, in the back of the bus, to entertain my fellow actors I offered my own fanciful parody of these good women. Later I revived the character for our end-of-season revue and decided to name her after my own nanny who was called Edna.'

'What happened to the real Edna?'

'I don't know. She was wonderful, but she was dismissed for some reason. I don't know why. I really don't. My mother never told me.'

Scene 4

4.00 p.m. Back in the apartment building, we are travelling up in the elevator. Barry has his gimlet eye fixed on a fellow passenger's high heels. 'You know, I could no more walk about in high heels than fly to the moon. Edna does things I could never do. Sometimes I have no idea – literally no idea – what she is going to say next.'

Humphries has created a series of characters in his time: Edna, the gloriously gross cultural attaché Sir Les Patterson, the wistful Sandy Stone (a Betjeman favourite). Currently he is working on a new one: a grasping Australian lawyer. 'I think there's potential there, don't you?' He started out as a jobbing actor: he's played Estragon in *Waiting for Godot, Long John Silver in Treasure Island,* Fagin in *Oliver!* (more than once); when he was

Orsino he'd rather have been playing Sir Andrew Aguecheek (he loves Aguecheek's line, mournful and pathetic, 'I was adored once too'); would he like to do more straight theatre? 'Yes, I might well go legit again. There's plenty of time. I could have a go at Malvolio, I suppose, and there are some roles in Ibsen I'd like to do. Oddly enough, I don't know many actors. I saw Derek Jacobi in a restaurant the other day (Jacobi is playing Uncle Vanya on Broadway) and we waved at one another. The company of actors can be rather tedious: that combination of vanity and insecurity.'

'But isn't that you?'

He laughs. 'You're right. It's a freakish formula, unattractive in others, but in me wholly engaging.'

In the apartment we find Barry's fourth wife, Lizzie Spender (daughter of the poet, Stephen), sitting on the sofa going through details of the forthcoming tour. While Barry is presenting Dame Edna in a dozen different cities, from Minneapolis to Seattle, Lizzie will be 'exploring America through its food' and writing about it. Barry has had four wives and numerous liaisons. He has lost touch with his first wife altogether, the second two are 'the mothers of my children' so he still sees them. He seems a devoted and conscientious father. 'I must remember that I have a family' is one of the plaintive lines that echoes from his drinking years. His daughters are grown-up and living in Australia. 'Emily is an artist. Tessa was in *Home and Away* for a while. I'm a grandfather now. It's hard to believe.'

Humphries is highly intelligent and wonderfully funny: as a companion for lunch or dinner, or a holiday in Venice (Italy or California), I can imagine no one better. But being married to a housewife superstar (even a caring one who seems quite unspoiled by his/her success) and travelling the road in their wake cannot be easy.

It's 4.30 p.m. and Barry goes off to bed for his pre-performance snooze. He leaves me in front of the television, watching a clip from one of his shows. It is a piece he particularly wants me to see: Sandy Stone is describing what happens when he attempts to toast a crumpet – a whole routine, surreal and brilliant, is created out of a simple everyday experience. It is what Barry Humphries does best and he knows it. As he dozes off in the next-door room, I hope he can hear me laughing.

Scene 5

8.00 p.m. The Booth Theatre on 44th Street. *Dame Edna: The Royal Tour* is playing to yet another capacity house. For two and a half hours Dame Edna has the audience in the palm of her hand. She is formidable (in both the English and the French sense), she is vulgar ('I know Bill Gates. Don't ask me why, but there's something about Microsoft that reminds me of my late husband, Norm'), she is so politically incorrect you want to cheer – and you do. In the second half, as she humiliates assorted members of the audience and parades a quartet of them dressed as Prince Philip, Prince Charles, Fergie and the Queen Mother, a thousand people are reduced to near hysteria. I look around the theatre and men, women and children (the audience ranges in age from ten to eighty plus) have tears streaming down their faces. The standing ovation is spontaneous and sustained. As we leave, a woman from Wisconsin turns to me and says, 'Is he the funniest man on earth or what? Jack Benny, Bette Midler, Jackie Mason, I've seen the best. This guy is better.'

Scene 6

11.00 p.m. Dame Edna's dressing room. Her frocks are hanging all around me. There's a never-ending line of shoes that would warm Imelda Marcos's heart. In the doorway stands Barry Humphries, looking twenty years younger than when I last saw him six hours ago. He is suddenly rather beautiful: debonair and decadent, it's Jack Buchanan meets Aubrey Beardsley.

'What did you think?'

'You were wonderful. Incredible. You must be very happy.'

'I am happier than I have ever been. Do you remember Michael Arlen's line: "All I want is the respect of my children and the love of head waiters"? Well, all I want is the respect of my wife and children and the love of an audience.'

'You've got it.'

'Yes, it was good tonight.'

Roman Polanski

Roman Polanski cannot travel to America because he will be arrested there. He will not travel to London 'because of the British press'. I met up with him in Paris, in May 2000.

' I am widely regarded as an evil, profligate dwarf.' Roman Polanski is no fool. He knows how we view him. He is the Polish-born French-based film-maker, celebrated for *Knife in the Water, Repulsion, Rosemary's Baby* and *Chinatown*, world-famous because his wife was brutally murdered in California in 1969, notorious because, eight years later, he was forced to leave the United States having had sex with a thirteen year old girl. 'The media laid my silhouette in a morgue a long time ago. The picture is set. There is nothing I can do to change it. Whatever I say will make no difference. Every interview is the same. Always.'

Polanski is 5′ 4″ and coming up for 67 in August, but he seems taller and younger. He is hardly classically handsome (he has piggy eyes and Pinochio's nose), but he is undeniably attractive, slim, fit, humorous, with beautiful manners, a beguiling broken accent and the seasoned charmer's ability to make you feel, at this moment, that you are the only person on the planet in whom he is interested. We are sitting upstairs in one of his regular haunts, a Paris brasserie, on the Avenue Montaigne, off the Champs Élysées. I tell him that I would like this interview to be different.

'Well, if we talk about my work, and not my private life, it will be.'

Fortunately, *The Ninth Gate*, Polanski's latest film, his sixteenth, a thriller starring Johnny Depp, revolves around sex, violence and satanism, and co-stars the director's current wife, Emmanuelle Seigner, so we may be able to get the best of both worlds.

'Can we talk about violence?'

He shrugs and smiles at me indulgently. 'If you like.'

Within the first forty seconds of The Ninth Gate, even before the opening credits have begun to roll, we witness a man's suicide in close-up and, as the film progresses, the grisly and sensational deaths pile up. Violence is a feature of Polanski's work and of his life. He survived a childhood under the Nazi occupation, living with a family of Polish peasants after escaping the Krakow ghetto on the day it was liquidated. His mother was gassed at Auschwitz-Birkenau. After the war, in his early teens, back in Krakow, he was the victim of a terrible assault. A man (subsequently tried and sentenced to death for three separate murders) attacked him with a stone wrapped in a newspaper and left the boy for dead. Polanski leans forward and pushes back his hair to show me the long, jagged scars that still cover his head.

'Yes, I have known violence and there is violence in some of my films, but the two are not connected. My art is fiction. I am not unbalanced. I see the distinction between a story and reality. The film I am going to do next is set in the days of my childhood, it is about a Polish pianist and the survival of Warsaw, but it is based on a novel. When Steven Spielberg offered me *Schindler's List* to direct, I said, "No, I have lived with those people, I have walked those sidewalks, I cannot turn it into a film, I cannot make it entertainment."'

I want to explore this further. Polanski's first film, *The Crime*, was made in 1957 when he was a student at Poland's National Film School at Lodz. It runs to three minutes, has no dialogue and simply features a man entering a darkened room and stabbing another man to death. I begin to ask him about this, but he interrupts. 'You know when all this crap began, this business of "monkey see, monkey do", this trying to link my life with my films? It began with Sharon's murder.'

On 8 August 1969, Charles Manson, psychopathic leader of a satanic cult, despatched four of his followers to an address in Bel Air with instructions to murder whoever they found there. That afternoon Polanski's young wife, Sharon Tate, eight months pregnant, and four others were variously shot and stabbed to death. Polanski, who had been in London working on a film, returned to California at once to be greeted not with sympathy but with suspicion. The year before he had made *Rosemary's Baby*, a thriller about a girl who is raped by the devil and gives birth to his baby; recreational drugs were found in the Polanskis' house; Polanski was reckoned to be a sexual libertine. The press and the public managed to connect the unconnected and, overnight, the feeling grew that, somehow, Polanski had brought this horror on himself. Why does he think that is? 'There was such unease in America, the killing was so terrible, they had to give it some meaning.'

I say to him that, if my wife had been butchered to death by the demonic followers of Charles Manson, I don't think I'd be making a film about satanic murders, let alone one in which my present wife played the part of the devil. He laughs. 'Why not? It's just a film. It has nothing to do with Sharon or with *Rosemary's Baby*. I wrote the script with John Brownjohn. We had terrific fun. I like black humour. I like the moment when someone slips over in the middle of a funeral. Anyway, how can you do a serious movie on the devil? You'd have to be out of your mind.'

Does he think about Sharon still? 'Yes, of course. I loved her very much. Her father is alive. I see her family. We were very happy together. When we lived in London, by Eaton Terrace, we had some of our happiest times. I would go back to London now, except for the press. They have used up so much ink and saliva on me, I don't need it any more. Thirty years later they are still rehashing the same story. Here in France they leave me alone. They accept me as an artist.'

They may also have a more relaxed approach to Polanski's penchant for young women. His wives, his girlfriends, his one-night stands have all been very young and wonderfully pretty. Nastassja Kinski, who later played the heroine in his film of *Tess of the D'Urbevilles*, was fifteen when she first met and slept with Polanski. (That first night, her seventeen-year-old girlfriend came too.) In 1977, when he was forty-four, Polanski was arrested and charged with raping and sodomising a thirteen-year-old girl while taking photographs of her at the Hollywood home of his actor friend Jack Nicholson. He spent forty-two days in jail, was found guilty of unlawful intercourse with a minor, but, out on bail, prior to sentencing, managed to slip out of the country. He is still unable to return to the US. The New York sequences in The *Ninth Gate* were filmed on the streets of Paris, with establishing shots of the Manhattan skyline provided by a second unit. Polanski does not apologise for his past. 'It is futile to ask me what I'd do differently. I'd take away all the unpleasantness, of course, but I'm here because of who I am and what has happened to me.' In the case of the thirteen-year-old, he pleads guilty to a moment of lust, but asserts that he believed the girl was older and more experienced than she proved to be.

At one point in his new film, with a wry grin a character around Polanski's age declares, 'My orgy days are over.' What about Roman's?

He laughs. 'Who wants to go to an orgy? And who cares about my private life? Who needs to know? I love girls. I have had some fun, that's all.'

In the autumn of 1985, when he was fifty-three and she was eighteen, Polanski met his present wife, the actress Emmanuelle Seigner. 'I feel very grateful to her. This has been a good period in my life.' Was he at all worried about the difference in their ages? 'Yes, at first, but I don't think it has been a problem – except she finds me a little conservative, a little too conventional. She is not conventional at all. I like her mind, her intelligence, her sense of humour.' (I want to chip in that I like her body – she appears naked, rampant and glossy in the film – but Polanski is talking about her with such reverence that I resist the temptation.) 'Emmanuelle is extraordinary. And we have two wonderful children. Our little girl, Morgane, is seven and fabulous. I think she is going to be an actress or a director. She saw *The Ninth Gate*. She liked it. Of course, it was made by her father.'

'Didn't she mind seeing her mother . . .'

'No, not at all. She knows it's just a movie. She knows how it's done. Elvis hasn't seen it. He is just two.'

'Elvis Polanski? I like it.'

'It's a great name, isn't it? I hope it won't be too heavy to wear.'

'Do you read to them?'

'Of course. I try to get maximum mileage with them. What do you think they like? Scary stories! And you know what is Elvis's favourite film? *Snow White*. He watches it all the time. Every night he goes to bed holding the seven dwarfs.'

What are Polanski's favourite movies?

'*Citizen Kane*, naturally. Olivier's *Hamlet*. Fellini's *8½*. And a picture by Carol Reed called *All the Men Out*. It has James Mason's finest performance.'

As he reverts to his children and rattles on enthusiastically about the joys of fatherhood, I am reminded of John Huston's line in *Chinatown*, most people's favourite Polanski: 'Politicians, ugly buildings and whores all get respectable if they last long enough.'

Is he a responsible parent?

'I try to be. Children must have maximum freedom. At the same time, they must know the limits or they are lost.'

Does he think that might have been his problem as a child? Because he was separated from his parents when he was seven or eight, because he lost his mother in the holocaust, he was never given any boundaries?

He doesn't answer my question. Instead, he says, 'You have to find the middle way. It's quite easy. When there is a dispute, I negotiate a settlement. They are obedient.'

Is control important to him?

'Control is what movie-making is about. You have to impose your vision. But as a film-maker, my real strength is perseverance. As a man, it is optimism. My weakness is my short temper. I have rows that I regret instantly. But I am a happy man. I win friends instinctively. I tell jokes. [The one he tells me is very funny, if unsuitable for a Sunday newspaper.] I am full of hope and ambition. I keep looking for the movie that I call my "opera", my great work. I haven't found it yet.'

Before we go, I ask him if he has any final thoughts he would like to share with the British public. He smiles and blows away a little ring of cigar smoke: 'No. Whatever I say is me saying it and therefore suspicious. For me to say anything at all is pointless.'

Later in the afternoon, we are standing in the street near his home being photographed. A small crowd has gathered. A batty old lady is prodding Polanski with a bony finger, muttering 'Bonjour Monsieur Bien-connu'. As I move the lady out of the shot, Polanski calls after me, 'There's something I want to say. Have you got your notebook?' I am standing quite a distance from him now. He is laughing. 'This is like a scene from a Woody Allen movie.'

I have pen and pad in hand. 'I'm ready.'

'When I was a boy I did have boundaries, you know. After the war, I became a boy scout. I remember running through the woods with the other boys, playing games. It was a good organisation. I took it very seriously. It gave me my identity. I learnt its virtues, its values. Whoever founded the boy scouts, I owe it all to him.'

Quentin Crisp

Quentin Crisp was born on 25 December 1908, and died on 20 November 1999. By chance, he gave me what turned out to be his final interview.

The week before he died, I had lunch with Quentin Crisp. We met in the Bowery Bar, in Manhattan on the Lower East Side, for crab cakes and whisky, and for two hours I sat and gazed in wonder at an old man with mauve hair, the self-styled 'stately homo of England', as – head held high and almost always in profile – he talked, in a gravelly, lilting voice, about life, and death, and his vision of the great hereafter.

He wore his trademark hat and chiffon scarf and lilac eye shadow. Knowing he lived alone in a small room he never cleaned in the heart of New York's Hell's Angels country ('You can't get any lower and that's a comfort'), I was surprised to find, as I helped him off and on with his coat, that his pale silk shirt, though frayed, was quite fresh, his jacket, though old, was newly pressed. He looked immaculate, like an Edwardian dandy: Max Beerbohm meets Hetty King. I helped him onto the banquette by the window: 'Mr Crisp's usual table,' said the waitress. He seemed mellow and amused, mentally alert, physically frail.

'Am I ready for the next world? Oh yes. I am 90 and my heart is not good. I am flying to England on Saturday and flying is bad for the heart. But I have been asked to go and I never say "no" to anything because I recognise that, as I lie dying on an iron bedstead in a rented room, I shall regret what I didn't do not what I did.'

Quentin Crisp died in Manchester last Sunday, on the eve of what he expected to be his farewell tour as a professional raconteur. He ended his days in a welter of glowing obituaries, celebrated on Radio 4's 'Thought for the Day' as 'a justified sinner, something akin to a saint', his 'genuine individualism' saluted in a leader in the *Daily Telegraph*: 'We have lost someone who was gay, not just in the modern sense, but also in the old.'

Mr Crisp began life as Dennis Charles Pratt, in Sutton, Surrey, on Christmas Day, 1908, the youngest of four children. His father was a suburban solicitor ('without much humour'), his mother a housewife with social pretensions.

'Were you brought up to believe in God?' I asked.

'I went to church as a child, but even as a child I recognised it was merely a social occasion. We were dressed in starched shirts and sailor suits and knew it had nothing to do with You Know Who.' With an elegant turn of his one good wrist, he waved his fork towards the sky. 'I became an atheist from the moment I thought for myself. When I was in Ireland performing my one-man show – I don't really act, I just say what I think – I told the audience I was an atheist and a woman got up and said, "Yes, but is it in the God of the Catholics or the God of the Protestants in whom you do not believe?"' Mr Crisp chortled softly and, without moving his head, glanced towards me to make sure I had enjoyed the joke. 'I don't believe in God and He doesn't believe in me, but let's pretend heaven is a possibility. I wanted to call my life story *I Reign in Hell*, but Jonathan Cape decided that wouldn't do, so when it was published in 1968 it was called *The Naked Civil Servant* and now, everywhere I go, I have to explain I was never a civil servant.'

As a child, he was a misfit. As soon as he could walk, he took to wearing his mother's clothes and imagining himself as a fairytale princess. At school he was beaten. As a young man, walking through London, asserting his individuality with hennaed hair, 'blind with mascara and dumb with lipstick', he was beaten up. He changed his name and drifted through assorted occupations (including some months as a male prostitute, 'disappointing and disappointed') until the war came. He tried to join the army, but was declared 'totally exempt, suffering from sexual perversion'. In 1942, he became an art school model and for the next thirty years worked in virtually every art school in and around London, usually posing naked in a variety of dramatic and exotic postures. (His crucifixion pose was a favourite.) He asked himself the question, 'Who would you be if there was no praise and no blame?' and then tried to live according to his answer.

'I have made only two decisions in my life. The first was to leave home, the second was to live in America. I left home when I was 22 because I felt I couldn't really go on eating my parents' food and taking their shelter and never doing a thing they asked, so I left. And it was very difficult because I had no money and I had to live in the worst parts of London – in King's Cross and Clerkenwell.' He rolled the names around his mouth and spat them out with haughty theatrical disdain.

'If there is a heaven it will be like America, because in America everybody is your friend. In England nobody is your friend. I've lived here for eighteen years and I've lived in my room for eighteen years. It's one room in a rooming house. It is probably the only rooming house left in Manhattan. I only pay $350 a month. I never felt safe in England. In New York you are safe wherever you go. You can get shot, which is nice, because that's the end, but you never get beaten up.

'The police are very cosy in America. They drive their cars at walking pace down Second Avenue and, if I look at them, they beckon me over and ask me my name. I say, "Am I illegal?" And they say, "Oh no, it's nothing like that. We just wondered how the show was going." No English policeman is ever going to ask you how the show is going. In England, if you like something you don't mention it, if you don't you do. In America, if you don't like something you don't mention it. What you do like you mention – so the air is full of praise, which is nice.'

'Don't you have some residual affection for England?'

Crisp Lines

'If at first you don't succeed, failure may be your style.'

'Never keep up with the Joneses. Drag them down to your level.'

'There is no need for housework, just keep your nerve. After the first four years, the dirt doesn't get any worse.'

'For flavour, Instant Sex will never supersede the stuff you had to peel and cook.'

'People who are lonely are those who do not know what to do with the time when they are alone.'

'Life was a funny thing that happened to me on the way to the grave.'

'Not really, because I didn't like England, and the English didn't like me. I do understand why. You see, the English don't like effeminacy. The English don't like effeminate women. English men say of their women, "Oh you know, she fiddles with her appearance and asks me 'How do I look?' and 'Do you love me?'". They find their women exasperating. But American men indulge their women. They call them "Sugar" and "Honey" and "Baby". My brother was never without a woman in tow. He sat her on a bar stool and every twenty minutes he said to her, "Are you all right?" And when she'd gone he'd say to me, "What a boring woman," and I'd say to him, "What did you say to which she could make a witty response?"

'Heaven will not be like England, that much is certain. I can tell you what heaven will smell like. When I was young there was a fur firm called

Revillon who made a perfume called "Latitude 50" and that smelled like having your teeth drilled. It was wonderful.'

'Is it a perfume you wore?'

'No, I wanted to express my femininity, but I didn't buy perfume because it was expensive. Make-up was cheap so I could wear that. I wore very little at first, but exhibitionism becomes like a drug. Eventually, you can take a dose of it that would kill anyone just starting out.

'The sound of heaven will be silence. I don't really hold with music because, to me, music is the most noise conveying the least information. If there has to be a heavenly choir, let it be led by Barbara Cook. She has a beautiful voice, very flexible, very emotional.

'I think I will like the food in heaven. I like food that tastes of nothing and I'm sure that's what they serve. Here, I eat most of my meals in the Cooper Diner on Second Avenue, where you can eat anything and it all tastes the same. I don't like kinky food. As you go up Second Avenue, you pass Thai restaurants, Tibetan restaurants, Chinese, Indian, but it all tastes very peculiar, so I avoid it. Usually I eat alone. I go to most places alone. When I receive an invitation I go, and if you can live on peanuts and champagne you need never buy food in New York. I am content with my fate.'

I said, 'But are you happy?'

'Yes. The secret of how to be happy is to remember that happiness is never out there, it's always in here.' He looked at me directly again (probably for only the second time) and cupped his hands around his heart. 'And, also, to live alone. I had no opinions about cohabitation until the last four or five years, but recently I have become a kind of mail-order guru, and people come to see me and tell me their problems. And all the problems concern the person they live with, so to be happy you have to live alone.'

'What about pets?'

'Oh no. Animals are a nuisance. There will be no animals in heaven. There will be people, which is fine, because I like people, but any people will do. I have my friends, but I'm mad about strangers—' He looked at me once more – 'because they haven't heard it all before.

'I would like my guardian angel to be like Elizabeth Taylor. She is now more famous than she was when she was a movie star and she has done it simply with the exertion of her personality. In England it's called "showing off". In America it's called "doing fame" and she does it to perfection. I've never met her, but I'd like to meet her, and when she gets to heaven I will.

'There are several actresses I hope to meet in heaven. I want to make small-talk with Joan Greenwood. I adored her voice and manner. She was the most affected actress ever and it worked perfectly. And I want to meet Edith Evans. I was quite young when I saw her in a Restoration drama. I couldn't believe how she performed the asides. She came down stage and spoke to the audience in an extraordinary voice: "The devil take him for wearing that livery." It was so funny.'

Mr Crisp's evocation of Edith Evans was spot-on. Not long ago he played Lady Bracknell in *The Importance of Being Earnest* off Broadway. 'It's a very good part, it's short and showy and the lines say themselves. You don't have to do anything.' He also appeared in several films, notably as Elizabeth I in Sally Potter's version of Virginia Woolf's *Orlando* ('twilight cinema, not as bad as art house, not as good as the real thing') and as himself in his own *Resident Alien* ('unabashed festival fare – I just wandered about the Lower East Side talking to myself'). 'If you don't want to be in a movie in America, you have to keep moving, because the moment you stand still someone comes up and says, "Would you like to be in our picture?"

'I am curious to meet Oscar Wilde because I think his whole life was built on a misunderstanding. He said, "In matters of great importance it is not sincerity that matters but style." He didn't understand that they are the same thing. Style is no good unless it tells you what the content is. You only know of the content what you receive through the style, so you can't separate the two. But he thought you could, which accounts for that terrible poetry he wrote. He thought that style was to allow a rain of bejewelled phrases to fall on banal material. I don't think it is, as I shall tell him.'

'Are there any great historical figures you would like to meet in heaven?'
'Yes. This has been the age of tyrants and they would be interesting to meet, especially in heaven where they couldn't carry on as they had carried on down here. Hitler murdered everybody. Stalin prevented Russians from reaching the outer world. And think of Pol Pot. He beheaded people who wore glasses. Isn't that weird? I want to meet Pol Pot in heaven and sit down with him quietly and ask him what he thought he was doing.'

Mr Crisp said to me, 'The secret of success as a performer is to make the audience like you. That's all you have to do.' I liked him at once. He didn't ask you to agree with him, simply to accept him. He may have become a gay icon, but he was never a gay activist. 'I am what I am and that's that.' He was special because he was true to himself. His favourite line belonged to Blanche Du Bois in Tennessee Williams's *A Streetcar Named Desire*: 'I never lied in my heart.'

After lunch, we found a cab and I dropped him off outside his rooming house. I enquired about his fellow tenants. 'They're nice. They carry my letters up for me because I can only go up and down the stairs once a day now my heart's so bad. My neighbours are kind, except for one of them who puts dead mice under my door. I think he wants to me to go. He probably wants my room.'

Did Mr Crisp have a last message for the English people? 'Yes, only one. Tell them they can be happy. There is no need to go on being miserable. The English are miserable to show they take life seriously. Well, why do they take life seriously? They can be happy.'

I shook his hand and told him what a privilege it had been being his stranger for today, and, as an afterthought, asked him if he had any plans for the millennium. 'I shall take no notice of the millennium. I am told it is only an excuse for a street party, so if you want you can be on an icy street, jumping up and down and having your pockets picked. This I do not want, so I won't be there. I shall be hiding. You won't see me any more. Goodbye. And thank you. It's been fun.'

Christopher Robin

Christopher Robin Milne was a phenomenon. He is probably the most famous real child in literature. I got to know him in the 1980s when, with Julian Slade, the creator of Salad Days, *I wrote a play about his parents, A. A. Milne and Dorothy de Selincourt. (In the play the part of Christopher Robin was played by another phenomenon of a kind: the boy soprano, Aled Jones.) Lesley Milne is a phenomenon too. As I discovered when I talked to her in March 2001, money does not matter to her.*

L esley Milne is not amused. The widow of Christopher Robin – he died five years ago, aged seventy-five she is now in her mid seventies, beady-eyed, feisty, formidable – is at home in Totnes with the telephone answering machine on and the front door firmly closed. Since word broke that the Disney Corporation is shelling out some £240 million for a twenty-five year extension in their rights to exploit Winnie-the-Pooh, Piglet, Eeyore and the rest of her husband's childhood companions – but Mrs Milne is not going to get a penny of it – she has been under siege. The world's press are frantic to know how she feels, but she is not inclined to tell them.

'I have just got rid of the *Daily Mail*,' she informs me briskly. 'I don't read the *Daily Mail*. I particularly dislike the *Daily Mail*. I don't read the *Sun* either, for that matter.' (Last week, in an unusually lengthy leader, the *Sun* lambasted the Milnes for allowing 'a great British asset to be sold off cheap'.)

'Who are you writing your piece for?' Mrs Milne asks me, rather sharply.

'The *Sunday Telegraph*,' I murmur silkily, offering the ultimate reassurance.

'That's no better,' she snaps 'I am a lifelong *Guardian* reader. So was Christopher.'

'Talk to me anyway,' I say 'Look on it as missionary work.'

She laughs. It is a small throaty chuckle, cynical but warm. She agrees to talk to me, partly because I knew her husband (yes, I shook the hand that held the paw of Winnie-the-Pooh: it is my proudest boast), partly because she wants to set the record straight. 'I am being portrayed as some sort of penniless widow who has been left out of the will. It's ridiculous.'

A. A. Milne wrote the stories about Winnie-the-Pooh and Christopher Robin in the 1920s. When he died in 1956 his literary estate was divided four ways: a quarter each going to his family (Christopher was his only child), his old school (Westminster), his club (the Garrick) and the Royal Literary Fund.

'About twenty years ago,' Lesley explains to me, 'we decided to sell half of our share to the Royal Literary Fund.'

'For just £150,000?'

'Yes, that was what it was worth at the time.'

'But now it's worth £30 million. You must regret that?'

'Not for a moment.' She takes a deep breath and repeats the phrase quite distinctly, 'Not for a moment.' She wants me to understand that there are still some people in this world for whom money isn't everything. 'I am entirely comfortable. When we were first married we were hard up, we had to count the pennies then, but now I've got everything I could possibly want. Please make that quite clear.'

'I will,' I promise.

'The other half of our share was put in trust for Clare.'

Clare is Lesley and Christopher Milne's only child. Now forty four, she was born in 1956, a few months after A.A. Milne's death, suffering from cerebral palsy.

'How is Clare?' I ask.

'Clare is very well, thank you. She's cared for in a home now. She has been for years. She is beautifully looked after.' She pauses. She senses I want more. 'Clare is lovely,' she adds. 'Clare is happy. She comes to visit me regularly. She likes nice clothes. She loves shopping. And she likes good food. And wine. She particularly enjoys wine.'

Clare, of course, could buy anything she wanted. Her current annual income from assorted royalties is around £500,000 and the latest Disney windfall will net her £30 million. 'What does Clare think of all this money that's coming to her?' I ask.

'She's rather vague about that sort of thing,' says her mother. 'She doesn't know the difference between £1,000 and £1,000,000. That's rather nice, don't you think? I think that's very nice, really very nice.'

This is the first time I have encountered Lesley Milne. In the early 1980s, when I came to know her husband – I was writing a play about the Milne family and kept a note of our conversations – he seemed to me to be at his happiest talking about Clare.

'The one question we always used to dread,' he said, 'was "And do you have any children?" In the early days I became adept at steering the conversation onto safer ground. Now I find it better to make the matter quite plain from the start: it saves later embarrassment. "Yes, a daughter. She has cerebral palsy." There follows a momentary pause; then, "Oh . . . I'm sorry to hear that." And then, after a few more words, we move to another subject.'

Christopher told me that his daughter had taught him 'a philosophy that parents don't usually expect to learn from their children'. 'Once we had accepted Clare's disability, there were plenty of other things we could be happy about, plenty to enjoy, plenty to be grateful for. And at the top of the list was her own very evident zest for life, her high spirits, her sense of fun, her cheerful acceptance of all she couldn't do, her delight in what little she could. She set us an example. We tend to think that, if someone is deprived of a blessing that we ourselves possess, their life is sadder. But in fact the man who has less than his neighbour is only unhappy if he had been hoping for more and chooses to feel jealous.'

When I first met him, Christopher had just turned sixty. He seemed older. He was a little bent, with owlish glasses and a mischievous twinkle in his eye. I had been warned that I would find him painfully shy, diffident about his parents, reluctant to talk about Pooh. In fact, he was consciously charming, courteous, gentle but forthcoming. He said at once, 'Of course, we must talk about Pooh. It's been something of a love-hate relationship down the years, but it's all right now. Believe it or not, I can look at those four books without flinching. I'm quite fond of them really.'

'Those four books' dominated his life. The first, *When We Were Very Young* was published in November 1924, dedicated to 'Christopher Robin Milne', just turned four; the last, *The House at Pooh Corner*, in October 1928. Within eight weeks the first collection of nursery verses had sold more than 50,000 copies; by the time the last book appeared each title in the series was selling several hundred thousand worldwide.

Christopher told me that, until he was eight or nine, he 'quite liked being famous'. He corresponded with his fans, made public appearances, even made a record. 'It was exciting and made me feel grand and important.' He felt differently when he went away to boarding school where he was teased and bullied. He learned to box to defend himself. He came to despise the boy in the books called Christopher Robin. He had a particular loathing of the child depicted in 'Vespers', the little boy kneeling at the foot of the bed. 'I vividly recall how intensely painful it was to sit in my study at Stowe while my neighbours played the famous – now cursed – gramophone record remorselessly over and over again. Eventually I took the record and broke it into a hundred fragments and scattered them over a distant field.'

'Fame can be counterproductive,' says Lesley Milne. 'Alan Milne spent the latter part of his life regretting that most of his work as a playwright, essayist and novelist was forgotten. Pooh made him rich, but not happy. Christopher Milne spent the early part of his life fighting for an identity separate from his father and those immortal playmates in the Hundred Acre Wood.'

According to Lesley, Christopher and Alan had 'a curious relationship'. Neither knew the other very well. 'It is difficult to imagine these days, when families are so close, how children were raised in an affluent middle-class family between the wars. A small child saw his parents only occasionally, however much they loved him in theory. A little boy or girl was more a pet than a companion: well washed, brushed, dressed up to be brought out, cute and lovable, on special occasions. He might be asked to sing or recite for teatime guests to coo over. I doubt that Christopher's parents ever saw him throw a tantrum or encountered dirty nappies.'

As a small boy the love of Christopher's life was his nanny, Olive Rand. She was the centre of his universe: 'for over eight years,' he told me, 'apart from her fortnight's holiday every September, we were not out of each other's sight for more than a few hours at a time'. Lesley says, 'They remained friends as long as she lived.'

Life for young Christopher was divided between London, a comfortable house in Chelsea, and the country, Cotchford Farm, near Hartfield in Sussex, on the edge of Ashdown Forest, the territory Pooh & Co would make world-famous. According to Lesley (who says this to me somewhat tartly), Christopher's mother loved London 'and New York – she was flighty, very actressy and superficial. She laughed a lot.' According to Christopher, in the country his mother loved her garden: 'she was good with her hands'. 'And if I wasn't a full-time job,' he said with a wry smile, 'I was at least a part-time hobby.' Mrs Milne dressed her son not as other boys of the period, as he would have liked, but 'girlishly', with 'golden tresses' and 'curious clothes' –

exactly as Christopher Robin appears in E. H. Shepard's famous drawings. A. A. Milne was either at the Garrick Club or at his desk. Lesley says he was 'a large, remote, godlike being', distant, guarded, ungiving. At the end of his life, Christopher was less harsh in his verdict: 'Some people are good with children. Others are not. It is a gift. You either have it or you don't. My father didn't.' Christopher came to believe that because his father could not play with his small son, didn't know how or where to begin, he created 'a dream son' on the page instead. And it was only when the children's books were behind him, when Nanny was no longer in the way, that father and son began to know one another.

Their friendship lasted nine years, the years of Christopher's adolescence. What did they do together? 'The Times crossword, and algebra, and Euclid.' They would putt on the lawn, throw tennis balls at each other, look for birds' nests, 'catch things in the stream, play cricket in the meadow'. Then came 'the inevitable parting'. There is a touching passage in A. A. Milne's autobiography where he anatomises the 'life-long process of saying goodbye' and pictures himself bidding his own father farewell: 'From now on we shall begin to grow out of each other. I shall be impatient, but you will be patient with me; unloving, but you will not cease to love me. "Well," you will tell yourself, "it lasted until he was twelve; they grow up and resent our care for them, they form their own ideas, and think ours old-fashioned. It is natural."'

Christopher told me, 'My father had me longer than most because we started later than most, and perhaps because we had been closer the drifting apart, when it came, was greater.' The separation began in 1938 when Christopher was eighteen and went to Cambridge (he won a scholarship to Trinity), then to war (the Royal Engineers, North Africa, Italy), then back to Cambridge to finish his degree. It was after the war, when Christopher was in his mid to late twenties, that his resentment of his father came to a head. 'Six years in the army don't qualify a man for employment,' says Lesley. 'Being a storybook hero doesn't help either.' Briefly Christopher worked for the Central Office of Information, he tried retailing (for a year and a half he worked for the John Lewis Partnership, starting in the lampshade department at Peter Jones), he had a go at writing, without success. He failed to find a niche and held his parents responsible for his plight. He came to believe that 'my father had got where he was by climbing on my infant shoulders, that he had filched from me my good name and had left me with nothing but the empty fame of being his son.'

This was Christopher's worst period: he was bitter, resentful, a man with a household name but no role in life. Meeting Lesley in the spring of 1948 saved him, certainly, but distanced him still further from his parents. Lesley was his first cousin on his mother's side, but Lesley's father and Christopher's mother hadn't spoken to one another for thirty years. 'Mine was a very peculiar family,' says Lesley in a matter-of-fact way. 'They were cut out of my grandfather's will because they wouldn't go into the family business. They were deprived of all their money. There was lots of falling out, lots of rows and long silences. My father became a teacher. He was lovely. My aunt wasn't.'

The cousins, Christopher and Lesley, were married in July 1948 and, soon after, set off for Devon to start a new life as booksellers. Christopher's mother, who, according to her son, 'always hit the nail on the head no matter whose fingers were in the way,' was incredulous. 'I thought you didn't like "business",' she said to him, 'And you're going to have to meet Pooh fans all the time. Really it does seem a very odd decision.'

It was an odd decision, but it worked. The marriage, the bookshop, his own eventual success as a writer (a selection of his memoirs, *Beyond the World of Pooh*, is just out in paperback), each helped him come to terms with who he was, who he had been. But he wasn't reconciled to his parents. In his father's last years he rarely saw him. 'My father's heart remained buttoned-up,' he said. After A. A. Milne's death in 1956, Mrs Milne lived on for fifteen years. In all that time, her son saw her only once.

Tentatively, I ask Lesley what she feels about her parents-in-law now?

'I didn't like them,' she says crisply. 'They weren't likeable. It's as simple as that.'

In the early years of their marriage, when they were establishing their bookshop, Christopher and Lesley struggled financially, but they remained fiercely independent, rejecting the idea of financial help from anyone. As Christopher explained to me the last time I saw him, 'To have taken a lift from my fictional namesake of all people would have been the final insult.' In time, of course, he did take the money. 'I had to accept it,' he said, with a modest smile and a shrug, 'for Clare's sake.'

Christopher told me that his chief delight in life – greater by far than any satisfaction he derived from his writing or any pleasure he got from his hobby of studying insects and caterpillars and weeds – had been using his hands to adapt and make everyday things for Clare: a chair, a tricycle, an unbreakable plate, a fork and spoon, a special egg whisk to help her make a cake. He had this fantasy that one day they might launch into business together: 'C. R. Milne & Daughter – Makers of Furniture for the Disabled'.

When I remind Lesley of this, she gives a little laugh and says, 'Well, in a roundabout way it could happen. Have I told you the news? We are going to create a special charity to help disabled people. It will be called The Clare Milne Trust. It will be launched this autumn. Isn't that marvellous? What do you think?'

I do think it is marvellous. The story has a happy ending: the Disney mega-millions that are surplus to Clare's modest everyday requirements are to go in their entirety into a fund to help others who are physically and mentally handicapped. There's a honeypot at the end of the rainbow. And down in Totnes, with the telephone answering machine back on and the front door firmly shut, is a remarkable old lady who speaks her mind, who enjoys her garden, and her glass of wine, who wants neither fame nor fortune, who doesn't want her photo in the paper ('thank you very much') or another penny in the bank, who remembers her husband for who he was and not what he was called, who loves her daughter for what she is and not what she might have been.

Richard Branson

Sir Richard Branson is a phenomenon: a self-made British billionaire. I interviewed him in February 2001.

T he last time I sat down for a two-hour conversation with Richard Branson was in August 1967. We were both teenagers then, bright-eyed boys, fresh out of school, burning with ambition. Richard was planning to launch his first venture – a magazine called *Student* – and, out of the blue, wrote to me (editor of my school magazine) inviting me to come on board. According to my diary, we met in a basement flat off the Edgware Road and got on rather well. Over a sandwich lunch, he outlined his plans to conquer the world and suggested we go into partnership. 'We'll be rich and famous,' he said. I had my doubts. I knew I could deliver, of course, but young Richard seemed to me to be all over the place. Frankly, I didn't rate his prospects, so, there and then, firmly and forever, I said, 'Thanks, but no thanks.'

Last week, three and a bit decades on, I took the Central Line to Notting Hill Gate and trudged up Campden Hill to the London headquarters of the Virgin Group, to renew my acquaintance with Richard Branson, self-confessed billionaire, knight of the realm and – according to at least seven surveys – most admired man in Britain.

He was looking good. At seventeen, he struck me as a young orang-utan on the loose. At fifty, he is cooler, calmer, apparently taller (his posture is improved), more the well-groomed king of the jungle. On 1 January this year he weighed fifteen stone. He gave up alcohol for six weeks and is exercising daily. Now he weighs thirteen and a half. Is this a response to a mid-life crisis? 'No, I just wanted to get in shape. On Friday, I was due at the BBC in White City, but the taxi didn't arrive so I decided to run. I couldn't have done that two months ago. Two people from Virgin Cars were running after me and, as we were crossing Shepherd's Bush Green, a couple of very big black guys jumped on them because they thought they were chasing me.' He laughs: the nostrils flare, the huge white teeth are bared. Is the laugh engaging or slightly sinister? I can't decide. Branson is a puzzle.

The people love him (he gives me a piece of market research, dated 26 January, to prove it), but the establishment is wary. When I was the government whip at the Department of Transport in the early 1990s at a ministerial meeting I raised the possibility of a knighthood for Branson. A senior civil servant quickly put me in my place: 'If you knew what we know you would realise that Mr Branson will never be the recipient of a knighthood.' What does Sir Richard make of this?

'It's true.' His brow is furrowed: he speaks quite softly. 'The chattering classes are suspicious of me. If you look back at the history of entrepreneurs in Britain, very few have found favour with the establishment. Publicly politicians say how much they welcome entrepreneurs, but entrepreneurs threaten the status quo. At Virgin we have tried to upset the way things are done, change the things that are done, whether that's in financial services, air industry, rail industry, soft drinks, telephone, across the board. And some people won't like that. Last week we were at the EC trying to complain about the way the car industry behaves. A lot of these companies have non-executive directors that move from one company to another. Take George

Russell as an example. He was chairman of the ITC when we bid for Channel 5. He turned us down, despite the fact that we bid the best price. At the same time he was chairman of Camelot – nothing wrong with that – but, if you look, in Britain there's quite a lot of criss-crossing that goes on between the individuals who are involved in a lot of companies we take on. We've had our run-ins with BA. You'll find the directors who are directors of BA are directors of other companies. Then you'll find some of those people end up working with the Millennium Dome.'

I have come to see Branson on behalf of the *Sunday Telegraph*, a paper that recently rejoiced in his failure to secure the National Lottery and has long been a minor thorn in the entrepreneur's flesh. (By a wide margin, the *Sunday Telegraph* rates more mentions in his autobiography than any other newspaper.) My task is to confront Sir Richard with his failures, to quiz him on his financial probity, to question the financial viability of his empire, to delve into his psyche.

It isn't easy because he is surprisingly inarticulate. He gives me complete concentration. His manner is relaxed, gregarious, unguarded. His staff gurgle and beam at me like labrador pups. The atmosphere could not be more open and encouraging. But his answers to my questions when they come and they come slowly, littered with ums and ers, sentences that trail away, long silences, even the occasional 'I've forgotten the point I was going to make, sorry' – don't give a great deal away.

We are sitting on small sofas on a raised dais at one end of his office, eating tuna salad (leaving the potato, declining the French bread), drinking sparkling water flavoured with elderflower. For much of the time Richard perches on the edge of his seat, bent forward, hugging himself tightly, gazing at the floor or his food. Now and again he gets up and rummages on his desk for a document to show me. He is looking to the future: he wants me to see the photographs of the new tilting high-speed trains that are going to transform the West Coast main line within five years. 'They will be absolutely and utterly beautiful,' he promises.

I want to start with his immediate past: the failure of the People's Lottery. Over thirty years he has ridden an extraordinary commercial roller-coaster, building up a business that now encompasses 200 companies and 40,000 employees worldwide, but, as the new millennium dawned, Branson said his over-riding ambition for the twenty-first century was to secure the running of the National Lottery. He failed. How does that feel?

'It's counter-productive to dwell on failure. I'll try very hard to succeed if I believe strongly in something, and then the moment I've failed I am quite good at moving on, and it's quite nice to be able to move on.'

But he hasn't moved on. He is still bleating about the costs of the process and who should pay them. 'As far as I'm concerned asking for the costs back is simply handing it over to the lawyers and saying write a letter, get the costs back. We want whatever is right legally. I am not tossing and turning at night on this. At the same time if you feel wrongfully done, it's important to clear it up. And I think actually even the Lottery Commission have admitted to us that they realise that they messed up and please send us in the bills and we'll seriously consider it. We haven't made a claim yet, but the chances are we will.'

We are almost into the second hour of our time together and I am getting anxious. I have forty pages of notes, but I haven't got beneath the tan, the beard, the perma-grin. He answers every question and concedes nothing. I tell him there are people who think he is a bad man. He says you cannot be successful in life unless you deal with people well. I tell him he has been accused of stashing away millions by being less than open about Virgin's finances and avoiding paying capital gains tax by channelling funds into offshore trusts. He assures me that honesty and fair-dealing in business are what pay and that he has always taken detailed legal advice. I tell him that I am troubled by his enthusiasm for grabbing people at parties, lifting them in the air and turning them upside down. 'It's to make people laugh,' he says cheerily. 'It's to encourage my staff and friends to have a good time. If you are a leader of people, you can either stand in the corner and drink sherry with your fellow directors or you can have a good time.' I tell him I have been told he has a fearsome secret temper. He smiles and denies it absolutely.

In the hope of coaxing him into a little self-revelatory introspection, I suggest we attempt an old-style business school SWOTS analysis, looking at his weaknesses and strengths, and the opportunities and threats that now face him and his businesses. He doesn't look very hopeful. 'I'm not very good at those sorts of things. Bill Gates asked me to go over to see him the other day. He invited thirty top chief executives from around the world and he asked if I would do a ten-minute presentation. Just before I stood up to do it he handed out forms to everybody and said, "I think everybody should be judged. If you wouldn't mind marking Richard one-to-ten for his presentation." I thought, "Fuck, I want to get straight on the plane and go home. This is the most strange thing I've come across."'

'What did you do?'

'Well, I had on my left the guy who runs Amazon and I said to him, "I'll mark you ten out of ten if you mark me ten out of ten." And I turned to the woman on my right . . .' He laughs. 'I'm not a great believer in that kind of approach. I think people know when they're performing well. I don't think people should be marked all the time.'

I won't be deflected. 'Your strengths?' I ask.

'Motivating people, drawing the best out of people, knowing how to praise people, realising that criticising people is counter-productive.'

There is a long pause. He is clutching himself and staring at the floor. 'I am quite good at focusing on what matters in life. I see things quite simplistically in order to compensate for mild dyslexia . . . It was only last year . . .' He hesitates. I wait. Eventually he says, 'I had sat through board meeting after board meeting not knowing the difference between net and gross and really struggling. And then, finally, last year, somebody said to me, "Now look, Richard, we know you're never quite sure whether it's good news or bad news when we give you the figures, but think of the Atlantic and think of the fish all over the ocean. If you've got fish in the net that's what you've caught – all the rest is the gross." I thought, "Fantastic. I've finally got there."'

Since silence has fallen once more, I suggest some strengths for him: physical courage, daring, an enviable capacity for taking risks, chutzpah, resilience, staying power. He doesn't respond, then he says, almost to himself, toying with a forkful of tuna: 'Quite determined. Don't like to take No for an answer. Will never give up. Three or four attempts to fly around the world in a balloon . . . Once beaten, I was happy to move on.'

What about his family? Aren't they a source of strength? Branson has some extraordinary relations. His father's father was a cousin of Scott of the Antarctic. His Uncle Jim taught the SAS how to eat – and live off – grass. At 89, his mother's mother became the oldest person in Britain to pass the advanced Latin-American ballroom-dancing examination and, aged 90, the oldest golfer to hit a hole in one. What about his parents?

'They were always praising, never criticising. My mother was determined to make us independent. When I was four years old, she stopped the car a few miles from our house and made me find my own way home across the fields.'

Branson had a comfortable middle-class upbringing, reared in Surrey, educated at Stowe. Academic work was not to his taste. He took one A Level, Ancient History, and cheated during the exam. When he left school, aged 17, his headmaster said to him, 'Congratulations, Branson. I predict you will either go to prison or become a millionaire.' Within four years the first half of the prediction was fulfilled. Branson devised a scam enabling him to export records without paying purchase tax. He was arrested and spent a night in the cells. His mother rode to the rescue and secured his bail. He negotiated a settlement with Customs & Excise and avoided a criminal record. On the way home, his mother said to him, 'You don't have to apologise, Ricky. I know that you've learnt a lesson. Don't cry over spilt milk.'

I suggest to him that his mother is the source of his resilience, determination and ambition. He nods. 'She's quite amazing. She's 78 now. We've been fortunate in having a very close family.'

What about weaknesses?

'I suspect my biggest weakness is an inability to say No. I have to have people around me trying to hold me back. Take the Dome. I've had ideas about what to do with the Dome for some time. I've been trying to think: shall we? shan't we? But then there are only so many things you can do.'

No other weaknesses?

'Beautiful women and sticky puddings are my wife's usual complaint.'

Branson is ready to be remarkably candid about his lively love life, especially the early years. Age thirteen, he was asked to leave his prep school following nocturnal visits to the headmaster's eighteen-year-old daughter.

Three years later he lost his virginity to a nameless girl at a party. There was so much thrashing and panting on her part that Richard assumed he had inspired 'ecstatic multiple orgasms' until he discovered, after the event, that the unfortunate creature was a chronic asthmatic.

His first marriage, to a twenty-year-old American girl, Kristen Tomassi, didn't last long. According to Richard, they had 'a bizarre sexual allergy to each other. Whenever we made love, a painful rash spread across me which would take about three weeks to heal. We went to a number of doctors, but we never resolved the problem. I even had a circumcision to try to stop the reaction. Being circumcised aged twenty-four is not a good idea, particularly if the night after your operation you find yourself watching Jane Fonda's erotic film *Barbarella*.'

He met his present wife, Joan Templeman, exactly 25 years ago. 'She's a very down-to-earth Glaswegian.' What did she make of his kiss-and-tell autobiography? 'I don't think she's read it. She is busy with her friends. She has got better things to do than read about Richard Branson.' What are her passions? 'Her children. She's a wonderful mother.' The Bransons have had three children: a premature baby, Clare, who died aged four days, Sam, now 15, and at St Edward's, Oxford, and Holly, 18, on her gap year in Canada. 'It would be nice to have a young prince or princess to help promote the Virgin brand, but my daughter is off to become a doctor and I want her to do her own thing. The last time I asked Sam what he wanted to do when he grew up was three years ago. He said he wanted to climb trees and rescue cats.'

Is vanity one of his weaknesses?

'I try to defend my reputation. Reputation is one of the few things you have in life. Since I use myself to promote my businesses – whether it's for personal reasons or business reasons, I don't know – we do try to protect our reputation as best we can. Virgin as a brand is now stronger than myself. It's the most respected brand among men, the fourth most respected among women. I'm now fifty, and there's no question that the personal appeal will be less as I grow older. These days we try to get the headline "Virgin to do this" rather than "Branson to do that".'

What happens when he dies?

'Just as you arrived I was signing my will. Because of my boating and ballooning activities, I got into the frame of mind of having to plan for the future. If I am run over, we have a good team of people in place who would continue things.'

Could the Virgin empire come to an end?

'Certainly. It wouldn't be for me to decide, but empires always end up getting broken up anyway – and sometimes it's in their interests. Take the Soviet Union.'

Time is running out and we've reached Opportunities and Threats. What does the future hold for Sir Richard? Politics? The House of Lords? 'I don't think so. Unless you've got the top job in politics, you can achieve more being an international businessman and if you want to campaign on a particular issue people do not suspect your motives, but if you're a politician they do.' He claims not to have decided which way he will vote at the general election. He likes William Hague. 'If you meet him personally, he comes across very well . . . but I think from the public's point of view, if Kenneth Clarke had been there, he would have had Labour on the ropes

right now, whereas Hague somehow . . . Also one or two of the people he's
got around him . . . Widdecombe, she doesn't exactly . . .' And what about
the Blairs and the line Cherie Blair is reported to have uttered at a Downing
Street reception: 'I've been talking to Tony and we agree that we must do
something for you'? Mrs Blair has subsequently denied saying it and
Branson has no recollection of hearing it.

What about the threats? He is no stranger to debt mountains. He has
been close to the wire time and again. In the city some liken him to a
whirling dervish spinning a bucketful of manure above his head: as long as
he keeps spinning at sufficient velocity the manure stays in the bucket.
Rumour has it that a number of his businesses are dangerously over-
extended. Is that true? 'That's been said for about thirty years. I'm not
somebody who believes in money sitting on deposit in bank accounts.
When I make money I reinvest it straight away into new ventures. We're
Britain's largest group of private companies. Last year we turned over
around £3 billion. In three years' time I expect that to be six billion. Around
the world, we have some two hundred companies. Are they all profitable?
No. Those that have been going for more than two years are.'

Is another threat that he might lose interest? 'Yes, that is a danger.' For a
moment, he looks directly at me and suddenly seems utterly exhausted.
Have I glimpsed the future? Is the man who once boasted that he lived on
havoc and adrenaline going to throw in the towel? Within five years will we
see Richard Bowker (mark the name), 34, Branson's new blue-eyed boy and
Virgin Group Commercial Director, taking the helm? No, I am imagining
things. Almost at once Richard rallies and remembers why he is giving me
an audience. 'Virgin is so full of variety and I've still got quite big business
challenges to complete.' He has the world to conquer yet. 'I spend 250 days
a year abroad. In America, in South Africa, in Australia, Singapore, Japan,
in most European countries, we're developing a number of companies. I'd
love it if ten years from now Virgin could be the most respected brand
globally – not the biggest, but the most respected.'

Why does he keep pushing himself? What's the point? 'We're here to test ourselves and those around us. See what you can create with what you've got. Aspire for the best. No point in being second best.' Does he have a maxim, a motto he lives by? 'Yes. Nothing ventured, nothing gained.' And a final word? 'Yes, Gyles. Goodbye. And see you again in thirty years.' He is laughing. I still can't decide if the laugh is engaging or slightly sinister.

Richard Whiteley

Richard Whiteley is a bizarre phenomenon: the man who has made more
appearances on British television than any other. I first met him when
Countdown *was launched in November 1982. I interviewed him in October*
2000.

I have only one piece of advice to offer parliamentary candidates in the
run-up to a general election. When out canvassing, don't knock on
any doors between 4.30 and 5.00 in the afternoon. That's when Middle
Britain is watching *Countdown* and does not wish to be disturbed.

If you've not heard of *Countdown* I'm surprised. It's a broadcasting
phenomenon: the first, and most consistently popular, programme on
Channel Four, a simple words and numbers game (imported from France)
that attracts a daily audience of four million and, over eighteen years, has
transformed its amiable host, Richard Whiteley (56, 5´ 9″ ins, 14½ stone)
from a regional news presenter into the unlikeliest cult figure of our time.

Whiteley – trademarks: loud jackets, louder ties, appalling puns;
previous claim to fame: being attacked in the studio by a ferret – is an old
chum. Over the years I have been a regular guest in *Countdown*'s

'Dictionary Corner'. More than once, in the early days, I said to Carol Vorderman – then, as now, the numbers guru on the show – '*Countdown* is perfect for Richard. He's a provincial presenter going nowhere. But a bright girl like you shouldn't be in television. It's a terrible cul-de-sac. You must make something of your life. Get out while you can.'

Richard and I are chuckling over the quality of my career counselling, mulling over old times, taking tea, and scoffing roast beef sandwiches. We have got together to celebrate the publication of his autobiography. It isn't out until next week, but already a reprint looks likely. A raft of men's magazines – *FHM*, *Maxim*, *Loaded* – are running profiles of the TV tea-time idol. He has been honoured by *The Oldie* ('Most Inexplicable Survivor'), *Woman's Own* are giving him a make-over, *The Lady* are inducting him to their hall of fame. Bunter-like, Richard is blinking at me from behind his giglamps and beaming from ear to ear. 'Students watch *Countdown*. Grannies watch *Countdown*. When I met Princess Margaret she said, "I do believe my sister watches it after the racing." I thought, "Who's her sister?" Then I realised. She meant the Queen.'

Why is the programme so popular?

Richard chortles: 'It can't just be me, with my adenoidal voice and nasal twang. I'm hardly an oil painting. No, people watch because they like to play the game. It's a habit, like doing the crossword. But more than that, I think it's a point of security in an uncertain world. Nobody knows where they are any more. It's not *News at Ten*, it's *News at When?*. But there's one thing in this life you can be sure of: on Channel Four at half-past four, come what may, you will find me and Carol waiting for you. I sometimes think we're the Wilfred and Mabel Pickles of our day. Wilfred Pickles came from Yorkshire too, you know.'

Yorkshire, nostalgia, innocence, the security of known relationships – these, I reckon, are the keys to Richard Whiteley (whose own all-time favourite TV programme, unsurprisingly, is *Upstairs Downstairs*). Richard was born on 28 December 1943, Innocents' Day, at the Duke of York's

Nursing Home, Bradford. 'My parents met at Heaton Tennis Club. My mother was a hairdresser. My father was the third generation of Thomas Whiteley & Co, worsted manufacturers of Eccles Hill, Bradford. We made cloth for quality women's suiting. Whiteley's mill chimney was the highest point in Bradord.' As he says this, Richard's mouth is full of sandwich, but his eyes are shining. 'Once upon a time Bradford was the centre of the world for textiles. By the time I came along business wasn't so good. I followed my father to Giggleswick, but paying the school fees was quite a struggle.'

Giggleswick is Yorkshire's second oldest public school, founded in 1512. 'I love the place. I loved it as a child. I love it now as a governor. When I went I was thirteen, the youngest boy in the school and quite apprehensive. I had asthma and dreaded what would happen if I had one of my attacks in the middle of the night. I can picture the dormitory now: the iron bedstead, the bit of carpet on the floor, the jerry cans under the beds which we emptied in the morning. I remember the night that a bat flew in the window and was drowned in one of the pots.

'The chapel was the place I loved most of all. You felt quite close to God there. I loved the full-throated singing of the boys, and I can still hear the powerful voice of our headmaster, Mr Benson, reading the lesson or giving the blessing. The memory of it fills me with awe. At the end of term we always had a special service. The chapel was in darkness, lit by just two candles. We came in to the Londonderry Air. We sang "O God our help in ages past". There was the Magnificat by Harwood, Psalm 121 ("Praise Him in His noble acts"), a reading from Ecclesiastes ("Cast thy bread upon the waters") and then "Lord dismiss us with thy blessing." That's the service I want when I die.

'As a boy I loved the idea of religion. It wasn't a million miles away from my thoughts to become a clergyman. I am a believer. I say my prayers regularly, every night, in bed, before I go to sleep. Praying is important.'

'Is it easy?' I ask.

'You can get leaflets, you know, to help you pray. The only time I found praying difficult was when my sister, Helen, was ill. She died of liver cancer, four years ago, when she was forty-nine. I have dedicated my book to her memory. I miss her so much.'

Richard blows his nose and takes another bite of sandwich. 'Yes, I like knowing where I am, I like closed communities, I like being in a safe world. When I got to Cambridge I liked it at night when the college gates were closed and we were shut in, safe and sound.'

By the time Richard emerged from Cambridge (he edited *Varsity* and got a Third), he had abandoned all thoughts of the church and was set on a career in broadcasting. 'As a teenager I was obsessed with television. In chapel I would pretend it was an outside broadcast and work out the best camera angles. I waited for Friday for the *Radio Times* to come out. I bought the *BBC Year Book* and learnt who did what.' He begins to recite the names and job titles of BBC executives, circa 1965. 'I wanted to be a BBC trainee, I wanted to be editor of *Panorama* and then head of current affairs. Unfortunately, at Cambridge I discovered every third person wanted to be a BBC trainee.' He went instead to ITN and then, aged 24, to Yorkshire TV in Leeds. He has been there ever since. 'I love everything about Yorkshire. Just seeing the word Leeds on the motorway fills me with pride.'

For 27 years he presented YTV's early evening news programme. 'I was happy being Mr Yorkshire. I didn't think I wanted anything more of life. And then along came *Countdown*, quite by channe of the executives had seen it in France and bought it for a summer try-out. We had Ted Moult with the dictionary and a girl doing the sums who couldn't add up. I think we only had eight letters to begin with and the clock ran for forty-five seconds. It was low-tech and very slow, but it got an amazing reaction from the audience. We sharpened it up, brought in Carol, sold it to Channel Four, and here we are, eighteen years on.'

The sustained success of *Countdown* has brought Whiteley fame and fortune. He earns several hundred thousand a year. He has featured on *This is Your Life* and *Have I Got News For You*. His chat-show was a sell-out at the

Edinburgh Festival last year. He is about to embark on a nationwide tour of British universities.

Why is he so popular with student audiences? 'I've no idea.' Could they be sending him up? 'Possibly, but they seem to like me.' I am sure they do. Richard may have the soul of Alan Partridge and the wit of Nicholas Parsons, but he also has the warmth of Fozzie Bear – and the reputation of Errol Flynn.

'Now, don't start that, Gyles. Once upon a time it might have been twice-nightly-Whiteley, but now it's once-yearly-nearly.'

Sex does not feature in his conversation or his book. 'I'm a tea-time presenter. Sex starts after the watershed. People ask about me and Carol. Well, the closest it got was when I discovered there was a hole in the wall between her dressing room and mine. I was tempted to report it to studio security, but I thought, "To hell with it, let her look."'

He chuckles at this sally. He looks less happy when I press him to talk about his private life. 'I was married once, when I was twenty-eight, to an interior designer from Harrogate. She was incredibly beautiful. When she came into the canteen heads would turn. It lasted two years. When we split up, I wore a black tie on television for a whole year. Nobody noticed. Since then I have had a series of very understanding partners.' I have known at least four of Richard's girlfriends and found them to be intelligent, attractive, likeable, long-suffering. His current partner is Kathryn Apanovich, forty, one of the presenters of *Live Talk* on ITV. She does not feature in the index of his memoirs.

When I suggest to Richard that perhaps he has a problem with commitment, he looks at me blankly. When I ask him about his love-child, he blinks. He leans forward. He furrows his brow. Interviewing a friend isn't easy. 'It's a fact that I have a thirteen-year-old son called James. I am very proud of him. He lives in London with his mother. We speak on the telephone about twice a week. I see him when I can.'

Does Richard feel he has fulfilled his potential? 'I haven't built anything,

I haven't created anything, I haven't improved anyone, but I think I've used my gifts very well indeed. I dumb down to make Carol look good.'

Does he still have ambitions? 'Well, I have appeared on television 10,000 times, more than anyone else, and I haven't yet won an award. And I would like to be invited to David Frost's summer party. He's my hero, you know.'

My friend is looking twitchy. I am thinking that I may have touched too many raw nerves, then I see him glance at his watch and the penny drops. It is just on five o'clock. We have talked right through *Countdown*. There is a television in the room and we haven't switched it on. 'Never mind.' He pops a last bite of sandwich into his mouth. 'I can catch it at 5.30 in the morning. It's repeated then, you know. Chinese waiters all watch the early morning edition. One of them told me it's the prostitutes' favourite programme.'

'Do you watch it whenever you can?'

'Oh yes, at four-thirty in the afternoon: a cup of tea, a KitKat and *Countdown*. Who could ask for anything more?'

Foreign Assignments...

Walter Cronkite

At the end of 1999, I was sent to New York to interview the twentieth century's most celebrated newsman, Walter Cronkite.

'Jeez, you're meeting Walter Cronkite? I don't believe it. Uncle Walter, man, whoa!' My cab driver spoke for the American people. I was in New York, on West 52nd Street, on my way to meet a national hero. In my time I have been privileged to walk with princes, presidents, prime ministers, but this was something else. This was a world exclusive: the pre-millennial audience with the one and only Walter Cronkite, broadcasting legend and, according to opinion polls across four decades, 'the most trusted man in America'.

Mr Cronkite is a reporter. For thirty years he was the face of CBS News, for twenty he presented the United States' most watched television news programme, signing off each night with a phrase he made his own: 'And that's the way it is.' He was the original 'anchorman' – the word was coined for him – but Cronkite didn't simply read the news: somehow he made you understand how you should feel about it as well. He has received more awards than any broadcaster in history (many more), he was the first newsman to be honoured with the Presidential Medal of Freedom. Roll together the reputations of the Queen Mother, Sir Trevor McDonald and the late Richard Dimbleby and you begin, just, to get a measure of the reverence in which this man is held.

I emerged on the nineteenth floor of the CBS building, home of 'The Cronkite Unit'. The great man is 83 now, it is eighteen years since he last presented the evening news, but the fan mail still pours in and a staff of five are in attendance. 'Does he really need all this?' I asked one of the assistants. She looked at me quite dewy-eyed: 'With someone of Mr Cronkite's integrity, standing and stature, you can't let things drop, you simply can't.' Clearly this was the Emerald City and I was Dorothy on my way to meet the mighty Oz.

'Mr Cronkite will see you now.'

And, suddenly, there he was – the man who broke the news of Kennedy's assassination – and, of course, he wasn't terrifying at all. Seated behind his desk, sucking a throat lozenge, he was Bert Lahr as the Cowardly Lion: avuncular, benign, twinkly, almost bashful: 'Oh, for gosh sakes, come in, have you been kept waiting?' He was eager to please and happy to help. He swallowed the lozenge. 'Now, my friend, what's the plan?'

I volunteered my bright idea: 'You've interviewed everyone from Harry Truman to Frank Sinatra, there's a Walter Cronkite School of Journalism at Arizona State University, so I thought maybe you – the great reporter – could tell me – the English novice – how I should do the interview.'

'Oh, for goodness sakes,' he laughed. 'What are you looking for?'

'Your take on the news that made the twentieth century.'

'Okay.' The great reporter took a sip of water, cleared his throat and turned his head towards my microphone. 'Let's go. I was born in 1916, in the week President Woodrow Wilson was elected, the week of the Battle of the Somme.'

'When did you know you were destined to become a newsman?'

'At the age of six I went running down the hill through our Kansas City neighbourhood to spread the news of President Harding's death. And three years later, I started peddling the *Kansas City Star*, so I guess that's when I knew the die was cast. My mother was horrified and frightened, as I suppose many mothers have been, or should have been, when their children got into newspapering. A year later we moved to Houston, Texas, and at high school I began interviewing my schoolmates and, when I was alone, I would imitate the radio announcers I most admired. I landed the job as sports editor for the *Campus Cub* and discovered the sacred covenant between newspaper people and their readers. We journalists had to be right and we had to be fair.'

'Do we need something about your family?'

'Just a line. My father was a dentist and an alcoholic. My mother was a good and gracious lady who lived to be 102.'

'Should we have some anecdotes about them?'

'Not here. You know, this is for a British audience, so around now we should get to England, don't you think?'

'Of course. What brought you to England?'

'The war. I dropped out of college to work for the Hearst News Service in Austin. I did my apprenticeship on the *Houston Press*. I learnt the basic rules of news: get the stories fast, get them accurate. I joined the United Press wire service and, when the war came, in September 1939, I was summoned to the foreign desk in New York, and sent on to London via Glasgow.

'The British Isles took some getting used to. My first day I was shocked to see the headline in the *Glasgow Herald*, "Knockers-up on Strike". I didn't know that few British labourers had alarm clocks, so factories and mines employed people to go and wake them up in the morning.

'England was so damp and cold. Wartime scarcities severely limited the menu and, let's face it, British cooking was never one of the world's great accomplishments. I remember, in London, there was a large brick building in the West End that called itself "Mrs Bradford's School of Cookery". I maintained it was the only four-storey structure in the world dedicated to the art of boiling.

'The blackout was total, accentuated by the smog – the natural fog off the Thames thickened by the heavy coal smoke that hung over the city. The girl conductors on the buses, the clippies, had a special job. They walked in front of the buses, guiding them along the street by flashlight.

'As we males made our way down Piccadilly in the impenetrable darkness we would hear the clicks of heels announce the arrival of a lady of the night. Wearing cheap perfume, she would run her hand along our pants leg. This might have seemed the opening to a street corner mating dance. Wrong. This was economic foreplay. By feeling the pants' cloth, the ladies could tell whether the male concerned was in the American or British Army and was an officer or an enlisted man. On that determination hung the price at which she would open the bidding.

'This was the environment into which the cream of American youth was plunged. Too many assumed that what they experienced was typical of England, just as the English assumed that the behaviour of tens of thousands of young men, barely out of adolescence, uprooted from home and family, was typical of American manhood. It's too bad that the GIs, restricted most of the time to their fully Americanised bases, had such little opportunity to observe the strength of the British people.

'In my view, Britain stood against the Germans not because of its military, which was ill-prepared, ill-supplied and too often ill-led, but because of the unyielding strength of British civilians. They suffered with unbelievable stoicism the Luftwaffe's terrible bombing. Never before in history have any people so patriotically accepted economic dictation as did the British in responding to rationing. Of course, there was a black market, but it was so despised that those who dealt on it, even for the most modest supplies, were shunned by friends and neighbours.

'Luxuries were few and far between. I remember, after D-Day, coming back to London from Normandy with my musette bag loaded with some of

Normandy's famed Camembert cheese. At that time, the trademark of an officer returning to London from the front was unmistakeable: the heady odour of Camembert.'

'So, in the twentieth century, the Second World War represents Britain's finest hour?'

'Without question. And Churchill her greatest leader.'

'Did you enjoy the war?'

'Well, put it this way: the most miserable twenty-four hours I ever spent was riding an RAF coastal command flying boat on a submarine patrol along a box pattern out to Iceland and back. It was cold, the sandwiches were soggy, the coffee frigid. We dropped bombs on one suspected submarine and it turned out to be a whale.'

Mr Cronkite has a soft spot for heroes (he has a bust of Churchill on his shelves), but no fondness for war. 'I have seen quite a bit of it. It was during the Korean war at the start of the fifties that I joined CBS News. Broadcasting has changed the conduct of war in this century. Yes, there were fine war correspondents in the nineteenth century, but their dispatches were read far after the fact. We have brought war into the homes of the populace and this has transformed the entire propaganda effort, altered the entire atmosphere of war.

'It's important that we bring the battlefield into the living room as often and as intimately as we can. Unless the people at home understand what they are sending their young people into and understand the horrors that they are having to endure, we're never going to get a handle on any serious effort to achieve world peace. Sure, it makes it difficult for governments to wage war. Whatever the truth of the matter, the Pentagon, the military bastions in Washington, still believe that in Vietnam it was the press that did them in.'

Mr Cronkite is widely credited with swinging American public opinion towards US withdrawal from Vietnam. In 1968, following a trip to the war zone, Cronkite concluded a special report on the Tet offensive with a personal editorial: 'It is increasingly clear to this reporter that the only rational way out will be to negotiate, not as victors, but as an honourable people . . .' It was as if, said *Newsweek*, 'Lincoln himself had ambled down from his memorial and joined an anti-war demonstration.' Watching the broadcast in the White House, President Johnson turned to one of his staff and said, 'If I've lost Cronkite, I've lost middle America.'

Was that Mr Cronkite's finest hour?

'No. It was a unique effort on my part – perhaps egotistically, believing that people did watch and believe in our broadcasts – to try to throw a little light on a terribly clouded and difficult situation. I don't think we caused President Johnson not to run again, but I think we were another light straw on the very heavy load he was carrying on his back. I do not believe the government should ever operate in the dark, even in wartime.

'You know, the Pentagon was electrified and heartened in 1982 by the conduct of the Falklands War by Margaret Thatcher. The British forces severely limited reporters' access, kept TV cameras away from the fighting, censored dispatches, provided poor communications facilities and, on occasion, misled newsmen. And Thatcher got away with it.'

'But she would have said your kind of reporting could have sent out negative signals, damaged morale, jeopardised the mission.'

'I think that's probably true. There is a conflict, definitely, between government objectives – I'm not saying democratic objectives, government objectives – and what the people should know. Mrs Thatcher's handling of the Falklands conflict may help explain what happened a year later, when her fawning admirer President Reagan decided that Fidel Castro's Cuban Communists had gone too far on the island of Grenada. The American tradition of giving journalists open access to the battlefield, a tradition at least a century and a half old, came to an abrupt end. When the US forces landed on Grenada, newsmen were excluded for the first two days of the operation, until it was virtually over.

'I believe in censorship. You can't reveal size of troops, disposition of troops, and so on, and expect to conduct a successful war effort, but all these things should still be covered, reporters should be there, cameramen should be there, so an historical record is available. We have no impartial record of the Persian Gulf effort, the press was totally limited in covering that war by the military. That's not right. People must know how troops behave in their name.

'We seem to forget that the German people gave away their rights to innocence when they applauded Hitler's clamping down on the press and broadcasting. At that point they became guilty of anything Hitler did in their name.'

President Kennedy thought Cronkite was a closet Republican. Nixon assumed he was a Democrat. All his professional life Mr Cronkite has been careful to remain way, way above party politics, but, talking to him, it is clear that he is a tender-hearted liberal who got away with it because he looks like a middle American conservative.

My time is up. 'What should the last question be?'

'Don't ask me what I hope to be remembered for. Let's avoid the clichés. We want to keep it to the theme, but finish with something from the heart, yes?'

'Yes. How do you rate this century against those that have gone before?'

'Good question. This has been the best century in the improvement of people's living standards around the world, particularly those of the developed nations, and we have seen the slow, if much too slow, spread of that improvement into other areas of the globe.

'The disappointment to me, as I get ready to leave this existence, is that I don't see any real improvement in our basic philosophy. We call ourselves civilised and yet we still believe that the way to settle our arguments is to kill each other. We're really the least developed of all the animals in that regard. Other animals don't plot to kill. They kill for survival. But we plot destruction, we plan it, we build the weapons to accomplish it. How can we call ourselves civilised when that's the best we can do? If we spent the three hundred billion dollars a year that we spend on weapons on peace instead, couldn't we achieve it? What's wrong with us? I just don't understand what's wrong.'

'Mr Cronkite, the United States is the century's most successful country and you are arguably its most respected citizen, and we're ending the interview on a pessimistic note. Is that right?'

The legend smiled and shrugged and said, 'That's the way it is.'

The event of the century

I asked Mr Cronkite to name the most significant event of the twentieth century.

'Man's landing on the moon. Definitely. Without a question of a doubt.'

'You put the lunar landing ahead of the discovery of penicillin, contraception, the computer—'

'Or even the splitting of the atom, yes, for heaven's sakes. The development of vaccines, the X-ray, all the rest, fall in some way behind. Of course, the advent of the birth control pill has changed the whole societal relationship between the genders and helped to elevate women to an equal role with men, but the landing on the moon is in a different league – not because I was there to report it, but because it marks man's first escape from his environment on earth. One of the few dates the modern American child knows is 12 October 1492, the day Columbus landed in the new world. One day people will be living on other moons, flitting about at the speed of light, and they will look back to a time they can barely imagine when three men climbed into a funny little vehicle they called a spaceship and took almost four days to reach their destination. Five hundred years from now the one year of our century that will be memorised by schoolchildren – if they are still going to school, they may be getting their education by osmosis, who knows? – but the one year they'll know is 1969, when man first walked on the moon.'

Royalty

I asked Mr Cronkite about his encounters with royalty.

'Towards the end of the war, King George paid his first visit to British troops on the Continent, a brief sortie of a few hours. The British army named a pool of correspondents to cover the royal arrival at Eindhoven Airport and I was the American representative. I was wearing an airborne combat outfit. I was rather proud of my combat boots, my pants legs tucked into them in best paratrooper fashion. Before we were escorted to the airport, Montgomery's press aide, a Brigadier Neville, came into the press room. He was a complete caricature. He carried a riding crop that he whipped at his boots as he walked, as if to urge himself along.

'"Pool correspondents," he announced, "Attention! Inspection!"

'Ridiculous, pompous, unprecedented orders to a gaggle of civilian correspondents, but the subservient British press marched forward. I slouched after them. They passed Neville's inspection. I did not. He looked with particular disfavour on my boots. "Get this man a pair of gaiters," he ordered.

'"Brigadier Neville," I said, "we Americans dumped a helluva lot of tea into Boston Harbour in 1773 to avoid wearing those gaiters and I'm not about to start now." It may have been my finest hour. The British Empire wilted before my determination and I met the King in my good American combat boots.

'When I covered the coronation of Queen Elizabeth it was the most watched event in history. The challenge was to transport the BBC's television coverage across the Atlantic as quickly as possible. We set up a studio and production centre in an abandoned tower at London airport and had two rapid film developers that could take pictures off the television tube and deliver them in just fifty seconds, and we had a commentary booth so that I could inject an American angle to the story. The idea was to fly the film across the Atlantic in a Canberra bomber. Unfortunately, the pilot took the reels out of their cans so that he could fit them into the tiny cockpit. At the other end, the engineers had no idea which reel was which. They just grabbed one reel and slapped ii on the air. It just happened to be the reel of the coronation ceremony itself. The other networks started as the Queen's day began. By sheer fluke, we showed the coronation first. That's how scoops are made.

'Much later, in the 1960s, I became quite friendly with the Duke of Edinburgh. He appeared to me to be highly capable, charismatic, a man denied a chance at real leadership because of his curious role as consort to the Queen.'

Assessing the presidents

Which US presidents will be remembered one hundred years from now?

'The wartime presidents, Wilson and FDR. One of the reasons we remember wartime presidents is that so much of the democratic procedure is suspended in wartime. They can act on their own initiative, do more or less as they please.

'I wouldn't want to put the presidents I've known in a particular order. Any of us close to power see the clay feet. I remember Truman for his courage and his cocky certainty that he was right. Eisenhower said his intention was to calm the nation down and he succeeded. He said his plan was to do nothing, literally nothing, to let the war wounds settle. He could not utter a single sentence that parsed, but you knew what he meant and he meant well.

'Cut short as it was, the Kennedy presidency has left little that's noteworthy for the history books, but Jack's charm, his style and his rhetoric captured the imagination of a generation of Americans to a degree unmatched by any other occupant of the White House this century, even including the Roosevelts, Franklin and Theodore. And, yes, he showed courage in the missile crisis in 1962 when we didn't know how that would come out.

'An image that will always live with me is that of the newly-sworn-in president and his beautiful First Lady sitting in the back of their open limousine as it pulled away from the Capitol for the parade back to the White House. I was at the microphone in an open car immediately in front of them. The President tilted his top hat toward me and Jackie gave me a wave and a dazzling smile. I have thought since how similar the scene must have been to the one in the open car just before it passed the Texas Book Depository in Dallas not three years later.

'Lyndon Johnson lived up to that bromide that he was bigger than life. He really was. Hard to describe, he was hard to live with. The first time he came for an interview, he produced a sheaf of papers from his pocket. "Boys, here are the questions you'll ask me." I explained that we didn't use prearranged questions. "That's all right with me," he said, and he took back the papers and walked right out the door. His achievement as President was to get the civil rights legislation through Congress. I don't think Kennedy could have done that.

'I got along rather well with Nixon. He was stiff, uncomfortable, totally incapable of even halfway sensible small talk, and we all know that he had a psychological problem, no question, but he showed amazing political courage in following Kissinger's lead and opening up China. He studied foreign policy, more than any other president at least in the second half of the century. Gerald Ford, who succeeded him, was a nice man who played a good game of golf.

'Now this may surprise you, of all the presidents I have known since Herbert Hoover, the best brain was possessed by Jimmy Carter. His accomplishments were few, but his mind was remarkable. He had an incredible ability to absorb knowledge, filing it away, almost like a computer, except he was more reliable than most computers. You could just punch a button and he could recite any number of facts and figures. His presidency was a failure because he lived up to his campaign promise. He said he'd turn his back on Washington. Well, you can't turn your back on Washington and run the federal government. His liaison with Congress was virtually nil.

'Reagan had a personality that could sell almost anything. As a matter of fact, that was his original role in life: he was a commercial announcer for television and he became the commercial announcer for the set of beliefs of the people who surrounded him and put him in the presidency – and they did a great job of what they intended to do, which was to dismantle the New Deal. They won the plaudits of their part of the population in doing so.

'Every visitor to the Oval Office left impressed with the Reagan modus operandi. Before answering questions or introducing new topics, he slid his top desk drawer open just enough to read from a set of pre-prepared cards. But, by golly, he was affable. After our last interview, when I'd announced I was stepping down from the CBS *Evening News*, he invited me into the Oval Office with some of his key people. We had cake and champagne and spent two hours in an hilarious exchange of stories – most of them dirty.

'The problem for President Bush was that his party affiliations prevented him from acting as his heart would have wanted to. His instincts were liberal, but he was forced into positions on the Right. And that brings us up to Bill Clinton, who we've had now for almost eight years – an extraordinary individual. The moral burden he has carried will ensure that he is an asterisk in history – there for ever, for that reason alone.'

The giants of the twentieth century

'Who are the giants of the century? Mao Tse Tung. Lenin. Not Stalin. Not Hitler. There was a diabolical single-mindedness about Hitler, but I don't think that makes him interesting as a world leader. I would have liked to interview Hitler, not because there is any great mystery to him, but to confront him with all that he was responsible for.

'After the war, I covered the Nuremberg trials. Day after day, I sat gazing at the Nazi high command, twenty-one of the archvillains of our time, or perhaps of any time. I wanted to spit on them. I don't recall that it had ever occurred to me to want to spit on anyone before, but this was what I wanted to do. Hermann Goering, second only to Hitler, was on the stand for nine days, displaying all the arrogance with which he had once set out to rule the world. He calculated that the tribunal and subsequent historians would not tamper with the transcripts of the proceedings, so he laid out in exquisite detail the Nazi philosophy and programme.

'And the good people of our time? Gandhi. Mandela. Both of them in different ways symbolic of the century's changing attitude to race. When I was at school I knew a black delivery boy called Louis who was sent to deliver a quart of ice cream to a distant address. He went along a back alley in a white neighbourhood to reach the customer's back door. As he passed between the houses, the customer's next-door neighbour killed him with a single shotgun blast. The neighbour said the boy was a peeping tom. The police accepted that and the neighbour was never charged. In those days, no white was ever indicted for assaulting, or even killing, a black.

'Well, in the last half of this twentieth century, what we have done to begin to achieve equality between the races has been positive. We haven't gotten there yet by any means, but we are much further ahead than we were. That said, here in the US, there has been an interesting and disturbing development just lately: resegregation by the blacks themselves. As the blacks come into the middle class, they are finding they would rather live in their own communities than to continue to fight their way to social equality in the white communities.'

Sheikh Mohammed

In March 2000 I travelled to Dubai to meet one of the world's most successful racehorse owners and, I reckon, one of the world's most remarkable leaders.

His Highness General Sheikh Mohammed Bin Raschid Al Maktoum, Crown Prince of Dubai, and one of the richest men in the world, is staring fixedly at me with his big brown eyes. He speaks softly, calmly, with a definite Omar Sharif accent, and a quiet authority that brooks no argument. 'Horseracing is one per cent of my life. One per cent. At most. This is the truth.'

If Your Highness says so, one per cent, of course, but it's hard to believe all the same, given the awesome global impact the Sheikh and his brothers have had on racing in recent years. They own, breed, and run hundreds of the finest horses in the world. Since 1994, when Balanchine became the first non-European trained Classic winner, taking the Oaks and then beating the colts in the Irish Derby, the Maktoum family's private stable – named Godolphin after one of the three founding stallions of the modern thoroughbred – has annexed fifty-five Group One races around the world. The Maktoums have poured millions – some say £1 billion plus – into their hobby and reaped the rewards. Over several continents people are employed simply to collect and catalogue their trophies. At the Nad al Sheba racetrack in Dubai they have opened an elegant museum to celebrate their triumphs. (Their favourite jockey Frankie Dettori's signature was in the Visitors' Book just above mine. Alongside his autograph he'd written: 'Come on me!')

Inevitably, not everyone is comfortable with the Maktoums'contribution to the Sport of Kings. These chaps are a bunch of Bedouin tribesmen after all. They come from a country not much bigger than Kent. Some say their oil-gotten gains have distorted the market by pushing up prices artificially. Even the Queen Mother is reported to have reservations about 'all this Arab gold'. Sheikh Mohammed is unconcerned. He will not be riled or provoked. He believes Godolphin's success is about much more than cash. 'It is about quality – of horses, training, facilities, people, leadership. You cannot buy enthusiasm, you cannot buy loyalty. You cannot buy the devotion of hearts, minds, or souls. You must earn these.' He takes satisfaction that what began as 'an experiment' little more than a decade ago has evolved into 'the world's most potent racing force'. People said it couldn't be done. They wouldn't believe that horses wintering in Dubai, bred and trained by outsiders, could conquer the world. 'One of life's greatest pleasures is doing what others think you cannot do.'

The Sheikh is prone to gnomic utterances. 'Stride on, and the world will make way for you.' 'Every obstacle is a stepping stone to your success.' 'You don't fail when you fall. You fail when you refuse to get up.' Ask him for the thinking behind his decision to move part of his breeding operation from Britain to France and he says, with a smile: 'Unless you try to do something beyond what you have already mastered, you will never grow. In the race for excellence, there is no finish line. I want the best for my people. We go for good prize money. It is important. Not for me, I do not need it, but for others, for the stable lads. Where will you find the world's richest race meeting? Yes, here in Dubai, next Saturday.'

I am talking to His Highness in his principal palace on the outskirts of the city, not far from the racecourse. I am honoured and surprised to be with him. Before I set off for Dubai I went to see an old Gulf hand who explained the pecking order within the Maktoum family. 'They're all descended from Maktoum Bin Butti who settled the area with about eight hundred tribesmen in the 1830s. Mohammed is the third of the four brothers, but he's the one who counts. He's the one to see. He runs the show. He's fifty. The oldest is Maktoum, he's the Ruler, but he's a figurehead, he's not really interested in the job. He's smitten with his new Morroccan wife. Then comes Hamdan, who's Deputy Ruler. He's got various government jobs, but his real passion is the horses. And the youngest is Ahmed. What can you say about him? He eats, he sleeps. He looks good in a uniform, but that's about it. He's not even interested in horses.'

When I arrived in Dubai I understood I was to see Sheikh Mohammed right away. In fact, my first encounter was with His Excellency Dr Khalifa Mohammed Ahmed Sulaiman, 'Director of His Highness the Ruler's Court' and former ambassador in London: 'Sheikh Mohammed will see you, but I cannot say when. You must remember we have a different perception of time. I was born in 1950 or 1951, but I do not know when. In those days in this country we had nothing, literally nothing, no records, no papers, no paper. We did not write. We had no schools, no electricity, no roads. We had no watches, no clocks. Perhaps there was a clock in the mosque, but nowhere else. We had no concept of time as you have it. If someone said, "I will see you this evening", it simply meant that they would see you some hours later. I hope His Highness will see you before sunset.'

In the event, it was thirty-six hours later that the call came. And even as I was swept towards the palace (Intercontinental Hotel meets Buckingham Palace with a pleasing touch of Ali Baba), past the sentry posts, past the gorgeous peacocks and floodlit fountains, I was warned that the meeting might still not take place. 'The American astronaut Buzz Aldrin came to see the Sheikh. We were assured His Highness was ready and waiting, but when we walked into the room His Highness had disappeared. We were told, "His Highness has gone to catch the bustard." Mr Aldrin was quite confused. He did not appreciate that it is a tradition that each October the Sheikh must capture the first bustard seen in the desert sky.'

The court of Sheikh Mohammed is a bizarre blend of ancient and modern. There he stands at the top of the stairs, surrounded by twenty or thirty courtiers, a true Arabian prince, tall, dark, handsome, in traditional dress, mobile phone in hand, ready to extol the virtues of modern Dubai, 'the communications and commercial hub of the Gulf'.

As I approach, the sea of courtiers parts. I bow, he shakes my hand and leads me through to a drawing room the size of a tennis court. He indicates the sofa where I am to sit. Arabic coffee is served. I begin to tell him how wonderful Dubai appears to be. He says nothing. I tell him how wonderful he appears to be. Still he says nothing. I am thinking this is going to be an impossible interview, when a servant steps forward and collects our coffee cups. The Sheikh smiles: 'We Arabs do not talk until we have finished our coffee.'

Throughout our meeting, which lasts two hours, courtiers come and go, messengers approach and retreat: sometimes he receives them, hears what they have to say, takes a document from them, sometimes he raises a hand and silently they back away. I feel I am in a scene from one of Shakespeare's history plays: 'My liege, I bring news from France!'

The Sheikh is seeing me because he wants Western readers to know about modern Dubai – sunny, civilised, sophisticated, a place to invest, a place to visit. They don't eat sheep's eyes, they don't cut off people's hands, you can dress as you please and they happily serve you alcohol. I am seeing him because it is clear that he is an unusual man. Everywhere I have been they talk about him. He is revered. The managing director of the Internet City project (designed to make Dubai the e-commerce capital of the Middle East) is positively dewy-eyed: 'He is a real leader. He is there for me twenty-four hours a day. I can call him on his mobile anytime. You fall in love with your leader and you work hard. He pushes you to be creative. He is a simple man. You see him in a shopping mall, walking by himself. He is one of us, but he is a hero too. He rides 160 miles on horseback in endurances races. He is amazing.' (Incredibly, this appears to be a universal verdict. The population of Dubai runs at around a million, of whom only twenty per cent are native Dubaians, the rest expatriates, mostly workers from the Indian subcontinent. Everyone I quizzed, from the Home Counties MD of the Dubai Dry Docks to a gaggle of Filipino housemaids, spoke of Mohammed with admiration tinged with awe.)

I say to the Sheikh, 'Clearly you are a good leader.'

'I do not know if I am a good leader, but I am a leader. And I have a vision. I look to the future, twenty, thirty years. I learnt that from my father, Sheikh Raschid. He is the true father of modern Dubai. I follow his example. He would rise early and go alone to watch what was happening on each of his projects. I do the same. I watch. I read faces. I take decisions and I move fast. Full throttle.'

It could seem absurd, except that the achievements are there to be admired. In forty years the country has progressed eight hundred. What was a sandbowl is now an oasis. Oil came on stream in 1969, but Raschid and son quickly realised it wouldn't last: it has fallen from 450,000 barrels a day to 250,000 and by 2020 will have run out. They set about diversifying, developing tourism, turning Dubai into the re-exporting, trading and service centre for the Gulf. 'What you see now is only ten per cent of what we want to do.' Drive around the city in your Rolls-Royce Silver Seraph (retail price £158,333: there is one being raffled every day this month as part of the Dubai Shopping Festival: the odds are 5000 to 1) and you see fabulous hotels, skyscrapers, golf courses burgeoning everywhere. Go out into the villages and grub around the back streets and still you see prosperity and meet contented people.

Of course, Sheikh Mohammed has the advantage in that what he says goes.

'I am running my country myself, with my people. I do not have advisers. I think they are a waste of time.' Will democracy ever come to Dubai?

'What do you want? What they have in Russia now? Or Algeria? Or Palestine? What is democracy? My people can see me whenever they want to. They come to Majlis. They tell me what they think, they give me their problems.'

Majlis is an open meeting at which any Dubaian can come and meet the Sheikhs. At the Ruler's Court I am shown the sofas where regularly, usually at lunchtime, the Sheikhs sit to receive the petitions and views of the people. A British journalist tells me he went to one Majlis and heard a man pour out his heart to the Sheikh, telling him about a bad debt that was going to ruin his business. The Sheikh reached for a newspaper, tore off a scrap and there and then wrote out a banker's draft for £10,000.

'We look after our people. We give them education, land, pensions. And we listen to our people. When the price of petrol went up, I remember all the taxi drivers came to Majlis. They stood there and they shouted at me. That is democracy. I know what my people think. All people are selfish, but a leader must not be selfish. He must put his people before himself.'

I say, 'But you and your brothers are good men. Yours is a benevolent oligarchy. But what about your sons and grandsons? How do we know your successors will be good?'

'I am the Crown Prince. I will choose my successor. It may be one of my sons or it may be someone else. I will choose.'

'But you will not give your people the vote?'

'What is democracy for? To make people happy and safe. My people are happy and they are safe.'

Well, certainly all the ones I encountered were, blissfully so, but then I didn't meet any women. I saw some.

'And you will see more,' said the Sheikh. 'Now we are educating the ladies. Every single girl now coming out of university will have a job. We are pushing women. Yes, it is late, but we have ladies in the police, in the army. You will find them at immigration and at the new stock exchange.'

'Still in the traditional dress?'

'Of course. We are not Europeans. Our tradition is different. It does not mean it is wrong or will not change.'

What about the practice of men having more than one wife? 'That is usually for a reason, to do with health or other problems.' He smiles. 'I have only one wife. She is here in the palace.'

But the Sheikha does not appear in public. With the exception of the Ruler's young Moroccan bride, the Maktoum wives and daughters are kept well under wraps.

I ask the Sheikh about the woman accused of adultery who has recently been sentenced to death by stoning. 'That is in another of the Emirates, Fujairah, and it will not happen. In Dubai we do not do this. We have had executions, but not many. There is very little crime here.'

This appears to be true. The handful of British expats I met (there are around 20,000 in all) told me they do not lock their doors at night. There was a problem with an influx of Russian prostitutes a year or two ago, but apparently the police quickly had the matter under control. Drugs are not a feature of Dubai society.

'You must have some problems here, Your Highness? Money laundering? Corruption? Bribery?'

'Some foreigners do try bribery. They think it is expected. They are wrong and we are after them. From your society we try to take only the good things.'

'Is there a free press?'

'Yes. We have laws that must be obeyed, of course, but the press can say what they like . . .' There is a pause. 'About policy. They cannot say what they like about people.' From my reading of the two English-language papers, they are cringeingly respectful of the Sheikh and his brothers. At the Ruler's Court Dr Khalifa explained, 'In Dubai we respect our leaders. When I was in England and America I saw how your media mocked Margaret Thatcher and Ronald Reagan. Is that healthy? Is that good? I think not.'

Sheikh Mohammed is evidently all-powerful. How rich is he? He won't say. According to various rich lists his net personal fortune is in the region of $12 billion, but who knows? It is impossible to untangle the Maktoum wealth from that of the state. Dubai doesn't reveal its reserves, doesn't publish a budget. Why not?

'We do not publish figures because people would discuss them. We would be restricted. This way we are flexible. We do what we believe is right.'

It also makes life a lot simpler. At the airport I met the Sheikh's uncle, head of the department of civil aviation and chairman of Emirates Airlines. 'When I need to buy a new aeroplane I go to Mohammed and tell him what I want. We go through it together carefully, but it will take no more than half an hour to take a decision to spend several million dollars. The line of command is very short and the decision-making process very simple.'

Sheikh Mohammed has eleven children and a twelfth is rumoured to be on the way. How does he ensure that his offspring are not spoiled? 'I was not spoiled. When I went to school here I was treated like the other boys. Then I was sent to a language school in England, at Cambridge. I had £3 a week to spend. When the money for the gas meter ran out, I went cold. At Mons, where I did my officer training, they treated everyone the same. It is so with my children. I took my daughter away from the school where they gave her ten out of ten.'

Mindful of Disraeli's dictum ('Everyone likes flattery and when you come to royalty you should lay it on with a trowel') I conclude the interview by telling the Sheikh that he is wonderful, what he has achieved for his country is extraordinary and, should he be on the look-out for a British bride for his nineteen-year-old son, I will gladly put either of my daughters at his disposal. I think he is amused, but I am not sure. He shakes his head. 'You ask me strange questions.'

I ask one more. 'What is your secret?'

Without hesitation he says, 'God. Faith is everything. It gives you the strength, the energy, the power. I am a leader because it is a gift from God. I am a happy man because I never keep things in my heart. If something is wrong, I tell people. I take decisions. I don't feel burdened. I sleep well.'

'How much do you sleep?'

'Four hours, two hours.'

'Truly? Look into my eyes and tell me the truth.'

He leans forward and pushes his face into mine. 'I tell you the truth. In the day it is all rush. At night it is quiet. I am alone. I write my notes with my green pen. I read. I read a lot of classical Arabic. It is a beautiful language. How many words did Shakespeare use? Forty thousand? In Arabic there are forty thousand words for different fish. At night, I write my poetry. And I think. I am never idle.'

'Do you have a message for the British people?'

'Yes.' He sits back and laughs. 'Come and have a nice time in Dubai.'

'And for me?'

'For you? For you? Every morning in Africa a gazelle wakes up. It knows it must outrun the fastest lion or it will be killed. Every morning in Africa a lion wakes up. It knows it must run faster than the slowest gazelle or it will starve. It doesn't matter whether you're a gazelle or a lion, Mr Brandreth. When the sun comes up, you'd better be running.'

Postscript: The Thoughts of Sheikh Mohammed

I told Sheikh Mohammed that the day of our meeting happened to be my birthday. 'I will give you a present,' he said. For a fleeting moment I pictured an Arab stallion or even a Rolls-Royce coming my way, but he could sense I wasn't one for mere material gewgaws. He gave me a collection of his love poetry and a calendar featuring photographs of his favourite horses and nuggets of his wisdom.

'Extraordinary determination. That's what makes ordinary people real leaders.'

'At the root of all creation is imagination, because before you achieve you must first conceive.'

'It is the leader who sets the pace of the pack.'

'Begin when you are sure of yourself, and don't stop because someone else is unsure of you.'

> 'Go to the edge, the voice said. No, they said, we will fall.
> Go to the edge, the voice said. No, they said, we will be pushed over.
> So they went . . . and they were pushed . . . and they flew . . .'

> 'Watch your thoughts, they become words.
> Watch your words, they become actions.
> Watch your actions, they become habits.
> Watch your habits, they become character.
> Watch your character, it becomes your destiny.'

Sheikh Yamani

I interviewed the world's great 'oil guru' to mark his seventieth birthday on 30 June 2000.

O nce upon a time Ahmed Zaki Yamani was one of the most powerful men on earth. What he said, what he did, touched, and changed, all our lives. From 1962 to 1986 he was the Saudi Arabian oil minister, the public face of the revolutionary policy that, in the early 1970s, sent the cost of petrol through the roof, threw the global economy into chaos and altered the balance of world power. Today, he is sitting in a first-floor drawing room at the top end of Knightsbridge, plying me with tiny, bitter chocolates ('I make these myself') and ladling spoonfuls of thick honey into my coffee. 'You like coffee Mecca-style?'

If you were around in his heyday, when, with a prince's retinue and surrounded by armed guards, he crisscrossed the world explaining why and how the Gulf states must reduce oil production and raise oil prices (a five-fold increase in 1973 alone), you will recall the headline, 'Yamani or your life!', and recognise the face. It was everywhere. Twenty years on, amazingly, it hasn't changed: still round, smooth, beguiling, smiling, with a neat goatee beard, thick black hair (unretouched, I reckon) and what my mother used to call 'bedroom eyes'. I can describe his voice for you exactly: it is David Suchet as Hercule Poirot. Yamani has something of the Belgian detective's manner about him too: he is dapper, courteous, softly spoken, consciously charming, fully aware of his own genius.

In the week that OPEC gathers in Vienna, I have come to see the Sheikh (the title is honorific: Yamani is a commoner) both to wish him a happy birthday and to pick his brains. 'Your excellency,' I begin, 'no one knows more about oil than you.' He smiles and gives a courtly bow. He doesn't disagree.

In Vienna the ministers from the eleven oil-producing countries have agreed a new production quota of 27.3 million barrels a day, an increase of 2.6 per cent but less than expected. The price per barrel is now edging perilously close to the $30 mark. What happens next? 'The price will stay high for the moment because of the high demand in the US, where they need two million barrels a day to refine to have about one million barrels a day of gasoline, and because of unexpected demands in Asia – for example, in China where they have a requirement of 1.4 million barrels a day. But down the road, as you call it, I have no illusion: I am positive there will be sometime in the future a crash in the price of oil.'

'A crash?'

'Oh yes.' He smiles complacently. I look dumbfounded. If he is the all-seeing, all-knowing Poirot, I must be the unfortunate Captain Hastings. 'A crash.' He is nodding and looking me in the eye. Why am I not using the little grey cells? 'It is coming because oil companies who generated a huge profit from this price of oil are spending so much on exploration and developments. The discoveries which took place in the last three months are very significant. A huge field discovered in Kazakhstan: 5.2 billion barrels of recoverable reserve, which means they can easily produce 1 million barrels a day from that. The Russians have discovered a huge field at the northern part of the Caspian Sea.'

I raise my eyebrows. There has been no mention of this in my briefing notes.

'It's not yet announced,' says Yamani, silkily, 'but we know about it from different sources. It is well above ten billion barrels of recoverable reserve. They can easily produce two million barrels a day – easily. In Yemen, in Egypt, they make discoveries. Then you go to the west coast of Africa, to Angola, Nigeria . . . It all adds up.'

He waits until I have finished scribbling. 'Now we add the Iraqi factor. I don't think the Iraqis will be out of the market for long. Sooner or later the situation will change. We don't know when. It is only a matter of time. The Iraqis are capable of producing at least 6.5 million barrels a day. They have the reserves. All they need are foreign companies, foreign capital – and I think they would open the door for that.

'So, my friend, on the supply side it is easy to find oil and produce it. And on the demand side there are so many new technologies, especially when it comes to automobiles. The hybrid engines – the Japanese started that – will cut gasoline consumption by something like thirty per cent. Then – and it's a proven technology – you have the cell-fuel cars. This is coming before the end of the decade and will cut gasoline consumption by almost 100 per cent. Imagine a country like the US, the largest consuming nation, where more than fifty per cent of their consumption is gasoline. If you eliminate that, what will happen?

'I can tell you with a degree of confidence that after five years there will be a sharp drop in the price of oil. This, of course, if we don't have some political surprises. The middle east is not the most stable part of the world. Two-thirds of the world reserve is still in the Gulf. If anything happens there in one of the major producing nations, then definitely the price will shoot up to $40 or more. The oil market is full of surprises. That is the beauty of it.'

And in the longer term?

'Thirty years from now there will be a huge amount of oil – and no buyers. Thirty years from now, there is no problem with oil. Oil will be left in the ground. The Stone Age came to an end not because we had lack of stones, and the oil age will come to an end not because we have lack of oil.'

From the viewpoint of the west (and the environment) this is cheering – if unexpected – news, but what are the prospects for the Gulf?

'We have no alternative but to reform on all fronts – economic, political, social, everything. Every country in the middle east will be forced to do that. If they don't, they will be swallowed. I am a Saudi and I know we will have serious economic difficulties ahead of us.'

Yamani came to prominence under King Faisal, who valued and promoted him. He fell from grace under Faisal's brother, the ailing King Fahd, who had long been wary of him and eventually dismissed him in 1986. 'I was dreaming of getting out. I am grateful to King Fahd for fulfilling my dream. That is all I can say. I wish him good health.' It is evident from the Sheikh's body language and from what he says once my recorder is switched off that he sees no happy prospect for his country during the present king's time. He gives me a book his daughter has written. The epigraph is a quotation from King Faisal: 'In one generation we went from riding camels to riding Cadillacs. The way we are wasting money, I fear the next generation will be riding camels again.'

How did Yamani, a middle-class boy without royal connections, end up as the most powerful man at the court of King Faisal?

'I came from a scholarly environment. My father was a great jurist, my uncles were professors at the Grand Mosque of Mecca where I studied literature, Arabic, jurisprudence. From Mecca I went to Cairo and studied law. Then I went to NYU and to Harvard. I went back to my country where I was working for the government as a legal adviser in the tax department and the oil department, and I was writing in a lot of newspapers. King Faisal asked me to come to him. He was reading my articles. I think he liked them. To compare what he was to what we are now is not a good comparison.'

'What was the essence of his greatness?'

'He was modest in a glorious way. He lived in homes that today a middle-class Saudi would not accept. He never took money from the Treasury for himself.' (Yamani says this as though this fact alone makes the king unique.) 'He was a reformer. He was strongly for the education of women. At that time it was forbidden. He used to send girls from his own pocket to study outside the country. One of his achievements was to abolish slavery, and I was an instrument in that. He was a believer in the Arab cause and in Islam without being fanatic. He was shrewd. I am almost positive he can read minds. He was so disciplined. You can correct your watch on his movement.'

In March 1975 Faisal was assassinated, murdered in his palace by a young royal nephew. Yamani was at the king's side. 'When I remember how he was shot, how he fell into my arms, and the blood that was everywhere . . . It was twenty-five years ago, but as I tell the story I cry.' Yamani shakes his head mournfully, sniffs and smiles. 'The boy wanted to kill me too.'

1975 was a year of close calls. In December, at the OPEC headquarters in Vienna, Yamani and fellow Arab oil ministers were taken hostage by a group of pro-Palestinian terrorists led by Carlos Martinez, 'The Jackal'. 'They discussed who was going to kill who. They were all ready to kill the Iranian, but they said, "We don't think Yamani deserves to be killed". Carlos said, "But it's part of the plan. He has to be killed. I will kill him." Carlos told me, "I don't want you to think this is against you. We respect you. We like you. This is against your country. If the Austrian government don't publish our statement by five o'clock, at five-thirty I will kill you."

'I said, "Can I write my will?" They gave me paper. I had a pen. I started writing my will. It is a very strange thing. I did not think about death. I was thinking about my wife, my children, my mother. What occupied my mind was not fear. I was thinking what I wanted to achieve. I was writing very quickly and suddenly I saw someone grabbing me. I looked up and it was Carlos. I looked at my watch. It was 5.20. I was angry. I found myself arguing with him. I said, "I have ten minutes more". He smiled and said, "No, you have much longer than that. They have published the statement."'

Yamani laughs and claps his hands. 'What a feeling! What it is inside you will not be known until the event is there.'

'You no longer need bodyguards?'

'I have some, but only for my children because I don't want them to be hurt. When you go to Italy or somewhere where they kidnap, you have to be careful.' (As I come and go, I notice a burly figure, arms folded, stationed on the landing. Possibly you have to be cautious in Knightsbridge too.) He has homes in Sardinia, Switzerland, Jeddah, Mecca and Surrey. I tell him I understand he is enormously rich.

'Not really enormously rich, no, honestly. I have good real estate in Saudi Arabia and elsewhere. I have my investments, I am a good long-term investor, cautious, moderate. I don't gamble. I don't drink. I don't care for nightlife. My houses are good enough, not extravagant.' He gets about the world by private jet, but it is one he shares with friends.

If you ask him to name-drop he will. Hirohito, Marcos, Suharto, the Shah of Iran, Saddam Hussein, Franco, Ronald Reagan, George Bush, Ayub Khan, he's known them all. King Faisal apart ('He is unique'), who stands out from the crowd?

'I tell you a story, my friend. I was the inventor, the engineer of the idea of the North–South dialogue. I never forget a conference we had – it was chaired by both Pierre Trudeau – he was a good friend of mine – and the President of Mexico. There were twenty-one heads of state and government at this conference. I can tell you without any reservation that among the twenty-one there were only two who did their homework and were shining people, worthy of the highest respect: Indira Gandhi and Margaret Thatcher – the two women! You raise your hat for them and you bow.'

He has lived through exciting times.

'Difficult, difficult.'

'But you miss them, don't you?'

'No. Too much light hurts the eyes. If you get away from it and have just enough to see your way you are a happier person.

'I am a husband. My wife travels with me everywhere. I am a father and grandfather. I collect and study manuscripts. I cook. I design my own cloth. I am an expert in perfume.'

I look surprised.

'Oh yes. Making perfume in the Arab tradition is an art like impressionist painting. In the old days when a man is in love with a girl he will make a perfume for her which reflects his feelings.

'Let me tell you about a perfume created by a man called Al Kindi almost thirteen centuries ago. He created it for the wife of Haruna Rashid and she took it and, because it is pure oil, she put it in her mouth, and when the Caliph kissed her he was fascinated! Of course, she asked Al Kindi not to give the perfume to any other woman. In time, she passed away and all the ladies of Baghdad said, "Now she is dead, give us this perfume." Al Kindi would not give it to them, but he left the formula and – yes, my friend – I have a laboratory and I was able to reproduce it. It is fantastic!'

Poirot could not have unravelled the mystery more memorably. But there is a coup de théâtre to come. Sheikh Yamani raises his finger and beckons me towards him. 'Give me your hands.'

He produces a perfume bottle from the drawer of his desk and pours the thick sweet-smelling oil onto my palms. 'Rub it very hard. Put it in your hair. Yes, now. It is very exotic. It is pure oil. It will wait on you for a long, long time.'

I do as I am told and, an hour later, when I am sitting on the Piccadilly Line attracting curious glances, I think to myself, 'If he can persuade a middle-aged Englishman to do that, he must have a certain something.' Clearly, even now, you don't say no to Yamani.

Arthur C. Clarke

To mark the advent of 2001 I made a personal odyssey to Sri Lanka to meet Sir Arthur C. Clarke.

' I may have saved the human race, you know.' Sir Arthur C. Clarke rolls his wheelchair back from his desk and, baring an alarming set of pearly-white dentures, drops his jaw and grins at me. I had been thinking how like P. G. Wodehouse he looks. Suddenly he is Dr Strangelove. He laughs triumphantly and tosses two documents towards me: papers from NASA and the British National Space Centre detailing strategies for protecting the earth from devastation by asteroids.

Clarke – who, in the 1940s, developed the basic theory of communication satellites (for which he was nominated for a Nobel prize) and, in 1948, anticipated, in detail, man's first landing on the moon – turns out too to be the man who has inspired 'Safeguard', the international programme that will keep lethal near-earth objects at bay and, 'with a bit of luck', he says, ensure the future of the planet, 'at least for a while'. He chuckles. 'I try to be helpful if I can.'

As the pre-eminent science fiction writer of his generation (with more than eighty titles to his credit and sales of 50 million plus) and the undisputed prime seer of the space age, Sir Arthur's claims to fame are many: he was the first to predict reusable spacecraft, the millennium bug, and the proliferation of the mobile phone. He inspired Gene Roddenberry to create *Star Trek*. Most famously, with Stanley Kubrick, he wrote *2001: a Space Odyssey*, for many the definitive space movie. 'It's a film I still enjoy,' he says. 'Whenever I hear that opening music the hair on my neck stands on end.'

Clarke, a Somerset farmer's son, was born on 16 December 1917. When he left school (Huish's Grammar in Taunton), he joined the civil service. During the war, in his early twenties, he volunteered for the RAF and worked in radar. When he was demobbed he went to King's College, London, read Mathematics and Physics, and took a First. An obsessive 'sci-fi nut' since childhood, he published his own first stories in the 1940s and – as author and visionary – never looked back.

In the early 1950s a passion for underwater exploration took him first to the Great Barrier Reef of Australia and then to Sri Lanka, the beautiful war-torn island in the Indian Ocean that has been his permanent home for more than thirty years. Here he lives, honoured and tax free, Chancellor of the local university, the first person in the nation's history to be granted 'Resident Guest' status.

I have come to Colombo – where the sun is shining brilliantly and the street stalls are overflowing with inflatable Father Christmases – to wish the great man a happy birthday, to salute his achievement, to secure his predictions for life beyond 2001, and (if I have the courage) to ask him about the allegations that, in his time, he has paid for sex with doe-eyed Sri Lankan boys.

We are sitting in his workroom, on the first floor of his rambling, slightly ramshackle villa, in one of Colombo's smarter residential areas (the Iraqi ambassador lives next door). The room boasts a personal computer and a widescreen TV, but, these apart, the feel is more faded 1950s writer's study than twenty-first-century space module.

We are not alone. Throughout the interview, assorted servants – a secretary, a valet, a personal assistant, two houseboys, a lady bearing tea and sweetmeats – come and go. Beneath the desk, Pepsi, Sir Arthur's one-eyed 'killer chihuahua' ('she's ten years old and the love of my life') dozes fitfully. Across the room, slumped in front of the television, headphones clamped to her ears, is a fair-haired, long-legged seventeen-year-old girl. 'She is Cherene,' explains Sir Arthur, looking at her with pride.

'She is one of my three "adopted daughters". They are everything to me, especially the youngest one. I love them more than I can tell you.' Sir Arthur shares his home with the girls' parents: his partner in a deep-sea diving business, Hector Ekanayake (formerly Sri Lanka's flyweight boxing champion), and Hector's Australian wife, Valerie. 'More people should live in extended families,' says Sir Arthur cheerily, tucking into his second slice of cake. 'It works extremely well.'

Sir Arthur is in a wheelchair because, in Sri Lanka in 1962, he contracted polio. He made a good recovery, but is now the victim of 'post-polio syndrome' which means that he cannot walk unaided and is subject to sudden fatigue. When I arrive he seems full of beans, his voice rasping but strong, his accent 'old Somerset' with a touch of Transatlantic.

Once tea has been served and he has checked (and double checked) his screen for e-mails, and given me a copy of his standard handout for journalists explaining that he no longer talks to the press ('except in the event of a major development – e.g. a genuine message from space or an ET landing on the White House lawn'), he says, quite crisply, 'I have to play table tennis at five. That means we've got two hours. Where shall we start?'

'With where you went wrong?' I suggest, a little hesitantly.

'Good place to start,' he laughs. (To my surprise, he laughs a lot.) 'I thought the hovercraft would be really big. I even went out and bought one. That was a mistake. Hovercraft are wonderful over ice and excellent for military purposes, but they've not become universal in the way I thought they would. And the timescale in 2001 is a bit adrift. We thought we'd be well established on the moon by now. We've discovered more about the solar system than I envisaged, but not done as much human exploration as I had hoped. There isn't a Hilton in space quite yet, but Mir is a sort of hotel in space – only one and a half stars of course.'

What about HAL, the walking-talking-thinking computer that became the star of 2001?

'HAL is certainly possible now. We're a long way down the road with the development of artificial intelligence. There will undoubtedly be machines at least as intelligent as man by around 2020.'

'Will they be able to develop a conscience, a sense of moral values?'

'Some say no, but I'm not so sure. I like to quote Marvin Minsky, "Can a machine think? I'm a machine, I think." I like to quote J. B. S. Haldane too: "The universe is not only stranger than we imagine. It is stranger than we can imagine." All I will say is this: if there is a war between man and machine, I know which side will start it.'

When will we discover life on other planets?

'To date we haven't the slightest positive evidence that there is any life out there. I'd settle for a microbe on Mars, but so far nothing. That said, there are a hundred thousand million suns and a hundred thousand million galaxies so it seems to me 99 per cent certain there must be other forms of life. I've a feeling that by about 2030 we will have made contact with intelligent life on other planets. Of course, the first messages we pick up may have taken millions of years to reach us and come from lost civilisations.'

What are the immediate Clarke predictions for life on earth?

'I prefer to call them extrapolations rather than predictions. The greatest technological invention of the twentieth century has been the microchip. The great discovery of the next century – which does not begin until 1 January 2001, by the way – will be new forms and sources of energy: cold fusion, hot fission, goodness knows what. And there'll be a change in our personal fuel too. We'll be able to synthesise all our food quite soon. All it will take is water, air and a few basic chemicals. Unquestionably, we are going to see the end of agriculture and the end of animal husbandry, so called. That could happen within my lifetime.

'And for the next generation, of course, the impact of genetic modification will be profound, and not only in terms of health and longevity. Athletics, for example, will be transformed. You'll have swimmers with webbed feet and built-in snorkels.'

The Peter Pan in me is suddenly aroused. 'Will we be able to fly?'

'No, I don't think we'll have flying men on earth, but there will be space tourism and huge domes on the moon where you can go for flying holidays. You will be able to travel on my space elevator: a carbon-fibre cable car to the stars. I want the first one to be tethered to Sri Lanka's highest point, Adam's Peak. Look.'

With boyish glee, he produces another NASA report showing that the concept that began as a twinkle in his eye is now being developed as a real possibility. Within an hour of my arrival, the table in front of me is piled high with reports, documents, books, videos he is urging me to borrow so that I can explore his ideas further. He wants to show me the pictures he has taken of the moon using the 14″ telescope on the roof. He is so full of good humour and infectious enthusiasm that I am rapidly coming to the conclusion that to raise the sorry matter of the allegations made against him is going to be so downright discourteous as to be impossible.

Just then, Valerie comes into the room. She is forty-something, slim, attractive, friendly, forthright. She has brought in the draft of a letter she plans to send to her youngest daughter's school. She wants Sir Arthur to read it. While he is looking over it, she turns to me and – without any hostility – explains that they've been somewhat wary of journalists 'since that paedophile crap'.

She smiles, she says she hopes she'll see me later, she leaves. The unmentionable subject has been raised. Clearly, it hovers in the air all the time. Three years ago, just as he was awarded his knighthood in the New Year's Honours list, the *Sunday Mirror* produced a front-page story suggesting that the legendary writer chooses to live in Sri Lanka for more than the sun and Scuba-diving. It accused Sir Arthur of 'paying for sex with young boys'. Immediately, he angrily denied the charges and threatened legal action.

The accusations coincided with Prince Charles's visit to Colombo to mark the fiftieth anniversary of Sri Lanka's independence. The Prince had planned to knight Sir Arthur during the visit. In the event, the ceremony was called off.

Sir Arthur is looking straight at me and smiling. I glance towards the photograph of him with the Prince of Wales on the wall and say, 'Given what he's had to put up with himself from the press, didn't you think it was a bit feeble of Prince Charles to chicken out of the ceremony in the face of one unsubstantiated Sunday tabloid story?'

Sir Arthur leans across the table urgently. 'No, no, he didn't chicken out. I withdrew. I didn't want to cause him any embarrassment. We met up at the banquet. He couldn't have been friendlier.'

'So when did you get your knighthood?'

'A year or so later, at the British High Commission. I missed out on the dubbing, but I got the gong eventually. Better late than never.'

'Why didn't you sue the paper after all?'

'Time and money. It would have cost a fortune and dragged on for years. These things always do. I'd have won, then they'd have appealed. It would still be going on now. I'm an old man. It wasn't worth it. My conscience is clear. Having always had a particular dislike for paedophiles few charges could be more revolting, but they didn't stand up. I knew I was innocent, so I wasn't troubled.' (No other paper has followed up the charges. For what it's worth, my own sleuthing in Colombo has turned up nothing new. I met a young man who regularly played table tennis with Clarke twenty years ago – at the club where he was alleged to have picked up boys – and he had no evidence of any kind to offer against him.)

What are Sir Arthur's views on homosexuality?

'When impertinent reporters ask if I'm gay, I say, "I'm mildly cheerful."' I go along with Mrs Patrick Campbell: "I don't mind what people do in the

bedroom, so long as they don't do it in the street and frighten the horses."'
He shakes his head, a touch despairingly. 'People have strange attitudes to
homosexuality.'

I take this as my cue to mention a surprising essay of Clarke's that I
happen to have come across. Entitled 'The Gay Warlords' it is an ironic
squib that mocks those who want to keep homosexuals out of the armed
forces. Citing the Spartans, Alexander, Hadrian, Richard the Lionheart,
even Gordon of Khartoum, Clarke suggests that the real reason to keep gays
out of the military is that 'they're too bloodthirsty and warlike'. The piece
concludes with the true story of the turn-of-the-century commander-in-
chief of the Ceylon forces, Sir Hector Macdonald, VC, known as the bravest
soldier in the British army, who achieved the astonishing feat of winning
promotion all the way from private to general. 'Alas,' writes Sir Arthur, 'to
the great embarrassment of the local Brits (and doubtless the amusement
of everyone else), Fighting Mac was caught in flagrante with some
Colombo schoolboys – not the natives, by gad! – at least they were burghers
(upper-class Eurasians). Whitehall recalled the general prontissimo; he got
as far as Paris, and shot himself . . .'

The author narrows his eyes. 'What did you make of that?'

'Of the piece? I liked it. I thought it was remarkably sane, humane and
very funny.'

'Good, good,' he says, smacking his lips. 'No one has picked up on it
before. It's been out there a year now and no one in the world has noticed
it before you, no one at all. I'm glad you liked it.'

I liked the piece and I have decided I like Sir Arthur too. He is self-
absorbed, self-obsessed, self-regarding (of course he is: he has been a star
for half a century), but he is original and brilliant too and (this is the
surprise) wonderfully funny and almost touchingly eager to please. He has
a fund of good stories and no time for humbug. His lifestyle and his views
may not be to everybody's taste, but he is hearteningly unapologetic about
them. He doesn't smoke, he barely drinks ('two bottles of Harvey's Bristol

Cream per year'), but he believes – firmly – that all narcotics should not only be 'unbanned' but also be made free, 'so that those who want to kill themselves with them can, and the rest of us can get on with life.'

He has decided he will never leave Sri Lanka again. 'Travelling is simply too tiring for me now. And if I want to go back to Somerset all I have to do is close my eyes.'

Does he have any regrets?

'I wish I had learnt to play the piano. I bought one, but then the computer came along and I was distracted.'

What about his marriage? He was briefly married to an American, Marilyn Mayfield. Does he regret that?

'No, everybody should be married at least once. In 1952 I went to the United States and went swimming with my aqualung. I stayed at Key Largo and met Marilyn. A week later we were married. It didn't work out, but we stayed friends until she died.'

What about children?

'No. With my extended family, I've had all the fun with none of the responsibility.'

Will the three girls inherit his money?

He glances towards Cherene who is still sitting fixedly in front of the TV screen. 'Yes, if there's any left. I'm not in the Stephen King class, you know, and I've got about fifty people dependent on me in different parts of the world.' I suspect money is quite a preoccupation.

He pauses. 'I regret the fact that I never really knew my father. I was thirteen when he died. I would have liked to have known him properly. And I'm quite surprised by how much I miss Stanley Kubrick. We didn't see each other that often, but he was the most intelligent man I ever knew. We talked about mathematics together. He was fascinated by transfinite numbers – the numbers beyond infinity. He introduced me to my favourite line from Thackeray: "Good or bad, guilty or innocent – they are equal now."'

Does Sir Arthur think much about death?

'When I was last in New York I met Woody Allen and I agree with him. "I'm not frightened of death. I just don't want to be there when it happens." When I joined the RAF they put me down as "C of E". I got hold of the man handling the paperwork and made them change it to "pantheist". Now I say I'm a crypto-Buddhist, but I'm anti-mysticism and I have a long-standing bias against organised religion. I don't believe in God or an afterlife.'

'So you won't be joining the ranks of the great immortals?' I say, packing away the assortment of papers he has given me to study overnight.

He is struggling to his feet. 'I didn't say that,' he chuckles. 'Far from it. In fact, not long ago a guy came and removed six strands of my already scanty hair. Those hairs have now been launched in a satellite. Yes, my DNA is on its way to the stars. So, who knows, I might be created all over again. Think of that: a million years from now half-a-dozen Arthur C. Clarkes floating round the galaxies.'

'Incredible.'

'No, quite credible. Remember Clarke's law: "Any sufficiently advanced technology is indistinguishable from magic."'

The exorcist

In October 2000, for Hallowe'en, I travelled to Rome to meet Father Gabriele Amorth, the exorcist.

On the bumpy flight to Rome I read the Bible all the way. The passenger on my left – a wiry businesswoman from Wisconsin – found this disconcerting. As the turbulence worsened and I moved from Jude to Revelation, she hissed at me, 'Do you have to?' 'It's only background reading,' I murmured. She grimaced. 'What for?' I turned to her and whispered, 'I'm going to meet the exorcist.' 'Oh Christ,' she gasped, as the plane lurched and hot coffee spilled over us.

But I was. And I did. And I found the encounter both extraordinary and oddly moving.

Father Gabriele Amorth is indeed the exorcist, the most senior and respected member of his calling, a priest for fifty years, Rome's chief exorcist, the Pope's neighbourhood demon-buster, honorary president-for-life of the International Association of Exorcists. He is 75, small, spry, humorous, and wonderfully direct. 'I speak with the Devil every day,' he says, grinning like a benevolent gargoyle. 'I talk to him in Latin. He answers in Italian. I have been wrestling with him, day in day out, for fourteen years.'

On cue (God is not worried by clichés) a shaft of October sunlight falls across Father Amorth's pale, round face. We are sitting at a table by the window in a small high-ceilinged meeting room at his Rome headquarters, the offices of the Society of St Paul. Father Amorth has come to exorcism late in life, but with impressive credentials. Born in Modena, in northern Italy, the son and grandson of lawyers (his brother is a judge), in 1943, Gabriele Amorth, in his late teens, joined the Italian resistance. Immediately after the war, he joined the fledgling Christian Democratic Party. Giulo Andreotti was president of the Young Christian Democrats, Amorth was his deputy. Andreotti went into politics and was seven times prime minister. Amorth, having studied law at university, went into the church. 'From the age of fifteen I knew it was my true vocation. My speciality was the Madonna. For many years I edited the magazine *Madre di Deo* (Mother of God). When I hear people say, "You Catholics honour Mary too much", I reply, "We are never able to honour her enough."

'I knew nothing of exorcism – I had given it no thought – until 6 June 1986 when Cardinal Poletti, Vicar of Rome, asked to see me. There was a famous exorcist in Rome then, the only one, Father Candido, but he was not well, and Cardinal Poletti told me I was to be his assistant. I learnt everything from Father Candido. He was my great master. Quickly I realised how much work there was to be done and how few exorcists there were to do it. From that day, I dropped everything and dedicated myself entirely to exorcism.'

Father Amorth smiles continually as he tells his story. His enthusiasm for his subject is infectious and engaging. 'Jesus performed exorcisms. He cast out demons. He freed souls from demonic possession and from Him the church has received the power and office of exorcism. A simple exorcism is performed at every baptism, but major exorcism can be performed only by a priest licensed by the bishop. I have performed over 50,000 exorcisms. Sometimes it takes a few minutes, sometimes many hours. It is hard work – *molto duro.*'

How does he recognise someone possessed by evil spirits?

'It is not easy. There are many grades of possession. The Devil does not like to be seen, so there are people who are possessed who manage to conceal it. There are other cases where the person possessed is in acute physical pain, such agony that they cannot move. It is essential not to confuse demonic possession with ordinary illness. The symptoms of possession often include violent headaches and stomach cramps, but you must always go to the doctor before you go to the exorcist. I have people come to me who are not possessed at all. They are suffering from epilepsy or schizophrenia or other mental problems. Of the thousands of patients I have seen, only a hundred or so have been truly possessed.'

'How can you tell?'

'By their aversion to the sacrament and all things sacred. If blessed they become furious. If confronted with the crucifix, they are subdued.'

'But couldn't an hysteric imitate the symptoms?'

'We can sort out the phoney ones. We look into their eyes. As part of the exorcism, at specific times during the prayers, holding two fingers on the patient's eyes we raise the eyelids. Almost always, in cases of evil presence, the eyes look completely white. Even with the help of both hands, we can barely discern whether the pupils are towards the top or the bottom of the eye. If the pupils are looking up, the demons in possession are scorpions. If looking down, they are serpents.'

As I report this now, it sounds absurd. As Father Amorth told it to me, it felt entirely credible.

I had gone to Rome expecting – hoping, even – for a chilling encounter, but instead of a sinister bug-eyed obsessive lurking in the shadows of a Hammer Horror film set, here I was sitting in an airy room with a kindly old man with an uncanny knack for making the truly bizarre seem wholly rational. He has God on his side and customers at his door. The demand for exorcism is growing as never before. Fifteen years ago there were twenty church-appointed exorcists in Italy. Now there are three hundred.

I asked Father Amorth to describe the ritual of exorcism.

'Ideally, the exorcist needs another priest to help him and a group nearby who will assist through prayer. The ritual does not specify the stance of the exorcist. Some stand, some sit. The ritual says only that, beginning with the words "Ecce crucem Domini" ["Behold the Cross of the Lord"] the priest should touch the neck of the possessed one with the hem of his stole and hold his hand on his head. The demons will want to hide. Our task is to expose them, and then expel them. There are many ways to goad them into showing themselves. Although the ritual does not mention this, experience has taught us that using oil and holy water and salt can be very effective.

'Demons are wary of talking and must be forced to speak. When demons are voluntarily chatty it's a trick to distract the exorcist. We must never ask useless questions out of curiosity. We must interrogate with care. We always begin by asking for the demon's name.'

'And does he answer?' I ask.

Father Amorth nods. 'Yes, through the patient, but in a strange, unnatural voice. If it is the Devil himself, he says, "I am Satan, or Lucifer, or Beelzebub". We ask if he is alone or if there are others with him. Usually there are two or five, twenty or thirty. We must quantify the number. We ask when and how they entered that particular body. We must find out whether their presence is due to a spell and the specifics of that spell.

'During the exorcism the evil one may emerge in slow stages or with sudden explosions. He does not want to show himself. He will be angry. And he is strong. During one exorcism I saw a child of eleven held down by four strapping men. The child threw the men aside with ease. I was there when a boy of ten lifted a huge, heavy table. Afterwards I felt the muscles in the boy's arms. He could not have done it on his own. He had the strength of the Devil inside him.

'No two cases are the same. Some patients have to be tied down on a bed. They spit. They vomit. At first the demon will try to demoralise the exorcist, then he will try to terrify him, saying, "Tonight I'm going to put a serpent between your sheets. Tomorrow I'm going to eat your heart."'

I lean towards Father Amorth. 'And are you sometimes frightened?' I ask. He looks incredulous. 'Never. I have faith. I laugh at the demon and say to him, "I've got the Madonna on my side. I am called Gabriel. Go fight the Archangel Gabriel if you will." That usually shuts them up.'

Now he leans towards me and taps my hand confidentially. 'The secret is to find your demon's weak spot. Some demons cannot bear to have the Sign of the Cross traced with a stole on an aching part of the body; some cannot stand a puff of breath on the face; others resist with all their strength against blessing with holy water.

'Relief for the patient is always possible, but to completely rid a person of his demons can take many exorcisms over many years. For a demon to leave a body and go back to hell means to die forever and to lose any ability to molest people in the future. He expresses his desperation saying, "I am dying, I am dying. You are killing me; you have won. All priests are murderers."'

How do people come to be possessed by demons in the first place?

'I believe God sometimes singles out certain souls for a special test of spiritual endurance, but more often people lay themselves open to possession by dabbling with black magic. Some are entrapped by a satanic cult. Others are the victims of a curse.'

I interrupt. 'You mean like Yasser Arafat saying to Ehud Barak, "Go to Hell" and meaning it?'

'No.' Father Amorth gives me a withering look. 'That is merely a sudden imprecation. It is very difficult to perform a curse. You need to be a priest of Satan to do it properly. Of course, just as you can hire a killer if you need one, you can hire a male witch to utter a curse on your behalf. Most witches are frauds, but I am afraid some authentic ones do exist.'

Father Amorth shakes his head and sighs at the wickedness of the world. At the outset he has told me he is confident he will have an answer to all my questions, but he has a difficulty with the next one. 'Why do many more women seem to become possessed than men?'

'Ah, that we do not know. They may be more vulnerable because, as a rule, more women than men are interested in the occult. Or it may be the Devil's way of getting at men, just as he got to Adam through Eve. What we do know is that the problem is getting worse. The Devil is gaining ground. We are living in an age when faith is diminishing. If you abandon God, the Devil will take his place. All faiths, all cultures, have exorcists, but only Christianity has the true force to exorcise through Christ's example and authority. We need many more exorcists, but the bishops won't appoint them. In many countries – Germany, Austria, Switzerland, Spain – there are no Catholic exorcists. It is a scandal. In England there are more Anglican exorcists than Catholic ones.'

These days there is a tension between Father Amorth and the hierarchy of the Roman church. The Catholic establishment is happier talking about 'the spirit of evil' than evil spirits. Devil-hunting is not fashionable in senior church circles. The Vatican recently issued a new rite of exorcism which has not met with Father Amorth's approval. 'They say we cannot perform an exorcism unless we know for certain that the Evil One is present. That is ridiculous. It is only through exorcism that the demons reveal themselves. An unnecessary exorcism never hurt anybody.'

What does the Pope make of all this? 'The Holy Father knows that the Devil is still alive and active in the world. He has performed exorcism. In 1982, he performed a solemn exorcism on a girl from Spoletto. She screamed. She rolled on the floor. Those who saw it were very frightened. The Pope brought her temporary freedom. The other day, on 6 September 2000, at his weekly audience at St Peter's, a young woman from a village near Monza started to shriek as the Pope was about to bless her. She shouted obscenities at him in a strange voice. The Pope blessed her and brought her relief, but the Devil is still in her. She is exorcised each week in Milan and she is now coming to me once a month. It may take a long time to help her, but we must try. The work of the exorcists is to relieve suffering, to free souls from torment, to bring us closer to God.'

Father Amorth has laughed and smiled a good deal during our three-hour discussion. He has pulled sundry rude faces to indicate his contempt for the pusillanimous bishops who have a monopoly on exorcism and refuse to license more practitioners. He has told his tale con brio and with conviction. In his mouth it does not seem like mumbo-jumbo or hocus pocus. He produces detailed case histories. He quotes scriptural chapter and verse to justify his actions.

Given his shining faith and scholarly approach, I hardly dare ask him whether he has seen the notorious 1973 horror film, *The Exorcist*. It turns out to be his favourite movie. 'Of course, the special effects are exaggerated, but it is a good film, and substantially exact, based on a respectable novel which mirrored a true story.' The film is held to be so disturbing it has never been shown on British terrestrial television, nor until 1999 could it be rented from video shops. Nonetheless, Father Amorth recommends it. 'People need to know what we do.'

And what about Hallowe'en? The American tradition has made no inroads in Italy. 'Here it is on Christmas Eve that the Satanists have their orgies. Nothing happens on 31 October. But if English and American children like to dress up as witches and devils on one night of the year that is not a problem. If it is just a game, there is no harm in that.'

It is time to go to the chapel where our photographer is waiting. Father Amorth raises an eyebrow at us indulgently as he realises the photograph is designed to heighten the drama of his calling. He is accustomed to the ways of the press. Pictures taken, he potters off to find me a copy of one of his books.

'What did you make of him?' asks the photographer. 'Is he mad?'

'I don't think so,' I say. The *Telegraph*'s award-winning Rome correspondent, who has acted as interpreter for the interview, and is both a lapsed Catholic and a hardened hack, is more emphatic: 'There's not a trace of the charlatan about him. He is quite sane and utterly convincing.'

Surprised at myself I add, 'He seems to me to be a power for good in the world.'

With a smirk, the photographer loads his gear into the back of the taxi. 'So he's Peter Cushing then, not Christopher Lee,' he says as he clambers into the cab, chuckling.

Father Amorth reappears with his book and smiles. 'Remember, when we jeer at the Devil and tell ourselves that he does not exist, that is when he is happiest.'

Desmond Tutu

In April 2001, I was sent on a day trip to Cape Town for an Easter interview with Archbishop Desmond Tutu.

'I wonder whether they have rum and Coke in Heaven? Maybe it's too mundane a pleasure, but I hope so – as a sundowner. Except, of course, the sun never goes down there. Oh, man, this Heaven is going to take some getting used to.'

Desmond Tutu suddenly slaps the table and explodes with laughter. His tiny eyes disappear, his massive nostrils flare: he hoots, he honks, he shakes with merriment. He cackles with delight. Over the next two hours it happens again and again: sometimes a wild burst of merriment, at others a long, soft, giggling tee-hee. Surprisingly, it isn't irritating. It's simply Tutu. The man is a bundle of joy.

And he has prostate cancer. I am told that this could be his last interview, that I will find him frail and easy to tire. In fact, as he potters round his kitchen fixing me a fruit juice, he looks remarkably robust. He is 5′ 5″ but sturdy, and clearly full of beans. 'I've been having cryosurgery to zap the cancer,' he explains. 'They freeze the prostate, freeze it, and zap it.' Another paroxysm of laughter. 'They don't freeze everything around there, man. I want to celebrate my golden wedding in style!'

Desmond Tutu will be 70 in October. He will have been married to his wife, Leah, for fifty years in 2005. They live in a spacious house, airy and modern (car port at the front, small pool at the back), in a comfortable suburb of Cape Town, where Tutu was Archbishop for ten years, until 1996, and where, famously, on 9 May 1994, on the Town Hall balcony, he ushered in the new South Africa and presented his country's first freely elected president to a rapturous crowd: 'This is the day of liberation. This is the day of celebration. We of many cultures, languages and races are become one nation. We are the Rainbow People of God . . . I ask you: welcome our brand-new State President, out of the box, Nelson Mandela!'

I have come to see Archbishop Tutu, Africa's most persuasive orator, and, since 1975, when he became Dean of Johannesburg, the unquestioned moral force of the anti-apartheid movement, to talk, not of politics but of God. It is Easter and my host – Nobel laureate, winner of every humanitarian honour imaginable, recipient of 55 honorary degrees – has been voted most inspiring church leader in the world.

As we sit together at one end of his dining-room table, beneath a small painting of the Last Supper, and I take out my notepad, he gently puts his hand on mine and says, almost in a whisper, 'Let us say a prayer together. Let us pray for God's blessing on our conversation, and on your article, and on all the readers of the *Sunday Telegraph* – in Jesus's name. Amen.'

Our prayer done, the Archbishop – who was wearing full purple fig when I arrived, but has now changed into a loose black tee-shirt – leans towards me and chuckles, 'If this is going to be my last interview, I am glad we are not going to talk about politics. Let us talk about prayer and adoration, about faith – and hope – and forgiveness.'

First, however, we talk about death. 'When you have a potentially terminal disease,' he says with a suitably beatific smile, 'it concentrates the mind wonderfully. It gives a new intensity to life. You discover how many things you have taken for granted: the love of your spouse, the Beethoven symphony, the dew on the rose, the laughter on the face of your grandchild.' At this exact moment, an enchanting six-year-old, Naniso, the daughter of Mpoe, one of his own three daughters, skips through the room singing 'Jingle Bells' and looking for an Easter egg. She kisses her grandfather on the nose before dancing off.

'When I die I will miss my family so much. I will miss the rugby and the cricket and the soccer too.'

'What will you be glad to leave behind?'

'Personally? Illness, exhaustion, the diminishment in one's powers. I will be glad too to say goodbye to hatred and war and injustice and oppression, to the long, ragged lines of refugees, to all the things that have scarred this beautiful planet. I will be glad to be somewhere where you know accidents are not going to happen anymore.'

'What do you think Heaven will be like?'

The Archbishop closes his eyes to ponder and spreads his palms out on the table. 'It will be spatially, temporally different, of course. It is difficult for us to conceive an existence that is timeless, where you look at absolute beauty and goodness and you have no words. It is enough just to be there. You know how it is when you are sitting with someone you love and hours can go by in what seem like moments? Well, in Heaven, eternity itself will pass in a flash. In Heaven we will never tire. We will never be bored because there will always be such new sides of God that will be revealed to us.'

'Will there be people in Heaven?' I wonder.

He looks directly at me and grins. 'Oh, yes. Heaven is community. A solitary human being is a contradiction. In Africa we say that a person is a person through other persons. That's why God gave Adam that delectable creature, Eve.'

'Will we recognise them as people?'

He furrows his brow. 'I believe so, though what form or shape we'll have in Heaven I don't know. Saint Paul tries to explain it when he talks of "a spiritual body". It is a kind of oxymoron, but he is saying that in the next life we will be recognisably ourselves, but in an existence that is appropriate to Heaven.'

'Who do you hope to see in Heaven?' I ask.

'I'd love to meet my parents again. My father died in 1972 when I was teaching theology in Lesotho. My mother died in 1984, the year we got the Nobel Peace Prize. And then I have an older brother who died in infancy. I'd love to meet him. And I want to see my younger brother again. He died as a baby, but I remember he had this engaging gurgle if you tickled him.'

'Will he still be a baby?'

'I think so. There are babies in heaven, definitely. But no nappies. It really is Heaven, you see.' He is laughing again, rolling from side to side, his eyes shining, his right hand tickling the tummy of his imaginary baby brother. 'The little children will be very important in Heaven because they will be the ones asking those extraordinary questions that are so profound – "But, God, who made you?"'

Another explosion of wild laughter, near hysterical this time. And then, once the wave has crashed onto the shore, a sudden calm. 'In Heaven,' he whispers, 'I would want to meet St Francis of Assisi. And I would love to encounter Mary Magdalene because I think she is a gorgeous creature. She was abused, you know. I believe she was a prostitute, and yet she could love Our Lord so deeply, passionately, extravagantly. She offered unconditional love, not for any utilitarian purpose, but for the sake of it. Quite fantastic.

'I'd also like to meet Origen. He was an Alexandrian father, third century, one of the brightest minds of the early church. I am drawn to him because he taught "universalism" which says that, ultimately, even the devil is going to be saved because no one is going to be able to resist the attractions of the divine love.'

'So Hitler and Stalin and those responsible for the Sharpeville massacre are going to find a place in Heaven?'

Archbishop Tutu narrows his eyes and smiles. 'The wonderful thing about God's love is that maybe we are going to be surprised at the people we find in Heaven that we didn't expect, and possibly we'll be surprised at those we'd thought would be there and aren't. God has a particularly soft spot for sinners. Remember, Jesus says there is greater joy in heaven over one sinner who repents than over ninety-nine needing no repentance. Ultimately it all hinges on one thing: our response to the divine invitation. There is hope for us all. God's standards are quite low. Think of the thief on the cross. He has led a dissolute life. He gets his come-uppance. But all he has to say is "Please remember me" and that small spark of repentance is enough to get him an assurance that he will be in Heaven.'

I am thinking, 'God can forgive, but can we honestly expect a mother to forgive the murderer of her child?' I begin to say it, but the Archbishop – who chaired South Africa's controversial Truth and Reconciliation Commission – is ahead of me.

'Forgiving is not easy. Forgiving means abandoning your right to pay back the perpetrator in his own coin, but, in my experience, it is a loss which liberates the victim. Forgiving is not being sentimental. And in forgiving, people are not being asked to forget. At Dachau, the former concentration camp, they have a museum to commemorate what happened there. Over the entrance are the words of the philosopher George Santayana, "Those who cannot remember the past are condemned to repeat it."'

'When you get to Heaven,' I ask, 'what do you think will happen when you come face to face with God?'

The Archbishop shrieks. 'Will I survive? You remember Gerontius? He longs to be in the presence of God and his guardian angel takes him to God and the moment he comes into the divine presence he cries out in anguish, "Take me away." In the blinding presence of holiness, who would survive?'

It is my turn to smile. 'I think you might,' I say.

The Archbishop chuckles softly. 'So, God in God's goodness tones down the wind for the shorn lamb . . .'

'What would you ask God?'

'A great deal,' he says, earnestly. 'Why, God, did you make suffering so central to everything? Why? Why? Why?'

'Yes,' I respond. 'And what will his answer be? Why does God seem to spit on Africa?'

The Archbishop sighs and takes a deep breath. 'God says, "I obviously had the choice of making all kinds of different worlds, but I wanted to make a world of creatures who would love me, who would choose to love me, and that would not have been the case if they had been automatons. They had to have free will: they had to be free. And this is how they have used their freedom . . ."'

'Have you ever had doubts?'

'No, not doubts, but I have been angry with God on quite a few occasions. I remember I was chaplain at Fort Air university at a time when it was taken over by the apartheid government and the students who protested were expelled. I went into the chapel and I wept at the altar. I was so angry with God. I said, "How can you sit there and do nothing in the face of such blatant injustice?"'

'And what did God say?'

'I'm afraid I didn't give God the chance to reply. I've had a few such moments.' Another burst of laughter, another moment of calm. 'Can I say something about prayer? Our trouble has been that we have thought of prayer as conversation, where we use words and ask God for things. We forget that actually the heart of prayer is adoration – just being there with the beloved. Most of us have had that experience where you sit with someone you are deeply fond of and you don't have to use words, you seem to communicate at a level you didn't know existed. When you sit quietly with God, you will find the silence is a pregnant silence. It is not the absence of noise. It is something positive.'

'Have you always been a Christian?'

'My father was headmaster of a church primary school and my mother, although she was uneducated, was also a Christian. I would have been about twelve when I met up with Trevor Huddleston [the English missionary, and later Bishop of Stepney, who went to South Africa in 1943] and went to live in Sophiatown in a hostel that the Community of the Resurrection was running. I was nurtured by people like Trevor and, gradually, slowly, the flower opened up. In 1946, when I was fourteen or fifteen, I went to hospital suffering with TB. I got to the point where I was haemorrhaging and coughing up blood and I'd seen that most of the people who went through that stage died. I remember going to the toilet and coughing up quite a bit of blood and – it sounds like bravado at this distance, but I said,' – he speaks these words gently, lightly, imitating a child – ' "Well, God, if you mean that I'm going to die, it's okay. If not, it's okay." I accepted God's will. And I really did have an extraordinary sense of peace from that moment on.'

'What do you think now are your weaknesses, your frailties?'

The Archbishop beams at me. 'I have a very strong weakness for being liked. I want to be popular. I love to be loved. One has enjoyed the limelight. I am guilty of the sin of pride. Sometimes I find it very difficult to be humble – that is why it is so good to have Leah. She pulls me down a peg or two. To her I'm not an archbishop with a Nobel prize: I'm just a not-very-good husband who likes gardens but won't do any gardening. Your family is there to do what your guardian angel is supposed to do: keep your ego manageable and remind you that you are just a man. "Thou art dust and to dust thou shalt return".'

Archbishop Tutu is one of the most celebrated and admired people of our time. I ask him, 'What has been the high point of your life on earth?'

He replies without hesitation: 'The most gorgeous moment would be when I became a father for the first time, 14 April 1956, when our only son, our Trevor, was born. I was so proud and so happy. It made me feel a little like God.' He pauses and adds, slowly (it is the only time he is hesistant in our entire conversation), 'And, later, with the way Trevor has lived his life, taking the wrong turns and causing pain and anguish, I have learnt something of the impotence God feels as he watches his children making the wrong choices. Sometimes, in my own life as a father, I have felt very like God looking at us and thinking, "Whatever got me to create that lot?"'

Everywhere you look in the Archbishop's home, in the living room, the dining room, his study, alongside the trophies, medals, certificates and awards, are framed photographs of his family, dozens of them. 'What is Trevor doing now?' I ask.

'He's some sort of consultant. He is a very gifted person, very charming, when he is sober. He destroys himself, or seems to want to destroy himself, when he drinks. He has been in touble with the police. But there we are.'

He looks at me, and blinks away the tears, and claps his hands. 'You can't be so stingey as to give me only one moment in my life to remember? Can't I have another?'

'Of course,' I say, 'as many as you like.' The man is irresistible.

'The day that Nelson Mandela was released from prison, after twenty-seven years. He came to spend the night with us. It was like a miracle. In all the time of the struggle, it seemed there was no light at the end of the tunnel. It was all gloom and darkness and then, suddenly, there he was. This guy, who a few weeks before had been a terrorist, was a free man and the calls were coming in from all over the world, from the White House, from 10 Downing Street. It would be easy to say those twenty-seven years were a shameful waste. I don't think so. Those years and all the suffering they entailed were the fires of the furnace that tempered his steel, that removed the dross. Perhaps without that suffering he would have been less able to be as compassionate and magnanimous as he turned out to be. And that suffering on behalf of others gave him an authority and credibility that can be provided by nothing else in quite the same way.

'Of course, he is only a human being. He has his failings. As a speaker, he can be deadly dull, but, it's a cliché to say so, he is a truly remarkable person. And what he does show – and Mother Teresa and others have shown it too

– is that the world that is supposed to be so cynical and hard is actually extraordinarily sensitive to goodness. Nelson Mandela was not the leader of some mighty military machine or even a country with a powerful economy. South Africa is hardly a blip on the screen. He is famous the world over and people warm to him because he is good.'

And, of course, I have warmed to Archbishop Tutu for just the same reason. I remind him that the purpose of my visit has been to collect an Easter message. He laughs. 'You have travelled to the Dark Continent for an Easter message for your readers. God has a great sense of humour. Who in their right mind would have imagined South Africa to be an example of anything but awfulness? We were destined for perdition and were plucked out of total annihilation. God intends that others might look at us and take courage. At the end of their conflicts, the warring groups around the world – in the Balkans and the Middle East, in Angola and the Congos – will sit down and work out how they will be able to live together amicably. They will, I know it. There will be peace on earth. The death and resurrection of Jesus Christ puts the issue beyond doubt: ultimately, goodness and laughter and peace and compassion and gentleness and forgiveness will have the last word.

'Jesus says, "And when I am lifted up from the earth I shall draw everyone to myself", as He hangs from His cross with out-flung arms, thrown out to clasp all, everyone and everything, in a cosmic embrace, so that all, everyone, everything, belongs.'

The Archbishop has finished his homily, but somehow he can sense that I am not wholly satisfied. He smiles. He recognises a lapsed Anglican when he sees one. He leans towards me one last time and, in a voice barely above a whisper, says, 'You are like so many, my friend. You have everything, but, inside, you feel there is something missing: deep down, somewhere, it's not quite okay. Do not worry, do not feel troubled, do not be perplexed. God loves you as you are – with your doubts, with your intellectual reservations, with your inability to make the leap of faith. God says, "I made you, actually, and I made you as you are because I love you. Don't try to titivate yourself. Just be you and know that I affirm you. You are precious. You matter enormously to me. You matter as if you were the only human being and, you know something,'" – he pauses for a moment and smiles a wonderful smile – "'I create only masterpieces. I have no doubt at all about your worth. You don't have to do anything. Your worth for me is intrinsic. Please believe I love you. You are not going to find ultimate satisfaction in anything out there because I made you like me. As St Augustine says, 'Thou hast made us for thyself and our hearts are restless until they find their rest in thee.' I made you for a worshipping creature – and you have worshipped money and fame, I know it – but, ultimately, I am the only one worth worshipping. I won't let you go, my child. I won't give up on you – ever. I won't. I will sit here like the father of the prodigal son, waiting. Come back home, come back home to me, and our celebration will be mindboggling.'

A final explosion of laughter and the Archbishop pushes back his chair and says, 'Come, we will go outside and watch the sun falling on Table Mountain and smell the flowers together. God is good, man, and he is waiting for you.'

How to . . .

How to keep a diary

1 January 2000.

Today's the day. Tomorrow won't do. If you are going to keep a diary, can there be a better place to start than the beginning of a new millennium?

If you have not tried it before, let me warn you: diary writing calls for commitment, discipline and stamina. I know. I've been at it since I was nine. I started at the same age as Tony Benn, veteran MP and Britain's most prolific diarist. 'It's a dreadful burden,' he says. 'I began in 1934: "Got up, had breakfast, it rained today". My diary was a bit patchy in the early years and, during the war, it was illegal. You weren't allowed to keep a diary in case it fell into the hands of the enemy. But from 1950 I've kept it conscientiously. It must run to twelve million words or more by now. It's a big chunk of my life. I'd say an hour a day. I can't go to bed unless I've done it. It could be three in the morning, I still have to do the diary.'

My favourite political diarist is Sir Henry 'Chips' Channon, MP for Southend from 1935 until his death in 1958. With a pen dipped alternately in champagne and vitriol, he offers an unputdownable portrait of the

English establishment across four decades. His son, Sir Paul (MP for Southend since 1959 though not a diarist), agrees that immediacy is the essence: 'My father wrote it all down there and then. He'd come in from the Commons, return from the Coronation, and write it at once – and never look at it again.'

I once asked Alan Clark for the secret of his success as a diarist. He offered me 'the four "I"s: 'A diary should be immediate, indiscreet, intimate, and indecipherable.' Clark wrote his diary in a deliberately crabbed hand. (The apparent extracts that appear as endpapers in the published volume were specially manufactured: at his publisher's behest Clark made up and wrote out some legible 'sample pages', and included a deliberate cliff-hanger to tease the reader.)

Samuel Pepys wrote much of his diary in a shorthand quite common in his day and, for the passages concerning his extra-marital dalliances, in a complicated Spanish-based code of his own devising. Woodrow Wyatt wrote his diary in secret. 'Father would come home and lock himself in his study,' remembers his daughter Petronella. 'We had no idea what he was up to. We thought he was writing a play.'

Virginia Woolf's favourite time for writing her diary was immediately after tea, after her day's work and before the onset of evening, dinner, husband, friends. My favourite time is early in the morning, before either post or papers have arrived, in bed, with tea and Marmite toast. When I was an MP and setting off for the Commons before 7.00 a.m., I used to catch up with the diary in the chamber or in committee. The rules of the House do not allow you to read books in committee, but you can write them. (If you are crafty you can, in fact, read them too. A colleague completed *War and Peace* while serving on the Finance Bill: in the Library he photocopied fifty pages at the start of each day and brought them to the Committee Room tucked inside the Budget Red Book.)

When he was in government, Tony Benn scribbled notes through cabinet meetings and then returned to his department and wrote them up immediately, if necessary sacrificing lunch in order to do so. As a government whip, attending cabinet committees, I followed Benn's example. Occasionally it proved a risky enterprise. Towards the end of the 1992–7 parliament, when the Major government was in freefall, I was witness to a late-night encounter between the Chancellor of the Exchequer and the Foreign Secretary, apparently at irreconcilable odds over a central issue of policy. In the Commons library, at 2.00 a.m., mildly squiffy, I wrote my colourful account of the meeting. The following morning, sober and aghast, I realised I couldn't find my papers. (I don't keep my diary in a book, but on lined sheets of A4.) I called my wife: she searched high and low: I hadn't taken them home. I called the government car service: my driver hadn't seen them. They weren't on my desk in the whips' office. They weren't in my secretary's room. Suddenly, I recalled where they were. Walking as rapidly as the whips' rules allow (a whip never runs: everything is under control, always) I made my way to the quiet room at the end of the library. Standing by the table we sometimes shared, apparently leafing through my papers, was Peter Mandelson. My heart stood still. The Prince of Darkness looked up and smiled. 'I've found it.' He had been looking for his filofax.

'I wonder why I do it?' Virginia Woolf asked herself. I do it, I think, because it makes me feel more alive, more aware of what's happening to me, consequently more in control, more real. It's like checking in a mirror to make sure you're still there – and reasonably comfortable with what you see. I do it too because I have always been fascinated – and excited – by famous people (the achieving, the celebrated, even the notorious) and I still find it exhilarating to get a close-up snapshot of a household name. (Going back forty years, one of my first diary entries reads: 'Met Charles de Gaulle today. He is very tall and President of France.' And, last week, on the same day, I found myself, consecutively, with Margaret Thatcher, Joanna Lumley and Posh Spice. Yeessss!)

Tony Benn says: 'The only teacher is experience. With a diary you get each experience three times, first as it happens, then when you record it, then when you read it again.'

Some keep a diary with future generations (if not immortality) deliberately in mind. It worked for James Boswell: 'I thought that my son would perhaps read this journal and be grateful to me for my attention to him . . . My wife, who does not like journalizing, said it was leaving myself embowelled to posterity . . . but I think it is rather leaving myself embalmed. It is certainly preserving myself.'

Some keep a journal simply 'for the record'. Sir Peter Hall's diaries (1972–80) offer a fascinating account of his time as director of the National Theatre, but you will go through almost five hundred pages before you reach a personal revelation: '25 December 1979. New York: I didn't go home for Christmas. I have always kept this diary professional and un-personal, but now it's beginning to seem ridiculous if I cannot say – or will not say – what is in my heart. I am deeply in love with Maria Ewing, and have been with her here. We plan to make our life together in the new year when she will come to London.'

For others their diary is a confessional and consolation. Sir Edward Marshall Hall, the great turn-of-the-century advocate, kept a diary of the first six years of his career at the Bar and of his married life, the one a public triumph, the other a private nightmare. He could tell his diary what no one else knew: while he and his bride were still in the carriage that drove them away from the church on their wedding day, she told him she could never care for him as he cared for her. On 24 June 1882, during their honeymoon in Paris, he recorded: 'Ethel told me she would be just as happy without me as with me, which is not altogether a cheering prospect.' The next day: 'She said she did not love me at all now. I went down to breakfast, and meanwhile E went out without my seeing her. I then went out to shop and bought her a ring, but, as there were no signs of Ethel at four o'clock, I started out all over Paris looking for her . . . At last, when I was quite in despair, I saw her in the Rue Castiglione. I induced her to have some dinner and then pacified her grief a little, but I fear her love is almost gone for ever. I wish I were dead.'

In April 1988, when Kenneth Williams died from an overdose of barbiturates washed down with alcohol, the kind-hearted coroner brought in an open verdict. But it's clear from Williams's diaries that he used what he called his 'hoard of poison' to take his own life. He was in pain ('oh, this bloody ulcer and spastic colon'), he had given up smoking (a lifelong recreation), and he was waiting to go into hospital ('how I HATE those places') for an operation he dreaded. He was frightened. And he was fed up. He knew he had painted himself into a corner. Professionally and personally, he had nowhere left to go. The final words in the journal he kept so conscientiously for more than forty years summed it up: ' – oh – what's the bloody point?'

Kenneth Williams told me he did not want to see his diaries in print: 'Some sides of my character aren't presentable.' For him, the diary represented a safe house, what he called 'a secure place for my insecurities'. He used the diary to record his hopes, fears, frustrations, fantasies. We first had lunch together on 9 July 1979: 'Went to see Gyles Brandreth . . . I found him very engaging & because of this I became more and more forthcoming & was eventually talking in terms of the confessional: "My sexual indulgence is all masturbatory . . ." etc.' (I looked rather different twenty years ago. Thirty years ago I looked very different indeed. In December 1969 Richard Crossman saw me on a television programme and decribed me in his diary as 'a young Tory, handsome, good-looking, waving his delicate fingers about.' Crossman's verdict on what I had to say is more telling: 'The young man had no ideas or ideals . . . [he] didn't stand for anything.')

While there is not much point in a diary that does not at least attempt to be honest, inevitably a diarist only records the truth as he sees it. On 21 June 1985 Kenneth Williams came to dinner. According to my account of the evening: 'Kenneth was on manic overdrive – gloriously on song, wonderfully funny, but no one else got a word in edgeways. Kenneth didn't listen to a word anyone else had to say.' How wrong can you get? Kenneth's account of the same evening carefully records the names of each of the guests and his particular pleasure at the way one of them, Roddy Llewellyn, put across a joke. 'Roddy told a story about a man going into the home of two spinsters to view a Ming vase & seeing a french letter lying on the piano stool. The old lady explained, "We found it lying in the grass on the common & it said Place on organ to avoid infection and we haven't got an organ so we put it on the piano & do you know we've neither of us had any colds this year!" He's one of the few people I've ever come across who knows how to tell a story.'

Tony Benn, Richard Crossman and Tam Dalyell once compared diary entries of an evening they had spent together. Each had recorded a quite different highlight to their conversation. The only common factor, according to Tony Benn, was the way 'we had each insulted the other for not listening properly or understanding the case we were trying to put.'

What makes a diary publishable? According to Ion Trewin, Alan Clark's publisher at Weidenfeld and Nicolson, 'The quality of writing is key. That's why, for me, Woodrow Wyatt doesn't work. All he was thinking about was the gossip and the scandal. Name-dropping on its own isn't enough. You can pick up Chips Channon and, even not knowing who the characters are, you become absorbed at once.'

Trewin is clear that you shouldn't set out to write a diary for publication. 'If you have an eventual audience in mind – whether it's your grandchildren or the readers of a Sunday newspaper – you become self-conscious, you begin to self-censor. The whole thing becomes artificial.'

Trewin also has reservations about dictated diaries. 'They tend to be long-winded. They ramble. They just don't read so well.' Tony Benn, who has taken to dictating his diary in recent years, disagrees. 'Yes, there's a risk of being more verbose, but there's also a greater immediacy. And no prospect of correction or revision. When you hear the diarist's own voice speaking you know exactly how he felt at the time. Once I flew to Tokyo and

I tried taping the diary when I arrived, utterly exhausted. I've got on tape the moment I lost consciousness. 'Of course, a dictated diary can lead to misunderstandings in transcription. I found "cuddly Pooh" in the middle of one entry and took a while to work out that the sentence should have read "Hugh Cudlipp who . . ." And for one awful moment I thought I'd had a forgotten relationship with a Russian actress, Zinovia Flotta, until I realised the words I'd dictated were "Zinoviev Letter".

Ion Trewin, whose firm have published more diaries than any other, says, 'Different diaries work in different ways. Some will evoke a particular class or world, like those of Cecil Beaton or Noël Coward. Others will be social documents, portraits of an age and way of life, like the journals of Parson Woodforde or the Reverend Francis Kilvert. The most moving are testaments to courage, like those of Anne Frank or the wartime diaries of Victor Klemperer. And the most fascinating are diaries that are a witness to history. The first I worked on were those of Jock Colville, Churchill's wartime secretary. He shouldn't have kept a diary, of course, but he did, thank God. Frequently the best diaries are written not by a main player, like Churchill, but by someone like Colville, a relatively dispassionate observer close to the centre of events. We like a diarist to be our eyes and ears, eavesdropping on history.'

The one essential is candour. As Chips Channon put it in his own journal: 'What is more dull than a discreet diary? One might as well have a discreet soul.' Be yourself and damn the consequences. Alan Clark's weaknesses were his diaries' strengths. He acknowledged their failings: 'Sometimes lacking in charity; often trivial; occasionally lewd; cloyingly sentimental, repetitious, whingeing and imperfectly formed . . . But they are real diaries.' And they sold 300,000 copies.

So keep a diary, and, who knows, one day it may keep you. You know the rules: do it on the day (or at least not later than the morning after the night before); don't hide anything; don't revise; don't look back; don't write for publication; pace Tony Benn, don't dictate. If you happen to walk with history, don't record what we will get in the official record: simply tell us what it was like to be there. And if history has passed you by, and you're not even on nodding acquaintance with a prime minister or a Spice Girl, don't despair. According to Ion Trewin, 'Of the diaries that have stood the test of time, several of the best make no mention of great people or events. They are beautifully observed portraits of everyday life. It's the domestic detail and the quality of observation that make them so absorbing. In the hands of a true diarist, even the dull days can be good.'

Siegfried Sassoon on 13 January 1921: 'Rainy weather. Does the weather matter in a journal? Lunched alone; does that matter? (Grilled turbot and apple-pudding, if you want full details.)'

But just before you throw down the paper and search for your notebook and pen, a final word of warning. Diaries can be dangerous. They become a compulsion. You will get hooked. Anais Nin, who began to write her diary aged eleven, frequently felt her journalising was overwhelming her life and, over fifty years, tried repeatedly to break herself of the habit, without success: 'The period without the diary remains an ordeal. Every evening I want my diary as one wants opium.'

Of course, you may be about to throw down the paper for a different reason. There is something irritating, self-regarding, self-indulgent about a diarist. It's not your style. Besides, you are too busy living life to want to write about it. As Tallulah Bankhead observed: 'Only good girls keep diaries. Bad girls don't have the time.'

How to get a gong

1 January 2001.

If you didn't get a mention in this weekend's New Year's Honours List, and would rather have liked one, don't despair. Read on. For the past year I have been making a television documentary about honours in Britain and I now know how the system works. Finding out hasn't been easy because the civil servants who run the show won't talk ('Let not daylight in on magic' is still their line) and, according to the Cabinet Office, 'there is not a government minister responsible for honours so we do not have anybody available for interview'. Happily, I managed to unearth a Whitehall mole willing to spill the beans and found a number of former cabinet members ready to reminisce. I also remembered that when I left government myself in 1997 (I was in the Whips' Office) I brought with me a secret document marked 'Honours In Confidence'. I think the time has come to give its contents wider currency.

So, if you are suffering from knight starvation and feel Her Majesty has yet to give you your just deserts, welcome to Brandreth's Rough Guide to the Honours System. Pitch yourself at the right level and play the game by the rules and you will find your gong is as good as guaranteed.

What's on offer?

Plenty. Some 2,000 honours are awarded each year, with a bumper crop expected in 2002, to mark the Queen's Golden Jubilee. They come in a bewildering array of shapes and sizes. Top of the range is the Order of the Garter (founded 1348) given for 'exceptional service to the nation'. Tony Benn once asked a senior courtier why it was felt that the Duke of Kent (a decent cove, but not quite the Duke of Wellington) should be the recipient of this special distinction. 'The Queen is the fount of all honour,' Benn was told, 'so inevitably those close to the fount will get splashed.'

The Order of the Thistle (1687) is Scotland's equivalent of the Garter, with another royal relation, Princess Anne, the genial Princess Royal, the most recent recipient. The Royal Victorian Order (1896) is for personal service to the sovereign and comes in five classes: on retirement tweenies at Balmoral become 'members' (MVO), senior royal retainers, friends and family become Knights and Dames Grand Cross (GCVO). The Order of Merit (1902) is for 'high personal intellectual achievement' (Lucian Freud, Tom Stoppard) and the Companion of Honour (1917) is comparable but less glorious. (It is also a bonbon proffered to retiring politicians: Mo Mowlam is next in line: service in Northern Ireland virtually guarantees it.)

In 1399 the first knights of the Order of the Bath actually took one, as a symbol of spiritual purification. Today the Order is reserved for senior members of the home civil service (the very chaps who run the honours system) and military personnel (even, occasionally, real heroes), while the Order of St Michael and St George (1819) is now confined to diplomats and those 'who have given service to Britain overseas'.

All of the above go to a tiny handful of people. Most honours – more than ninety per cent – are now given within the Order of the British Empire, founded by George V in 1917. This, frankly, is where you are most likely to come in.

Who gets what and why?

Why does Barbara Windsor become a Member, Joanna Lumley an Officer, and Ned Sherrin a Commander of the Order of the British Empire? Because – according to my secret document – there is a formula applied to each candidate that measures 'length of service', 'quality of achievement', 'the degree of responsibility carried' and whether 'national, regional, local or parochial'. According to my mole, 'Snobbery comes into it too. Writers, classical actors, members of the Garrick Club, get a higher level of award than TV personalities and soap stars.'

Since 1993, when John Major overhauled the system, the rule has been 'no awards to people occupying particular posts simply because they are occupying that post: they have to earn an award by merit.' The only exception is the case of High Court judges who get an automatic K on appointment. According to the Cabinet Office, 'this recognises both their status and the need for judges to be free from the influence of later offers of an honour.' John Major told me that he had hoped to abolish this judicial perk, but was advised that, if he did, he wouldn't have any judges.

Who decides?

Ultimately, the Queen on the recommendation of the prime minister. In practice, the permanent secretary in each government department is key. He's the one to nobble. In the early 1990s, when Stephen Dorrell was the reluctant culture minister (and I was his eager-beaver parliamentary private secretary) I had a number of secret encounters ('You understand this meeting is not taking place, Gyles') with Sir Hayden Phillips CB, the department's permanent secretary, smoothest of Whitehall mandarins and noted Mr Fix-It in the field of honours and the arts. Hayden relished honours as a connoisseur savours fine wine. 'A CBE for Alan Bates feels right, don't you agree? A knighthood for Donald Sinden? Mmm . . . He hasn't been on the list in my time, but I don't see why not. Shall we give it a try?' With the help of my friend Danny Finkelstein (Director of the Conservative Research Department) on the back of an envelope (I have it still) I drew up a list of twenty candidates ripe for recognition, from Delia Smith to Norman Wisdom. I am happy to report all of them have since received their due.

Each government department's list of nominees is then assessed by one of the 'central committees of advisers expert in the various spheres of interest'. When she was Secretary of State Virginia Bottomley asked Sir Hayden who served on the advisory committee for the arts. 'It is not for you to know, minister', was the gist of his reply. Says Bottomley, 'I thought the secrecy was somewhat extreme, but there wasn't much I could do about it.'

My mole says, 'The secrecy is to prevent the committee members from being got at. Candidates can be blackballed. That has to be done anonymously.'

If your candidacy survives this stage, the final hurdle is the 'central honours committee' chaired by the Head of the Home Civil Service. If you've got his backing, bingo.

Where do you start?

You can be the beneficiary of a permanent secretary's patronage (see above). The prime minister can put you on the list. (If he does, make sure he knows who you are. Harold Wilson sought an honour for Harry H. Corbett, the actor who played Steptoe Junior and was a Labour Party supporter. The OBE was offered to Harry Corbett, the creator of Sooty, the glove puppet.) You can be nominated by an organisation, national association or public body. You can even be nominated by an individual: admirer, friend or relative. They will need to submit your name on a special four-page form available from the Ceremonial Branch, Cabinet Office, Ashley House, 2 Monck Street, London SW1P 2BQ. (Send an s.a.e. Personal callers are not welcome.) If this is your mode of entry, critical to your success will be the letters of support accompanying the completed form. According to my mole, 'Quality rather than quantity is what counts. We particularly welcome endorsements from Lords Lieutenant and senior figures in the same areas of endeavour. The file needs to be fat enough to show breadth and depth of support for the candidate, but not so voluminous as to suggest a concerted campaign. We don't like to feel we're being "bounced".'

Some 9,000 nominations are made each year and around ten per cent are successful. If you are female or non-white your chances are enhanced. Currently a third of those honoured are women and three per cent come from ethnic minority communities. The powers-that-be would like to improve the percentages.

Can you buy an honour?

Yes. When Lloyd George was prime minister there was a set tariff: a knight-hood cost £10,000, a baronetcy £30,000, a peerage upwards of £50,000. Lloyd George took the view that 'the sale of honours is the cleanest way of raising money for a political party' and in five years, 1917–22, the distribution of 25,000 CBEs/OBEs/MBEs and 1,500 knighthoods garnered more than £2,000,000 for Liberal Party funds.

It is done with more subtlety these days. Ivan Massow, millionaire businessman, gay activist and sometime prospective Conservative candidate for the post of London Mayor, told me he was offered a peerage by William Hague's men. 'They're not totally blatant,' he admits. 'They don't say, "Give us the money, support us, and you'll get a peerage." But it's clear what's on offer. They use phrases like "you'd look good in ermine, you'd be so effective in the upper house." It's more like a flirtation, sizing up someone over dinner before you decide whether you're going to sleep with them.'

A long-time Conservative Central Office insider maintains that, when the Tories were in government, the standard practice of party fund-raisers was to solicit loans from wealthy supporters. In due course, the individual making the loan would receive recognition – a CBE, a K, even a peerage – and the expectation was that, on receipt of the honour, the loan would become a gift. In the insider's fifteen-year experience the system failed only once: the benefactor got his peerage and then asked for his money back.

Of course, no one doubts that the Tory Party's current treasurer, Lord Ashcroft, was worthy of ennoblement for reasons beyond and above his multi-million-pound munificence to the Conservatives, just as a raft of New Labour peers – David Puttnam, David Sainsbury, Melvyn Bragg – merited recognition regardless of any financial contributions to the Labour Party's cause.

These days the political parties try to avoid honouring out-and-out crooks. Lloyd George gave a CBE to a Glasgow bookie with a criminal record in recognition of his 'untiring work in connection with various charities'. Harold Wilson knighted and ennobled his friend and benefactor Joseph Kagan who was imprisoned for theft and false accounting. In John Major's day, at a Conservative Party Ball where I was conducting the auction, I was briefed not to take bids from 'a doubtful group of characters' at a certain table. 'We'd like their money,' I was told, 'but we can't have them being photographed with the prime minister. They'll be wanting knighthoods next.'

Around half of the modern honours are given in recognition of 'voluntary service' and, for the non-politically minded, giving handsomely to charity is another way of securing your bauble. The secret is to choose a charity with sufficient clout and the right connections. According to Geordie Greig, editor of *The Tatler*, 'The House of Lords is now stuffed with political place-men, so a peerage is quite devalued. A knighthood given for charitable services has much more style.'

Will the skeletons in your cupboard prove fatal to your chances?

Not necessarily. According to the confidential guidelines: 'It is important that those recommended for awards have a private character which reflects the high standard expected of recipients of honours. Nor should there be anything in their past history which would make the person unsuitable to receive an honour.'

In practice, homosexuals have featured on the list since well before the decriminalisation of homosexuality in 1967 and even prosecution for lewd behaviour is not a long-term bar. The actor John Gielgud, for example, both knighted and fined for importuning in Coronation Year, went on to earn a CH and an OM, so, while Gary Glitter is almost certainly beyond the pale, there's hope yet for Hugh Grant and George Michael.

A colourful private life (Elton John, Barbara Windsor) and living abroad (Julie Andrews, Elizabeth Taylor) are no longer obstacles to preferment, but outstanding liabilities to the Inland Revenue will still be damaging to your prospects. The critic Sheridan Morley told me that he had written to Margaret Thatcher suggesting that David Niven 'who had stood for Britain in countless Hollywood films' should receive a knighthood. According to Morley, 'Thatcher replied that, yes, indeed, an honour for Niven was an excellent idea and would certainly be forthcoming once he had regularised his tax affairs. The good news was relayed to Niven whose response was "Bugger that!" Niven died wealthy, but undubbed. A year or two later, exactly the same thing happened with Rex Harrison. But Rex decided to pay up and got his K in consequence.'

(Once you have got your gong, it is best to keep your nose clean because what the Queen giveth she can also take away. Tax evasion cost Lester Piggott his OBE and, when he was revealed to be a spy, Sir Anthony Blunt was stripped of his KCVO.)

How long will it take?

According to my secret document, 'it is unusual for a person with less than twenty years' overall service to receive an honour'; you are unlikely to get a knighthood before you are 50; you won't be offered a second honour within five years of receiving your first; and if you are expecting your gong on retirement, if you don't get it in the list immediately following your retirement, bad luck, you've missed the boat.

Once your name has been fed into the system it can take anything from six to eighteen months before that letter from 10 Downing Street marked 'Urgent, Personal and Confidential' flops onto your doormat: 'The prime minister has asked me to inform you, in strict confidence, that he has it in mind to submit your name to the Queen . . .'

Time was when premature publicity of any kind would have kiboshed your chances. Now, 'spin' can work to your advantage. When Donald Dewar vetoed the proposed knighthood for Sean Connery because of Connery's support for the Scottish Nationalist Party, the ensuing press furore guaranteed Connery his K next time round. Special pleading on behalf of Michael Caine accelerated his knighthood and (I am told) the fall-out from the OBE given this summer to J. K. Rowling is going to ensure belated recognition for Anthony Buckeridge, the creator of another schoolboy hero, Jennings.

Buckeridge is 88 and frail. According to Max Clifford, PR adviser to the 'stars' (and Mohammed Fayed), 'If I had a client who wanted a gong, I'd put it about that they had some kind of terminal illness. That usually clinches it.'

Will it change you?

Tony Benn, who disclaimed a peerage and would turn down the Garter if it were offered, says, 'Politicians shouldn't accept honours. My father used to say, "Pastry chefs don't eat cakes". The effect of the honours system is subtle and pernicious. I've seen what it can do. The hope of preferment can persuade even the best people to watch what they say, to trim their sails. The patronage system in this country is thoroughly corrupt. It should be brought to an end, and the sooner the better.'

The Queen takes a different view. Not only does she give out honours, she accepts them too. (She is the most decorated woman on the planet, with at least 75 foreign gongs, ranging from Denmark's Order of the Elephant to Spain's Order of the Golden Fleece.) Her view is that honours cost very little and give a great deal of pleasure. 'The system does discover people who do unsung things,' she points out. 'And I think people need pats on the back sometimes. It's a very dingy world otherwise.'

How to write a love letter

14 February 2001.

L et me tell you about Chrissie. She was a girl with green eyes, long auburn hair, a perfect mouth, and an amazing way with words. She was the sister of a girl in my class (I went to Bedales, the coeducational boarding school in Hampshire) and when our relationship began she was eighteen and I was four years her junior. She was no longer at school herself: she was out in the big, wide world, but one weekend she came to

> ## Robert Schumann to Clara Schumann, 1838
>
> What a heavenly morning! All the bells are ringing; the sky is so golden and blue and clear – and before me lies your letter. I send you my first kiss, beloved.

Bedales to visit her sister and happened to see the school play, T. S. Eliot's *Murder in the Cathedral*, in which I had a walk-on part as one of the monks.

I had not heard of Chrissie and had no idea who she was until two or three days after the performance when I received a ten-page letter from her that began, 'My dearest, darling Gyles, I saw you in the play on Friday and I have to tell you that I am now in love. Don't laugh. This is real. This is true. This is beautiful.' This is odd, I thought, but not unpleasant.

She enclosed a photograph, taken in a nightclub in Beirut (this was the 1960s), and an invitation to me to write back and share with her my 'hopes and dreams and innermost, innermost thoughts'. I did write back. I have no

---

Napoleon Bonaparte to Josephine Bonaparte, 1796

I have not spent a day without loving you; I have not spent a night without embracing you; I have not so much as drunk a single cup of tea without cursing the pride and ambition which force me to remain separated from the moving spirit of my life. In the midst of my duties, whether I am at the head of my army or inspecting the camps, my beloved Josephine stands alone in my heart, occupies my mind, fills my thoughts. If I am moving away from you with the speed of the Rhône torrent, it is only that I may see you again more quickly. If I rise to work in the middle of the night, it is because this may hasten by a matter of days the arrival of my sweet love.

---

idea what I said: I didn't keep copies of my letters, but I have kept every one of the hundred and more increasingly intimate letters, notes and cards she sent to me over the next two years. She wrote wonderful letters, full of energy, excitement, sunshine and sex. I came of age with Chrissie. She described her body, she anticipated mine. Now and again, she scrawled an erotic doodle in the margin. She was a fabulous correspondent.

One day, when I was sixteen, I was lying on my bed in my dormitory reading, when a boy came in and said, 'Your friend Chrissie is in the quad. She wants to see you.' In two years, Chrissie and I had never met. Beirut was a long way from Hampshire. I hesitated. Another message came. I got up, combed my hair, brushed my teeth, and went down into the quadrangle. She was there, alone, looking irresistible, even more lustrous than her photograph. I recognised her at once. She didn't recognise me at all. Within three minutes we had worked out that the young man she had wanted to correspond with had been another of the monks in *Murder in the*

Edward, Prince of Wales, to Mrs Freda Dudley Ward, 1919

My vewy vewy own precious darling beloved little Fredie –

I can never never tell you how I loathed our parting this morning angel, although only for a fortnight; 2 weeks out of the short 10 weeks that remain before my next f-cking world trip!! . . . I'm just going to bed so as to be asleep by midnight (according to your orders) but I just can't till I've written you a few lines to say how I'm missing you & wanting you tonight & how hopelessly lonely & lost I feel!! . . . I'll finish this tomorrow as I'm so so thleepy & you must be too; baby mine pleath do take the greatest care of your precious little self; now it's my turn to preach!!

Be vewy vewy careful of the 'hunt horses' they might give you to ride if you do hunt as one can't trust them & then you haven't ridden for such ages!! I'm vewy vewy worried at the idea of your riding rotten horses, you just mustn't!! If only – but then it's the usual reason why I shouldn't lend you horses, merely because I'm the bloody f-cking P of W!

Cathedral. Chrissie's sister had identified me by mistake. Chrissie had been writing to the wrong guy. I never heard from her again.

I am sharing this traumatic adolescent moment with you to explain why, in the thirty-plus years since Chrissie left my life, I have been wary of love letters, either the writing or the receiving of them. Of course, I am now a happily married man and, as a rule, married men don't write love letters – at least, not to their wives. There are exceptions. Winston and Clementine Churchill wrote affectionately and copiously to one another over more than fifty years, but affairs of state – and a different taste in holidays – meant they were frequently apart and separation is a spur to letter-writing. Love letters also thrive (at least for a while) on frustration and adversity. For sheer passion, John Keats's frantic letters to Fanny Brawne could hardly be bettered, but his ardour was fuelled by non-consummation. Had he got the girl, would he still have wanted to be buried with one of her letters in his hand?

Mine has been a relatively tranquil life. My wife-to-be said yes (eventu-

---

Lord Byron to Teresa Guiccioli, 1819

My dearest Teresa . . . My destiny rests with you, and you are a woman, eighteen years of age, and two out of a convent. I wish that you had stayed there, with all my heart – or, at least, that I had never met you in your married state. But all this is too late. I love you, and you love me – at least, you say so, and act as if you did so, which is a great consolation in all events. But I more than love you, and cannot cease to love you. Think of me, sometimes, when the Alps and ocean divide us – but they never will, unless you wish it.

Byron

---

ally) and there was no Mr Moulton Barrett of Wimpole Street standing in our way. In consequence, I realise that when it comes to love letters (at least ones from me) the dear creature has been short-changed. I would like to put matters right, but, frankly, I am out of practice, which is why, this week, in anticipation of Valentine's Day, I have been seeking guidance in the art of love-letter writing. I have taken soundings from a number of authorities (all female), ranging from women of experience (Lady Antonia Fraser has compiled the definitive anthology of love letters) to three unattached ITN journalists, aged 26, 27, and 30. I even made a pilgrimage to Ladbroke Grove and, over whisky and Rioja, took a masterclass from Margaret Drabble, who in her new novel evokes Robert and Elizabeth Browning – 'their story is the paradigm of perfect love', she says – and has read more widely, more wisely, than anyone I know.

So, if you want to woo and win – or simply wow – the one you love, here are the rules: the seven essentials of successful love-letter writing.

1. Be passionate. 'A love letter must be full of fire,' says Drabble. 'Napoleon wrote cracking good love letters to Josephine. William Wordsworth wrote quite passionately to Mary. Jane Carlyle poured energy and all her literary talent into the letters she wrote to Thomas Carlyle. Jane Austen would write you a witty letter, but she was too proper to be passionate. A good love letter takes risks, feels dangerous. Women, of course, were

---

A letter written by Ludwig van Beethoven but never sent. It was found in a drawer after his death.

My angel, my all, my other self. Just a few words today, and that in pencil. Tell me, could our love exist other than by sacrifices, by not desiring everything? Is it your fault that you are not wholly mine, that I am not wholly yours? For the moment look at the loveliness of nature and calm your spirit about what has to be. We will surely see each other soon. You are suffering. I know from your letters you are suffering, my dearest treasure, but we must be patient. Wherever I am, there you are also. I shall make it possible for us to live together – and then what a life it will be!

Angel, the post leaves early today so I must finish this so that you can get it as soon as possible. Be calm, my love, today, yesterday, tomorrow. I long with tears for you. You! You! YOU! My life, my everything, farewell. Only go on loving me and never deny the true heart of your loving L. Yours eternally, mine eternally, ours eternally.

---

not allowed to take the initiative in these matters, but had they been, I think Charlotte Bronte would have written you a letter that was suitably impassioned.

'I would have welcomed a letter of admiration from Lord Byron. He wrote brilliant love letters to everyone – girls, women, men, boys, Caroline Lamb, his half-sister, the sixty-year-old woman with whom he was having an affair when he was half her age, even his wife. I wouldn't want a letter from Robert Browning. He belongs to Mrs Browning. They were equally in love and it was a love that endured. But Byron was different. You could have a fling with Byron and move on. No harm done.'

2. Be thoughtful. According to Lady Antonia Fraser, looks count. 'How important is the actual physical appearance of the letter! A thousand years ago at the court of the Japanese Emperor, no gentleman would have dreamt of spending a night with a lady without sending round a letter of appreciation the morning after – a letter in which the thickness, size, design and colour of the paper all helped to indicate the emotional mood that the writer wished to suggest – the finishing touch being supplied by the branch or spray of blossom which it was de rigueur to attach to it.'

It seems times have changed. One of the ITN journalists I spoke to (Natalie, 26) showed me her pager bearing a text message from her man: 'ImRdy4Luv' it read, 'MkeMyDaSa+!' (Translated from text-speak that's

---

Winston Churchill to Clementine Churchill, 1935

My darling Clemmie, In your letter from Madras you wrote some words, vy dear to me, about my having enriched yr life. I cannot tell you what pleasure this gave me, because I always feel so overwhelmingly in yr debt, if there can be accounts in love. It was sweet of you to write thus to me, & I hope & pray I shall be able to make you happy & secure during my remaining years, and cherish you my darling one as you deserve, & leave you in comfort when my race is run. What it has been to me to live all these years in yr heart & companionship no phrases can convey. Time passes swiftly, but is it not joyous to see how great growing is the treasure we have gathered together, amid the storms & stresses of so many eventful, & to millions tragic & terrible years?

'I'm ready for love. Make my day, say yes.') 'Not much of an invitation, is it? But it's better than nothing, I suppose. The truth is I don't want a text message or an e-mail or a phone call. I want an old-fashioned love letter written in ink on proper paper in a hand I can read. I want to feel that some time and effort and thought have gone into it.'

Margaret Drabble is confident that electronic communication won't supplant the traditional letter, because the letter is tangible and portable. 'You can carry a letter with you, hide it under the pillow, keep it in a shoe box with all the others as solid proof of love.' Antonia Fraser quotes Edith Wharton summing up the crucial moment of the letter's arrival: 'the first glance to see how many pages there are, the second to see how it ends, the breathless first reading, the slow lingering over each

---

Zelda Fitzgerald to F. Scott Fitzgerald, 1920

I look down the tracks and see you coming – and out of every haze & mist your darling rumpled trousers are hurrying to me – Without you, dearest dearest I couldn't see or hear or feel or think – or live – I love you so and I'm never in all our lives going to let us be apart another night. It's like begging for mercy of a storm or killing Beauty or growing old, without you. I want to kiss you so – and in the back where your dear hair starts and your chest – I love you – and I can't tell you how much – To think that I'll die without your knowing – Goofo, you've got to try to feel how much I do – how inanimate I am when you're gone – I can't even hate these damnable people – Nobody's got any right to live but us – and they're dirtying up our world and I can't hate them because I want you so – Come quick – Come quick to me – I could never do without you if you hated me and were covered with sores like a leper – if you ran away with another woman or starved me and beat me – I still would want you I know –

Lover, Lover, Darling -

Your Wife

---

phrase and each word, the taking possession, the absorbing of them, one by one, and finally the choosing of the one that will be carried in one's thoughts all day, making an exquisite accompaniment to the dull prose of life.'

3. Be yourself. Drabble offers reassurance for those who feel they may not have a professional writer's facility with words. 'With a love letter, passion, feeling, sincerity are what count. Simplicity of expression can be a virtue. Good writers don't necessarily write exciting love letters.

Fine words can stand in the way of true love. Bernard Shaw is a good example of a writer who managed to hide his feelings behind his words.'

4. Be prosaic. In 1857 Baudelaire sent a collection of his poetry to his mistress, Madame Sabatier, with a covering note: 'Farewell, dear lady. I kiss your hand as a sign of my utter devotion. All the verses contained between page 84 and page 105 are yours alone.' Shakespeare, Byron, the Brownings all wrote love letters in the form of poetry, but Drabble advises, 'Unless you are a poet, save your blushes and stick to prose.'

Seven years ago this week a tender-hearted Tory MP (Hartley Booth, Mrs Thatcher's successor at Finchley, a married man, a father of three, and a lay preacher) succumbed to the charms of his twenty-two-year-old researcher and was forced to leave the government when samples of his maudlin love poetry found their way into the pages of the *News of the World*. Apparently there was no affair, simply a sentimental attachment. The Chief Whip was not to be mollified. 'Whether he's giving her one or not is immaterial,' he barked. 'What we can't have is any more of his atrocious poetry getting into the public domain. It's a disgrace to the administration.'

Nathaniel Hawthorne to Sophia Hawthorne, c 1839

Dearest – I wish I had the gift of making rhymes, for methinks there is poetry in my head and heart since I have been in love with you. You are a Poem. Of what sort, then? Epic? Mercy on me, no! A sonnet? No; for that is too labored and artificial. You are a sort of sweet, simple, gay, pathetic ballad, which Nature is singing, sometimes with tears, sometimes with smiles, and sometimes with intermingled smiles and tears.

But if you are determined to put poetry into your love letter, make it your own. Antonia Fraser tells the story of how her father, the Earl of Longford, courted her mother with Tennyson's line 'Now sleeps the crimson petal now the white', adding solemnly, 'I wrote that.' Lady Antonia says, 'He was felt to have gone rather far in his assumption of her ignorance of English literature.'

John Keats to Fanny Brawne

My dearest Girl,

This moment I have set myself to copy some verses out fair. I cannot proceed with any degree of content. I must write you a line or two and see if that will assist in dismissing you from my Mind for ever so short a time. Upon my Soul I can think of nothing else. The time is passed when I had power to advise and warn you against the unpromising morning of my Life. My love has made me selfish. I cannot exist without you. I am forgetful of everything but seeing you again – my Life seems to stop there – I see no further. You have absorbed me. I have a sensation at the present moment as though I was dissolving – I should be exquisitely miserable without the hope of soon seeing you. I should be afraid to separate myself far from you. My sweet Fanny, will your heart never change? My love, will it? I have no limit now to my love . . .

Yours for ever,

John Keats

---

5. Be sexy. My trio at ITN expressed enthusiasm for love letters that are 'a bit raunchy'. 'Sexy is good,' said Julia (30), 'Prince Charles wanting to be Camilla's tampon is yuk.' I showed them Chopin's letter to his mistress Delphine Potocka in which he explains that the sexual act robs him of his creativity – 'a man wastes his life-giving precious fluid for a moment of ecstasy' – and counts the cost: 'Who knows what ballades, polonaises, perhaps an entire concerto, have been engulfed in your little D flat major . . .' 'I'm sorry,' said the girls, pulling a face in unison, 'that's a real turn-off.'

According to Margaret Drabble, 'James Joyce wrote some very

outspoken letters to Nora Barnacle – open, sexual and very persuasive. He made it clear what he wanted and she certainly gave in to it. The secret, I think, is to pace yourself. A letter should contain surprises. Unexpected explicitness is very powerful.'

6. Be positive. Drabble and Fraser report that many of the most compelling love letters in literature have been riven with angst, fuelled by frustration, inspired by adversity, but the young women at ITN are

---

An anonymous suicide note

No wish to die. One of the best of sports, which they all knew. Not in the wrong, the boys will tell you. This bastard at Palmer's Green has sneaked my wife, one of the best in the world; my wife, the first love in the world.

---

adamant that they want joyful love letters, filled with hope and humour, not anxiety. 'And I want a letter that's more about me than it is about him,' says Sara, 27. 'A self-absorbed lover is a real bore, especially if he's always down-in-the-mouth. If you can find a bloke who gives the impression that he's more interested in you than in himself you're onto a winner.'

7. Be sparing. Antonia Fraser believes that when it comes to love persistence pays. She quotes Ovid approvingly: 'In time refractory oxen come to plough, in time horses are taught to bear the pliant reins, an iron ring is worn by constant use . . . Only persevere, you will overcome Penelope herself.'

Margaret Drabble isn't so sure. 'Distrust a man who writes too many letters,' she says. 'Not only can the weight of the correspondence be a bit overwhelming, but you have to ask yourself if love-making by letter isn't a substitute for love-making in fact. Some people use the letter as a way of keeping the relationship at bay. There are six hundred pages of Kafka's letters to Felice Bauer. They were twice engaged, but each time he called it off. He had a commitment problem, clearly, and found more satisfaction in writing the letters than in marrying the lady.'

Drabble's ideal correspondent would not write too frequently, nor at too great a length. His letters would be passionate, bold, reckless, surprising – and heartfelt, at least at the time. I suggest to her that it's a tall order. She raises her whisky to me: 'If you can't manage it, don't despair. You can always go for the Cyrano option and call in the professionals. There's a respectable tradition of inarticulate chaps getting articulate chaps to write their love letters for them.'

Happily, such a service is currently available in London – free of charge – to visitors to Tate Modern's 'Century City' exhibition. In the Bombay

---

The Prince de Joinville to the actress Rachel Felix, c 1840:

Where? – When? – How much?

Her reply:

Your place. Tonight. Free.

---

section the artist Shilpa Gupta invites you to dictate a love letter into the microphone attached to a computer. Next, you select the type of paper on which your letter should be written and the scent with which to perfume it. The artist, working with a back-up team in Bombay, will then hand-write your letter for you and send it to the object of your affection. For tongue-tied lovers Gupta offers a ready-made missive, which you can adapt to your personal situation by choosing appropriate words from pull-down menus.

I have checked out the Gupta web-site (www.sentiment-express.com) and, while I like the look of it, I feel my wife would prefer something entirely home-made. Whatever I come up with – and I shall follow the rules and do my best – I know it will not rival my favourite love letter, written by the playwright Eugene O'Neill a few months before he died: 'To darling Carlotta, my wife, who for twenty-three years has endured with love and understanding my rotten nerves, my lack of stability, and my cussedness in general. I am old and would be sick of life, were it not that you, sweetheart, are here, as deep and understanding in your love as ever – and I as deep in my love for you, as when we stood in Paris, July 22nd 1929, and both said "Oui".'

PS Chrissie – If you're reading this, would you drop me a line?

Anthony Clare:
how to be happy

In January 2000, in search of happiness, I went to Dublin to meet the eminent psychiatrist, Professor Anthony Clare.

I want to be happy. How about you? If you know me, you probably think I am happy, almost irritatingly so. Well, I'm not. At least, not all of the time. I should be, of course. I count my blessings: I've got a good job, a fair income, a perfect wife (truly), three children with whom I'm still on speaking terms (That's the joy of money: it keeps you in touch with your offspring). I've got it all, and yet . . . You know what I mean, don't you? Something's missing, something's wrong. Perhaps I am expecting too much? Perhaps this is just a touch of post-millennium blues? There we were, at the end of December, with such high hopes. Here we are, at the end of January, and nothing's changed.

So I have been to see a psychiatrist. Indeed, I have been to see The Psychiatrist, the famous one off the radio, the one with the lilting Irish accent and the charming, disarming, penetrating way with him. Dr

Anthony Clare is 57, married with seven children (his parents were firm
Roman Catholics, but he is not averse to contraception: he and his wife just
like children), and as delightful in person as he seems on the wireless. He is
slight, twinkly, amused, amusing, attractive, wiry, beady-eyed, engaging:
Gabriel Byrne meets Kermit the Frog.

He is medical director of St Patrick's Hospital in Dublin, Ireland's first
mental hospital (founded by Jonathan Swift in 1757). To reach his office
from reception I travel through a labyrinth of corridors and stairwells, past
sullen young women with eating disorders, past alcoholics and depressives,
past shuffling figures muttering to themselves, past rows of old people
sitting sadly in armchairs gazing vacantly into the middle-distance. By the
time I arrive at the great man's room I am feeling suitably shame-faced.

His welcome is wonderfully warm. 'And what are you after?'

'I am looking for the elixir of happiness.'

He laughs. 'If it's an elixir you're after, Dublin's not a bad place to start.'

'No,' I persist, 'I'm serious. I want to be happy, I want to be happier. I
want you to point me – and my readers – in the right direction.'

He smiles. He may be celebrated as a media shrink, but he is serious too.
He is professor of clinical psychiatry at Trinity College, a research scientist
and a scholar. He pours coffee, invites me to take my place in the psychiatrist's chair, and suggests we might begin with a definition. 'What is
happiness?' There is a long pause. He sits behind his desk. He closes his eyes,
screws up his face. Eventually, eyes tight shut, he speaks.

'I pause because so many people talk about happiness as a physiological
state – that's to say certain kinds of hormones are flowing around your
system and, as a consequence, you feel a certain way – but others believe
that isn't so much happiness as ecstasy, or some kind of elation.'

Another pause. The eyes open. 'I would say happiness is a cognitive state,
an intellectual perception or understanding of you, the person, and your
relationship with your environment. It does have pleasurable components,
but that's not the essence of happiness. The essence of happiness is a

conscious appreciation of the rightness of being.' He looks me in the eye, to make sure I'm following. 'And it's a state. It's not a permanent trait. People aren't "happy" – they have experiences of happiness. Most people's customary state is one of balance between conflicting needs and desires and emotions, and happiness comes into play as one of those experiences which people from time to time describe and clearly aim for.'

'For example?'

'For example, one of my happy situations would be sitting in the Italian sunshine, mid-morning in Umbria, and laid out on the table there's wine and cheese and tomatoes with oil dribbled over them, and with a few friends I'm sitting there talking about something like this – happiness – and, so long as the wine's drinkable and the cheese smells like cheese, frankly I don't care, I'm happy. The people are key. Having people around you who make you feel good and think you're good is important.'

'You can describe a happy experience. Can it be measured?'

'There's amazing stuff going on now with imaging scanners, looking at centres of the brain that light up when people are feeling good, when they're listening to Mahler or Mozart or they're watching a favourite movie. A number of biological systems are bound up with our feelings. Take the role of the endogenous opioids. These are opiate-like substances that we produce inside us, and sometimes activities that we engage in can stimulate them – jogging for example, or some of these arousal jags that people put themselves into, climbing mountains, putting themselves in danger. You do something that prompts a natural high. It's almost as if you've got access to your own fix. And that's led to a lot of interest in the possibility that people who are prone to taking external substances – opiates, hallucinogens, amphetamines and so on – are people who, for one reason or another, have an internal opioid system that doesn't work very well, so they need external stimulation.

For a moment, the flow falters. 'The reason I'm pausing here is that while the biological systems may be a prerequisite to happiness – if your seratonin is low or your endogenous opioids are blunted, then it may indeed be difficult to feel happy – just because they are functioning well doesn't mean that you are going to be happy. As in every human feeling state there are a number of components, all of which have to be present. You need a reasonably healthy functioning system and then circumstances of a cognitive kind, of a personal and inter-personal kind that have meaning and that you pursue.

'To test happiness, I look at the areas of life that people over the centuries have identified as the mainsprings of human happiness. Jung pulled them together in a listing. He identified things like having a philosophy of life, having reasonable physical health and reasonable mental health. He thought an education mattered, but he didn't mean a narrow scholastic education. He meant an openness to the world, an openness to the arts, the sciences, human knowledge, an outward-looking approach. For inward-looking people it isn't easy. It's not impossible, but introspective people have problems being happy.

'If you sat here, Gyles, and I was testing you, I'd look at your philosophy of life – is it positive or negative? It doesn't mean you can't be happy if you think life is an absolutely pointless exercise, but it's starting to tilt the balance a bit. What are you doing with your life? Freud thought "to love and to work" were the two elements of happiness. Well, there's some truth in that. So, what's your work? How do you feel about it? Is it satisfying? Do you feel you are making a contribution and that it's valued? What about love? Do you love and are you loved?'

I have quite complicated answers to these questions at the ready, but I don't offer them. I don't want the degree of my introspection to become too apparent too soon. Instead, I change tack. 'Do we have a right to be happy?'

'According to the American constitution "the pursuit of happiness" is an inalienable right. The Americans, of course, have changed the way we think about the whole subject. The arrival of psychoanalysis in the United States and what the Americans did with it is important in terms of the modern attitude to happiness. The Americans took Freud and adapted him to their own purpose. Freud, of course, was a European pessimist. He didn't see the warring ego, id and superego as being resolved, but the Americans, with their passion for self-perfection and their notion of perfection being achievable on earth, took Freud's theory and turned it into a therapy to make you happy. And the result is that now, along with our air-conditioned four-door car and our house and our couple of holidays a year and a reasonable standard of health, we all expect happiness too.

'I remember in one of the prayers we used to say when I was a child there was a reference to life as "a vale of tears". Happiness was not for this world. Indeed, the notion of happiness on earth was a delusion and a snare. Happiness was the state you would arrive at after you were dead – if you did everything the right way. Heaven was happiness. You might get a glimpse of heaven on earth, but no more. When, in Irish Catholicism in the fifties and sixties, they were trying to come to terms with sexuality, some of the more complicated priests or nuns, who were supposed to know nothing about it, would assume that sexual ecstasy was a glimpse of heavenly happiness.'

'Bless them.' We both laugh. (Professor Clare laughs a lot. As you read this, remember there's a half-smile on his face most of the time.)

'Indeed. Now we demand heaven on earth. All the psychological theories today assume some kind of maturing balance between emotion and perception and cognition and will and impulse control. To what end? Perfection. A mental state of perfection is happiness. And the psychoanalyst has become the secular priest who will take you to happiness.

'While people want to be happy, admitting you are happy is a different matter. I think it was Shaw who said, "People rarely admit to being happy", rather as people rarely admit not to be stressed. People are wary of saying they're happy. Why? Perhaps because it sounds like an invitation to fate. Or it sounds smug. Or it sounds insensitive. Aldous Huxley in *Chrome Yellow* has a character sound off about "happy people" being "stupid people", completely insensitive. There's the noise and the screams and the roars of life out there, and the happy people just don't hear them. How can you be happy when you see on television what's happening in Kosovo or Uganda?'

'Well, how can you?'

'It's difficult. I remember discussing this with R. D. Laing, who was a very suffering man in many ways, but who recognised that if you allow suffering to overwhelm you you're not going to be of any use to anybody. So perhaps this process of being happy has an evolutionary purpose. It allows you to do things, to move forward. If you were too ready to become – understandably – unhappy, you'd be paralysed.'

'Why do some people talk of the war as the happiest time of their life?'

'Among those who fought in the Second World War there was a comradeship. People who might otherwise have found it difficult to socialise were thrown in together. They had no choice. And there was a shared philosophy, a common purpose. The basic fighting man felt he was doing something worthwhile. That was why the 1939-45 war was so different from Vietnam, or even the Gulf. And those engaged in the war were testing themselves. That seems to be rather important. Happy people are rarely sitting around. They are usually involved in some ongoing interchange with life. Of course, we're talking about people who survived the war, not those who were wounded or killed. And I'm not sure how many back home felt that way, other than those in the blitzed cities where again there was this comradeship.

'During the deepest troubles in Northern Ireland, in the Shankhill and the Falls, while people might not have described themselves as happy, they certainly felt a bond, a sense of community. One of the things that was destroyed when the slums of Dublin were moved to the suburbs was that sense of comradeship, of being together. I don't glory in the tenements of the thirties, Sean O'Casey's tenements in the city here, but my God they did produce a sense that people mattered to one another.'

'What about individual circumstances that are conducive to happiness? Is health important?'

'It can be an important component, but not necessarily. You will find disabled people who describe themselves as happy, and people who have led terrible lives who, because of a philosophical view of life and of suffering, describe themselves as happy too.'

'Does appearance matter? Do looks help?'

'Being reasonably attractive is a help. People come towards you, warm to you. But you can be too beautiful. Extremes are difficult for human beings to cope with. Marilyn Monroe wasn't very happy.'

'What about family circumstances?'

'It may be relevant where you come in a family. There's some evidence that first-borns, who get all the initial attention and love, are more contented, more confident. They may also be more conservative, less radical because they like the world as they see it. A second or third child is immediately in a more competitive and challenging situation, so there may be a tendency for first-borns to be happier.'

He shifts a little uneasily on his chair and lowers his voice: 'This is a terribly politically incorrect thing to say, but, on the whole, it's better to have two parents than one. This is not meant as an attack on single parents and, of course, we all know plenty of one-parent families that are successful and two-parent families that are a disaster, but as a general rule two-parent families are more conducive to happiness.'

'What about marriage?'

'In essence, marriage is good for men; and can be, but is not necessarily, good for women. If you take the four categories – married men, single men, married women, single women – it does appear that married men are the happiest and single men are the unhappiest. With women it gets more complicated. For instance, married women with a poor level of education are unhappier than single women, but educated married women are relatively happy.

'Married men do badly when they're bereaved, very badly. They either quickly remarry or they die. You'll often hear men say they can see their wives surviving without them, whereas all women think their husbands will marry again. Women just don't believe their men can function without the kinds of support that marriage can give them, and it seems they're right. Women cope with bereavement far better. There's no evidence, as I understand it, of a higher mortality rate among women in the two or three years after bereavement, but there is with men.'

'What about money?'

'It has suited all sorts of people to equate material possessions with a state of happiness, because that keeps you pursuing them. But money and material things are a means to an end. I do not knock them. Often they free people. It is difficult in situations of struggle to be happy, but it doesn't follow that in situations of plenty you will be happy.'

'So winning the lottery won't make me happy?'

'Not of itself. Money is an enabler, but our society has got it horribly wrong and confuses the enabler with the end.'

I have been with the psychiatrist for nearly two hours, but I tell him I can't leave yet. 'In fact,' I say, 'unless I get what I came for I can't leave at all.'

'You want "strategies for happiness", do you?'

'Yes, please. I have come to see the wise man and I can't leave empty-handed. I want the secret recipe: Anthony Clare's Seven Steps to Happiness. This is the bit I and my readers are going to cut out and stick on the fridge door.'

'Oh God.'

'Go on, please.'

The professor smiles. He laughs. He is going to oblige. But first, the caveats: 'Remember, psychiatrists are very much better at exploring the pathological and the diseased and the malfunctioning, so you've got to be wary of those who come to the issue of health from disease or come to the issue of happiness from mental illness. Remember too that the things that I'm going to recommend are not all easy to do. If they were people would have no problems being happy.'

He closes his eyes once more. He rubs his thumb against his forefinger until he's ready. 'Okay. Here goes. Number one: cultivate a passion. How important it seems to me in my model of happiness it is having something that you enjoy doing. The challenge for a school is to find every kid some kind of passion – something that will see them through the troughs. That's why I'm in favour of the broadest curriculum you can get.

'Next, be a leaf on a tree. You have to be both an individual – you have to have a sense that you are unique and you matter – and at the same time you need to be connected to a bigger organism, a family, a community, a hospital, a company. You need to be part of something bigger than yourself. Yes, a leaf off a tree has the advantage that it floats about a bit, but it's disconnected and it dies.

'Some very interesting stuff has been done over the years on the issue of networks. The people who are best protected against certain physical diseases – cancer, heart disease, for example – in addition to doing all the other things they should do, seem to be much more likely to be part of a community, socially involved. If you ask them to enumerate the people that they feel close to and would connect and communicate with, those who name most seem to be happiest and those with least unhappiest. Of course, there may be a circular argument here. If you are a rather complicated person, people may avoid you. If, on the other hand, you are a centre of good feeling people will come to you. I see the tragedy here in this room where some people may sit in that chair and say they don't think they've got very many friends and they're quite isolated and unhappy, and the truth is they are so introspective they've become difficult to make friends with. Put them in a social group and they tend to talk about themselves. It puts other people off. So that's my third rule: avoid introspection.

'Next, don't resist change. Change is important. People who are fearful of change are rarely happy. I don't mean massive change, but enough to keep your life stimulated. People are wary of change, particularly when things are going reasonably well because they don't want to rock the boat, but a little rocking can be good for you. It's the salt in the soup. Uniformity is a tremendous threat to happiness, as are too much predictability and control and order. You need variety, flexibility, the unexpected, because they'll challenge you.

'Live in the moment. Look at the things that you want to do and you keep postponing. Postpone less of what you want to do, or what you think is worthwhile. Don't get hide-bound by the day-to-day demands. Spend less time working on the family finances and more time working out what makes you happy. If going to the cinema is a pleasure, then do it. If going to the opera is a pain, then don't do it.

'Audit your happiness. How much of each day are you spending doing something that doesn't make you happy? Check it out and if more than half of what you're doing makes you unhappy, then change it. Go on. Don't come in here and complain. People do, you know. They come and sit in that chair and tell me nothing is right. They say they don't like their family, they don't like their work, they don't like anything. I say, "Well, what are you going to do about it?"

'And, finally, Gyles, if you want to be happy, Be Happy. Act it, play the part, put on a happy face. Start thinking differently. If you are feeling negative, say, "I am going to be positive," and that, in itself, can trigger a change in how you feel.'

The professor slaps his hands on his desk and laughs. 'That's it.'

'And it works?'

'Well, it's something for the fridge door. Try it and see.'

Postscript:
a fond farewell

Thank you for reading this book – or for dipping into it – or for happening to flick it open at the car boot sale and chancing upon this page: it has been good to have your company. You probably aren't the sort of reader who writes to authors out of the blue, but just in case you are, just in case you have been toying with the idea of dropping me a friendly line, here's a final piece – by way of warning.

O scar Wilde liked to boast that so great was his celebrity he was obliged to engage two secretaries to cope with the demands for copies of his signature and locks of his hair: 'Within three months, one had died of writer's cramp; the other was entirely bald.' I know just how Oscar felt because I was adored once too. For seven years, 1983–90, I sat on the TV-am sofa alongside Anne Diamond and Roland Rat, the twin icons of breakfast broadcasting. Millions tuned in. Thousands of them wrote to me. Alarmingly, hundreds still do.

I have returned from holiday to find my desk doubled-decked with unsolicited correspondence from professed admirers. What am I to do? Really big stars can afford staff to handle their fan mail. Really good people do their best to reply personally to as many letters as they can. She won't thank me for telling you, but I happen to know that Joanna Lumley (actress and saint) spent every day of the Bank Holiday weekend, from dawn to dusk, sitting alone at her kitchen table conscientiously working her way through the avalanche.

John Cleese's approach is more robust. Write to him out of the blue and this is the reply you get: 'Thank you for your recent letter. The problem is this. For some time, I have been struggling to create a routine whereby I have enough time to pursue my own interests. Unfortunately, I find – and I'm not exaggerating – that I've almost no time for my own major activities, like writing, because I have a constant stream of meetings and mail and telephone calls to attend to, eighty per cent of which derive from other folks' attempts to involve me in their projects, which – while splendid and very worthwhile – are still not as essentially interesting as my own. So, I'm afraid I'm giving a blanket "No" to all requests for the foreseeable future, in the hope that I can discharge all my other obligations and then actually be able to focus on my own projects for a time. Good luck.'

I have neither Lumley's heart nor Cleese's courage. I get an average of fifty unsolicited letters a week – on a par with a regional TV weather presenter, I'm told. I can't reply to everybody, but nor do I want to be seen to be blowing a giant raspberry in the face of so many friendly people, most of whom are writing to me on behalf of undeniably worthy causes. This is my compromise. I have been through the backlog piled high in the in-tray and I am going to deal with it here and now, once and for all. I am taking the ten most common requests and setting down my full and final response to each one. In future, if you write to me, kindly enclose an s.a.e and I will send you an individually autographed copy of the following.

1.   If you are asking for money, the answer is No. It's not that I haven't got any, it's just that I want to hang onto to it. Let me add – and this is a line

I was given a few years ago by the lovely Katie Boyle (prototype TV celebrity, the Joanna Lumley of the 1950s) – 'I already have three favourite charities I support financially and very much wish I could do more for. I am sure you will understand.' (Of course, they won't understand, but there you are. I sent a letter along these lines to a young drama student the other day and she wrote back, indignantly: 'Timothy West sent me £500. Surely you can spare a few hundred? If I don't get the money I won't be able to finish my training.' Timothy West is notoriously generous to would-be actors, as is Sir Anthony Hopkins, as was Sir John Gielgud. I am afraid I'm not.)

2. If you are asking for an item to raffle or auction, sorry, but I'm clean out of stock. In my time, I have filled jiffy bags of every size with assorted jumpers, teddy bears, books, ties, cartoons, cuff-links, autographed underpants and trundled down the road to line up at the post office with my offerings. No more. Lady Thatcher might send you a handbag, but I don't have anything of value to offer and it's probably better to disappoint you with this answer than disappoint you by sending something you won't want. I attended a charity auction recently for which Ken Dodd had kindly donated a tickling stick. The organiser was not impressed: 'We expected something worthwhile, not a ruddy feather duster.'

3. If you are inviting me to make a speech / give away the prizes / run an auction / join you bungy-jumping, abseiling or walking up Ben Nevis, sadly I must decline 'on doctor's orders'. (This is a totally bogus excuse, but it was suggested to me by another pioneer celeb, the late Fanny Cradock. 'Darling, if you tell them you can't do it on medical grounds, suddenly they feel sorry for you. It never fails.' That's not entirely true. Years ago, Godfrey Winn, then England's highest paid columnist, had agreed to speak at a charity lunch. Unfortunately he died a week before

the event and I called the organisers to explain that, as Mr Winn couldn't make it, I would be coming in his place. 'But Mr Winn must come,' protested the charity's chairman. 'He promised.' 'You don't seem to understand,' I said, 'the poor man can't come, he's dead.' 'He must come,' persisted the chairman. 'You don't seem to understand: we've had the menus printed.')

4. If you are a budding writer wanting to know how to get started, I recommend application and pass on Mark Twain's advice: 'Apply the seat of the pants to the seat of the chair.' If you are a student hoping for help with your homework/project/thesis, may I recommend the public library, undervalued and under-used these days. If you are wanting me to share with you the best advice I ever got, I picked it up from General MacArthur: 'Have a good plan, execute it violently, do it today.'

5. If you are compiling a celebrity cookbook, I'm not surprised. Every famous name I know (from Jane Asher to Franco Zeffirelli) has a recipe ready and waiting for you on the word processor. Down the years, my offerings have ranged from the ridiculous (chilli con lobster) to the sublime: take an egg, place in a pan of boiling water for three and half minutes and serve with thick fingers of white bread and butter. If you're after something more subtle and substantial try the weather girl at Anglia TV: she sends out a three-page recipe for a delicious onion cream tart. I like the standard offering from writer Alan Sillitoe: 'Try this at 2.00 a.m. as a pick-me-up during Chapter Seven: black olives (from oil rather than brine), rye bread, Hungarian sausage (or Italian salami), with a couple of tiny glasses of neat vodka.'

6. If you are compiling a book of tips and wrinkles, good ideas and helpful advice, and want to know the best tip yet to come my way, I'm happy to oblige. When I was an MP I found that, almost every weekend, I would

have to show a face at constituency functions, party events, coffee mornings, barbecues, assorted fund-raising 'dos'. These proved to be cumulatively costly because at each of them there was a raffle and, as the local MP, I was expected to buy tickets, by the strip and in every colour. One day, in the House of Commons tea room, I happened to be sitting at a table with John Major. I told him my dilemma. The prime minister smiled. 'I'll let you into a little secret,' he said. And from out of his breast pocket he pulled three strips of different coloured raffle tickets. 'I keep them in my jacket and, as I arrive at an event, I pull them up, like so. Nobody asks me to buy any tickets because they assume I've already bought them.'

7. If you want to know my all-time favourite funny story (and, bizarrely, most weeks someone does) I really can't make up my mind. I'll give you my current favourite and trust you'll settle for that. It's true. It has John Mortimer interviewing the late Kingsley Amis and being alarmed to learn from the great writer that he had recently attacked his son, Martin, with a hammer. The week after Mortimer's interview was published, he was obliged to print an apology explaining that he had misheard Amis pére. What Kingsley had said was, 'I'm feeling terrible because I've hit my thumb with a hammer.'

8. If you want to know who are the most interesting people I have met, I could send you a book – but you seem to be holding it already.

9. If what you are after is the worst experience of my professional life – and, after recipes, and item 10, this is the most frequent request I get – again I am happy to help. This incident took place thirty years ago, but I have nightmares about it still. I was twenty-two and making a documentary for ITV called *The Saint and the Cynic*. The saint was Thomas à Becket, the eight-hundredth anniversary of whose martyrdom was the

peg for the film, in which I was supposed to play the cynic and cross-question the then Archbishop of Canterbury, the prelate with the eyebrows and the twinkle, Michael Ramsey. Music was to be provided by Yehudi Menuhin (no less), playing unaccompanied Bach on the very spot in the crypt of Canterbury Cathedral where the four knights had cut down the turbulent priest in 1170.

We had one day for filming and on the afternoon of that fateful day the Archbishop and I were standing at the top of the stone steps leading down to the crypt when Yehudi Menuhin arrived. I was surprised to find that he had his violin case handcuffed to his wrist.

'For the insurance people,' he explained. 'It is a very valuable instrument, a Stradivarius.'

'Oh, how exciting,' I exclaimed, as the great virtuoso unlocked the handcuff, opened the case and took out his violin.

'It is beautiful,' I gushed.

'Certainly, it has a beautiful tone,' said Menuhin.

'May I hold it a moment?' I asked.

'By all means,' said Menuhin, 'but be careful.' He handed me the precious instrument. I took it with both hands.

'My, my,' I murmured appreciatively. 'Have you seen this, Your Grace?' I said to the Archbishop, who was standing a few steps away from me. 'To think I am holding Yehudi Menuhin's Stradivarius!' I must have turned to face Dr Ramsey with a touch too much youthful exuberance because, as my body swivelled round, the instrument flew – suddenly, swiftly, easily – out of my hands. I made to catch it and, as I did so, tilted the edge and sent it spinning towards the crypt. It bounced its way elegantly – and audibly – down the ancient stone stairway – boing, boing, ping, boing – and landed, with a crash, bridge and all strings broken, at the foot of the steps, about a yard from the spot where Becket had been murdered.

Yehudi Menuhin's many years of meditation and macrobiotic dieting had been but a preparation for this moment in his life. He did not offer a word of reproach. He closed his eyes for a second, bit his lip and took a deep breath. Then, quite calmly, he walked down the steps to retrieve his shattered instrument.

'I will have to use the other one,' he said quietly.

'You have another violin with you then?'

'Yes,' he said, 'it's in the car.'

'Let me get it for you,' I volunteered.

Briefly his face did seem to twitch. 'Er, no, I'll fetch it myself. Thank you all the same.'

10. And I'm finishing with the question most often asked. What is your favourite quotation? Under the circumstances, it dictates itself. *Hamlet*, Act V, Scene 2, line 369: 'The rest is silence.'